Aesthetics: 50 Puzzles, Paradoxes, and Thought Experiments is a teaching-focused resource, which highlights the contributions that imaginative scenarios—paradoxes, puzzles, and thought experiments alike—have made to the development of contemporary analytic aesthetics. The book is divided into sections pertaining to art-making, ontology, aesthetic judgements, appreciation and interpretation, and ethics and value, and offers an accessible summary of ten debates falling under each section.

Each entry also features a detailed annotated bibliography, making it an ideal companion for courses surveying a broad collection of topics and readings in aesthetics.

Key Features:
- Uses a problem-centred approach to aesthetics (rather than author- or theory-centred) making the text more inviting to first-time students of the subject
- Offers stand-alone chapters, allowing students to quickly understand an issue and giving instructors flexibility in assigning readings to match the themes of the course
- Provides up-to-date, annotated bibliographies at the end of each entry, amounting to an extensive review of the literature on contemporary analytic aesthetics

Michel-Antoine Xhignesse is an Instructor of Philosophy at Capilano University, in North Vancouver, Canada.

PUZZLES, PARADOXES, AND THOUGHT EXPERIMENTS IN PHILOSOPHY

Imaginative cases—or what might be called puzzles, paradoxes, and other thought experiments—play a central role in philosophy. This series offers students and researchers a wide range of such imaginative cases, with each volume devoted fifty such cases in a major subfield of philosophy. Every book in the series includes: some initial background information on each case, a clear and detailed description of the case, and an explanation of the issue(s) to which the case is relevant. Key responses to the case and suggested readings lists are also included.

Recently Published Volumes:

EPISTEMOLOGY
KEVIN McCAIN

FREE WILL AND HUMAN AGENCY
GARRETT PENDERGRAFT

PHILOSOPHY OF LANGUAGE
MICHAEL P. WOLF

AESTHETICS
MICHEL-ANTOINE XHIGNESSE

Forthcoming Volumes:

ETHICS
SARAH STROUD AND DANIEL MUÑOZ

BIOETHICS
SEAN AAS, COLLIN O'NEIL, AND CHIARA LEPORA

PHILOSOPHY OF MIND
TORIN ALTER, AMY KIND, AND CHASE B. WRENN

METAPHYSICS
SAM COWLING, WESLEY D. CRAY, AND KELLY TROGDON

For a full list of published volumes in **Puzzles, Paradoxes, and Thought Experiments in Philosophy**, please visit www.routledge.com/Puzzles,Paradoxes,andThoughtExperimentsinPhilosophy/book-series/PPTEP

AESTHETICS

50 PUZZLES, PARADOXES, AND THOUGHT EXPERIMENTS

Michel-Antoine Xhignesse

Routledge
Taylor & Francis Group

NEW YORK AND LONDON

Designed cover image: baona / Getty Images

First published 2023
by Routledge
605 Third Avenue, New York, NY 10158

and by Routledge
4 Park Square, Milton Park, Abingdon, Oxon, OX14 4RN

Routledge is an imprint of the Taylor & Francis Group, an informa business

© 2023 Taylor & Francis

ISBN: 978-1-032-43635-7 (hbk)
ISBN: 978-1-032-43639-5 (pbk)
ISBN: 978-1-003-36820-5 (ebk)

DOI: 10.4324/9781003368205

Typeset in Bembo
by codeMantra

Pour toutes mes familles. J'espère que ça vous donne un aperçu!

CONTENTS

ACKNOWLEDGEMENTS

First, I'd like to extend my gratitude to Andy Beck, without whose careful guidance this book wouldn't exist.

I am especially grateful for the assistance of the Aesthetics Anonymous FB group, on which I relied for help identifying promising paradoxes, puzzles, and thought experiments, and whose members I consulted about sources. In particular, I'd like to thank Antony Aumann, Aili Bresnahan, Elisa Caldarola, Ley Cray, John Dyck, Saul Fisher, Michalle Gal, Deborah Knight, Tom Leddy, Erich Hatala Matthes, Shelby Moser, Jonathan Neufeld, Nick Riggle, Elizabeth Scarbrough, Mark Silcox, Brian Soucek, Jonathan Weinberg, and Mary Beth Willard for their help with cases and sources, as well as Matt Strohl, who let me have a sneak peek at his book.

Chris Bartel, Miguel F. Dos Santos, David Friedell, Erich Hatala Matthes, and Aaron Meskin were kind enough to cast an eye over some draft chapters and helped me to avoid at least some embarrassing mistakes. They did what they could but the buck, unfortunately, stops with me.

Thanks are also due to my brother Xandar for his horrifying fake food memes, which offered a peculiar sort of inspiration for certain chapters.

Finally, I owe my greatest thanks to Loki, who slept through it all, and to Thieves!, who kept us company. And Alice, of course, whose contributions are too many and varied to begin to list, but whose help and support mean the world.

And 'hello' to Jason Isaacs.

PREFACE

It is sometimes claimed that there is a scarcity of thought experiments in aesthetics. especially compared to epistemology, ethics, and meta-physics.[1] This claim is manifestly false—except insofar as it's true.

It's false insofar as there are thought experiments under every rock in aesthetics. But it's true insofar as these have occupied a different role with respect to research in the field. In ethics, for example, you'll find entire cottage industries of trolley problems and ticking bombs, as well as any number of articles devoted to in-depth discussions of drowning children and helpless violinists. The same can't really be said of aesthetics; we have many thought experiments whose influence would be hard to overstate (e.g., *The Gallery of Red Squares, Guernicas*), but the discussion has not tended to place them front and centre in the same way. Thought experiments in aesthetics are more like spiders than the scorpions of other subfields: they lurk in the background, pulling the threads of a vast web rather than lying in wait inside a careless someone's boot.

I suspect that the reason for this difference in emphasis is largely due to the subject matter of aesthetics, which, like the philosophy of science, is closely tied to the real, practical world. A lot of aesthetics is about *art*, after all, so it's only natural that it would draw many of its puzzle cases from the artworld. In fact, analytic aesthetics has long been characterized by a heavy reliance on artworld puzzle cases. Since today's artworld is chock full of artists trying to outdo one another along various dimensions, it should come as no surprise that the real world is a rich source of genuine counterexamples for any given philosophical theory or set of intuitions about art. Unfortunately, this focus on artworld cases has tended to be rather narrow, and often picks up on the same tired handful of artworks from the early-to-mid twentieth century, Duchamp's *Fountain* (1917) chief among them.

This focus on real cases is critical, since so much of aesthetics draws its subject matter from the artworld—but it also tends to obscure the role that *imaginative* cases and philosophers' *intuitions* have played in advancing the discourse in aesthetics, particularly in the last several decades. My hope is that by gathering together fifty puzzles, paradoxes, and thought experiments in aesthetics I can highlight the role that imaginative cases in particular, and our intuitions more broadly, have played in the development of contemporary analytic aesthetics.

The purpose of this book is to offer a starting point for students and researchers interested in aesthetics. As such, each chapter is accompanied by a brief annotated bibliography of ten sources. These are not intended to exhaust each topic—how could they?—but rather were chosen as a representative sample of what discussion of the topic at hand looks like, and the different directions in which it has headed. I have largely refrained from citing historical sources, since these are for the most part obvious and very well-documented already—if, for example, someone doesn't already know about Kant's influence on aesthetic attitude theories, even a brief excursion into the contemporary literature will serve to make it clear. Likewise, although many of the cases date back several decades, I have tried to give readers a glimpse of contemporary work on the issue. So, for example, it would have been entirely possible to spend the entire chapter on artifactuality (*The Whale and the Driftwood*) talking about work from the 1960s, but I judged that the reader's interests would be better served by a broader sampling.

Similarly, it would not have been unreasonable to cite the same few foundational works again and again—especially Goodman's *Languages of Art: An Approach to a Theory of Symbols* (1968), Wollheim's *Art and its Objects: An Introduction to Aesthetics* (1968), Wolterstorff's *Works and Worlds of Art* (1980), Danto's *The Transfiguration of the Common-place* (1981), and Walton's *Mimesis as Make-Believe* (1990). These are the foundational texts of contemporary analytic aesthetics, to be sure, and anyone interested in aesthetics would do well to read them. But not everyone will have the time to wade through these tomes before tackling a particular issue of interest, so instead I have chosen to focus primarily on the rest of the specialized literature which followed. Nor have I limited my surveys of the literature to work which explic-itly discusses a given thought experiment. Since that kind of focus is unusual in aesthetics, I have used the lists of suggested reading to focus attention on the broader issues at stake in each puzzle, paradox, and thought experiment. I have tried to avoid repetition of sources across cases, even though many cases are closely interrelated. In a few instances, I have failed.

Likewise, it would have been possible to populate the book with fifty thought experiments drawn exclusively from the work of Arthur Danto, perhaps with a sprinkling of George Dickie and Kendall Walton. I have opted instead for more variety. The resulting list of cases is, I think, far more representative of the breadth of work and interests in aesthetics today. Some of these cases are old and venerable, but many are shiny and new and point in interesting new directions for research. Many, of course, overlap significantly (e.g., *The Problem of Museum Skepticism, The Puzzle of Cultural Appropriation,* and *The Puz-zle of Cultural Property*). For that reason, my choice of five broad parts into which to divide the cases is somewhat artificial, but needs must.

Finally, I suppose it's obligatory to say something about the distinc-tion between puzzles, paradoxes, and thought experiments. As I see it, puzzles are persistent and perplexing problems, and paradoxes and thought experiments are special kinds of puzzles. A paradox is a puzzle that seems to involve a contradiction, while a thought experiment is a puzzle specially designed to elicit judgements about a fictional sce-nario with tightly controlled parameters. Puzzles and paradoxes seem to arise naturally, whereas thought experiments are made things. All may mobilize our intuitions, but only thought experiments are specif-ically designed to do so. This falls well short of a philosophically robust definition in terms of necessary and sufficient conditions, but I trust it's a good enough working description to get along.

WORKS CITED

Arielli, Emanuele (2018). Is beauty in the folk intuition of the beholder? Some thoughts on experimental philosophy and aesthetics. *Rivista di Estetica* 69: 21–39.

Danto, Arthur C. (1981). *The Transfiguration of the Commonplace*. Cambridge, MA: Harvard University Press.

Goodman, Nelson (1968). *Languages of Art: An approach to a theory of symbols*. Indianapolis: Bobbs-Merrill.

Livingston, Paisley, and Mikael Pettersson (2017). "Thought Experiments in Aesthetics," in *A Companion to Applied Philosophy*, Kasper Lippert-Rasmussen, Kimberley Brownlee and David Coady (eds.). Malden: Wiley-Blackwell, 501–13.

Sorensen, Roy A. (1998) *Thought experiments*. New York: Oxford University Press.

Wollheim, Richard (1968). *Art and its objects*. Cambridge: Cambridge University Press.

Wolterstorff, Nicholas (1980). *Works and worlds of art*. Oxford: Clarendon Press.

NOTE

1 See, e.g., Livingston and Pettersson (2017), Sorensen (2018: 253), and Arielli (2018).

PART I

ART-MAKING

GENERAL BACKGROUND

Most philosophical discussions of art today take for granted the premise that art-making is necessarily an intentional activity of some kind. This is because artworks are artifacts (or performances), and these are usually distinguished from naturally occurring objects and processes by the fact that someone produces them intentionally. So, for example, the rustle of wind through oak leaves or the patter of raindrops on a tin roof cannot, considered by themselves, be artworks, since they are not the result of someone's intentional action. But a recording of these same sounds is an artifact, since it was intentionally produced, and it may even be or become a work of art in its own right, depending on what further conditions we think need to be satisfied for something to count as art. These fundamental ideas weren't always so widely accepted, however. They owe their popularity today to the discussion following the presentation of several thought experiments and the intuitions they elicit.

DOI: 10.4324/9781003368205-1

The cases in this section all explore some aspect of the *process* of art-making, from the artist's intentions and what it means for something to be an artifact or designed, to the prominent role we assign to creativity and artistic genius, and to the questions of who can revise a work of art, what counts as an 'authentic' work, why fiction tends to have just a single ending, and who counts as the 'artist' for multiply-authored works such as films.

APELLES'S HORSES (INTENTIONALITY)

CASE

According to legend, the Greek painter Apelles of Kos (c. 4th century BCE), famed for his realistic pictures, once tried to paint the myth of Poseidon's creation of the world. Apelles spent months labouring over his painting, getting every detail just right. But one detail always escaped him: the lather on his horses' mouths, which was intended to echo Poseidon's creation of horses from the swells of the sea. He tried again and again, using every trick and technique at his disposal, but could never quite get it right until, in a fit of rage, he threw his sponge at the offending painting and thereby achieved the very effect he'd been looking for.

Apelles's story has been told by a number of authors, chief among them Dio Chrysostom (c. 40–120 CE), Pliny the Elder (c. 23–79 CE), and Sextus Empiricus (c. 2nd–3rd centuries CE). Sextus Empiricus uses the anecdote to illustrate what he means by the state of 'ataraxia' (a kind of tranquillity and freedom from worry), which he thought of as life's purpose. More interestingly for our present purposes, Dio Chrysostom (2017) and Pliny the Elder concluded that the anecdote shows us that Apelles *needed* a bit of luck—rather than more skill—to finish his painting.[1] Without that lucky accident, he could never have

DOI: 10.4324/9781003368205-2

finished the picture he set out to paint. So far, so good! But: if the finishing detail was due entirely to a stroke of luck, can we really say that the painting as a whole is the product of Apelles's intentions? This might seem like a trivial question—Apelles painted most of the painting himself, after all!—but it picks up on a very important issue in the ontology of art: art's intention-dependence.

It is more or less universally accepted, among philosophers of art, that art-making depends in some way on the artist's intentions. This, we think, marks the difference between an artwork, such as a sculpture, and a natural object or event, such as a rock formation: somebody had to make the artwork, to carve the shape into the soapstone, whereas nobody was trying to do anything at all when a ginger root looks like a person, or when a cloud looks like a sheep (see also *The Whale and the Driftwood*). Artworks, we say, are *intention-dependent*— they need intentions. Natural objects and events, by contrast, don't: they're intention-*in*dependent.

Returning to poor Apelles, we can now see the outline of the problem: can we really say that his painting is an intentional object if its completion was totally dependent on a stroke of luck (an unplanned throw)? It seems Apelles is no better off than I would be if I planned to paint an action painting by dropping a can of paint onto a canvas from atop a ladder but, once I got to the top of the ladder, a loud *bang!* startled me and I accidentally dropped the can. The result certainly *looks* like an artwork—in fact, it looks just like what I envisioned—but is it really? After all, I never actually carried out my plan since the bang interrupted me.

RESPONSES

Apelles's case is not one which has drawn much attention from philosophers of art. What *has* drawn their interest, instead, is the puzzle that lies at its heart: what, exactly, does it mean to say that art-making is an intention-dependent activity? How much intention is required, just how unintentional can art-making be, and what role does *luck* play in the production of artworks (Livingston 2005, Ribeiro 2018; see also *Pinny the Who?*)?

Some have argued that art-making can be an unintentional activity—at least to some extent (Lopes 2007). Suppose, for example, that I intend to build a doghouse but that my skills aren't up to snuff, and so I end up with something *much* too small. But now suppose that I decide that my erstwhile doghouse, while not up to that particular task, could be put to better use as a birdhouse. In that case, I made the birdhouse, and I did so deliberately at every step—except, of course, that I didn't intend *to make a birdhouse*. I intended *to make a doghouse* and ended up with a birdhouse instead. So too with art: I might intend to make a quilt but end up with a work of textile art instead, or intend to durdle on the guitar but end up with a full-fledged song. This kind of 'unintentional' art-making is called *accidental art*, and it happens when someone intends to make something which isn't art and fails in their attempt to make their intended object but, in failing to do so, they nevertheless succeed in making an artwork.

On the other hand, sometimes people 'unintentionally' make something in the sense that they set out to make (or do) something without realizing that that thing can also be counted as an instance of something else. Someone with a tippy boat, for example, might come up with the solution of attaching pontoons to either side to stabilize the craft. In doing so, they would have created a catamaran—even if they know nothing at all about catamarans. So too with art: I might not know anything at all about art but nevertheless have a passion for drawing pictures of things. This kind of unintentional art-making is called *incidental art*, and it happens when someone intends to make (or do) something which also happens to satisfy the conditions for being a work of art.

But not everyone is on board with accidental and incidental art-making. Some, for example, have chosen to bite the bullet entirely, arguing that art-making requires a specific intention *to make art*—that is to say, one must explicitly decide that one is going to make an artwork, and so one must be in prior possession of the concept of 'art', which they deploy in each particular case of art-making (Binkley 1988, Clowney 2011). According to this model, accidental and incidental creations are just *non-art*. Others, however, think that we need to pay attention to the intentional activity involved in accidental and incidental creation because it results in *failed-art*—cases where an intention to make art wasn't successfully completed, for whatever reason (Mag Uidhir 2013). For these philosophers, the artworld is chock full of failed-art masquerading as full-fledged art.

Finally, it has been argued that our descriptions of this case are misleading, since they prompt us to run together several different stages in the artist's activity and to ignore others (Baxandall 1985, Xhignesse 2020, Anscomb 2021). In particular, we seem to have sanitized our descriptions of artistic intentions so that every artist starts out with a clear plan which she intends to follow, thereby ignoring the fact that many artists report on their work as a process of discovery, or rely on help from others (see *The Puzzle of Multiple Authorship*). Doing so need not undermine their intentional control over the final product, especially when partially outsourcing creative agency is part of the plan, and when the artist retains the final say over the work produced. Happy and unhappy accidents happen all the time, but artists seldom stop once they happen: they either decide to endorse the accident or try to fix it.

SUGGESTED READING

SEMINAL PRESENTATION:

1. Chrysostom, Dio (2017). *The Complete Works of Dio Chrysostom*. Translated by J. W. Cohoon. Hastings: Delphi Classics.
   Chrysostom relates the tale of Apelles in Discourse 63, using the legend to argue that luck is an essential feature of life, and that Apelles *needed* luck to finish his painting. There is no suggestion here that the presence of a lucky accident undermined his efforts.

DEFENCES:

2. Baxandall, Michael (1985). *Patterns of Intention: On the Historical Explanation of Pictures*. New Haven, CT: Yale University Press.
   Baxandall argues that we have to think of the artist's intentions as dynamic, rather than static. The artist may begin with a preliminary set of goals in mind, but she is not slavishly tied to them; they will inevitably change throughout the process of creation, responding to challenges and new ideas as they arise. The final product thus stands as a declaration *after the fact* of the artist's intentions.
3. Lopes, Dominic McIver (2007). Art Without 'Art'. *British Journal of Aesthetics* 47 (1): 1–15.
   Lopes argues that art-making can proceed without a concrete concept of 'art'. To that end, he identifies two kinds of art which can be characterized as 'unintentional', or as having been made without any clear concept of 'art' in

mind: accidental and incidental art. The upshot is that we can rightly classify the work of other cultures as 'art' even if their concepts do not appear to match up with our own; concepts are superfluous.

CRITIQUES:

4. Clowney, David (2011). Definitions of Art and Fine Art's Historical Origins. *Journal of Aesthetics and Art Criticism* 69 (3): 309–20.
   Clowney argues that practices in general are intentional: to pick up a rook and place it on a chessboard, with no clue how the game works and without regard for the rules, does not count as making a move in chess. So too with art-making: to make art is to make music, a painting, a dance, etc., and it's impossible to do these things unintentionally.
5. Mag Uidhir, Christy (2013). *Art & Art-Attempts*. New York: Oxford University Press.
   In Ch. 1 Mag Uidhir argues that art is necessarily intention-dependent and outlines the conditions which must be satisfied for something to count as the product of a successful art-attempt. The rest of his book charts the consequences of this analysis of art-making and failure.

FURTHER READING:

6. Binkley, Timothy (1988). The Computer is Not a Medium. *Philosophic Exchange* 19: 155–73.
   Binkley argues that computers cannot act as an artistic medium. In particular, he argues that the products of computer use are not properly intention-dependent: computers act more like active, creative partners than a passive medium for creation.
7. Livingston, Paisley (2005). *Art and Intention: A Philosophical Study*. Oxford: Oxford University Press.
   Livingston opens the preface to his book with the case of Apelles, from which he concludes that Apelles's fortuitous accident undermined his intended project: the whole point, for Apelles, was to show that his skills were up to the task of exactly reproducing the world, and on that score, he not only failed but *gave up*. The rest of the book is an attempt to come to grips with artists' intentions and the phenomenon of artistic luck.
8. Ribeiro, Anna Christina (2018). Aesthetic Luck. *The Monist* 101 (1): 99–113.
   Ribeiro argues that our aesthetic characters are subject to four kinds of 'aesthetic luck': constitutive, upbringing, sociogeographic, and circumstantial luck. Aesthetic luck is the kind of luck that influences a subject's aesthetic experiences of the world; as such, it is distinct from the artistic luck we are concerned with here, although the parallels are clear to see.

9. Xhignesse, Michel-Antoine (2020). Failures of Intention and Failed-Art. *Canadian Journal of Philosophy* 50 (7): 905–17.

I argue that art's intention-dependence imposes relatively weak constraints on art-making, namely, that art-making must be either deliberate or incidental, rather than accidental. But artistic plans can be partial, and the question of whether a particular instance conforms to those plans is settled after the fact.

10. Anscomb, Claire (2021). Creative Agency as Executive Agency: Grounding the Artistic Significance of Automatic Images. *Journal of Aesthetics and Art Criticism* 79 (4): 415–27.

Anscomb tackles the case of mechanically- and naturally-dependent forms of art-making, arguing that their means of production do not undermine attributions of control. She argues that creative agency is a species of executive agency and that the exercise of intentional control is more flexible and accommodating of delegation to others or mechanical processes than we sometimes allow.

NOTE

1 Note that Pliny the Elder ascribes the legend to Protogenes and Nealces rather than Apelles. Regardless of who, if anyone, the legend is about, Apelles's situation is one with which we are all intuitively familiar.

EMPTY AND UNIVERSAL FICTIONS (FICTIONAL TRUTH)

CASE

Imagine it's bedtime, and that your child (or perhaps they're a younger sibling?) is asking for a story. "Not one of those!" they exclaim as you turn to the bookshelf, "One of *your* stories." Put on the spot like that, you might well draw a blank; you might, in fact, wonder just what the bare minimum is you can get away with. Or, conversely, you might wonder just how much detail to go into to satisfy your diminutive charge's request—if your protagonist searches through the phonebook, should you list every name and number she sees in its pages, or should you cut to the chase?

We all have a pretty good innate sense of how much or how little we should include when we tell stories, although some of us are better at it than others. But, in a more philosophical mood, you might well wonder about the stories at the extremes of content—those with absolutely no content (empty fictions), and those with all possible content (universal fictions). How would you even tell such a story?

Let me show you how! Let's start with a completely empty story, a story with absolutely no fictional content whatsoever. For ease of identifying my story, I've drawn a rectangle around it so that you can

DOI: 10.4324/9781003368205-3

tell exactly where it is—but don't mistake the rectangle for part of the story! The rectangle is just a tool I've used to make sure you get it right, like using a highlighter to highlight certain portions of a text. OK, here goes—one empty fiction, coming right up:

That was easy enough. Now, for our next trick, let's try a universal fiction:

ALL THE THINGS

Once upon a time, there was a short story—this story!—in which anything and everything was true.

As it stands, however, *All The Things* is a little ambiguous: a logician might say that the range of the quantifier is unclear. Is it anything and everything *in the universe* that's true in the story, or just anything and everything that's contained in that particular story? If it's the former, then that's a lot of truths! But the latter interpretation could be satisfied by a story which only contained a single claim. What *I* mean when I talk about universal fiction is something like the former interpretation: a story in which all the things in the universe—each and every possible fact—are true. And *All The Things* struggles to communicate that without begging the question, so perhaps we had better try building our universal fiction some other way.

To wit:[1]

MAXIMUM

Whatever is not explicitly fictionally true in *Minimum*, the text of which is below, is fictionally true in *Maximum*.

MINIMUM

Notice that telling Maximum requires us to first tell an empty fiction, *Minimum* (this one has a title for ease of reference, but our initial empty fiction didn't, to avoid any potential unpleasantness in case titles are parts of stories; see *Retitling Art*). By pointing to an empty fiction, we can articulate what a universal fiction must be like: the perfect opposite of the empty fiction (Wildman 2019). *Minimum* has absolutely nothing to say for itself; *Maximum*, on the other hand, instructs us to take every proposition that is not told to us explicitly by *Minimum* (i.e., all propositions, since *Minimum* says nothing at all), and those are the propositions which are true in our new, universal fiction.

But maybe that seems like a dirty trick; after all, we don't have much of a *story* here! Instead, we have a bunch of silence and an instruction, and that's not very exciting. So let's try one last time to build a universal fiction (the following strategy comes from Wildman and Folde 2017):

The House-Hippo Nest

Once upon a time, I needed a suit. On my way to the ferry I noticed that a tailor's shop had sprung up by the dock—*Seams, No Stress*, it was called. The tailor was a small creature with elfin features who convinced me to have a suit made from a fabric called 'sour cherry and goat cheese'. Who was I to ask questions? A few days later my suit was ready. It had the most gorgeous dark pink pants. But when I put them on, they were a creamy white instead! I removed them in consternation and held them up to the light—sure enough, they were white, but they were pink. Flummoxed, I turned to the tailor but the shop had vanished into thin air, leaving me holding my pink and not-pink pants. Then I remembered Dr. Matthews's logic class—from a contradiction, you can validly infer anything at all. And sure enough, house hippo nests are built out of lost mittens.

It's short, and perhaps not very exciting, but at least this one has some sort of narrative. The universality comes in thanks to a law of classical logic known as the *principle of explosion*. Explosion tells us that whenever we have a contradiction, we can validly infer anything and everything from that contradiction. In the story above, the contradiction is that my pants are pink and my pants are not pink at the same time. Since I know that it's *true* in the story that my pants are pink, I also know that it's true that either my pants are pink *or* house hippos build nests out of lost mittens. And since I know that it's *false* that my pants are pink, the only way that the proposition that 'either my pants are pink or house hippos build nests out of lost mittens' can be true is if house hippos do, in fact, build their nests out of lost mittens. Therefore, we can conclude that house hippo nests are made of mittens![2]

Or should we?

RESPONSES

Generally speaking, the possibility of empty and universal fictions is widely accepted (see, e.g., Blumson 2015, Bourne and Caddick Bourne 2018, Estrada-González 2018, Wildman and Folde 2020, Nolan 2021a). It makes intuitive sense, after all—we tend to accept that authors can write whatever stories they like, so the only bar to writing such stories is going to be an author's imagination. Nevertheless, several philosophers have questioned whether the strategies offered for generating universal fictions are adequate.

Some, for instance, have argued that empty and universal fictions are utterly trivial—empty fictions because they literally have no content, and universal fictions because they have *all* content, and so cannot say anything in particular (Xhignesse 2021). We might even go so far as to say that they aren't properly *stories* at all. Similarly, some have argued that empty and universal fictions must (but cannot) overcome the hurdle posed by *The Puzzle of Imaginative Resistance*: we are typically unable or unwilling to actually imagine such stories, despite the guidance authors offer through their texts (Estrada-González 2018; see also Nolan 2021b). If story-content is closely tied to our acts of imagining, or to imaginability more generally, then we have good reasons to doubt the existence of properly empty or universal fictions. It is worth noting one promising avenue of response, however, which suggests that we can reconcile impossible (or unimaginable) fictional content with our intuitions about the author's power to make anything true. The key to doing so, it's argued, is instead to frame the impossible content not as a representation of impossibility, but rather as an authorial prompt to pay attention to some comparison or feature of the story (Bourne and Caddick Bourne 2018).

Others have couched their suspicion of universal fictions in their concerns about impossible fictions more generally (see Nolan 2021b). So, for instance, it has often been argued, going back to the earliest work on truth in fiction, that impossible fictions are the product of unreliable narrators—narrators who are either lying or mistaken. Alternately, it has been suggested that perhaps what apparently looks like inconsistent story *content* is actually part of what the author is communicating *outside* the fiction—so, e.g., the inconsistency in *The House Hippo* has to do with me trying to communicate something about a real-world logical principle, rather than actually being true in the story and making everything else true, too.

Still others have argued that the key stumbling block for impossible fictions is the assumption that authors have the power to make anything whatsoever true in their stories (Ricksand 2020). They argue that we aren't entitled to this assumption: there are hard limits on authorial say-so, such as the law of non-contradiction, which make it impossible for certain kinds of content to be true in a story, even if authors *can* sketch out the process for generating such a story or describe what it might look like (Xhignesse 2021). These limits include logical necessities, the influence of genre or reading conventions, the dictates of conversational pragmatics, and so on.

SUGGESTED READING

SEMINAL PRESENTATIONS:

1. Wildman, Nathan and Christian Folde (2017). Fiction Unlimited. *Journal of Aesthetics and Art Criticism* 75 (1): 73–80.

Wildman and Folde introduce and defend the possibility of universal fictions and offer a recipe for building new such fictions. The existence of universal fictions entails that, contrary to prevailing opinion, fictions are not necessarily incomplete.

2. Wildman, Nathan (2019). The Possibility of Empty Fictions. *Journal of Aesthetics and Art Criticism* 77 (1): 35–42.
    Wildman introduces the possibility of empty fictions and sketches five unsuccessful arguments for their possibility before introducing the complemental strategy for universal fiction.

DEFENCES:

3. Blumson, Ben (2015). Story Size. *Philosophical Papers* 44 (2): 121–37.
    Blumson explores the prospects for using mathematical insights to generate new stories, including zero-, infinite-, and indenumerably infinite-length stories. He argues that the minimum story length is 0, and there is no maximum length.

4. Wildman, Nathan and Christian Folde (2020). Defending Explosive Universal Fictions. *Journal of Aesthetics and Art Criticism* 78 (2): 238–42.
    Wildman and Folde respond to Ricksand's contention (below) that their recipe for universal fictions does not actually establish the existence of such fictions. In particular, they accept that saying something (fictionally) does not necessarily make it (fictionally) true, but argue that this fact does not undermine poetic license.

CRITIQUES:

5. Estrada-González, Luis (2018). (In Some Fictions) Everything is True. *Australasian Journal of Logic* 15 (2): 64–76.
    Estrada-González defends a more traditional kind of universal fiction ("Everything is true.") from Wildman and Folde's objections, arguing that their preferred recipe for generating universal fictions faces the very same shortcomings (such as they are). In fact, he argues that imaginative resistance suggests Wildman and Folde's fictions may not be universal at all.

6. Ricksand, Martin (2020). Fiction Is Always (Or Never) Unlimited: A Reply to Wildman and Folde. *Journal of Aesthetics and Art Criticism* 78 (2): 235–8.
    Ricksand argues that Wildman's and Folde's recipe for universal fictions is nothing more than that—just a recipe, rather than a demonstration of their existence. In particular, he argues that their recipe relies upon the truth of the principle of poetic license, but that they have not demonstrated that this principle is true.

7. Xhignesse, Michel-Antoine (2021). Exploding Stories and the Limits of Fiction *Philosophical Studies* 178 (3): 675–92.

I argue that our storytelling practices preclude the possibility of telling empty or universal "fictions". In particular, I argue that universal fictionalists must—but cannot—overcome the Says-Is Gap and deke out our conventional responses to story-level contradictions.

FURTHER READING:

8. Bourne, Craig and Emily Caddick Bourne (2018). Personification Without Impossible Content. *British Journal of Aesthetics* 58 (2): 165–79.

   Bourne and Caddick Bourne argue that the personification of abstract concepts in stories (e.g., Death in Terry Pratchett's *Discworld*) involves comparing a fictional character with what they personify, without the further assumption that these two things are identical. Personification is not a representation of impossibility, but rather an authorial prompt to pay attention to some comparison.

9. Nolan, Daniel (2021a). Impossible Fictions Part I: Lessons for Fiction. *Philosophy Compass* 16 (2): 1–12.

   Nolan explores the different potential sources for impossible fictions, showing that they are actually quite commonplace features of fiction. He offers a taxonomy of several different types of impossible fictions before exploring their significance for theories of fiction.

10. Nolan, Daniel (2021b). Impossible Fiction Part II: Lessons for Mind, Language and Epistemology. *Philosophy Compass* 16 (2): 1–12.

    Building on his work in Part I, Nolan explores what impossible fictions might mean for our theories of linguistic representation, mental content and concepts, and conceivability. After discussing these matters, he canvasses different strategies which have been offered for resisting impossible fictions.

NOTES

1 I have adapted this diagram (and this telling) from Wildman (2019, §2).
2 I have walked you through a short proof of explosion which relies on recognizing that a disjunction (an 'or'-type statement) is true as long as at least one of its disjuncts (one of the propositions on either side of the 'or') is true. Some readers may find it easier to grasp by reflecting on the definition of validity: an argument is valid so long as it's impossible for all of its premises to be true and its conclusion false. When we have an argument with a contradiction in the premise set, however, it is impossible for all the premises to be true at once, meaning that it's technically impossible for the argument to have all true premises and a false conclusion. Therefore, we can validly infer any conclusion whatsoever from a contradiction.

THE PARADOX OF AUTHENTICITY

CASE

For a time, the Canadian painter Emily Carr sold pottery and rugs with Indigenous motifs under the name 'Klee Wyck'. In December 2021, two white men misrepresenting themselves as Indigenous were arrested for selling masks, "totem" poles, and pendants on the Seattle art market (a market long known as the stomping ground of the "Seattle Tribe" of forgers). Aloha Poke is a Chicago-based restaurant chain "inspired" by Hawai'i, but with no actual ties to the islands and their people. These are all obvious cases of inauthenticity; they are, in a word, *fakes*. They purport to be works (or dishes) by and from a culture from which they aren't.

But what should we make of a *mabarung* performed for tourists (the usual audience is the gods) at a Balinese hotel (Davies 2007)? Similarly, Hawaiian hula divides into two main forms: Hula Kahiko, the traditional form which pre-dates Western contact, and Hula 'Auana, which features songs rather than chants and non-traditional (Western) instruments like the guitar and 'ukulele. One of these is clearly 'authentic', but what about the other? Or consider the African carver who toils away in a workshop that produces masks and figurines resembling those traditionally used in ritual practice but destined for

DOI: 10.4324/9781003368205-4

airport tourist shops, who nevertheless takes pride in their work and explicitly intends their carvings as objects of aesthetic appreciation (Kasfir 1992). These, too, are classed as inauthentic fakes.

Where artifacts are concerned, collectors employ very specific criteria of authenticity: an 'authentic' artifact is one that is made by (1) a member of a subaltern[1] group, (2) in that group's traditional style (i.e., free of Western influence; see also *The Transmogrifier*), and (3) intended for a traditional social or religious function. Only these objects qualify as Art; any artifacts made by someone from a different geographic 'style area', produced for money, or produced primarily as an object of aesthetic appreciation are either a fake or tourist kitsch— it is inauthentic.

We find ourselves in the ludicrous position of arguing that subaltern peoples don't have art—or don't share our concept of art—because their practices are so different from our own, so much more functional, even as we discount their explicit attempts to adhere to 'our' concept of art as inauthentic. Aleut ivory carving and beadwork thus qualify for support from the Alaskan State Arts Council, but activities which the Aleut think of as contiguous with these—such as harpoon-making—do not (Shiner 1994); but should one of them decide instead to carve, say, Dora the Explorer, or bead a Christmas stocking—well, that's *inauthentic*.

This tension is what I call the *paradox of authenticity*: on the one hand, authenticity demands a certain purity, a freedom from contaminating influences; but on the other hand, it sees us dismiss as inauthentic legitimate attempts to adhere to "our" sense of Art. If you go to the African Art exhibit of a major museum, after all, you probably aren't expecting to find video installations and conceptual art (Taylor 2016). But why shouldn't you?

RESPONSES

A number of very different issues find themselves grouped under the banner of 'authenticity' (see Young 2006, Taylor 2016), all of which may be at stake in different articulations of the paradox. Among these, in particular, are questions about genuineness as opposed to forgery (see *Faking Nature*), and about a work's artistic merit or value. Interwoven into these discussions, there is also a moral concern about the requirements embodied in the demand for authenticity.

A number of philosophers and art historians have argued that the demand for cultural products untainted by Western influence is rooted in the myth of pre-contact societies as having their own distinctive, entirely unique, and culturally uniform styles (Shiner 1994, Kasfir 1992, Taylor 2016). In fact, however, subaltern groups were and are not isolated from one another, or from the world: they, like everyone, have always adopted new techniques and styles, and adapted them to suit their present purposes. A culture's 'style', as distinctive as it may be, is not some fixed thing; it changes as its practitioners acquire new skills and goals. In fact, closer examination reveals that Western art itself is thoroughly contaminated by foreign styles and non-artistic (especially economic) motives (Dutton 2000).

The paradox of authenticity is thus clearly a double standard, and we can all agree that double standards are morally bad. But it can also arise out of a hesitation to impose Western cultural categories on subaltern peoples. At one end of the spectrum, for example, we should be wary of the impulse to assimilate Australian Aboriginal painting to the category of modern art, simply because it looks abstract or non-representational (Coleman 2001). But at the other end, we need to beware of the tendency to exaggerate differences, lest we forget that our own artistic practices, for example, are heavily influenced by religious and financial motivations (Dutton 2000, Davies 2007). Our museums and galleries, after all, are chock full of objects which have been removed from their original, functional contexts and put to new work as objects of aesthetic appreciation (Eaton and Gaskell 2009; see also *The Problem of Museum Skepticism*). This suggests a moral obligation to engage with the art of subaltern groups on its own terms, rather than as an assimilated or exoticized category.

Nor should we attach too much significance to claims that there is "no word for art" in some language. For one thing, it is not obvious that this kind of concept-matching is useful; French has no word that means exactly what 'evil' does in English, for example, but we somehow manage to get by with 'the bad'.[2] But for another, the 'no word' claim is not really a linguistic claim at all: it was a political slogan used to express Indigenous artists' alienation from the institutional artworld (Mithlo 2012). We should turn our attention away from talk of concepts or words and focus instead on a culture's practices, and which of those are recognizably artistic, if somewhat different from our own (Davies 2005).

One natural way of thinking about authenticity is in terms of aesthetic value. Authenticity may not be a perceptible property, but it *is* a *contextual* one (see *Guernicas* and *Pot People, Basket Folk*), and clearly we value it a great deal: it seems to be an aesthetic merit. One reason to value it might be that it puts us into contact with the object's history. This helps to explain some of the collector's priorities, since a present-day Inuit soapstone carving (made with power tools or, more commonly, an axe, file, and sandpaper) doesn't give the buyer the sense of being in direct contact with, say, the tenth century Dorset culture, which would have used different tools. Similarly, we might value the 'authentic' piece as a source of information about that history. A modern imitation, no matter how good, is not a direct source of information about the past.

Another possibility which might partly explain the collector's priorities, however, is a belief that the use of another culture's characteristic styles necessarily results in an aesthetically inferior product. If this 'aesthetic handicap thesis' (Young 2006) is correct, then collectors have a good reason to demand that their artifacts be genuine products of the relevant culture, since anything else will be of lesser aesthetic merit *even if it's perceptually indistinguishable from the real deal.*

There is certainly something to this idea, insofar as we clearly value originals over copies and forgeries, since these latter are derivative works. It is less clear, however, that an outsider's use of a culture's traditional styles *necessarily* results in an aesthetically flawed work, especially if those styles are being put to innovative, rather than derivative, uses (Young 2006). So while we might readily agree that the Inuit-imitator is not doing anything particularly impressive, we might change our tune if instead they try to make something radically new and different (and not just a Dorset knock-off).

So perhaps we are better off de-coupling authenticity from aesthetic value and focusing instead on the artist's *achievement*. In particular, perhaps we should be asking what the artist's aesthetic reasons were for appropriating as they did (Pearson 2021). Doing so allows authenticity to re-enter the discussion as an aesthetic merit or flaw, but only given the artist's aims and achievement. The result is that our talk of 'authenticity' is a shorthand way of thinking about the artist's aesthetic reasons, with the background understanding that imitative use of another culture's artistic expression is generally less valuable than innovative use, and that even innovative uses may sometimes prove morally suspect (Taylor 2016).

SUGGESTED READING

SEMINAL PRESENTATION:

1. Shiner, Larry (1994). "Primitive Fakes," "Tourist Art," and the Ideology of Authenticity. *Journal of Aesthetics and Art Criticism* 52 (2): 225–34.
   Shiner shows that our demands for "authenticity" from small-scale societies reflect a colonial nostalgia for pre-conquest cultures. According to this mindset, subaltern groups must remain pure and free of outside influence lest their cultural output become inauthentic tourist fakes.

DEFENCES:

2. Kasfir, Sidney L. (1992). African Art and Authenticity: A Text with a Shadow. *African Arts*, 25 (2): 40–53+96–7.
   Kasfir argues that our ideal of authenticity for African material cultures comes from the mistaken Victorian presupposition that they are unique due to their isolation from the world, internal coherence, and uniformity of style. She observes a tension between the demands of Western art and the criteria of authenticity deployed by collectors.

3. Dutton, Dennis (2000). "But They Don't Have Our Concept of Art," in *Theories of Art Today*, Noël Carroll (ed.), Madison: University of Wisconsin Press, 217–40.
   Dutton casts a critical eye on our tendency to jump from the fact that other cultures have different artistic *practices* from ours to the notion that they lack *concepts* of art consonant with our own. He argues that we often exaggerate cultural differences by performing inapt comparisons which minimize or ignore similar features of our own artistic practices.

CRITIQUES:

4. Young, James O. (2006). Art, Authenticity and Appropriation. *Frontiers of Philosophy in China* 1 (3): 455–76.
   Young distinguishes several senses of 'authenticity' and argues against the "aesthetic handicap thesis," the view that when people outside a culture employ that culture's aesthetic content, the resulting work is necessarily

aesthetically flawed. Appropriation can be morally or aesthetically bad, but 'inauthentic' works are not necessarily aesthetically inferior.

5. Eaton, A. W. and Ivan Gaskell (2009). "Do Subaltern Artifacts Belong in Art Museums?" in *The Ethics of Cultural Appropriation*, James O. Young and Conrad Brunk (eds.). Malden, MA: Wiley-Blackwell, 235–67.

    Eaton and Gaskell address the issue of whether it is acceptable to display the artifacts of 'subaltern' cultures in Western art museums, considering that doing so seems to exapt many of them for 'inauthentic' purposes. They argue that it is, provided museums do so sensitively, and address the asymmetry of long-term power relations.

FURTHER READING:

6. Coleman, Elizabeth Burns (2001). Aboriginal Painting: Identity and Authenticity. *Journal of Aesthetics and Art Criticism* 59 (4): 385–402.

    Coleman argues that our appreciation of Australian Aboriginal art should be sensitive to its particular aims, values, and mode of production rather than its perceived stylistic influences or similarities to Western art. Doing so need not require deep, perfect knowledge of "ideal" Aboriginal culture and values, but it does require us to take these works on their own terms.

7. Davies, Stephen (2007). Balinese Aesthetics. *Journal of Aesthetics and Art Criticism* 65 (1): 21–9.

    Davies canvasses Balinese artistic practices, especially in music and dance, paying particular attention to the ways in which Balinese practices seem to differ from our own. He argues that we must be careful not to force the practices of other cultures into the boxes we have created for our own. Careful attention reveals significant and surprising variation even in our own practices.

8. Mithlo, Nancy (2012). No Word for Art in Our Language?: Old Questions, New Paradigms. *Wicazo Sa Review* 27: 111–26.

    Mithlo surveys the history of the "no word" refrain in Indigenous art, showing that it doesn't reflect the linguistic or conceptual facts. It arose primarily as a rejection of standard categories of reception and as an expression of Indigenous artists' alienation from the artworld. She argues that the "no word" refrain and the artist-first (Indigenous-last) strategy it gave birth to do more harm than good and should give way to an Indigenous curatorial practice instead.

9. Taylor, Paul C. (2016). *Black is Beautiful: A Philosophy of Black Aesthetics*. Chichester: Wiley-Blackwell.

    In Ch. 5, Taylor surveys different ways of thinking about authenticity, especially as they pertain to Black aesthetics. He argues that talk of authenticity is—or should be—a heuristic device we use to guide our actions, rather than a litmus test used to evaluate art and artists.

10. Pearson, Phyllis (2021). Cultural Appropriation and Aesthetic Normativity. *Philosophical Studies* 178 (4): 1285–99.

Pearson argues that we should focus on the artist's achievement and ask what their aesthetic reasons were for appropriation. This *aesthetic externalism* returns the result that most acts of appropriation are *not* aesthetic achievements, though some may be. In particular, Pearson's account helps to explain why we typically think there is no problem with members of a minority culture appropriating a majority culture's cultural output.

NOTES

1 I am following Eaton and Gaskell (2009) in using 'subaltern' to designate groups who operate at a disadvantage to those who wield power in their society.
2 "Le mal."

4

THE PARADOX OF CREATIVITY

CASE

Imagine a marksman shooting targets. She knows exactly what she wants to do, which is hit the bull's eye, or as close to it as possible. She has a clear idea and view of the target, knows where the bull's eye is, and knows that success will result in there being a hole through that black circle at the centre of the target. She also knows how to achieve this end—how to stand or lie, how to breathe and squeeze the trigger, how to compensate for drift, and so on. Now, let's ask ourselves: is creativity in the arts like being a brilliant marksman?

The common answer here is 'no': artistic creativity sees the artist create something new and original, something which didn't exist before, and to do so the artist can't just follow a pre-existing set of rules. Unlike our marksman, the artist doesn't know exactly what her target is, or what success will look like. Success, for her, requires *inspiration*, whereas for the marksman success requires *control*.

At a first pass, this seems like a fairly plausible rendering of our ordinary intuitions about artistic creativity. We talk about it in terms of inspiration, of originality, and sometimes of a kind of 'madness' or possession by a muse. We do not, however, typically think of it as a

DOI: 10.4324/9781003368205-5

cold and calculating process of rigorous rule-following that can be described in a listicle, like "the twelve secrets of highly creative artists".

But this view of creativity leads us to a paradox: the artist does not know what they are aiming to do, but they have to know something about it, otherwise they couldn't correct mistakes or be aesthetically discriminating, since they don't know what results they are trying to achieve. This tension is known as *the paradox of creativity*. The artist isn't just a passive dreamer: they exert some sort of creative control over their output. But, according to our usual way of talking, the creativity doesn't lie in the skilled execution of their vision (that's just *craftsmanship*), it lies in the spontaneous moment of inspiration.

But the defining element of creativity can't just be that it's *unconscious*: imagine a carpenter is tasked with making a dresser, and suppose further that they are given very detailed post-hypnotic instructions for carrying out the task (Maitland 1976). We wouldn't say that they were acting creatively, especially if their actions were entirely unconsciously guided. So: creativity isn't just some kind of invisible force that guides the artist's hand, since the same can be said of our hypnotized carpenter, and their work is clearly not creative. How, then, should we explain artistic creativity?

RESPONSES

Although there was some historical interest in creativity—notably in Plato's *Ion*, in Kant's *Critique of Judgment*, and in Collingwood's *The Principles of Art*[1]—the paradox of creativity has primarily been a bugaboo of contemporary philosophers, and philosophical work on creativity has really only come into its own in the last few decades. These philosophers have tended to locate creativity in one of three places: in the process of creation, in the psychological makeup of the creative person, or in the products created.

Let's start with the process of creation. One intuitive explanation is just that creativity consists in doing something novel, and that great artists have a sort of unconscious feeling for what works and what doesn't (Tomas 1958). When the result is as it should be, it "feels" right; when it isn't, it doesn't. But this explanation doesn't explain much: what is this mysterious feeling, and how does an artist know which part of the artwork she's having a feeling of rightness or wrongness about, and how to fix it (Maitland 1976)? Far from solving the paradox of creativity, it seems we have just displaced it to another subconscious level.

Another natural suggestion is that creativity consists in creative problem-solving. This suggestion is leant some plausibility from the history of science, where it seems that a big part of Darwin's genius, for example, lies in his solution to the problem of speciation. But it isn't clear that the analogy to the history of science is apt. In particular, it's worth noting that the problems scientists face are *externally* set (e.g., what is the sun made of?), whereas those facing artists are *internally* set (e.g., how can I captivate my audience, tie up this plotline, etc.) (Dutton 2001). Moreover, an artist's previous attempts to solve her problems may be independently aesthetically interesting, whereas a scientist's failed attempts are of little more than historical interest. Indeed, this may well be an artifact of the fact that science and art typically claim different goals: truth (or, rather, its practical equivalent), versus audience interest and appreciation.

Besides: if creativity is a kind of problem-solving, then it's just as paradoxical as before to say that artists have some kind of fore-knowledge of the problems they will encounter and how to solve them (Maitland 1976). It might make some sense to think this way about some art forms, like poetry and literature, where the abstract medium—language—means that foreseeing a work can be coextensive with creating it. But in the material and performative arts, this kind of foresight can only ever be a plan that still needs to be executed, and its execution can bring surprising problems to the fore. So perhaps, instead, we are better off thinking of creativity as a kind of inspired and free *performance* which shows off the artist's achievement; in other words, it's a property we ascribe after the fact to the performance that generates a work (Maitland 1976).

Another tempting place to look for creativity is somewhere in the artist's psychological makeup: creativity is a capacity the artist has because of the way her brain is configured (Gaut 2010). She does have to have *some* idea of what she's doing and why—it can't all be down to subpersonal processes!—but there is room, too, for the artist to exploit happy accidents (see *Apelles's Horses*). Creative insights can sometimes occur spontaneously (as in Poincaré's case), but artists must lay down the conditions for them to do so: they must first choose some initial operating constraints, establish their expectations, and so on (Livingston 2009). Doing so helps artists to avoid floundering aimlessly, as well as to eschew clichéd approaches and overused habits. Under such conditions, an unbidden insight may sometimes occur and be of some use; but it is always subject to further conscious control and refinement. This is why successful artists can produce hit after hit, whereas mad geniuses (to use the cliché) possessed by inspiration don't seem to accomplish much at all. Alternately, the experiential account of creativity maintains that what makes a mental process creative is just the agent's (accurate!) experience of that process as new for them (Nanay 2014).

Finally, several accounts of creativity emphasize how new, original, surprising, or unusual the product is. These theories tend to locate creativity in that product itself, rather than in the artist's psychological makeup. When we focus on the product, it is hard not to notice that its value tends to be retroactively determined, in relation to the prior products that already exist in that same domain. Creativity, then, is a relational rather than an essential property of an object (Briskman 1980). This suggests that we cannot give a general theory of creativity, since doing so would require us to be able to specify in advance what would count as surprising and new in some domain, thereby robbing it of its surprise. It should come as no surprise, then, that great artists and scientists struggle to explain their creativeness and appeal, instead, to the mysterian metaphor of 'inspiration'. Creativity hinges on the unexpected.

Alternately, we might think that attributions of creativity are dependent on elements of all three locales: the process, person, and product. The computational theory of creativity posits that there may not be any one unified answer to what makes all creative things creative. Nevertheless, a natural place to start is by asking how it is that creative people do what they do, and what makes their results count as creative (Boden 2004 [1990]). We might then distinguish between different kinds of creativity—the kind we get from putting old ideas together in new ways, the kind we get from exploring the limits of a conceptual space, and the kind that utterly transforms existing conceptual spaces. It seems to follow that creative people are those who have a very good grasp of existing ideas and conceptual spaces, and who are equipped with the knowledge, determination, discipline, and intelligence to make surprising breakthroughs. Creativity is thus an aspect of general intelligence.

Similarly, the 'recombination theory' of creativity focuses on the first kind of creativity identified by the computational theory, rather than those pertaining to conceptual space (Novitz 1999). According to this model, creativity involves the deliberate or accidental recombination of ideas in a manner that is (1) surprising to its intended community, and (2) for an end-product intended to be valuable to that community. Methodical problem-solving, as in science, can thus satisfy the first criterion, but so can the happy accident of playing around until something cool emerges.

Note, however, that the second criterion smuggles in a moral component (see also *The Paradox of Bad-Bad Art*): developing ingenious new tortures or weapons, on this model, is not creative, even if our intuitions might claim otherwise. The computational theory speaks of creativity as arising out of an attempt to break free from a conceptual space inhabited by everyone else, and it is natural to think that those best placed to do so are those who have a comprehensive understanding of that conceptual space (Boden 2004 [1990]). But it's worth noting that conceptual spaces and their attendant conventions present serious obstacles and disincentives to creativity, too (Novitz 1999). We are attached to our traditional ways of doing–and valuing—things, to our friends and parents and teachers and their views, as well as to their material support. Not only does this make it difficult to go against the grain and be "creative", but it also means that some such attempts may not be recognized as such.

Of particular general interest is the recombination theory's appeal to communities of people who are surprised by and value the creative output. This suggests, as the product-oriented approach did, that there is a significant *social* aspect to creativity. In focusing on the processual or psychological aspects of creativity, it is easy for us to lose sight of the social pressures and constraints at work (Brand 2015). The arts are and were not equally open to all potential contributors: regardless of the originality of their work, their openness to new ideas, their ability to draw novel connections, etc., women (among others) have historically been excluded from the arts. Indeed, it is worth observing that we tend to run together the concepts of *creativity*, *originality*, and *genius*—and thus, our ascriptions of one or the other may tend to reflect cultural biases that unfairly devalue the contributions of some artists (Brand 2015; see also *The Problem of Genius*).

SUGGESTED READING

SEMINAL PRESENTATION:

1. Tomas, Vincent (1958). Creativity in Art. *Philosophical Review* 67 (1): 1–15.
   Tomas introduces the marksman thought experiment, arguing that creativity requires that artists not know what they are aiming to do. Creativity is not just skilled labour, nor is it consciously controlled: it is *originating* something, though with an element of critical control. This critical control is not shaped by a vision of the desired result, but by critical judgements—the "kicks" of inspiration—about what has already been done.

DEFENCES:

2. Livingston, Paisley (2009). "Poincaré's 'Delicate Sieve': On Creativity and Constraints in the Arts," in *The Idea of Creativity*. Michael Krausz, Denis Dutton, and Karen Bardsley (eds.). Leiden: Brill, 129–46.
   Inspired by Poincaré's description of his creative process in mathematics, Livingston argues that creativity combines deliberate and involuntary elements. Conscious work helps to set the stage and orient the process by committing to a scheme with certain constraints and establishing expectations. Unconscious deliberation sifts much of the wheat from the chaff, but additional conscious deliberation is required to recognize and polish successful results.

CRITIQUES:

3. Maitland, Jeffrey (1976). Creativity. *Journal of Aesthetics and Art Criticism* 34 (4): 397–409.
   Maitland argues that the paradox of creativity is an illusion that rests on conflating creative problem-solving with creative performance. If creativity is a species of problem-solving, then it is paradoxical for the artist to have foreknowledge of the problems they will encounter and how to solve them. But creativity is *performative*; it is the exhibition of an achievement.

4. Briskman, Larry (1980). Creative Product and Creative Process in Science and Art. *Inquiry: An Interdisciplinary Journal of Philosophy* 23 (1): 83–106.
   Briskman argues that general theories of creativity are impossible we cannot specify in advance what will make something new and surprising. He treats creativity as a property of objects (or theories) rather than of actions or people, arguing that objects count as creative in relation to prior products in the same domain.

5. Novitz, David (1999). Creativity and Constraint. *Australasian Journal of Philosophy* 77 (1): 67–82.
   Novitz offers the 'recombination theory' of creativity which accounts for creativity in both art and science. A creative act, he thinks, (1) involves the intentional or accidental recombination of ideas, objects, and techniques,

(2) in a way that is surprising to a relevant audience, and (3) is intended to be of real value to people.

FURTHER READING:

6. Boden, Margaret (2004 [1990]). *The Creative Mind: Myths and Mechanisms.* 2nd ed. New York: Routledge.
   Boden focuses on creativity's surprisingness, which she argues can result from the recombination of old ideas, the exploration of the limits of a conceptual space, or the outright transformation of that conceptual space (see especially Ch. 4). She advocates a computational approach to creativity, according to which it results from the component parts of general intelligence (Ch. 10).
7. Dutton, Denis (2001). What is Genius? *Philosophy and Literature* 25: 181–96.
   Although broadly sympathetic to the characteristics of creativity identified by the Darwinian approach, Dutton is skeptical of the parallel between creativity in art and in science. In particular, a great artist's success-rate seems much higher than a great scientist's.
8. Gaut, Berys (2010). The Philosophy of Creativity. *Philosophy Compass* 5 (12): 1034–46.
   Gaut surveys work on the psychology of creativity, including the psychoanalytic, cognitive psychological, computational, Darwinian, sociocultural, and personality studies approaches. He advocates an agency theory of creativity according to which creativity is the capacity to more or less deliberately produce original and valuable work with flair.
9. Nanay, Bence (2014). "An Experiential Account of Creativity," in *The Philosophy of Creativity: New Essays.* Elliot Samuel Paul and Scott Barry Kaufman (eds.) Oxford: Oxford University Press, 17–35.
   Nanay argues that what makes a token process creative is the agent's experience of it as something novel. He distinguishes originality, which is a property of the products of mental processes, from creativity, which is a property of the mental processes themselves.
10. Brand Weiser, Peg Zeglin (2015). The Role of Luck in Originality and Creativity. *Journal of Aesthetics and Art Criticism* 73 (1): 31–55.
    Brand observes that in printmaking, 'originality' is primarily used by dealers as a guarantee of quality, whereas it has a psychological connotation for artists and aestheticians, who too often identify it with 'creativity' and 'genius'.

NOTE

1 See Plato (1997). "Ion," in *Plato: Complete Works,* John M Cooper and D. S Hutchinson (eds.), Paul Woodruff (trans.). Indianapolis: Hackett Publishing Company, 937–49; Kant, Immanuel (1987). *Critique of Judgment.* Werner S. Pluhar (trans.). Indianapolis: Hackett Publishing Company; and Collingwood, Robin George (1938). *The Principles of Art.* Oxford: Oxford University Press.

5

THE PROBLEM OF GENIUS

CASE

What does it mean to say, of some artists, that they are geniuses?

It means that they are very good, obviously! But what does it mean to say that they are very good? Do we mean that their work is highly original, that their creative vision is unique, or that they have mastered the technical craft of their chosen medium? Do we mean that they enjoy widespread acclaim and long-lasting fame, that they changed the course of art history, or do we mean something else entirely? Besides, there are *lots* of very good artists out there by *any* measure, but only some of these qualify as geniuses. The question is, which ones, and on what basis?

One way of approaching the question is inductively: we could list a few artistic geniuses and see what sorts of properties they have in common. Let's give it a try: pull out a pen and some paper, or open a new Word document, and list the top ten greatest artists of all time, in any medium (e.g., painting, sculpture, music, literature, etc.).

So, what does your list look like? I'm guessing you probably included da Vinci, Picasso, van Gogh, Beethoven and Mozart; perhaps even Michelangelo, for a little variety, and I suppose that we should

DOI: 10.4324/9781003368205-6

maybe add Vermeer, Caravaggio, Rembrandt, and Monet for good measure, and—oh, that's ten already!

I suspect that most of our lists will overlap substantially and will be populated primarily by artists known by a single name (as above). Suppose, for the sake of this thought experiment, that you'd come up with the list I generated above. It's not a bad list! Crack open any art history textbook, and you'll see their works. Each and every one of these artists was a master of his chosen medium, and it shows. But now, let's try our hand at the second part of the experiment: let's try to figure out what they have in common.

Well, for one thing, they're mostly painters—apart from Beethoven and Mozart, that is, and with the partial exception of Michelangelo, who preferred sculpture. But, looking at that list, you could certainly be forgiven for thinking that artistic geniuses are primarily painters, and sometimes musicians. Certainly, with a list like that, you wouldn't be inclined to argue that genius is evenly distributed among the arts. I mean, just try to name a single great embroiderer!

You could also be forgiven for thinking that most great art was produced between the fifteenth and eighteenth centuries, and all of it in Europe. Our list, after all, is entirely European and mostly features artists who lived squarely in those centuries. It's a list entirely devoid of Neanderthals and Zoomers, and pretty much everyone else in between, too.

Finally, you could be forgiven for thinking that artistic genius is male; none of our ten, after all, are women. With a little extra effort, now that you mention it, perhaps we can add Jane Austen to our list, and maybe we should remove Caravaggio, because he languished in obscurity for centuries before his rediscovery by Roberto Longhi in the 1920s. So: how does your list compare, overall?

The problem, of course, is that these conclusions are clearly risible. It beggars belief to suggest that, over the course of 40,000 years or more of art-making, nothing worthy of much notice was produced except in a 300-year period on a single continent, or by anyone who wasn't male. Where are the geniuses of Classical Greece or the present day, the geniuses of Africa, of North and South America, of Asia? How is it that, out of the roughly 107 billion people estimated to have ever lived on earth, not one of them was both a great artist and female (or only one, if you consented to the addition of Jane Austen)? And yet, that was our list.

RESPONSES

The analysis of genius has been a dominant topic of discussion in aesthetics for quite some time, particularly since the eighteenth century and in discussions of the history of aesthetics. As the nineteenth century drew on, non-rational sources of inspiration became increasingly important to the characterization of genius, changing it from a term describing the special talents most people possess to a spark of divine creativity which is the exclusive purview of a select few men (see *The Paradox of Creativity*, and c.f. *The Puzzle of Multiple Authorship*). Kant, for instance, emphasized the artistic genius' strength of character, which allows him to transcend the rules laid out by nature and impose his own rules upon his creative output. Schopenhauer likewise thought that the artistic genius achieves what others cannot even imagine, because his depth of vision allows him to perceive the world as it is, rather than as it is represented to us (Battersby 1989 surveys this history; Mumford and Lacerda 2010 offer a contemporary take on non-rational genius).

More recently, it has come under question for exactly the same kinds of reasons we developed when analyzing our top ten list above (see Korsmeyer 2020 for an overview). One prominent analysis which has come to dominate feminist aesthetics is that 'genius' is not so much a measure of innate ability, of originality, or of quality of workmanship, but rather a measure which tracks social influence and the kinds of things which particular people at particular times care about most (Nochlin 1971, Gates 1994). So, for instance, we can explain the preponderance of painters and musicians in our list by observing that these have traditionally been considered the epitome of art, in contrast to 'women's work' like embroidery and tapestry, mechanical reproduction like photography, or mere games.

But while some have argued that we need to be skeptical of genius, since the concept reflects matters of historical accident and social preference, others have been hard at work trying to rehabilitate it. The 1970s and 1980s, for example, saw significant efforts being made to rediscover women artists and justify their inclusion in the canon of the greats (see Eaton 2008, Meagher 2011). Others have argued that what is needed instead is either a reconceptualization of genius or the introduction of new criteria of genius which will better reflect the full panoply of artistic voices and traditions (e.g., Battersby 1989, Hein 2010). A key point of contention, here, is whether concepts like 'genius' are themselves gendered (James 2013), or whether they are gendered in their application only (e.g., Kivy 2001)—i.e., are women not 'geniuses' because the concept itself is inextricably male (and must thus be replaced), or is it a gender-neutral concept whose application to women has been stymied by social factors?

Such considerations have led a number of feminist theorists to argue for the existence of distinctively feminine arts with their own aesthetic (typically rooted in women artists' positions as a counterweight to the dominant male conception of art history). On the other hand, many have worried that this kind of project works to essentialize women and their artistic contributions, without regard for the many differences between women in different historical periods, or in different social and economic circumstances.

SUGGESTED READING

SEMINAL PRESENTATION:

1. Nochlin, Linda (1971). Why Have There Been No Great Women Artists? *ARTnews* 69: 22–39.

   In this classic paper, Nochlin upended art history by arguing that there are no 'great' women artists. This is not for lack of talented female artists, but rather due to systemically oppressive social conditions which suppressed their artistic development, due approbation, and uptake. Our concept of 'genius', she argues, is not based on quality of workmanship, but rather on relatively arbitrary and historically contingent social factors.

DEFENCES:

2. Gates, Eugene (1994). Why Have There Been No Great Women Composers? Psychological Theories, past and Present. *Journal of Aesthetic Education* 28 (2): 27–34.

   Gates critically canvasses the many modern psychological theories which have been offered for the supposed dearth of female composers, from the so-called variability hypothesis and the theory of the urges to studies of achievement motivation and hemispheric specialization. Following Nochlin, Gates argues that the likeliest explanations are sociological, not biological.

3. Kivy, Peter (2001). *The Possessor and the Possessed: Handel, Mozart, Beethoven, and the Idea of Musical Genius.* New York: Yale University Press.

Kivy explores some early conceptions of genius and charts their progress in the world of musical composition. He distinguishes between the Platonic conception of genius, according to which someone is possessed by divine inspiration, and the Longinian, according to which certain individuals are naturally endowed with superior abilities. The first, he argues, helps to explain one-hit-wonder masterpieces; the second, consistently great masters. Women's exclusion from the musical canon results from systemic discrimination, rather than some fault within the concept of genius itself.

CRITIQUES:

4. Battersby, Christine (1989). *Gender and Genius: Towards a Feminist Aesthetics.* Bloomington: Indiana University Press.

Battersby undertakes a genealogy of the concept of 'genius', from classical Rome to the present day. She argues that the concept is essentially and inextricably gendered—and sexualized—male, but also functions to bestow certain 'feminine' qualities upon the artist. The result is that although the concept of genius is extensively feminized, it nevertheless excludes women. Unlike Nochlin, she argues that feminist aesthetics should strive to reconstruct and highlight women's contributions to art and art history.

5. James, Robin (2013). Oppression, Privilege, & Aesthetics: The Use of the Aesthetic in Theories of Race, Gender, and Sexuality, and the Role of Race, Gender, and Sexuality in Philosophical Aesthetics. *Philosophy Compass* 8 (2): 101–16.

James surveys the ways in which the aesthetic is mobilized by systems of privilege and oppression, as well as the ways in which aesthetics constructs and legitimates these systems. James pays particular attention to the ways in which normative masculinity informs aesthetic concepts such as artistic genius.

FURTHER READING:

6. Eaton, A. W. (2008). Feminist Philosophy of Art. *Philosophy Compass* 3 (5): 873–93.

Eaton offers a critical perspective on the history of feminist philosophy of art (though not feminist accounts of our *aesthetic* responses), with a particular focus on the problem of canon formation in the arts, and the explanations marshalled for and against it.

7. Hein, Hilde (2010). "Looking at Museums from a Feminist Perspective," in *Gender, Sexuality, and Museums: A Routledge Reader*, Amy K. Levin (ed.). New York: Routledge, 53–64.

Hein offers some suggestions for counterbalancing our typical emphasis on individual creativity. She argues that we ought to pay closer attention to art produced outside the academic fine art system. In particular, she suggests that museums ought to place additional emphasis on "ordinary" objects.

8. Mumford, Stephen and Teresa Lacerda (2010). The Genius in Art and in Sport: A Contribution to the Investigation of Aesthetics of Sport. *Journal of the Philosophy of Sport* 37 (2): 182–93.

Lacerda and Mumford tie 'genius' to the concepts of originality and innovation, arguing that geniuses need not be aware of just how they manage to execute their superior aesthetic vision. After characterizing genius in the artworld, they extend their account to the realm of sports.

9. Meagher, Michelle (2011). Telling stories about feminist art. *Feminist Theory* 12 (3): 297–316.

Meagher argues that we should be skeptical of the tidy narrative of intergenerational strife which has come to characterize the history of feminist art. This narrative, she argues, functions primarily to distance later waves of feminism from the caricatured essentialism of prior waves.

10. Korsmeyer, Carolyn (2020). "Feminist Aesthetics," in *The Stanford Encyclopedia of Philosophy* (Spring 2020 Edition), Edward N. Zalta (ed.). https://plato.stanford.edu/archives/spr2020/entries/feminism-aesthetics/.

Korsmeyer offers an overview of the main issues in feminist aesthetics, with particular attention to the notion of creativity, the concept of genius, and feminist critiques of traditional aesthetic categories (e.g., beauty, disinterestedness, taste, etc.).

6

THE PUZZLE OF MULTIPLE AUTHORSHIP

CASE

Imagine I use my cell phone (and some free editing software) to make a home movie of my baby's exploits on a particular day. Intuitively, I am the author of the film, since I exercised control over every aspect of the process (save, perhaps, for what the baby was doing).

Imagine, now, that Jasmine has come into a large pile of money and wants to make a film. But although she watches a great deal of cinema, she doesn't know much about making films, so she hires people to fulfil each of the key roles, under her oversight. As the project takes shape, however, she realizes that she really doesn't have a very good handle on the business of filmmaking at all, so she outsources all of her decisions to a coin flip—especially when the director and the producer have differing ideas. By chance, the director and producer each get their way about half the time. Here, it seems that there is so much luck involved that neither Jasmine, the producer, nor the director is properly the author of the film—certainly, whatever else our intuitions claim, *Jasmine* isn't.

But now suppose, instead, that Mary Beth is a talented new filmmaker who partners with a helpful producer, with whose help she

DOI: 10.4324/9781003368205-7

generates all of her footage. But when looking at the rough cut, the producer thinks the film cannot be sold as-is. He informs her that she must sacrifice certain key scenes and ideas, or else he will fire her and find someone else to complete the project as he sees fit. After some reflection, she gives in. Here, it seems that Mary Beth's authorship is impaired by the directives from on high; the more substantial the cuts, and the less under her control the final product is, the less the degree to which she counts as its author.

So: authorship seems to involve a degree of creative control over the project. But now, suppose that a big-budget film is being produced over the course of many months. Making the film requires careful contributions from many different people—the director, producers, director of photography, actors, makeup artists, special effects techs, stunt doubles, camera crews and boom operators, set designers, choreographers, editors, and many, many more. Each one of these people contributes something aesthetically important to the final film. Are they all among its co-authors?

Suppose, further, that unbeknownst to them Maia, a rival filmmaker, breaks into the studio and sabotages the production in various ways by messing with the lighting, the placement of equipment like mics and cameras, subtly altering the sets and revising the dialogue, and so on. Each individual act of sabotage is small enough to go unnoticed, but their cumulative effect on the film is aesthetically significant. Imagine, further, that the alterations go unnoticed or, because of budgetary constraints, cannot be fixed. Is Maia one of the film's co-authors?

Presumably, your intuitions, like mine, suggest that she isn't. But why not? Maia has clearly contributed in aesthetically important ways to the film, and has exercised a degree of control over the entire affair, so why doesn't her contribution rise to the level of co-authorship? The home movie case seemed clear, but things get messier once other people are involved, since they too may make important contributions to the work. *The puzzle of multiple authorship* concerns how it is that we should go about distinguishing between people who merely contribute to an artwork and those whose contributions rise to the level of co-authorship. The literature on multiple authorship is best developed with respect to film, but the puzzle is as widespread as collaborative artistic practices are (see also *The Paradox of Creativity*).

RESPONSES

In cinema, auteur-theory postulates that the director is the author of a film, since they are in control of most aspects of production and are therefore responsible for the film's aesthetic properties (see Meskin 2008 for the history of debates over auteur theory; see also *The Problem of Genius*). So what we see is *un film de* George Lucas, Alfred Hitchcock, Steven Spielberg, Akira Kurosawa, etc.

The trouble, however, is that we also see *un film de* Aaron Sorkin (for screenwriting) or Wally Pfister (for cinematography), as well as a Dwayne "The Rock" Johnson or a Meryl Streep film. Worse still, even an iconic film series like *Star Wars* owes much of its aesthetic identity to the (largely uncredited and often belittled) work of editors like Marcia Lucas, George's wife, who also worked on the scripts with her husband and is responsible for key moments such as Obi-Wan Kenobi's death and spiritual guidance. The difficulty, then, comes with distinguishing who counts as a mere contributor versus a co-author.

A useful place to start looking for authors is by focusing on whoever it is who deliberately endows the work with its aesthetic properties (Gaut 1997, Mag Uidhir 2012, Bantinaki 2016, Wylie 2018, Anscomb 2020). We might then note that certain kinds of contributors are typically given more creative freedom than others (Wylie 2018, Anscomb 2020), such that their decisions come to shape the final product in important ways. This is true of Marcia Lucas's contributions to *Star Wars*, for example, but perhaps also of certain sound engineers for recorded music. Artists frequently delegate tasks to others who are more skilled in some respect than they are, but we should not rush to the conclusion that delegation entails a loss of intentional control, either (Bantinaki 2016, Anscomb 2020). The key is to determine the particular balance of directed control with spontaneous creativity for any particular project: co-authors have a high degree of autonomy, subject to coordinating their actions with the overall plan (Anscomb 2020). The reason, then, that we don't count the contributions of key grips and caterers—or of Jasmine and perhaps Mary Beth, above—as authorship is just that they are usually directed in highly specified ways by the intentions of others (Mag Uidhir 2012).

Perhaps another way of putting it is that to be a co-author is to be partly *responsible* for making something a work of the art-kind (e.g., comics, film, music, painting, sculpture, etc.) that it is (Mag Uidhir 2012, Hick 2014). Collective production, on its own, does not entail collective authorship: collective authorship rests on socially determined power relations, and typically sees each author assuming responsibility for the work as a whole (Hick 2014; see also *The Revision Puzzle*). Recognizing that a process of production was collective, however, might bear on the proper aesthetic appreciation of the work (Bantinaki 2016). What it is to be an author of a work in a given art-kind is determined by the appreciative and creative practices that characterize that art-kind, so that authorship in cinema may not look much like authorship in literature or theatre.

This is an important insight, because the case for single cinematic authorship, in particular, appeals to our intuitions about *literary* production, where a single person is usually responsible for all of a work's aesthetically significant properties. In fact, however, literature and film seem relevantly *disanalogous*, since no single person is responsible for _all_ of the work's aesthetic properties. In particular, it's not clear who should occupy the 'author' role with respect to film (Gaut 1997, Meskin 2008). Although directors are the most commonly named candidates, the fact is that screenwriters actually *write* the film's script, actors portray the characters, and so on, and these are all people who have a direct effect on the film's aesthetic properties. While it may sometimes be useful to postulate a single 'constructed' or ideal author for purposes of interpretation (see *Pinny the Who?*), it seems like any theory of authorship which emphasizes contributions to a work's aesthetic properties will tend towards multiple authorship for collaborative art-kinds like film (or comics).

This suggests that although contributing aesthetically relevant properties to the final work is perhaps necessary, it is not a sufficient condition for authorship. What we need is an account of what makes these contributions author-like versus not. And a natural place to look for guidance here is in the philosophy of action, which has a well-developed body of work on shared intentions. One possibility is that joint authorship requires the participants to share an intention to contribute to making a single, unified work (or: a work that makes a single utterance), of the form "*I* intend that we *D*" (Livingston 1997). That is to say, the relevant participants are each committed to working together, and acknowledge and respond to the actions and plans and sub-plans of the other participants. This isn't to say that authors must explicitly intend each and every utterance made by their work, but unintended meanings must result from work which *was* intentionally undertaken (see also *Apelles's Horses*). Although this model does an excellent job of characterizing the kind of active collaboration that takes place in small groups closely together, it is less clear how it applies to projects involving dozens or even hundreds of people, such as studio films. The relevant parties are certainly all committed to working together, but the scope of their interactions may be fairly limited. For such projects, perhaps no single group occupies the role of 'author'—perhaps 'authorship', here, is relative to the different concerns we bring to bear (i.e., are we interested in evaluating or interpreting the film, in talking about its style, or enforcing someone's legal rights?) (Meskin 2008).

Alternately, perhaps authorship requires people to individually commit to contributing to a shared goal, of the form "we intend to *D*" (Sellors 2007). The authorial team, then, is the group of people who share this we-intention; other contributors who don't share this we-framing are not co-authors. This model does a good job of capturing what goes on in improvisational performances, where performers are united by the intention to do something together but may not be aware of one another's particular sub-plans. The trouble is that the looseness of these requirements makes it difficult to distinguish contributors from co-authors. Think of the caterer on the film set, who contributes nothing to the aesthetic dimension of the film but who may be so charmed by the prospect of feeding the cast and crew that they form a delusional we-intention of this kind. They are contributing something important to the film, but they surely aren't a *co-author*!

One last suggestion is that co-authorship is a matter of group membership, which itself entails that members explicitly share certain commitments, obligations, and entitlements, and recognize one another as legitimate contributors to the final project (Bacharach and Tollefsen 2010). In particular, the case of the saboteur seems to suggest that co-authorship requires co-authors to have more than just certain goals in common: they need to coordinate their activity in pursuit of a joint goal. It is precisely because Maia is an outsider to the project that she isn't a co-author: she doesn't share a joint commitment to produce a coherent film with the other filmmakers (quite the contrary).

SUGGESTED READING

SEMINAL PRESENTATION:

1. Livingston, Paisley (1997). "Cinematic Authorship," in *Film Theory and Philosophy*, Richard Allen and Murray Smith (eds.). Oxford: Oxford University Press, 132–48.
   Livingston argues that joint authorship requires a shared intention to contribute to making a single utterance for which the authors are responsible. A shared intention is a state of affairs built out of individual commitments to working together by acknowledging and responding to the sub-plans of the other participants.

DEFENCES:

2. Meskin, Aaron (2008). "Authorship," in *The Routledge Companion to Film and Philosophy*. Paisley Livingston and Carl Plantinga (eds.). New York: Routledge, 12–28.
   Meskin surveys arguments for film authorship, focusing on the issues of multiple vs. singular authorship and whether film authors are real or constructed. He argues that cinematic authorship is context-sensitive, emphasizing different kinds of contributions depending on whether we are speaking about evaluation, interpretation, in terms of the style manifested, or about legal and moral issues.

3. Anscomb, Claire (2020). Visibility, Creativity, and Collective Working Practices in Art and Science. *European Journal for Philosophy of Science* 11 (1): 1–23.
   Anscomb compares collaborations in the arts and sciences, arguing that we should evaluate them based on the degree of autonomy granted to collaborators in the production of the work. A co-author is given a high degree of autonomy in formulating and realizing a work's salient features, such that they are directly responsible for some of the work's artistic properties.

CRITIQUES:

4. Sellors, C. Paul (2007). Collective authorship in film. *Journal of Aesthetics and Art Criticism* 65 (3): 263–71.
   Sellors defends the idea that films are the product of real, rather than constructed, individuals. He argues that authorship isn't derived from a text, but rather from an agent's intentional action which causes that text.

5. Bacharach, Sondra and Deborah Tollefsen (2010). We did it: From Mere Contributors to Coauthors. *Journal of Aesthetics and Art Criticism* 68 (1): 23–32.
   Bacharach and Tollefsen argue that the case of the saboteur shows that accounts of authorship which rely on shared intentions are either too strict in their requirements, or do not do enough to distinguish contribution from

authorship. They argue that co-authorship is tied to group membership, and the joint commitments, obligations, and entitlements that follow.

6. Hick, Darren Hudson (2014). Authorship, Co-Authorship, and Multiple Authorship. *Journal of Aesthetics and Art Criticism* 72 (2): 147–56.

   Hick uses the case of two posthumously published novels by Michael Crichton to challenge the view that mutual intentions about a project or coordination with one's co-authors are necessary components of joint authorship. Authorship, he thinks, is a matter of artistic practice, which rests on social power relations including those codified in copyright law.

FURTHER READING:

7. Gaut, Berys (1997). "Film Authorship and Collaboration," in *Film Theory and Philosophy*. Richard Allen and Murray Smith (eds.). Oxford: Oxford University Press, 149–72.

   For Gaut, authorship requires deliberate contributions to the final product's artistically significant properties. The arguments for single-authorship in cinema are based on a faulty analogy to literary authorship: the aesthetic contributions of actors, editors, and others are *internal* to the film itself, and thus differ significantly from contributions in the performing or literary arts.

8. Mag Uidhir, Christy (2012). "Comics & Collective Authorship," in *The Art of Comics: A Philosophical Approach*, Aaron Meskin and Roy T. Cook (eds.). Malden: Wiley-Blackwell, 47–67.

   Mag Uidhir argues that changes in the consumption habits of comics readers, along with certain technological innovations, have resulted in an environment in which various production roles have taken on new aesthetic significance, such that comics are now usually considered to be multiply authored. To count as an author of a comic, someone must be at least partly responsible for its being *a comic*.

9. Bantinaki, Katerina (2016). Commissioning the Artwork: From Singular Authorship to Collective Creatorship. *Journal of Aesthetic Education* 50 (1): 16–33.

   Bantinaki argues that creatorship and authorship are distinct categories: creatorship requires a contributor to use her own artistic creativity to inform some of the final product's aesthetic properties, whereas authorship requires the kind of direct responsibility and power of decision over the final product's artistic properties that is usually reserved for the commissioning artist.

10. Wylie, Caitlin Donahue (2018). Trust in Technicians in Paleontology Laboratories. *Science, Technology, and Human Values* 43 (2): 324–48.

    Wylie offers an informative parallel analysis of the work that technicians perform in scientific labs, focusing especially on the case of fossil preparators. She shows that preparators' work, though largely invisible, reflects significant aesthetic and creative decisions guided by a joint commitment to collaborating on the preservation, restoration, analysis, and mounting of fossils.

7

THE PUZZLE OF MULTIPLE ENDINGS

CASE

A story has a beginning, middle, and end.

Everybody knows that! Children's fables helpfully begin with 'Once upon a time', go on for a while, then end with 'The End', just to make sure we know what's up and don't get confused. But... *why*? Why don't stories typically have *multiple* endings?

They certainly *can*. Those of us of a certain age will remember choose-your-own-adventure novels (CYOA), which were quite popular—e.g., David Bischoff's *Time Machine 2: Search for Dinosaurs* (1984), R.L. Stine's *Give Yourself Goosebumps* series (1995–2000), or, somewhat more recently, Neil Patrick Harris's autobiography, *Neil Patrick Harris: Choose Your Own Autobiography* (2014). Some films have multiple endings, too: there's Jonathan Lynn's 1985 film adaptation of the classic board game *Clue*, which had three endings, each distributed at random to different cinemas; and Penelope Spheeris's *Wayne's World* (1992), which has two built-in endings; more recently, of course, there was *Black Mirror: Bandersnatch* (2018), an interactive film inspired by the choose-your-own-adventure genre which featured five main endings.

DOI: 10.4324/9781003368205-8

And then, of course, there are video games, many of which have multiple endings depending on just what the player does in the course of the game: there's the incomparable *Chrono Trigger*, as well as *Final Fantasy VI*, *Vagrant Story*, *Resident Evil*, and *Mass Effect 3*, and there's even a whole suite of visual novels with multiple endings, such as *Doki Doki Literature Club!*.

So, it's certainly possible for fictions to have multiple endings. But why do they tend to have just one ending, instead? This is the *puzzle of multiple endings*.

RESPONSES

One important first step here is to distinguish between *multiple* endings and *alternate* endings. When we talk about multiple endings, we're talking about works with two or more different, *authorized* endings, none of which is clearly preferred by the artist. Fan fiction rewrites are unauthorized, and so don't count. An alternate ending, on the other hand, is a different ending which *isn't* authorized, and which was clearly dispreferred for some reason (often for business and marketing reasons). This happens a lot in film when the studio intervenes and forces a director to change the ending (this is why we have director's cuts)—e.g., Ridley Scott's *Blade Runner* (1982), or Danny Boyle's *28 Days Later* (2002). It also happens in literature, though: just consider Charles Dickens's *Great Expectations* (1860–1), or Robert A. Heinlein's *Podkayne of Mars* (1962–3).

In fact, we can broaden the scope of the puzzle if we don't just focus on multiple endings. Taking our cue from the CYOA genre and from video games (especially open-world RPGs like the *Skyrim* series), we might notice that it's possible for some fictions to have very different kinds of *content*, up to and including their endings. One playthrough of *Final Fantasy XII*—and the story that thereby unfolds—might look radically different from another, even if they share an ending, depending on which side-quests each player chose to undertake. Given that this kind of variability of content is possible, why does fiction tend *not* to feature it?

The puzzle seems particularly acute because it raises problems for our traditional accounts of games, fiction, and fictional truth (Moser 2018, Willis 2019). Which ending, for example, is true of *Clue*, and which events are true in *Time Machine 2: Search for Dinosaurs*? More generally, they also raise worries about the pretence theories of fiction that dominate the philosophical literature (Cova and Garcia 2015), which maintain that we use the fiction as a prop in a game of make-believe. When fictions have variable content, what, exactly, is *the* prop that we're using (c.f. Tavinor 2005, Willis 2019)?

On the one hand, it seems like pretence theories are well-equipped to handle this kind of variability: when we engage with a fiction, we are making-believe that certain things are true, including certain facts about ourselves (e.g., I am fighting a red jelly). We can then distinguish between things which are true in the world of the story—things which are true on *any* telling of the story—and things which are just true in a particular game of make-believe. This seems like a perfectly natural way to handle the kind of interactivity that's characteristic of RPGs and CYOA novels: our engagement with them is pretty much the same as in childhood games of make-believe. But on the pretence model, this is true of our engagement with pretty much *any* fiction, so it doesn't help us to explain why some fictions are so much more variable than others. Indeed, it seems that we should expect a lot more variability among canonical fictions than we in fact find (Cova and Garcia 2015).

Another possibility is that in saying that fiction tends not to have multiple endings or variable story content we are ignoring the whole host of fictions which do—not just weird movies like *Clue*, but CYOA novels, visual novels, comic books, tabletop role-playing games (RPGs), and, crucially, *video games*. These are all kinds of fiction which typically—even prototypically—feature variable content, including multiple endings. So perhaps the puzzle is just predicated on a kind of cultural bad faith that ignores "low-culture" in favour of "high-culture" (see also *Utopia*).

There's certainly something to the idea that in formulating the puzzle we seem to focus our attention selectively on certain cultural products—e.g., novels and film; perhaps even Literature and Film with capital letters—and not on others. But perhaps the puzzle tracks a real difference between cultural products: perhaps it tracks a difference between *interactive* and *non-interactive* fiction (Tavinor 2005, Cova and Garcia 2015, Robson and Meskin 2016).[1] And some interactive fictions (*self-involved* interactive fictions) have us actively step into the driver's seat and take on the role of the protagonist, so that in engaging with them we are generating fictional truths not just about the story, but about ourselves, too (e.g., *I* beat Zombor on Zenan Bridge). Perhaps, then, we can explain the relative dearth of multiple endings by observing the relative dearth of self-involved interactive fictions.

It is worth noting that there is some doubt about the extent to which we really do place ourselves at the heart of interactive fiction; in particular, the first-personal way we talk about fictional events may be misleading (Patridge 2017). Nevertheless, focusing on the interactive nature of these variable fictions gives us a natural explanation for their variability: interactivity allows for repeated consumption to reveal a new story or interesting content that was missed the first time (Lopes 2001, Wildman and Woodward 2018). Variable content diversifies the interactive experience and so it's more desirable in interactive fiction than in canonical fiction, and the primary vehicle for introducing it is to leave the story incomplete at various junctures. Although canonical fiction is incomplete too (fiction is *necessarily* incomplete because no author has the time to spell out *all* of their story's truths), interactive fiction exploits a kind of forced-choice incompleteness, according to which we must decide which of two or more things are true in the fiction or cease engaging with the fiction altogether. In this limited way, interactive fiction allows us to step into the protagonist's or storyteller's shoes.

If we want to know why our fiction is predominantly canonical (if it is), then a promising strategy is to observe that singular fiction seems to have features which would tend to make it more culturally stable than variable fiction (Nichols 2002). Crucially, multiple endings and variable content are harder to remember and transmit in a culture without access to a recording medium (e.g., writing, film, etc.). This fact alone seems to offer a promising explanation for our cultural bias towards singular, canonical fiction, as well as for the comparatively recent development of variable stories and multiple endings.

Similarly, it may seem that multiple endings and variable content ought to be particularly pleasing to us, because they allow us to pick and choose the story we want; they allow us to actively participate in the process of content creation. This participation seems to be what distinguishes interactive arts from other art-kinds (Lopes 2001). But it's not clear that this is what we *do* want—at least, not most of the time. Canonical fiction seems to respond to a different desire: the desire to be *told* a story, and it may well be that this desire is more basic and more widely shared than the desire to tell a story of our own (Sharpe 2002). Indeed, the *surprising* aspect of non-interactive fiction may well contribute to the pleasure we take in it.

SUGGESTED READING

SEMINAL PRESENTATION:

1. Cova, Florian and Amanda Garcia (2015). The Puzzle of Multiple Endings. *Journal of Aesthetics and Art Criticism* 73 (2): 105–14.
   Cova and Garcia characterize the puzzle of multiple endings and consider a number of inadequate responses to it. After distinguishing between alternate and multiple endings, they draw an illustrative contrast between the scarcity of multiple endings in traditional fiction and their proliferation in interactive fictions, arguing that this contrast poses a problem for make-believe accounts of fiction.

DEFENCES:

2. Robson, Jon and Aaron Meskin (2016). Video Games as Self-Involving Interactive Fictions. *Journal of Aesthetics and Art Criticism* 74 (2): 165–77.
   Meskin and Robson focus their attention on self-involved interactive fictions (SIIFs), fictions which encourage appreciators to identify with the protagonist. They argue that such fictions characteristically see us generating fictional truths about ourselves, unlike canonical fiction. Variable content and multiple endings, they think, are standard features of SIIFs.
3. Wildman, Nathan and Richard Woodward (2018). "Interactivity, Fictionality, and Incompleteness," in *The Aesthetics of Videogames*, Jon Robson and Grant Tavinor (eds.). New York: Routledge, 112–27.
   Wildman and Woodward argue that interactive fiction is best explained in terms of a special kind of incompleteness: forced-choice incompleteness, according to which there is no prescription to imagine *p* and none to imagine not-*p*, but there *is* a prescription to imagine one or the other. Such prescriptions are permissive, but also *prescriptive*; the audience *must* resolve the incompleteness, or cease engaging with the work. In resolving the relevant incompleteness, the appreciator *makes something true* in their reading or playthrough.
4. Willis, Marissa D. (2019). Choose Your Own Adventure: Examining the Fictional Content of Video Games as Interactive Fictions. *Journal of Aesthetics and Art Criticism* 77 (1): 43–53
   Willis observes that interactive fiction is not only open to multiple endings, but also to variable content *throughout* the story. Interactive fiction is

thus much more like the performing arts, where correct performances are under-described by the notation. Willis argues we must distinguish between what's true in the game and true in a *playthrough*.

CRITIQUES:

5. Patridge, Stephanie (2017). Videogames and Imaginative Identification. *Journal of Aesthetics and Art Criticism* 75 (2): 181–4.
   Patridge cautions that we should not overemphasize the role of self-involved imagining in interactive fiction. While it can be present, it often isn't—even when the fiction explicitly invites identification with a character of avatar. Often, it is the game-like aspect that dominates our engagement with the fiction.

FURTHER READING:

6. Lopes, Dominic McIver (2001). The Ontology of Interactive Art. *Journal of Aesthetic Education* 35 (4): 65–81.
   Lopes argues that interactive artwork are types whose tokens are generated by our interaction with them. He distinguishes between weak interactivity, which gives users control over when they access content, and strong inter-activity, which prescribes a certain set of actions that users can take to help generate a work's content. Inspired by games, he argues for a type-token ontology of strongly interactive works.

7. Nichols, Shaun (2002). On the Genealogy of Norms: A Case for the Role of Emotion in Cultural Evolution. *Philosophy of Science* 69: 234–55.
   Nichols asks what makes some norms more likely to prevail than others, arguing that emotional responses play a critical role. In particular, he argues that the norms prohibiting actions which will arouse negative emotions are more salient and memorable, and thus more likely to survive over time than their affectively neutral counterparts. Singular endings might be more prevalent because they yield simpler, more memorable, and more attractive fictions.

8. Sharpe, Robert Augustus (2002). The Tale and the Teller. *British Journal of Aesthetics* 42 (4): 415–8.
   Sharpe asks the related question of why it is that we cannot—or do not—write our own endings for the stories we consume. Sharpe ultimately argues that the answer lies in our storytelling practices: we want to be *told* stories, not tell them ourselves.

9. Tavinor, Grant (2005). Videogames and Interactive Fiction. *Philosophy and Literature* 29: 24–40.
   Tavinor contrasts video games with canonical fictions, arguing that their characteristic interactivity and 'kinetic' narrative structure sets them apart.

He argues that the interactive nature of video games is well captured by analyses of fiction as make-believe, where the game itself takes the role of a prop able to represent new content for imagining depending on the player's input.

10. Moser, Shelby (2018). "Videogame Ontology, Constitutive Rules, and Algorithms," in *The Aesthetics of Videogames*, Jon Robson and Grant Tavinor (eds.). New York: Routledge, 42–59.

Moser observes that distinct playings of a videogame can result in its having different 'constitutive rules', unlike ordinary games. She argues that a game's identity is tied to its complete game algorithm (as distinct from its code), rather than to its constitutive rules, thus allowing for very different playthroughs of one and the same game.

NOTE

1 Film can sometimes be interactive, too: Radúz Činčera's *Kinoautomat* (1967) was the first.

THE REVISION PUZZLE

CASE

We know that musical works can change. Right?

In 2018, Bad Wolves changed The Cranberries' hit single *Zombie* by updating one instance of 'bombs' in the lyrics to 'drones' and giving it a not-so-heavy metal instrumentation. Mozart's *Requiem* was changed by his student Franz Xaver Süssmayr (among others), who finished the piece after Mozart's death, based on Mozart's sketches for the piece. And Anton Bruckner was notorious for revising his works in light of criticism; his *Eighth Symphony*, for example, was first composed in 1887 and subsequently revised in 1890. These all seem like musical works which were changed.

Nor is the phenomenon limited to music: when we perform Shakespeare's plays today, it's commonplace to cut out the boring scenes, to update the play to a contemporary setting, or to retell the story entirely, as with *The Lion King* (1994; based on *Hamlet*) or *10 Things I Hate About You* (1999; based on *The Taming of the Shrew*). When the varnish on a painting like Rembrandt's *Militia Company of District II under the Command of Captain Frans Banninck Cocq* (1642; colloquially known as the *Night Watch*) gets too dark with age and grime, we *restore* it to its former glory. And when viewers follow Félix González-Torres's

DOI: 10.4324/9781003368205-9

instructions and take a candy from the pile which is *Untitled (Portrait of Ross in L.A.)* (1991), they change the installation; eventually, if everyone follows his instructions, there is no more pile at all.

Now, someone might object that not all of these "changes" are comparable. When Bad Wolves covered *Zombie*, they changed one word of the lyrics and played with the instrumentation, but the song itself was still The Cranberries' *Zombie*, and recognizably so. Their *performance* of the song is certainly different, but it's not obvious that they changed *the song itself.*[1] Similarly, someone might object that plays are designed to have some parts omitted or adapted when they are performed, just as altering the pile of candy is part of the point of González-Torres's installation and thus part of the *work* itself, and that *The Lion King* and *10 Things I Hate About You* are different works inspired by Shakespeare's originals (much as his plays were inspired by older stories). Finally, our interlocutor might concede that restoration affects an artwork's surface properties, but only in service of re-communicating the authentic, original aesthetic experience it once delivered (if the painting is so grimy that a daylight scene looks set at night, after all, then something has gone horribly wrong).

A useful way of conceiving of this difference is in terms of a work's *intrinsic* vs. its *extrinsic* properties. Intrinsic properties are properties a thing has because of (*in virtue of*) the way it is—so, e.g., *contains speeches* is an intrinsic property of *Hamlet*, and *is animated* is an intrinsic property of *The Lion King* (well, the original, anyway). All the other properties of the work which are not intrinsic are *extrinsic*—so, e.g., *is dirtier than The Mona Lisa* was an extrinsic property of Rembrandt's *Militia Company* until it was cleaned, and *has 642 candies purchased in New York* would be an extrinsic property of González-Torres's installation at whichever point it's composed of that many candies.

With respect to musical works, we might then say that Bad Wolves have only changed the extrinsic properties of the Cranberries original—which makes sense, since it's just a cover song. They obviously haven't changed *the original*. But what about Süssmayr's completion of Mozart, or Bruckner's meticulous revisions? These seem like good candidates for changing the work itself but, if so, then we are left with what David Friedell (2020) has called *the revision puzzle*: why can't *I* change Bruckner's *Eighth Symphony*? What gives *Bruckner* the ability to change it, but not *me*? Similarly, why is it counted as vandalism if I destroy a Banksy, but when *he* shredded *Girl with Balloon* (2006) moments after it was auctioned off for $1.4 million, that was somehow counted as part of the work itself?

RESPONSES

One natural answer to the revision puzzle is just that Bruckner is the author of his eighth symphony, whereas I am decidedly not: only the original artist may change her work's intrinsic properties (Savile 1993). Relatedly, the default view in musical ontology has it that musical works are uncreated and eternally existing abstract objects such as types (e.g., Kivy 1987). According to this view, musical works cannot change: their intrinsic properties are fixed by the sound-structure that determines the type's identity-conditions. Deviations from that type are either malformed instances or wholly new works.

The trouble with these responses, however, is that they don't seem entirely true to the facts. Consider posthumous completion: it's fairly plausible that Mozart's *Requiem* changed when Süssmayr finished it, or that Robert Jordan's *Wheel of Time* was changed by Brandon Sanderson when he was commissioned to finish the series. Then again, perhaps it matters that Süssmayr and Sanderson were officially commissioned by the relevant authorities, so that their versions were sanctioned. But even leaving posthumous composition aside, we know that jazz standards and folk songs change all the time, without their creators' consent or sanction. *Yankee Doodle*, for example, has come a long, *long* way from its origins as a fifteenth-century Dutch harvest song with nonsense words.[2] And more generally, we change objects all the time without their creators' consent, such as when we re-finish furniture or renovate our houses. So, what prevents a more permissive account of artistic revision?

Alternately, we might think that musical works in particular, and artworks more generally, are *temporally flexible*—that is, that they are capable of changing their intrinsic properties over time (Rohrbaugh 2003, Evnine 2009, Hazlett 2012; c.f. *The Wrong Note Paradox*). This means that Bruckner's revisions of his symphony changed the original entity (by changing what it's made of: its sound-structure), rather than creating a new one. This helps us to preserve the intuition that musical works can change, but it doesn't do much to explain why Bruckner can access and alter his work's intrinsic properties but I can't.

Perhaps a better explanation is that it's just a matter of social conventions which have developed in such a way that only the original artist can alter a work (Friedell 2020; see also Grafton-Cardwell 2020, Fisher 2021); anyone else's alterations result in a similar and closely related, but different, work. This means that there is nothing in the nature of the work itself or in musical ontology more broadly to prevent revisions. At a deep ontological level, it's an entirely arbitrary and contingent fact: a different history of artistic practices would yield a different set of conventions of authorship. But the fact that it's arbitrary and contingent at a deep ontological level doesn't mean that it's arbitrary and contingent at the top level, at the level of the world in which we operate.

Consider speed limits (Friedell 2020): there's nothing about the ontology of roads themselves that mandates a certain speed limit, nor is the limit of 50kph (30mph) identical to or part of the road in question. It's an *extrinsic* property associated with a particular road thanks to a complex system of laws and legal institutions; and so too with musical works, or so the idea goes. Just as I can't change a road's speed limit unilaterally, neither can I revise someone else's artwork (without generating an altogether different work). Our social practices determine that speed limit changes can only be effected by the appropriate arm of government (and those acting on its behalf); likewise, our artistic practices are such that Bruckner, but not I, can change his eighth symphony.

Such a solution will be compatible with any model of musical ontology that treats changes to musical works (or other artworks) as changes to their *extrinsic*, rather than their intrinsic, properties.[3] Musical materialism, for example, treats musical works as concrete entities either composed of all their performances taken together (Caplan and Matheson 2006), or each performance of which is a temporal stage in a larger space-time object (sometimes called a 'worm') (Moruzzi 2022; see also *Unperformable Music*). On such a construal, any changes we might effect are changes to a performance or stage of the work, rather than to the underlying entity. Changing a work's extrinsic properties is a relatively easy thing to do, and a widespread practice; but such changes are often governed by social institutions and practices, just as the properties of our road networks are. Sometimes, the social world restricts the ability to change an artifact to institutionally sanctioned individuals. There is nothing deeply principled or ontologically necessary about such restrictions; it's just the way things are.

SUGGESTED READING

SEMINAL PRESENTATION:

1. Friedell, David (2020). Why Can't I Change Bruckner's Eighth Symphony? *Philosophical Studies* 177 (3): 805–24.

   Friedell introduces the revision puzzle using Bruckner's *Eighth Symphony* and argues that the answer lies in our social practices. These are contingent but they nevertheless determine the range of ways in which artworks can change, and who has the power to change them. What changes are an artwork's extrinsic properties; musical works have almost no intrinsic properties beyond being created abstract partless objects.

DEFENCES:

2. Caplan, Ben and Carl Matheson (2006). Defending Musical Perdurantism. *British Journal of Aesthetics* 46 (1): 59–69.

   Caplan and Matheson argue that musical works are concrete spatiotemporal objects composed of all of their performances (i.e., each performance is a temporal part of a four-dimensional object). This means that *Zombie* is composed of The Cranberries' performances as well as Bad Wolves', and others. Any changes I or others may make are changes to the performances of the work, and thus merely changes to the work's extrinsic properties.

3. Moruzzi, Caterina (2022). Everyone Can Change a Musical Work. *British Journal of Aesthetics* 62 (1): 1–13.

   Moruzzi argues that musical stage theory—which posits that musical works are instantaneous spatiotemporal stages—allows anyone at all to change a musical work. Some changes, however, are more significant than others, and these will be socially determined. In particular, social conventions tend to restrict the authority to change musical works to their composers.

CRITIQUES:

3. Kivy, Peter (1987). Platonism in Music: Another Kind of Defense. *American Philosophical Quarterly* 24 (3): 233–44.

   Kivy defends musical Platonism against two major objections, the first of which is that contextual properties are essential properties of musical works. Kivy argues instead that it is sound structures that are essential to musical works; everything else is contingent. Changes to a sound structure would change a work, but such changes are impossible since the work exists eternally.

4. Rohrbaugh, Guy (2003). Artworks as Historic Individuals. *European Journal of Philosophy* 11 (2): 177–205.

   Inspired by photography, Rohrbaugh argues that it is a mistake to identify repeatable artworks with types. He argues, instead, that they are concrete objects persisting through history which are paradigmatically susceptible to change in their *intrinsic* properties over time (i.e., they're temporally flexible), just like folk songs.

5. Dodd, Julian (2007). *Works of Music: An Essay in Ontology.* Oxford: Oxford University Press.

   Dodd offers a landmark defence of musical Platonism rooted in the metaphysics of types, arguing that musical works are eternally existing abstract objects. In Ch. 2 he dismisses the possibilities that musical works might be changeable or modally flexible, arguing that any successful change to a work of music would result in an entirely new work.

6. Evnine, Simon (2009). Constitution and Qua Objects in the Ontology of Music. *British Journal of Aesthetics* 49 (3): 203–17.

   Evnine argues that musical works are constituted by their sound-structures, which are indicated by their composers. A musical work like Yankee Doodle can change over time by coming to be constituted by a new sound-structure, but this marks a change in the work's intrinsic properties.

FURTHER READING:

7. Savile, Anthony (1993). The Rationale of Restoration. *Journal of Aesthetics and Art Criticism* 51 (3): 463–74.

   Savile argues that a work's properties are "fixed" by the original act of creation. Time, he thinks, may change a work's extrinsic, but not the intrinsic, properties we take as standard for criticism (although he does not himself distinguish between intrinsic and extrinsic properties). Only the original artist, then, can change her work, and that, only before it is finished and its properties fixed. Exactly when that is remains an open question.

8. Hazlett, Allan (2012). "Against Repeatable Artworks," in *Art and Abstract Objects*, Christy Mag Uidhir (ed.). Oxford: Oxford University Press, 161–78.

   Hazlett argues that there is an unresolvable tension between our intuitions that musical works are repeatable and that they are modally flexible (i.e., that they could have been different), with knock-on effects for temporal flexibility). Artworks, he argues, can only be repeatable if they are abstract objects. Abstract objects have all of their intrinsic properties essentially, but artworks don't (i.e., many of their intrinsic properties are *accidental*); therefore, there are no repeatable artworks.

9. Grafton-Cardwell, Patrick (2020). Debugging the Case for Creationism. *Philosophical Studies* 177 (1–2): 1–19.
Grafton-Cardwell argues that creationists (like Friedell or Evnine) and Platonists[4] about repeatable artworks are at a standstill. In particular, he considers the Platonic case for temporal flexibility, arguing that acts of composition establish and rely on certain social practices, all of which are extrinsic properties of the musical work. So, when Bruckner revises his *Eighth Symphony* he is changing the social practices previously established with respect to his work.

10. Fisher, Anthony R. J. (2021). Musical Works as Structural Universals. *Erkenntnis*: 1–23.
Fisher defends a musical *Aristotelianism*, according to which musical works exist entirely in their instances, rather than in some more abstract realm. This means musical works are created and can be destroyed. Musical works, he argues, are structural universals whose normative features are contingent, and thus subject to intrinsic change.

NOTES

1 Although judging from the number of YouTube videos crediting it as being by "The Cranberries/Bad Wolves", it may well be that we need to rethink this intuition for the contemporary moment!

2 It has also come a long way from its eighteenth-century version as a British taunt of their colonial troops.

3 That said, you might worry that changes to a work's extrinsic properties alone aren't genuine changes to the work (Fisher 2021); similarly, if you change your phone number, nothing about *you* seems to have changed. The conventionalist, however, is happy to bite this bullet and accept that changing a melody is like changing a phone number.

4 Note that creationism is a way of articulating Platonism; the two aren't necessarily opposed, although some Platonists (like Kivy and Dodd) are adamant that musical works are eternally existing and, thus, discovered rather than created.

9

THE TIME MACHINE (DESIGN)

CASE

Imagine inventing a time machine. You start by drawing up plans, of course: you need to specify its various component parts—the flux capacitor, phase discriminator, dial-home device, gravitic drift compensator, Helmic regulator, the heart of the TARDIS, etc. (There are no separate plans for each of these components, however.) Now, here is the crucial question: have you *designed* a time machine? Intuitively, it seems like the answer must be 'no': you've done some of the same things that we think of as required for design, like drawing up plans for some kind of object with a specific function, and the planning phase is clearly distinct from the execution phase. But something isn't quite right, something isn't quite there. What is it?

One possibility is that this can't be a genuine design for a time machine because no such things exist, and the prospects for their possible existence are decidedly dim—indeed, yours is just a list of parts cobbled together from fictional time machines! Then again, there are plenty of designs out there for objects which, once assembled, wouldn't work—Leonardo da Vinci's designs for various flying or submersible machines, for example. The mere fact that the object designed couldn't work as advertised doesn't seem sufficient to deny

DOI: 10.4324/9781003368205-10

that we have a design on our hands. It *might* suffice to say that it's a *bad* design, but that just means that we need to figure out whether our time machine is a case of bad design or not a design at all.

Perhaps a different way of cashing out the problem with the time machine's 'design' is simply that it's ridiculous on the face of it. Given what we know about space-time, and given that the components are themselves fictional, anybody who knows anything can tell just by looking at the plans that they're doomed. With da Vinci's drawings, on the other hand, there's a good case to be made that a well-informed fifteenth-century Italian could not have reasonably characterized them as hopeless. Fanciful and unlikely, perhaps, but certainly not risible, and perhaps even plausible. So: what are the necessary and sufficient conditions for design?

RESPONSES

At a first pass, it seems like we might be able to define design as the activity of deliberately imagining a novel solution to some problem by creating plans for a new kind of object which one genuinely believes would solve the problem in question (Bamford 1991). One virtue of such an account is that it leaves clear room for failure: there's no condition requiring that the object successfully solve the envisaged problem. So long as the plans were deliberately conceived as a novel solution to some problem, they were designs; that their successful execution could not have solved the problem simply suggests that they were bad designs. The result is that quite a broad range of activities will count as design, including the formulation of hypotheses and theories in science. But since we regularly talk of 'experimental design', that particular result doesn't seem very far-fetched.

The problem is that our starting thought experiment seems to satisfy these conditions, and yet we hesitate to call it a case of design: we can easily imagine someone who doesn't know that the parts in question are all fictional, a child, perhaps, drawing up elaborate plans for a time machine. But, as we saw above, any reasonable person would *immediately* see that the plans weren't up to the task. It may be a case of *imagining* a time machine, but it doesn't seem to be a case of *designing* one. So perhaps what's missing is an epistemic constraint: design is the deliberate creation of plans for a new sort of thing which solves a particular problem, *where those plans are not obviously a non-starter in principle* (Parsons 2015). That's not to say that the designer must be justified in the belief that the design will work; it's just that the plans can't be an obvious waste of time. Similarly, the cost of materials might be impractical, but that's no barrier to the plans counting as a genuine design; that the materials don't and can't exist, however, *is*.

It might be objected that this focus on primarily functional considerations ignores the fundamentally *aesthetic* aspect of design (Hamilton 2011). Design, according to this view, isn't just about solving technical problems; it's about doing it *with style* (see also *The Transmogrifier*). Designs aren't just solutions, they're *elegant* solutions; decoration and embellishment are inseparable from the concept of design. Designs are things which we can appreciate aesthetically for their visual, auditory, or haptic (touched) features. Alternately, we might say that a design is a configuration that's sufficiently striking as to suggest, to viewers, that it was intentionally produced by someone (even if it wasn't) (Dilworth 2001; see also *The Whale and the Driftwood*).

Aesthetic accounts of design immediately raise two questions, however: first, how is design distinguished from *craft*, and second, how is design distinguished from *art* (Parsons 2015)? Let's consider craft first. It's widely agreed that the concepts of 'craft' and 'design' have a common historical origin in the industrial revolution, with the development of a consumer society focused on displaying and expressing individual, rather than social, taste (Hamilton 2011, Shiner 2012, Forsey 2013, Parsons 2015, Fisher 2019). Although the activities of crafting and designing are clearly as old as tool use, they underwent a significant reconceptualization as standalone concepts (and categories of disciplines) in the eighteenth century, with their respective activities clearly separated out by the early twentieth (Shiner 2012). Today, 'craft' retains a crucial association with the handmade, with intense engagement with a material (Shiner 2012); 'design', by contrast, is largely *disassociated* from the process of making, so that the designer and the craftsperson are typically different people (designs need not even be executed by craftspeople in the first place).

As for art, it has been suggested that design is a fundamentally 'mute' enterprise (Forsey 2013): unlike art, design does not usually involve an act of self-expression, or of communication to an audience. Design, on this view, is an *object-centred* practice; the designer, unlike the artist, is largely anonymous, their identity unimportant save insofar as their intentions determine the function to which the designed object is to be put, and that function in turn shapes our aesthetic evaluation of the object (Forsey 2013). Although the product of a design can be put to many different uses, what matters is its *intended* function, since this is what determines the nature of the object and our initial engagement with it. The beauty of a design is what philosophers sometimes call 'dependent' (as opposed to 'free') beauty (see also *Pot People, Basket Folk*), since appreciating it requires us to have a prior concept of what the thing is, and what it's used for (Forsey 2013). By calling something a 'fork', for example, we associate the object with our cultural knowledge of a particular kind of artifact; if it turns out that the fork in question is completely unsuited to spearing or shovelling food, then that's a strike against the design (although not necessarily a fatal blow—see Favara-Kurkowski 2021).

This emphasis on intended function is a common one, but it's worth noting that it's not entirely unproblematic. With technological design in particular, the uses to which objects are put quickly outstrip their intended functions. Classic examples include the phonograph, which was intended as a dictation device rather than a music player, and the typewriter, initially conceived as a writing aid for the blind (Idhe 2008). Similarly, the 'same' design can be very differently culturally embedded, as is the case with fourth-century Tibetan prayer wheels, ninth-century European windmills, and contemporary wind turbines. This kind of contingency suggests, to some, that we ought to be wary of a 'designer fallacy' comparable to the intentional fallacy in literature (Idhe 2008; see *Pinny the Who?*).

Finally, it's worth noting the historical and conceptual connection between design and architecture. The comparison between the two fields is a natural one, since buildings—especially *special* buildings—have been subjects of design since antiquity, and since modern architecture involves a distinct planning phase whose participants are not usually directly involved in the execution phases (Parsons 2015). But while our colloquial concept of design may well be influenced by our folk understanding of architecture, philosophers have argued that a closer look reveals significant disanalogies. In particular, it's not obvious that architectural designs are solutions to particular non-aesthetic problems, rather than part of a process of just figuring out what to do, since these "problems" are not easily comparable (De Clercq 2012). So, for example, while there may be clear tradeoffs between the values of privacy and natural illumination, there are no rules for determining what counts as a "best" solution (De Clercq 2012).

Contrary to popular belief, architectural design can also overlap considerably with the construction process (De Clercq 2012, Fisher 2019): architecture frequently requires the "recalibration" of plans, and thus often features plans which are themselves incomplete or non-fixed (Fisher 2019). Architectural objects also shape the spaces in which they find themselves, and are often designed in response to their local environments; the same can't be said for most designed objects, however. In fact, most designed objects are, by their nature, *replicable*—indeed, they're usually designed with that goal in mind. But while architectural works are replicable in principle, in practice they are seldom repeated, as is reflected in our practice of naming certain buildings (e.g., the Parthenon, Fallingwater, etc.) (De Clercq 2012; see also Dilworth 2001, and c.f. Bamford 1991). Unlike a musical work, which is widely believed to be individuated by its score (see *The Wrong Note Paradox*), architectural works are typically identified with the concrete particular *building*, not its plan (De Clercq 2012). Ultimately, then, although architecture and design have elements in common, it seems like we can't quite classify architecture as a species of design, since the two are based on, and oriented towards, different kinds of aesthetic interests and practical concerns (Fisher 2019).

SUGGESTED READING

SEMINAL PRESENTATION:

1. Parsons, Glenn (2015). *The Philosophy of Design*. Cambridge: Polity.
   Parsons suggests our thought experiment in Ch. 1. He defines design as the intentional solution of a problem by the creation of *prima facie* plausible plans for a new sort of artifact. Although design often has an aesthetic aspect, he argues that it isn't necessary for the concept.

DEFENCES:

2. Bamford, Greg (1991). "Design, Science and Conceptual Analysis," in *Architectural Science and Design in Harmony: Proceedings of the joint ANZAScA/*

ADTRA Conference, Sydney, 10–12 July, 1990, Jim Plume (ed.). School of Architecture, University of NSW.

Bamford argues that most definitions of design in the non-philosophical literature are either too broad, too narrow, or both. He argues that design involves imagining or describing a novel or original solution for some functional problem.

3. Dilworth, John (2001). Artworks Versus Designs. *British Journal of Aesthetics* 41 (2): 162–77.

Dilworth argues that designing involves producing a plan for something and, thus, that designs are types. Types, of course, are always multiply realizable. A design is a configuration that can be considered as though it had been intentionally produced by someone: it's any configuration that's suitably striking to viewers, so as to suggest that it was intentionally endowed with that quality.

CRITIQUES:

4. Hamilton, Andy (2011). "The Aesthetics of Design," in *Fashion – Philosophy for Everyone: Thinking with Style,* Jessica Wolfendale and Jeanette Kennett (eds.). Malden, MO: Blackwell, 51–69.

Hamilton argues that functional considerations alone don't quite capture the notion of design, which has an ineliminable aesthetic component. Design both solves functional problems *and* improves the look or feel of its object. Fashion's practical function, however, is typically hidden by its social functions.

5. Forsey, Jane (2013). *The Aesthetics of Design.* Oxford: Oxford University Press. Forsey is skeptical of the prospects for a definition of design in terms of necessary and sufficient conditions. Instead, she offers a descriptive characterization of design that aims to capture the intuitions that design is functional, immanent, mass-produced, and 'mute'. These characteristics, she thinks, distinguish design from art and craft.

FURTHER READING:

6. Idhe, Don (2008). "The Designer Fallacy and Technological Innovation," in *Philosophy and Design: From Engineering to Architecture,* Pieter E. Vermaas, Peter Kroes, Andrew Light and Steven A. Moore (eds.). Dordecht: Springer, 51–60. Idhe contends that discussion of technological design is prone to the "designer fallacy", which parallels the intentional fallacy in literature. He argues that technological design is heavily constrained by its materials and their relative plasticity and that the uses to which it is put typically outstrip the functions the object was designed to serve.

7. De Clercq, Raphael. (2012) "Architecture," in *The Bloomsbury Companion to Aesthetics*, Anna Christina Ribeiro (ed.). London: Continuum, 201–14.
   De Clercq surveys the literature on the aesthetics of architecture and its historical connection to design. He shows that architectural design can overlap with the process of construction and need not involve pre-existing plans. Moreover, in cases of non-anonymous architectural design, we tend to associate the design with a single, concrete *building* rather than the plan.

8. Shiner, Larry (2012). "Blurred Boundaries?" Rethinking the Concept of Craft and its Relation to Art and Design. *Philosophy Compass* 7: 230–44.
   Shiner canvasses the history of the concept of 'craft', arguing that it co-evolved with that of 'design' in the late nineteenth century but that their respective statuses diverged by the early twentieth. He advocates treating craft, design, and high art as closely related practices.

9. Fisher, Saul (2019). When is Architecture Not Design? *Laocoonte: Revista de Estética y Teoría de Las Artes* 1 (6): 183–98.
   Fisher argues that architecture isn't a species of design: the two disciplines have very different historical paths of development, and although they share some activities in common, they operate very differently today. Architecture is tied to particular environments, uses, and users in a way that design isn't, and requires a degree of plasticity and responsiveness of planning that is absent from design practices.

10. Favara-Kurkowski, Monika (2021). In defense of Forsey's Aesthetics of Design. *Avant: Trends in Interdisciplinary Studies* 12 (3): 1–10.
    Favara-Kurkowski defends Forsey's account of design from the charge that characterizing design's appeal in terms of dependent beauty precludes us from appreciating (deliberately) impractical objects, or objects with complex functions.

10

THE WHALE AND THE DRIFTWOOD (ARTIFACTUALITY)

CASE

Suppose you're walking along the beach with a friend, as you do, and you see a somewhat deflated whale carcass washed up on shore. Your friend points to it and says, "Look, there's a dead seagull!"

Obviously, your friend is wrong. Merely calling the whale a seagull doesn't suffice to make it one (besides which, there's no such thing as a 'seagull' either, just different kinds of gulls). Now suppose they point to an ordinary piece of driftwood[1] and say "There's an artifact!" Again, they're just plain wrong: nobody made it, it's just ordinary driftwood. But suppose, instead, they pointed to the same piece of driftwood and said, "That's a lovely sculpture!" To be clear, they aren't announcing that they've now *made* a sculpture; they're simply describing the object they see *as* a sculpture. Are they still wrong to say so?

For a time, a significant contingent of philosophers of art answered in the negative, arguing that the recent history of art had shown that while most artworks are artifacts, they need not *all* be. Inspired by Wittgenstein's remarks on the impossibility of defining games (c.f. *Utopia*), they argued that art, too, is an 'open' concept, which is just to say that we can always imagine future developments which might require us to revise our use and understanding of the concept (Weitz

DOI: 10.4324/9781003368205-11

1956). On this model, there are no properties common to all artworks and all art-kinds, no necessary and sufficient conditions we can use to define 'art'; all there is, are similarities between them, and it's on the basis of these similarities that we classify certain objects as art, and say that others are not. This is known as the family resemblance theory of art, on the basis that the various members of a family may all be quite different, yet they share a certain resemblance to one another.

Early versions of the theory posited that anything that resembled a paradigm instance of art should be counted as art by virtue of that resemblance. These early accounts quickly came under fire for being incomplete, since they failed to specify what counted as paradigm instances in the first place. More troubling, however, was the fact that absent further specification, anything can resemble anything else. *Sinosauropteryx*, for example, was a small, feathered compsognathid dinosaur, and recent analysis has shown it to have had orange feathers and a striped tail. One of Eric Doeringer's *Stripe Paintings* (2009) is orange with white stripes. Should we conclude on this basis that *Sinosauropteryx* was an artwork?

RESPONSES

Art is typically thought to be *intention-dependent*, which means that the artist's intentions are a necessary component of art-making (see *Apelles's Horses*). This is because all artworks are supposed to be *artifacts* or *performances*, and the difference between an artifact or performance and a natural object or process, like the driftwood, is that the artifact or performance is the result of someone's intentional activity. By suggesting that the driftwood is an artwork in virtue of looking like a sculpture, skeptics like Weitz were denying that artifactuality is a necessary condition for art.

This contention drew a great deal of criticism: after all, we wouldn't say that a monkey's random typing was a poem—at least, not until someone who knew what they were doing presented it as such (M. Eaton 1969). If by an unlikely coincidence the wind and waves arranged some sticks to say "TIDAL WAVE IN ONE HOUR" approximately one hour before a tidal wave was to hit, we shouldn't—and wouldn't?—call that a message, since the wind and waves weren't trying to *communicate*. If, on the other hand, you had heard of an impending tidal wave, saw the sticks so arranged, and decided to leave them there as a handy warning, *that would* be a communicative act. You would have commandeered—appropriated—a natural occurrence for your own purposes. Without an intentional underpinning, there is no message there for anyone to *interpret*. So, it seems, the driftwood *becomes* an artifact and an artwork through someone's act of appropriation.

Similarly, others observed that the family resemblance model hadn't quite managed to extirpate artifactuality as a necessary condition for art, since the paradigm instances by reference to which a natural object like the driftwood comes to count as art are themselves all artifacts (e.g., Michelangelo's *Pietà* [1498–9]) (Sclafani 1970). Art, so the thought goes, is a fundamentally human activity, and thus intimately tied to our social practices. To strip away its artifactuality runs the risk of divorcing it entirely from the sphere of human activity.

Although skepticism about the definition of art was quite fashionable for a time, it soon came under heavy fire. In particular, it was observed that the metaphor of family resemblance itself suggested a different result: family members are not identified by virtue of their overt physical resemblance, but rather by the fact that they have a common *genetic* heritage (Mandelbaum 1965). This genetic heritage allows us to group together as related even individuals who look and behave absolutely nothing alike; and that suggests that perhaps something similar is true of art, too. The fact that our *classifications* of art have changed over the course of history (if indeed they have—see *Pot People, Basket Folk*) does not necessarily mean that the nature of art has, too. So, although the attempt to define 'art' in terms of *perceptual* properties is perhaps doomed to fail, it may be that we'd be better off focusing on its *relational* properties instead.

The search for these common relational properties yielded the beginnings of the institutional theory of art, according to which what makes something art is the fact that there exists a social context in which certain practices and objects are so-designated, and members of that social context have decided to treat the object in question as one of those objects (Dickie 1969). On its own, the driftwood isn't an artwork; but it can *become* an artwork once it's embedded in an artworld context, in which people accept and treat it as such. The question, then, becomes how it is that things become embedded in the right way in the right social context. According to the institutional theory, this happens when someone from that context (the artworld; this can be the artist, a curator, a critic, etc.) presents an artifact as a candidate for appreciation by the rest of the artworld.

Skepticism about the possibility of defining art thus somewhat paradoxically gave rise to a decades-long cottage industry of attempted definitions (see Adajian 2022 for a survey of the main moves). Nevertheless, some avenues remain open for a kind of skepticism inspired by the family resemblance model. The cluster theory of art, for example, maintains that 'art' has no *individually* necessary or sufficient conditions; what it has, instead, are a set of conditions which are *disjunctively*[2] necessary and *jointly* sufficient, and some subsets of which are likewise sufficient conditions for art (Gaut 2000). These conditions include properties like *being creative, being beautiful, being expressive, belonging to an established artistic tradition*, etc. Our disagreements about whether, e.g., readymades or found objects are art can then be explained by the fact that we're mistaking certain properties (e.g., *exhibiting skill in making*) for *necessary* properties of art. Note, however, that the cluster account *does* posit one generic necessary condition for being a *work* of art: artifactuality. Artifactuality distinguishes artworks from *natural* objects like the driftwood (until and unless it is selected and presented by someone), but not from the other products of human action.

These considerations raise broader questions about the nature of artifacts. One of these is whether and how artworks differ from other artifacts. On this front, philosophers of art have observed that although any artifact is suited to becoming a work of art, provided the putative artist does a little legwork to justify its designation as art, ordinary artifacts seem to be much more closely tied to their functions (Levinson 2007). So, for example, a javelin can't become a chair, because it's not suited for sitting. This suggests that although 'artwork' is a wholly relational concept, ordinary artifacts are constrained by functional considerations.

A second question these considerations might prompt is just what role intentions play in the creation of artifacts in general. The dominant view among philosophers is some form or another of *intentionalism*: an artifact's proper function is set by its maker's intentions. If you invent the fork, for example, then its function—to spear or lift food—is set by your design intentions, and it's by reference to this function that we determine which things count as forks, which are defective forks, etc. Some articulations of this kind of intentionalism are fairly thick, and require makers to have a substantive conception of the artifact they're making (e.g., Thomasson 2007)—so, for example, you have to have a fairly clear idea of what the fork will look like, what it will do, its approximate range of sizes, etc. Likewise, it is by reference to the maker's intentions that we determine which features of the artifact are required for another artifact to count as the same sort of thing: forks don't need to have four tines, but they do need to have at least two, since these are required for them to spear and stabilize food effectively, which was the whole point of developing a fork in the first place. Thus, understanding the meaning of an artifact-term entails having some grasp of the conditions under which the concept applies (its application-conditions). The result is that if someone just points to some driftwood and says "What a lovely sculpture!" they simply do not have a good grasp of what 'sculpture' means.

Although intentionalism is currently the dominant view of artifact function, it's not clear how those intentions then get transferred to the artifact, so as to take precedence over the "deviant" uses to which it may later be put (e.g., using a Rembrandt as a parasol, or a parasol as art). One significant alternative notes that most artifacts are not invented or created in a single sitting and by a single person; they develop incrementally over time and in response to the uses to which they're put (A.W. Eaton 2020). An artifact's proper function, then, is not best characterized as the product of a single thick conception (see also *The Puzzle of Multiple Authorship*), but rather as that function which is responsible for its selection for reproduction throughout its history. In other words: the proper function of a fork is to spear and lift food, because that is why we have continued to make and refine the design of forks to better suit our needs.

SUGGESTED READING

SEMINAL PRESENTATIONS:

1. Weitz, Morris (1956). The Role of Theory in Aesthetics. *Journal of Aesthetics and Art Criticism* 15 (1): 27–35.
   Weitz first raises the spectre of the driftwood, though not as a thought experiment. He argues that the concept 'art' has no necessary or sufficient

conditions, not even artifactuality, because we can intelligibly say of a piece of driftwood that it is a fine sculpture. Art-status, he thinks, is a matter of "family resemblance" to other acknowledged instances of art.

2. Eaton, Marcia (1969). Art, Artifacts, and Intentions. *American Philosophical Quarterly* 6 (2): 165–9.

   Eaton first formulates our thought experiment as such, although she argues, *contra* Weitz, that artifactuality *is* a necessary condition for art. We would not say that a monkey's randomly typed text is a poem, or driftwood arranged by the wind in the shapes of English letters is a warning, until and unless someone with a communicative intent so-designated it. Intentions convert objects into actions.

DEFENCES:

3. Gaut, Berys (2000). "The Cluster Account of Art," in *Theories of Art Today*, Noël Carroll (ed.). Madison: University of Wisconsin Press, 25–45.

   Drawing on the family resemblance model, Gaut proposes a cluster account of art that does not need to appeal to resemblance to paradigm instances. Instead, he offers a list of ten properties, none of which is individually necessary for art, but which are jointly sufficient for it, and some subsets of which are also sufficient.

CRITIQUES:

4. Mandelbaum, Maurice (1965). Family Resemblances and Generalization Concerning the Arts. *American Philosophical Quarterly* 2 (3): 219–28.

   Mandelbaum observes that what makes a resemblance a family resemblance is a *genetic* tie, not a similarity of appearance; and that genetic tie trumps any amount of dissimilarity between family members. He suggests, then, that we look for necessary and sufficient conditions for 'art' among the concept's *relational*, rather than its perceptual, properties.

5. Dickie, George (1969). Defining Art. *American Philosophical Quarterly* 6 (3): 253–56.[3]

   In this first formulation of his hugely influential institutional theory of art, Dickie argues that a work of art is (1) an artifact which (2) has had conferred upon it by some social group the status of candidate for appreciation. He argues that in the driftwood case, Weitz has conflated the descriptive and evaluative senses of 'art'. Natural objects can *become* art when someone makes them candidates for appreciation.

6. Sclafani, Richard (1970). "Art" and Artifactuality. *Southwestern Journal of Philosophy* 1 (3): 103–10.

   Sclafani argues that even on Weitz's family resemblance model, artifactuality looks like a necessary condition for art. The driftwood is counted as art by virtue of its resemblance to paradigm instances of sculpture, *all of which are artifacts*.

FURTHER READING:

7. Levinson, Jerrold (2007). "Artworks as Artifacts," in *Creations of the Mind*, Eric Margolis and Stephen Laurence (eds.). Oxford: Oxford University Press, 74–82.
   Levinson argues that an artwork's artifactuality differs from an ordinary artifact's in that artworks only require that certain intentional-historical conditions be satisfied, whereas ordinary artifacts are constrained by functional conditions. Thus, anything can become an artwork, but nothing not suited for sitting can become a chair.
8. Thomasson, Amie (2007). "Artifacts and Human Concepts," in *Creations of the Mind*, Eric Margolis and Stephen Laurence (eds.). Oxford: Oxford University Press, 52–73.
   Thomasson argues that human intentions determine the nature of artifacts. This is both because the artifact is the result of someone's substantive intention to make something fulfilling a particular function and because it is by reference to the maker's intentions that we determine which features count towards something's being the same sort of artifact.
9. Eaton, A.W. (2020). "Artifacts and their Functions," in *The Oxford Handbook of History and Material Culture*, Ivan Gaskell and Sarah Anne Carter (eds.). Oxford: Oxford University Press, 35–53.
   Eaton argues that artifacts acquire their functions through artificial selection rather than the creator's intentions. Most artifacts develop gradually over time, in incremental stages, each responding to the demands of the uses to which it is put. An artifact's proper function, then, is determined by those functions which explain the history of the selection of its traits.
10. Adajian, Thomas (2022). "The Definition of Art", in *The Stanford Encyclopedia of Philosophy* (Spring 2022 Edition), Edward N. Zalta (ed.). https://plato.stanford.edu/archives/spr2022/entries/art-definition/.
    Adajian offers a comprehensive overview of the many different attempts to define 'art', and the role that skepticism about definitions has played in shaping these accounts.

NOTES

1 I mean something like a gnarled old stump of a tree torn free by wind and washed out to sea by the spring melt. A log destined for the lumber yards but which escaped a logjam might be a different matter, since it was cut and shaped for a purpose.

2 In philosophy, a 'disjunction' is an 'or'-type statement, and it is true as long as at least one of its disjuncts (the statements on either side of the 'or') are true. So, 'Either I like ice cream or pizza' is true if I like ice cream, if I like pizza, or if I like each one (on its own); it's only false if I don't like ice cream *and* I don't like pizza.

3 Note that this was Dickie's first of many published attempts to articulate the institutional theory of art. Although the details changed over the course of its refinements, the core expressed here has remained constant.

PART II

ONTOLOGY

GENERAL BACKGROUND

Ontology is the branch of philosophy which is concerned with existence and reality; in particular, it asks what the basic entities are which compose the things around us, and how these are grouped together into categories. The ontology of art, then, is concerned with investigating what sorts of things count as works of art, or music, or painting, etc. and why, as well as what *kinds* of things artworks are (e.g., are they concrete individuals, types, or something else entirely?), whether artworks are created or discovered, and whether they're singular or multiple entities (and, if the latter, on what grounds we group all of the instances together).

The cases grouped together here all get at some aspect of the ontology of art, whether it's the status of copies, the importance of titles or musical scores to the identity of their associated works, why we think some things just *can't* be art, or the way that cultural practices and social conventions shape our artistic practices and their products. Whatever one concludes, the consequences of adopting a particular stance on the ontology of art are far-reaching and will influence the

DOI: 10.4324/9781003368205-12

lessons we draw from many of the other cases in this book. Endorsing a particular definition of music, for example, has knock-on effects for what we think about the practices of other cultures, and endorsing a particular musical ontology will affect how we characterize a composer's individual style, or whether we think it's possible for music to express emotional content.

11

DINOSAURS IN THE JUNGLE (PHOTOGRAPHIC TRANSPARENCY)

CASE

Suppose an intrepid explorer emerges from the swamps of Costa Rica—not the tourist swamps of the mainland, you understand; the *real* swamps on Isla Nublar (or was it Isla Sorna?), to the west. Making it out alive is an achievement all its own, of course, but *she* came back with a small pile of photographs of a *dinosaur*—probably a *Therizino-saurus* by the look of it! So long as nothing obviously dodgy went on in the processing of these photographs, they would presumably help to convince us that there's a dinosaur somewhere out there.

But wait! A second explorer has made it out alive, and he also saw a *Therizinosaurus*! Unfortunately, the rain and ambient humidity made his camera inoperable, so he did the next best thing: he drew some sketches. So: which explorer has the better evidence?

At first glance, it seems like our photographer is the winner here. But that's not necessarily so: the photographs might be a little too blurry, or have just captured the tip of the beast's tail or snout, or perhaps she's got a history of dodgy cryptozoological finds. The drawings, by contrast, might be highly anatomically specific and produced by a skeptic with an impeccable reputation. Regardless, there seems to be

DOI: 10.4324/9781003368205-13

a more fundamental difference between the two which grounds our intuition that photographs are generally more reliable than drawings: the drawings, even under the best of circumstances, reflect the artist's *belief* that there is a dinosaur in front of him, whereas the photos are entirely independent of the photographer's beliefs about what she sees.

The drawings tell us what the second explorer *thought* he saw. Provided he's a trustworthy fellow and a competent artist, we might trust that there really was a *Therizinosaurus* out there—but our information here is *second hand.* The photos, on the other hand, convince us that the dinosaur was really there: we don't believe there was a dinosaur because we believe the explorer, we believe her *because there was a dinosaur.* The photos give us *first-hand* information, they allow us to see the creature for ourselves.

Similarly, a photo of your grandmother shows *her,* even if it's not the greatest picture. By looking at it, you see her *directly,* just as if she were there before your eyes (or through your glasses). If you were looking at a painting of her, however, you'd see the artist's representation of her; you'd see her filtered through the artist's perception. Even a really good photo-realistic portrait's properties would depend on what the artist thought they saw. The same just isn't true of a photograph. The dinosaur case above may sound a little silly, but it's not all that different from one we encounter in real life, where photos purporting to be of cryptids like Nessie, the Ogopogo, Bigfoot, or the Chupacabra abound. The photos, when they exist, are real, and they really do actually show what they show—whether they show what they purport to show, however, is another question. That they are accurate renderings of what was in front of the camera does not prevent them from sometimes being misleading.

This difference between photographs and manugraphs (hand-drawn images) is typically characterized in terms of *transparency*: photography is a transparent medium, which just means that we see the world *through* it (Walton 1984). In this respect, photography is like the air, water, or a lens, except that it allows us to see things which are distant from us in both space and time. I can't look at my maternal grandmother through water or a lens any more, but I can *absolutely* look at her through a photo.

RESPONSES

Many philosophers have focused their attention on the epistemic implications of photography's transparency and have tried to explain whether and why photographs are epistemically superior to manugraphs. This has led some to doubt photography's transparency, however. Some have observed that giving us direct perceptual access to a thing is insufficient for transparency: a thermometer, for example, gives us a straightforward and entirely mechanical measure of temperature, but nobody thinks that it allows us to directly *perceive* gradations of heat and cold (Currie 1991). A thermometer is clearly a *representation* of heat, even though it's not an *intentional* one. The same, it has been argued, is true of photographs: they are natural representations, but representations all the same. In particular, we can tell that photographs are representations rather than directly perceptual because they do not preserve egocentric information, the spatial and temporal relations between ourselves and the object we're seeing. Sight, however, does. In fact, it's claimed, this explains the great epistemic advantage that photographs enjoy: they can convey information about an object's visually accessible properties without also being tied to the egocentric location of the object represented (Cohen and Meskin 2004). In other words, you don't actually need to be in front of your grandmother to see what she looked like or even exist at the same time as her.

In defence of transparency, it's been argued that we should focus closer attention on the causal processes involved (Mizrahi 2021). Any visual medium will transmit some kinds of information and not others: a microscope pointed at a drop of blood will show you something very different from what your naked eye sees. Thus, the fact that photography doesn't capture egocentric information is no different from the fact that telescopes are only good conveyors of macro-level phenomena far away, and microscopes of micro-level phenomena close by; it's a by-product of the structure of the medium, nothing more. Photographs are like mirrors in that they're literally opaque surfaces, but which reflect light in such a way that we *can* see through them—in the case of mirrors, to whatever is in front of the mirror, and in the case of photos, to whatever has been photographed. What makes photography special is that it *records* light impressions *in addition to* reflecting them.

Others have focused on the aesthetic implications of photography's transparency. In particular, they have noticed that photography's transparency seems closely tied to its *automaticity*: it doesn't reflect the photographer's beliefs about the subject because it creates an automatic record, whereas the painter's creative process is rather more hands-on. This is important, because a popular thesis in aesthetics (the 'twofoldness thesis') maintains that our engagement with representational art requires us to have a doubled awareness of the work: we have to be able to see it *as* a painting or a photograph, and also be able to discern the representational content *in* it (Wollheim 1980). The automaticity of the photographic process has suggested, to some, that photographs are independent of their author's beliefs and intentions, meaning that we cannot take an aesthetic interest in how these beliefs and intentions are on display (Scruton 1981; see also *The Driftwood and the Whale*). If this is correct, then photography is not—cannot be!—a representational art.

This was a dominant view in the early days of photography, but it has not held much popular sway since (see Costello 2017). On this 'orthodox' view, any manipulation of the photograph or the causal process which generates it is an illegitimate deviation from the objective truth. But, as has been amply documented, the orthodox view is premised on a naïve folk understanding of the photographic process which does not survive close scrutiny: the photographer and their intentions are *intimately* involved in the process (Costello 2017).

Nevertheless, it is only comparatively recently that philosophers of art have mounted a concerted attack on the orthodox view. In particular, contemporary philosophers have argued that even if photographs are transparent, this fact does not entail that they are *invisible*: we are perfectly capable of taking an interest in them *as photographs* by considering those aspects over which the photographer exercised control: e.g., setting and framing the scene, emulsion and exposure time, focal length, depth of field, the selection and display of particular prints, etc. (Lopes 2003). Each of these is a step in the process that reflects the artist's creative intentions, and thus in which we can take an aesthetic interest. Transparency is perfectly compatible with the photographer's interventions. Seeing through the surface does not prevent us from seeing the surface itself.

A related line of attack argues that the causal processes which generate photographs do not entail that our aesthetic interest is in the photo's 'bare' subject (Davies 2009). Consider Whistler's painting of his mother, *Arrangement in Grey and Black No. 1* (1871). We can certainly approach it as just a picture of his mother, Anna Matilda, but the artist has also taken a particular perspective on his mother, he has arranged the composition so, chosen just these colours, and given it a strange title. Every one of these decisions is aimed at directing our gaze and our aesthetic appreciation: the painter uses the tools at his disposal to *shape* our aesthetic engagement. The same, it's argued, is true of photography, though the tools at the photographer's disposal are different: the photographer shows us *how* to see her subject.

Indeed, the fact that a photograph even *has* a subject in the first place is significant (Phillips 2009). The causal processes which generate photographs don't generate subjects; they simply record the light reflected by the objects before the lens. This means that a photograph of a cat on a couch could just as well be about the pattern of the couch's fabric—or anything else in the picture—as it is about the cat. Conversely, paintings are generated by causal processes too, but nobody thinks the interest we can take in a painting is limited to paintbrushes. To assign a subject to a photograph requires an intention which we can take an aesthetic interest in discerning.

SUGGESTED READING

SEMINAL PRESENTATION:

1. Walton, Kendall L. (1984). Transparent Pictures: On the Nature of Photographic Realism. *Critical Inquiry* 11 (2): 246–77.
    Walton argues that we see literally through photographs to their subjects. In looking at a picture of my grandmother, then, I see her directly, just as I would see her directly through a window. Seeing her through a painting, however, is fictional: it depends on how the artist interprets what she saw, not on what was really there.

DEFENCES:

2. Mizrahi, Vivian (2021). Seeing Through Photographs: Photography as a Transparent Visual Medium. *Journal of Aesthetics and Art Criticism* 79 (1): 52–63.
    Mizrahi defends photography's transparency, arguing that the causal processes involved are just like those we observe in perceptual media like mirrors and

screens, which are opaque but reflective surfaces. Any visual medium transmits some properties and not others; photographs don't convey egocentric information because that's just not the kind of information that is stored and transmitted by the medium.

CRITIQUES:

3. Currie, Gregory (1991). Photography, Painting and Perception. *Journal of Aesthetics and Art Criticism* 49 (1): 23–9.

   Currie argues that we do not literally see through photographs, since photographs do not preserve the egocentric information conveyed by sight, which allows us to orient ourselves and the object of perception relative to our surroundings. Photographs, he argues, are representations.

4. Cohen, Jonathan and Aaron Meskin (2004). On the Epistemic Value of Photographs. *Journal of Aesthetics and Art Criticism* 62 (2): 197–210.

   Cohen and Meskin distinguish between the visual and egocentric information carried by a photograph, arguing that their failure to convey egocentric information not only distinguishes them from plain sight, it also helps to explain their epistemic value. There is no need, then, to rely on automaticity or direct causal relationships to explain why we treat them as veridical.

FURTHER READING:

5. Wollheim, Richard (1980). "Seeing-as, Seeing-in, and Pictorial Representation," in *Art and Its Objects*, 2nd ed. Cambridge: Cambridge University Press, 205–26.

   Wollheim expands upon his 'twofold thesis', arguing that we can attend to pictures in two ways: either we attend to the image's (painted) surface, or we attend to its representational content. No matter how realistic the image, we don't mistake it for the real thing—because we see it *as a picture*. But we can also focus our attention on what it's representing. In other words, we're visually aware of both things at the same time.

6. Scruton, Roger (1981). Photography and Representation. *Critical Inquiry* 7 (3): 577–603.

   Scruton explains photography's epistemic privilege in terms of its *automaticity*: a pure (i.e., non-fine-art) photograph enjoys a strictly causal relation to its objects, and thus is not subject to any of its photographer's intentions or beliefs. This means we can't take an interest in the way the subject is represented and, thus, that photography is not a representational art.

7. Lopes, Dominic McIver (2003). The Aesthetics of Photographic Transparency. *Mind* 112 (447): 434–48.

   Lopes thinks that seeing through the photograph is just a species of generic seeing. But while photographs are transparent, this does not mean that they are invisible; we are perfectly capable of also taking an interest in the photographic surface itself. Thus, we can either see the subject itself or see the photograph *as a photograph*.

8. Davies, David (2009). Scruton on the Inscrutability of Photographs. *British Journal of Aesthetics* 49 (4): 341–55.

   Davies argues that the direct causal relationship between a photograph's subject and what we see does not entail that our aesthetic interest is in the photograph's 'bare' subject. Seeing a photograph is never just perceptual, it's always also inferential, just like seeing a painting: the photographer directs the path of our gaze, showing us *how* to see the subject.

9. Phillips, Dawn M. (2009). Photography and causation: Responding to Scruton's scepticism. *British Journal of Aesthetics* 49 (4): 327–40.[1]

   Phillips argues that paying proper attention to the causal processes involved in photography shows that the fact that there is something—e.g., a cat—in the photograph does not entail it is a *picture of* that cat. It's also a 'photograph of' dappled sunlight, the pattern of the rug, etc. All these are part of the causal process which generated it, but its *subject*, if it has one, is given by the photographer's intentional activity.

10. Costello, Diarmuid (2017). *On Photography: A Philosophical Inquiry*. New York: Routledge.

    This book surveys the history of philosophical thinking about photography, with a particular focus on the tension between photography's epistemic value and its art-status. Ch. 3 concerns transparency, and stresses that the mind-independent thesis which falls out of it is insufficiently sensitive to the particulars of the photographic process.

NOTE

1 Phillips is now Dawn M. *Wilson*.

12

FAKING NATURE
(AUTHENTICITY)

CASE

Suppose your parents asked what you wanted for your birthday, and that money was no object (far-fetched, I know!). And suppose, further, that you replied that you would like a painting by Jacques-Louis David (perhaps even more implausible, but since I'm writing the example I get to choose the artist!). And, indeed, on your birthday you awake to find David's *Napoleon Crossing the St. Bernard* (1801–5[1]) hanging on the wall opposite your bed. Holy carp! But wait—while you're busy profusely thanking your parents for the extravagant gift, they tell you that it's an exact reproduction of the first Versailles version of the painting, and that if you would prefer a copy of one of the four other versions, they have 30 days to exchange it. How would you feel?

I think it's fair to say that most of us would be disappointed, even if there was no discernible difference between the original and the replica. And that's because even if there are no aesthetically relevant differences between the two, they are nevertheless different in important historical respects: they have different origins. One of them is old, was touched by a master painter and commissioned as a gift to Napoleon himself from King Charles IV of Spain; the other is new, never came into contact with David, and was commissioned as a gift

DOI: 10.4324/9781003368205-14

for *you* by *your parents*. It seems like these different histories matter, and matter a great deal, to our engagement with and appreciation of the object before us. That difference seems to be reflected in the economics of the situation: the two paintings are (presumably!) not of equal monetary value, because one is old and by a famous artist, and the other is not.

If this seems like a plausible story to you, then the upshot is that two objects which are exactly alike are not necessarily equally aesthetically valuable (see *The Gallery of Red Squares* and *The Parable of the Pawn*). The aesthetic value we place on something clearly depends in part on its physical properties. But it's not just a matter of being delighted by some object, of taking pleasure in it or thinking it's beautiful, although these are certainly part of the equation. How we relate to that object seems to be influenced by *non-perceptible* features as well, such as its history; the discovery that something is a replica comes as a palpable *disappointment* to someone who initially approached the object as the genuine article.[2] For instance, think back to the first (or last) time you saw a dinosaur skeleton on display in a museum. *Did you know that most of the dinosaur skeletons in museums are not actually dinosaur skeletons?* They're casts taken from the real deal and loaned or sold to the museum in question (Rieppel 2016). Isn't that just *crushing*?

Originally, this kind of thought experiment was used by environmental philosophers to argue against the desirability of restoring natural landscapes which had been exploited by humans. It's much better, they argued, not to destroy the environment in the first place, since restoration can never fully recapture the value of the original (Elliot 1982).[3] If it's an aesthetic value then it is presumably imperceptible, otherwise we wouldn't be justified in denying that the replica possesses it. But then, what *is* it, exactly?

RESPONSES

On the environmental side of things, one popular explanation for the original's superiority to the restored environment is that the original has a certain aesthetic value that the restored environment does not: its 'naturalness' (Elliot 1982). The original environment was wholly the product of nature; by definition, the restored environment is the product of human intervention, even if it exactly copies the original.

The natural world reflects the order of nature, so to speak, and that is or can be a fundamentally awe-inspiring thing: it's more impressive, after all, when millennia of erosion balance a boulder atop a tiny pillar (e.g., Idol Rock in Brimham Moor) than when a human achieves the same look using a crane or a jackhammer.

Drawing on this reasoning, some philosophers have attempted to offer a general characterization of our aesthetic appreciation of nature that runs roughly parallel to our appreciation of art (see *Guernicas*). For artworks, our judgements are said to be framed and constrained by our understanding of the work's correct categories; for the aesthetic appreciation of nature, it's suggested that scientific knowledge plays the same kind of role (Carlson 1993). So, for example, my appreciation of the *Gorgosaurus libratus* skeleton at the entrance to the second floor of the Redpath Museum at McGill University is framed against the knowledge that it was bipedal and carnivorous (rather than quadrupedal—awfully silly, considering its tiny arms!—and herbivorous). These considerations show the creature in rather a more terrifying light than the alternative.[4]

This example raises two concerns, however: (1) does this show that scientific knowledge is *necessary* for the aesthetic appreciation of nature, or simply that it *enriches* it (Turner 2019), and (2) perhaps this kind of appreciation, guided as it is by the categories of science, isn't actually *aesthetic* in the first place (Carroll 1993) We don't need *any* scientific knowledge to be impressed by how huge a *Brachiosaurus* is: simply standing under it is enough to overawe anyone. But knowing that the sauropod respiratory system made extensive use of air sacs—like the avian respiratory system—helps us to understand how they got so huge and introduces interesting new points of contemplation (you can see the relevant indentations in the bones) and comparison.

Scientific knowledge can enrich our experience by showing us how to put flesh on the bones, by steering us in correctly imagining how the creature lived, and by guiding us in appreciating interesting or distinctive aspects of its anatomy. In addition, scientific knowledge and aesthetic considerations are both intimately involved in generating the display itself, from the initial preparation and uncovering of the bones to their assembly, display, and even their location in the museum. The same can be said for other kinds of knowledge, too, such as historical or Indigenous knowledge, so we might hesitate to put all of our cognitive eggs in the scientific-category-basket (Brady 2000). And if we accept that scientific knowledge has a role to play in the aesthetic appreciation of nature, then it seems likely that knowledge is relevant to aesthetic appreciation *more generally* (this is the core of what is called '*aesthetic cognitivism*'—see Gibson 2008; see also *The Problem of Museum Skepticism*). On the other hand, the more I describe explicitly thinking about the skeleton in light of scientific information, the more… clinical… the experience starts to sound. This is clearly appreciation, but is it *aesthetic* appreciation? Perhaps we were better off sticking just to the emotional responses nature draws out of us (Carroll 1993).

On the artifactual side of things, such considerations have prompted some philosophers to focus on our immediate sense of awe and wonder and being transported back to the distant past as a candidate explanation for the aesthetic value of originals over replicas (Korsmeyer 2008). Genuineness, the argument goes, is a non-perceptible aesthetic property and a key feature of a particular experience we sometimes have of being put in touch with the past—often quite literally. I might be so moved by the ludicrously large skeleton before me that I reach out to touch it: this is a reaction that makes sense if the skeleton before me is made of real bone turned to real stone, a lingering trace of the past, but it seems kind of weird if it's just a plaster cast.

Others have argued that the importance of provenance depends on what our purposes are: whereas mechanical reproduction ensures objectivity for epistemic purposes, where aesthetic appreciation is concerned it seems to preclude creativity (Rieppel 2016). Granted, it seems to matter a great deal in the context of religious experience that the Shroud of Turin be the genuine article. But if we think that aesthetic appreciation has a genuine cognitive component—if we think that the artifact can tell us something about the world and its history, or that knowledge of the world and its history is relevant to its aesthetic appreciation—then it is important to note that a replica might be *preferable* to the original, or at least just as good (Sandis 2016, Matthes 2018). The original, for example, might be too degraded to adequately convey its relevant aesthetic content, as with Gustav Klimt's *Philosophy* (1900), which was destroyed in 1945; or it might be too fragile to allow widespread access to it, as with Chauvet Cave in France; or it might just be inaccessible, like da Vinci's *Mona Lisa* (c. 1503–6), which can hardly be seen for the crowds and its bulletproof case.

These are circumstantial benefits, to be sure, but they suggest that as long as the replica is faithful, it should function as a point of contact with the original and thus, transitively, with the kind of aesthetic experience we might aspire to glean from the original. True, the walls of the *Caverne du Pont-d'Arc, Chauvet 2* are not Chauvet's; but the whole point of going there is so that I can experience *Chauvet*, which I otherwise could not. While I can certainly aesthetically appreciate it as a replica, the whole point of seeing it is to aesthetically appreciate *the original*, just as the point of an art history textbook is to give students epistemic access to the history of art.

SUGGESTED READING

SEMINAL PRESENTATION:

1. Elliot, Robert (1982). Faking Nature. *Inquiry: An Interdisciplinary Journal of Philosophy* 25 (1): 81–93.
   In this classic essay in environmental philosophy, Elliot compares the act of restoring a natural environment to that of forging a work of art. But a key value of nature, he thinks, is non-perceptible: its authenticity or 'naturalness'. And an environment's naturalness cannot survive the process of destruction and restoration.

DEFENCES:

2. Carlson, Allen (1993). "Appreciating Art and Appreciating Nature," in *Landscape, Natural Beauty and the Arts*, Selim Kemal and Ivan Gaskell (eds.). New York: Cambridge University Press. 199–227.
   Carlson argues that the appreciation of art gives us two models for the appreciation of nature: appreciation for its design features ('design appreciation'), or for the ordering of its pattern ('order appreciation'). Since nature isn't designed, design appreciation cannot guide our appreciative responses.
3. Korsmeyer, Carolyn (2008). Aesthetic Deception: On Encounters with the Past. *Journal of Aesthetics and Art Criticism* 66 (2): 117–27.
   Korsmeyer argues that even though replicas may have greater *cognitive* value than derelict originals, the original object has more, and more direct, *aesthetic* value. The differences may be perceptually trivial, but they are aesthetically significant: originals with real age value put us in contact with the past, and replicas do not.

CRITIQUES:

4. Rieppel, Lukas (2016). Casting Authenticity. *Extinct: The Philosophy of Palaeontology Blog*, 1 February 2016. http://www.extinctblog.org/extinct/2016/1/28/casting-authenticity.
   Rieppel observes that most fossils on display in museums are casts rather than original fossils and that this fact does not seem to trouble us, whereas it *would* trouble us if a gallery contained reproductions rather than originals. He argues that this is because the appreciation of natural history and of art are governed by different epistemic standards and different standards of authenticity.

5. Sandis, Constantine (2016). An Honest Display of Fakery: Replicas and the Role of Museums. *Royal Institute of Philosophy Supplement* 79: 241–59.
   Sandis argues that the importance of provenential authenticity is relative to the purposes to which a display is put, or which a museum serves. He argues that for cognitive purposes, a replica may well be preferable to an original, since it enables closer contact and inspection under better conditions, without causing harm to either the observers or the artifact.

6. Matthes, Erich Hatala (2018). Authenticity and the Aesthetic Experience of History. *Analysis* 78 (4): 649–57.
   Matthes accepts that non-perceptual properties can be relevant to aesthetic experiences and that an object's historical value can impact that experience. But he argues that we should not tie historical value too closely to authenticity; so long as they are true to the original, replicas can facilitate just as much aesthetic contact with the past as originals do.

FURTHER READING:

7. Carroll, Noël (1993). "Being Moved By Nature: Between Religion and Natural History," in *Landscape, Natural Beauty and the Arts*, Selim Kemal and Ivan Gaskell (eds.). New York: Cambridge University Press, 244–66.
   Carroll worries that cognitivist accounts which take external knowledge to be necessary for appreciation exclude our more common visceral aesthetic responses, particularly to nature. He argues that appreciation guided solely by scientific knowledge seems like it isn't *aesthetic* appreciation at all. He advocates for an 'arousal model' of the appreciation of nature instead.

8. Brady, Emily (2000). *Aesthetics of the Natural Environment*. Tuscaloosa: University of Alabama Press.
   Brady canvasses the history of environmental aesthetics and the aesthetic appreciation of nature, arguing for a kind of appreciation she calls the 'Integrated Aesthetic'. In Ch. 4, she offers a critical account of cognitivism in environmental aesthetics. She worries that cognitivism privileges scientific knowledge at the expense of other kinds of knowledge and engagement with natural environments, including Indigenous knowledge and history.

9. Gibson, John (2008). Cognitivism and the Arts. *Philosophy Compass* 3 (4): 573–89.
    Gibson gives an overview of the debate over cognitivism in aesthetics, canvassing several promising attempts to salvage the view. One of these is the experiential approach, according to which art helps us to inhabit a particular perspective—either by offering us a simulation or by giving us a more direct experiential knowledge. Gibson is skeptical that this suggestion is *literally* true but argues that it *is* plausible that adopting these perspectives puts us in a better position to recognize truths about ourselves and the world.
10. Turner, Derek D. (2019). *Paleoaesthetics and the Practice of Paleontology*. Cambridge: Cambridge University Press.
    Inspired by Carlson's scientific cognitivism and Elliot's thought experiment, Turner identifies 'historical cognitivism' as the broader thesis that knowledge of a thing's history enriches (but is not necessary for) our aesthetic engagement with that thing. This short book is devoted to showing that scientific knowledge can enrich our aesthetic engagement with fossils and that historical sciences like palaeontology have distinctively *aesthetic* goals.

NOTES

1   There are five slightly different versions of the painting in existence, all painted between these dates.
2   Note that we're talking about replicas here, rather than forgeries: forgeries aim to deceive, whereas replicas aim to convey all of the relevant information conveyed by the original.
3   Similar arguments have been made about the desirability of de-extinction projects, such as mammoth revival.
4   Not that you *shouldn't* be scared of giant quadrupedal herbivores with tiny forelimbs.

13

GUERNICAS (CONTEXTUALISM)

CASE

Imagine a painting you know well. The original thought experiment uses Picasso's *Guernica* (1937), but any painting at all will do, so long as you can form a clear picture of it in your mind.

Now that you have it fixed in your mind's eye, imagine a society for which there is no art of painting—that is to say, they do not have any established artistic practice of applying pigment to wood, canvas, or plaster to generate a two-dimensional abstract, non-representational, or representational surface. What they have, instead, is a practice of applying pigment to a surface to generate guernicas (or whichever other painting you selected)—pictures which look exactly identical to the real-world *Guernica*. There is one important difference between Picasso's *Guernica* and these guernicas, however: guernicas manipulate the painted surface's bas-relief dimensions. In other words, they are appreciated for their three-dimensional properties, for the ways in which different elements physically protrude or recede, are bumpy, rough, or smooth. If it helps, think of the category of guernicas as works which are appreciated primarily for their *impasto* technique.

We think of the original painting as flat, even though it has a surface over which the paint was unevenly applied. That's just because we

DOI: 10.4324/9781003368205-15

don't usually take much, if any, aesthetic or artistic interest in a painting's surface-level properties. We might note an *impasto* technique, but we don't ascribe any artistic significance to just how thick the paint is in one location, or which bits stick out more than others. But we *could*, and the point here is that our imaginary society *does*, at least where guernicas are concerned. For them, even our 'flat' *Guernica* is an interesting guernica—or, well, perhaps they would think it is especially dull and empty. The point is just that they're interested in its surface-level properties, and we aren't. They would notice its flatness, whereas we take it for granted. Nor is this unusual: for any given artistic medium, there are some features of works in that medium which we attend to with great interest, and others which we don't.

What this thought experiment seems to show is that our aesthetic judgements—including, and especially, our attributions of certain aesthetic properties to a work—are dependent on our category judgements (Walton 1970). Seen as a painting, *Guernica* is exciting and vibrant; seen as a guernica, it's kind of boring. Similarly, *Showgirls* (1995) is a bad musical, but a good piece of satirical exploitation cinema (see *The Paradox of Good-Bad Art*). Put differently, a work's category membership seems to affect its aesthetic properties, where its 'category' is understood as a work's genre, medium (art-kind), style, etc. (basically, any perceptually distinguishable category to which it might belong[1]). But relativism lurks around the corner: after all, we could just as easily say that *Showgirls* is a subversive piece of sculpture, a repetitive series of photographs, etc. For any judgement we care to make, there's bound to be a category out there relative to which it's a reasonable judgement. So, we'd best revise our thesis somewhat: a work's *correct* category membership seems to affect its aesthetic properties.[2] What counts as a correct category, we might say, is subject to several different criteria: it should minimize contra-standard properties and maximize the work's aesthetic value, reflect society's category judgements and cohere with the artist's intention, and might also be subject to considerations pertaining to the processes used to produce the work.

But *how*, exactly, do a work's correct categories affect its aesthetic properties? They do so by determining which kinds of properties are considered standard, contra-standard, or variable for those categories. A *standard* property is one that typically characterizes the category (e.g., a sonnet has fourteen lines of iambic pentameter); a *contra-standard* property is one which tends to disqualify the work from being classified in a particular category (e.g., having three lines of five, seven, and five syllables is standard for haikus, but contra-standard for sonnets); and a *variable* property is one which has nothing to do with a work's being classified in a category (e.g., rhyme and prose are variable properties of poetry). Some works in a category may lack some standard property of the category, or contain some contra-standard properties—that is how a category's boundaries are pushed, after all. But generally speaking, that a work possesses certain standard properties is a defeasible reason to categorize it as we do, and that it possesses contra-standard properties is a defeasible reason not to.

The upshot is that formalism in art (sometimes called 'empiricism')—the view that all of a work's aesthetically relevant properties are perceptual—must be false, since just what a work's perceptible properties *are*, exactly, seems subject to a prior judgement about its correct categorization. In other words, *categories* are aesthetically relevant, but categories are not merely formal properties of artworks, so formalism must be false.

RESPONSES

It is impossible to give a full accounting of the enormous and incredibly wide-ranging literature that has sprung up in response to this thought experiment. I will offer a snapshot that I hope is representative, but which is necessarily hopelessly incomplete.

Historically speaking, this thought experiment sounded the death knell for formalism and paved the way for the *contextualist* positions which dominate today (see also *Pot People, Basket Folk* and *The Gallery of Red Squares*). Contextualists have drawn the (perhaps somewhat stronger than originally intended) lesson that an artwork's aesthetic properties *necessarily* depend on many of its non-perceptible properties, such as the artist's identity and oeuvre, the work's historical period and how it compares to other works in, before, or after that period, etc. (Levinson 1980). Some have even gone so far as to argue that the correct appreciation of an artwork under its relevant categories first requires us to engage with it under a more fundamental *ur*-category, that of an artifact—i.e., an entity that is the product of someone's intentional activity (Davies 2020; see *The Whale and the Driftwood*). When we take artifactuality to be a standard property of the entities under consideration, so the suggestion goes, we are then in a position to determine which properties count as standard, contra-standard, and variable for the *kind* of artifact we're considering.

We can ask the further question of what guarantees that the contextualist's classifications, and the properties we take as standard, contra-standard, and variable for each classification, are appropriate or correct. For formalists, the answer is straightforward: the relevant properties are there in the work and directly available to perception. Although Walton originally offered some criteria for identifying a work's correct categories (that it possesses many standard properties of the category; that judging it under the category yields an aesthetically richer work; that it was intended for that category; that its intended category was recognizable in the culture), these fall short of explanations. But contextualists can embrace this uncertainty: they need simply maintain that the origins of our categories are thoroughly conventional (Xhignesse 2020). This means that our categories are rooted in arbitrary and historically contingent clusters of properties; but once those clusters are culturally established, they exert the kind of normative pressure that ultimately makes some correct and others incorrect.

Not all formalists have accepted their fate, however. Some have argued that while the case of guernicas shows that an *extreme* formalism (according to which all of a work's aesthetic properties are purely perceptible) must be wrong, more moderate versions can accommodate the challenge. In particular, these moderate formalists have argued that there are at least *some* artworks whose properties are purely formal (e.g., highly abstract or non-representational art; instrumental pure music); and while they concede that this class of artworks is limited in extent, they maintain that the appreciation of a work's perceptible (i.e., aesthetic) properties is crucial to the appreciation of *any* artwork (Zangwill 2000). They have also taken refuge in the apparent fact that appreciators—especially novice appreciators—are not typically aware of the influence of categories on their judgements, which suggests that these judgements are made independently of categories altogether, and solely on the basis of the work's perceptible features. A novice wine appreciator's moment of epiphany, when they suddenly taste all of the complexities of a really good wine, is said to be like this (Sackris 2013).

Indeed, there is some disagreement about just how strongly the original thought experiment motivates contextualism. Some, for instance, have argued that Walton's reference to perceptually distinguishable categories indicates a certain sympathy towards formalism: whatever a work's correct categories are, we literally perceive them in the work itself (Laetz 2010). Just what this perception amounts to, or how it is effected, however, is unclear. One suggestion, itself quite friendly to contextualism, is that art-historical experience and expertise support *perceptual learning*, such that our repeated exposure to certain categories causes an enduring change in our perceptual systems (Ransom 2020). So, for example, someone familiar with the technique of cross-hatching will see it as indicating tone and shading, rather than as a layer of mesh overlaying the scene. The concept of perceptual learning might thus help to explain why it is that appreciators aren't typically aware that they are making category-dependent judgements. This is an important tool for contextualists, who struggle with the fact that the more contextual knowledge they require of aesthetic properties, the less likely it seems that aesthetic properties are perceived in the first place.

Contextualists have exported these lessons to other aspects of aesthetics beyond the visual arts, notably to literature and to environmental aesthetics. In the philosophy of literature, for example, the language of standard, contra-standard, and variable properties lends itself neatly to the characterization of literary genres and can help us to avoid having to characterize the fiction/non-fiction distinction in terms of necessary and sufficient conditions (Friend 2012). Environmental aesthetics, meanwhile, has resisted the suggestion (present in Walton's original article) that the appreciation of nature is directly perceptual and not subject to category judgements. In particular, it has been argued that we appreciate natural beauty in light of its *scientific* categories (Carlson 1981). The fact that these categories are derived scientifically rather than culturally, in turn, explains which are correct and why, thus avoiding the relativism lurking around the corner in cases of art appreciation.

SUGGESTED READING

SEMINAL PRESENTATION:

1. Walton, Kendall L. (1970). Categories of Art. *Philosophical Review* 79 (3): 334–67.
   Walton formulates the *Guernica* thought experiment as a challenge to aesthetic formalism, arguing that our aesthetic judgements of artworks are not solely based on their perceptual features; we judge artworks relative to the properties which we take to be standard, contra-standard, and variable for the categories to which they belong.

DEFENCES:

2. Laetz, Brian (2010). Kendall Walton's 'Categories of Art': A Critical Commentary. *British Journal of Aesthetics* 50 (3): 287–306.
   In this critical exegesis and overview of responses to Walton's original article, Laetz argues that (1) commentators have misinterpreted Walton's guidelines for discerning a work's correct category as guidelines for determining category membership, and (2) that Walton is much more sympathetic to formalism than commentators have taken him to be.

3. Davies, David (2020). 'Categories of Art' for Contextualists. *Journal of Aesthetics and Art Criticism* 78 (1): 75–9.
   Davies argues that appreciative engagement with art requires us to engage with it under the category 'art'—that is, as the product of someone's agency, as an *artifact*. In other words, correctly determining a work's aesthetic properties requires us to treat artifactuality itself as a standard property which determines a subset of the standard, contra-standard, and variable properties for the kind of artifact we have on hand.

4. Ransom, Madeleine (2020). Waltonian Perceptualism. *Journal of Aesthetics and Art Criticism* 78 (1): 66–70.
   Ransom argues that the argument from guernicas does not entail that our bare perceptual judgements are dependent on contextual knowledge. She argues that perceiving artworks in a given (correct!) category takes experience and training which actually changes our perception (it's not just propositional knowledge).

CRITIQUES:

5. Zangwill, Nick (2000). In Defence of Moderate Aesthetic Formalism. *Philosophical Quarterly* 50 (201): 476–93.
   Zangwill argues that a more moderate version of formalism survives the challenge from guernicas. A moderate formalist thinks that aesthetic properties are crucial for appreciation and that there are limited classes of artworks

whose aesthetic properties are purely formal. To appreciate something *aesthetically* is to glom on to its direct perceptual features. Appreciation of non-formal properties is an intellectual, not an aesthetic, exercise.

6. Sackris, David (2013). Category Independent Aesthetic Experience: The Case of Wine. *Journal of Value Inquiry* 47 (1–2): 111–20.

   Sackris argues that the experience of wine tasting shows that at least some aesthetic judgements (viz., moments of epiphany) are independent of category judgements. Although he concedes that experience *can* direct our attention to appreciate particular features of a wine, he thinks that the properties it directs our attention to are available to direct perception: a purely formal evaluation is also possible.

FURTHER READING:

7. Levinson, Jerrold (1980). What A Musical Work Is. *Journal of Philosophy* 77 (1): 5–28.

   Inspired by Walton, Levinson argues for a contextualist analysis of musical works, according to which non-perceptible properties of a work—such as its composer's identity, its historical period, the rest of its composer's oeuvre, how it compares to other works, etc.—are relevant and necessary determinants of the work's aesthetic properties.

8. Carlson, Allen (1981). Nature, Aesthetic Judgment, and Objectivity. *Journal of Aesthetics and Art Criticism* 40 (1): 15–27.

   Carlson argues that we can extend Walton's views to the appreciation of nature without succumbing to category relativism: our appreciation of natural beauty is subject to prior considerations of which category the entity belongs to. Determining which of these judgements is correct is a matter of deferring to scientific categories (natural kinds) rather than cultural factors. This view has come to be called *scientific cognitivism*.

9. Friend, Stacie (2012). Fiction as a Genre. *Proceedings of the Aristotelian Society* 112 (2pt2): 179–209.

   Friend develops a contextualist account of genre and of the fiction/nonfiction distinction, and shows that the inclusion of contra-standard properties can push a genre's boundaries such that it changes in response. She argues that non-perceptual properties can be just as integral to category classification as perceptual properties, and that classification as fiction/non-fiction depends on clusters of non-essential criteria.

10. Xhignesse, Michel-Antoine (2020). What Makes a Kind an Art-kind? *British Journal of Aesthetics* 60 (4): 471–88.

    I argue that what makes some of our kind-categorizations art-relevant is entirely a matter of convention, where conventions are understood as patterns of behaviour that reproduce largely due to the weight of precedent (consciously or unconsciously). This means that our categories of art are not always perceptually distinguishable. It also means that the ontology of our categories of art is fundamentally arbitrary and historically contingent, even if they're robustly applied by today's artworld.

NOTES

1 There is a tension here between Walton's definition of categories in perceptual terms, and some of the criteria he later gives for identifying a work's correct category, not all of which are perceptual (see Laetz 2010).
2 Note, however, that any work of art will correctly belong to several different categories—e.g. *Guernica* is both a painting and a work in the cubist tradition. It is also a surrealist work (Laetz 2010).

14

POT PEOPLE, BASKET FOLK (CONTEXTUALISM)

CASE

Imagine two groups of people, separated by forbidding mountains; call one the Pot People, the other the Basket Folk. Each group makes both pots and baskets. Each group's pots look the same: they're short and squat, with wide mouths and a semi-circle pattern around the neck. Their baskets are also indiscernible, woven out of thick reeds individually dyed rust-red, sickly yellow, and queasy-green, arrayed in a layered triangle motif, with high sides and a single hooped handle around the centre. The Pot People care an awful lot about pots: their God is a pot-maker, and so simply seeing a pot puts them in touch with God and the cosmic order. Potters are thus honoured artists, but baskets are just functional containers for them. The Basket Folk, meanwhile, hold parallel views of baskets and basket-weavers. So far, it shouldn't seem especially controversial to suppose that Pot People pots and Basket Folk baskets are artworks or, at least, art-like in important respects not disanalogous to religious art in the Western tradition.

Now suppose that Pot People pots and Basket Folk baskets are put on display in a major art museum, while Pot People baskets and Basket Folk pots are sent to the appropriate wing of a natural history museum, where an informative diorama shows the sacred role pots

DOI: 10.4324/9781003368205-16

play for the Pot People and baskets for the Basket Folk. But as a guided tour walks by, a child pipes up and says that they can't see a difference between the venerated Pot People pots and the pots strewn about the Basket Folk diorama. Suppose further that there *is* a difference, but it's not a perceptible difference—the two sorts of pots use clay with slightly different isotopes, for example, or the two sorts of baskets use different sub-varieties of reed. This difference clearly doesn't explain what makes Pot People pots or Basket Folk baskets special to each group but not the other. So: does it matter that the child can't see the difference between them?

The intuition being pumped by this thought experiment is the *contextualist* intuition that the relevant difference comes from their contexts of origin, from the network of meaning in which Pot People pots, but not baskets, and Basket Folk baskets, but not pots, are embedded (see also *Guernicas*). Basket Folk pots are every bit as well decorated as Pot People pots, after all, but they clearly aren't artworks in Basket culture: they're useful tools, nothing more, as the diorama makes clear.

If, however, you find yourself sympathetic to the child's concern, then you're tending towards formalism, the view that all that matters to an artwork's appreciation and art-status are its aesthetic properties. And since both sets of pots (or baskets) have the same aesthetic properties, it follows that either both are art, or neither are. This is the same result as we would expect in cases of forgery or exact replication (see also *Faking Nature* and *The Supercopier*). The possibility that the child raises is that a pot's meaning to the Pot People (or baskets to the Basket Folk) is *irrelevant* to the aesthetic appreciation of the artifact.

RESPONSES

Although this thought experiment represents one of many moves intended to vitiate contextualism in contemporary aesthetics, our focus in this section will be on the distinction it invokes between artworks and ordinary functional objects (for more on indiscernibility and contextualism, see *The Gallery of Red Squares*).

Lurking in the background here is an important historical issue: the distinction between art and craft. Under the influence of a pair of papers by Paul Oskar Kristeller (1951–2), it has long been the orthodox opinion among art historians and philosophers of art that 'art' is a comparatively new concept in the West, which arose in the eighteenth century (see, e.g., Shiner 2001, Kivy 2012). The ancients, it's thought, had a very broad conception indeed of what was included in the arts, including such things as cooking, magic tricks, mirrors, mimicking animal noises, and sophistry. The sixteenth century saw a further distinction between art and craft, but it wasn't until the eighteenth century, with the work of Batteux, that we see the modern 'system' of the arts—painting, sculpture, music, poetry (i.e., everything literary), and architecture—take shape (Kristeller 1951–2; Shiner 2001). In particular, it was with Batteux that the concept of fine art achieved autonomy from practical or moral concerns: art is to be appreciated and evaluated for its own sake.

The upshot, if this is correct, is that most of the works produced in the history of Western art were not produced under the concept of art as we recognize it today, meaning that many of the most famous works in our galleries are the products of a different kind of activity—one with more immediate practical purposes, such as the religious. In short, they aren't artworks. In this, they are not all that far removed from the works of subaltern cultures (see *The Problem of Museum Skepticism*), which tend to be intricately designed everyday artifacts.

The trouble is that this influential interpretation of art history does not bear scrutiny. Although it's true that the ancient Greeks and Romans included many activities under the umbrella terms '*ars*' and '*teknē*', it simply isn't true that they didn't group together certain arts as special and different from the others: Aristotle called these the 'imitative' arts: music, dance, poetry (i.e., the literary arts), and painting (Young 2015). And while it's true that the ancients had a broad conception of 'art' in general, so do we: we speak of the art of war, the liberal arts, etc. The important point is that their conception of the imitative arts closely matches that of the 'fine' arts found in Batteux, other eighteenth-century writers, and in the present day. Indeed, Batteux himself explicitly cites Aristotle as the source for his grouping (Porter 2009, Young 2015). To be sure, some arts have been added and subtracted from the category of the fine arts at various times—e.g., gardening, architecture, and photography—but the core four have proven remarkably stable over the millennia. The disagreement, rather, mostly stems over issues of why and how imitation characterizes the fine arts, since not all imitations are artworks (cf. imitating animal noises), whether the fine arts can be sources of knowledge (see *The Paradox of Authenticity*), and art's role as a source of pleasure. Finally, art history simply does not bear out the thesis of increasing autonomy, especially from considerations of moral utility (Porter 2009).

We are thus led to the contrary conclusion that the art/artifact distinction is not overly robust, and seems rather to reflect social attitudes about the various arts. It seems, then, that art is found everywhere, in all human cultures: but this raises the question from our thought experiment, namely, how do we distinguish between the objects which are artworks and those which are artifacts?

One answer is that we can't rely on the object's perceptual properties to guide us, and nor should we expect the difference to be marked by a special word in the relevant culture's language (Danto 1988). Instead, we have to look at the network of meanings in which the artifact is embedded: if it's a rich network of meanings that sees special attention being paid to the object, then it's an artwork. This isn't to say that the artifacts should be "placeless" in the culture—that they should be autonomous objects of appreciation, in Kristeller's sense. On the contrary, requiring placelessness just serves to pre-emptively exclude subaltern artifacts from the sphere of art. To be art, thinks Danto, is just to express a meaning, and ordinary artifacts don't express any meanings when taken out of their ordinary contexts of use. Art, however, does: it speaks to everyone, even if it tells us all different things based on our background knowledge.

Indeed, it seems that *all* art is functional in some respect—whether because it's guided by an intention to educate, to overawe us with religious sentiment, to make money, or simply to reward sustained attention. Art seems to develop when certain behaviours or objects 'become special'; they get exaggerated or stereotyped, and become ritualized rather than purely utilitarian (Dissanayake 1988). 'Making special' describes the deliberate elaboration of an object and its investiture with meaning. But the fact that all art is functional does not seem to preclude us from appreciating it for its own sake; on the contrary, it seems like consideration of the artwork's primary function is *always* relevant to its aesthetic evaluation (Davies 2006): there's not much sense, after all, in trying to appreciate the marble boat at the

Summer Palace in Beijing (the *Boat of Purity and Ease* [1755]) as anything other than a boat-shaped pavilion on the water.

Although today most philosophers of art seem to agree that the art/artifact distinction is not particularly robust, several have taken issue with the way in which Danto's thought experiment presents the issue. So, for instance, we might worry that the focus on meaning is still insufficient to distinguish artworks from artifacts, since so many artifacts which Danto, at least, might want to exclude from the purview of art actually participate in symbolically dense systems of meaning (Gell 1996). Consider the Drakkar, a longboat used by Vikings to carry raiding parties (and their spoils) around the world. These were works of very fine craftsmanship, but they were also home to the men who sailed them for months on end. They represented safety and wealth; they were handed down through families; they earned names, like *Ormrinn Langi* (The Long Serpent) or *Reinen* (Reindeer), and fame; and they were decorated with elaborately carved prows which were fitted with intricate serpents when nearing hostile waters, to frighten the spirits of the land (hence the appellation 'dragon-ship'; the sails were the dragon's wings, the rear its tail). As a means of transport, they were tools, but they were clearly symbolically dense for their users. Should we class them as art, too? We certainly *can*, but the question is whether we *should*; whether as a class of objects they could express their meanings outside their contexts of use in iron-age Norse society.

Others have observed that the thought experiment's initial plausibility trades on the experience of bewilderment so many of us have when presented with works from artistic traditions about which we know nothing (Dutton 1993): to the uninitiated, one Balinese *gamelan* sounds much like another, for example, and Coast Tsimshian "totem" poles look rather like Haida or Kwakwaka'wakw poles. But it's no accident that we notice *these* objects rather than others and think of them as potential artworks: it's precisely because they are perceptually striking in some way—where the "totem" poles are concerned, for example, they stand alone and reach dizzying heights, and feature intricate painted designs. But, not knowing anything about their context and background, we are not equipped with adequate criteria for distinguishing—or even appreciating—them; we don't realize that different peoples used different combinations of colours for their poles, or used shallow vs. deeply etched reliefs, etc. In other words, the gallery public of New York may not be able to tell Pot People and Basket Folk pots apart, but Pot People probably can. Learning about the work's and practice's context thus doesn't so much reveal hidden meaning as it does otherwise inaccessible aesthetic properties.

SUGGESTED READING

SEMINAL PRESENTATION:

1. Danto, Arthur C. (1988). "Artifact and Art," in ART/ARTIFACT: *African Art in Anthropological Collections. Exhibition Catalogue.* New York: Center for African Art and Prestel Verlag, 18–32.
   Danto introduces our thought experiment to show that what makes something a work of art is its *meaning*, not its perceptual properties. Artworks are appropriately treated as ends in themselves; artifacts, by contrast, are embedded in a system of meanings: their use *is* their meaning.

DEFENCES:

2. Davies, Stephen (2006). Aesthetic Judgements, Artworks and Functional Beauty. *Philosophical Quarterly* 56 (223): 224–41.
   Davies argues that *all* art is functional and, thus, that utility is not an appropriate criterion for distinguishing between art- and non-art objects. We can appreciate art for its own sake while also acknowledging that it serves extrinsic practical purposes. Consideration of the artwork's primary function—whether it's inducing religious awe, warding off evil, entertainment, moral education, etc.—is *always* relevant to its aesthetic evaluation.
3. Dissanayake, Ellen (1988). *What Is Art For?* Seattle: University of Washington Press.
   Dissanayake contends that looking for the function of art is a more promising task than searching for its definition. In Ch. 4, she argues that art 'makes special'; it involves a degree of elaboration which sets the artwork apart from everyday objects in the relevant culture, but without, for all that, placing it in an autonomous aesthetic realm. She offers an evolutionary account of the development and adaptiveness of 'making special'.

CRITIQUES:

4. Dutton, Denis (1993). Tribal Art and Artifact. *Journal of Aesthetics and Art Criticism* 51 (1): 13–21.
   Dutton argues that Danto's argument and thought experiment mistakenly leave out the aesthetic dimension of subaltern art. In the real world, utilitarian and expressive art traditions are not indistinguishable, because people

normally invest a great deal of special care in the creation of meaningful artifacts. It's no accident that we think certain subaltern artifacts (rather than classes of artifacts) are artworks: they are perceptually striking in some way.

5. Gell, Alfred (1996). Vogel's Net: Traps as Artworks and Artworks as Traps. *Journal of Material Culture* 1 (1): 15–38.

Although Gell is sympathetic to Danto's suggestion that artworks embody meanings and are not distinguished by their perceptual properties, he argues that Danto relies on an over-idealized distinction between functional and meaningful artifacts. Ethnography, he argues, shows us that many of the artifacts we'd class as merely functional have an important symbolic dimension, and often are embedded in highly ritualized practices.

FURTHER READING:

6. Kristeller, Paul Oskar (1951–2). The Modern System of the Arts: A Study in the History of Aesthetics Part I *Journal of the History of Ideas* 12 (4): 496–527; Part II in 13 (1): 17–46.

Kristeller argues that our modern concept of art was first formulated in the eighteenth century, by Charles Batteux. Previously, our conception of art was very broad and included many crafts; with Batteux, we first singled out poetry, painting, sculpture, music, and architecture as a unified sphere of human activity, free from moral or utilitarian objectives.

7. Shiner, Larry (2001). *The Invention of Art: A Cultural History*. Chicago: University of Chicago Press.

Shiner expands upon Kristeller's thesis, paying particular attention to the rise of artworld institutions (e.g., museums, secular concerts, and academies) and the ways in which they regulate artistic practice. Ch. 15 deals with the art/artifact distinction, arguing that institutions have a vested interest in promoting the art/craft dichotomy.

8. Porter, James I. (2009). Is Art Modern? Kristeller's "Modern System of the Arts" Reconsidered. *British Journal of Aesthetics* 49 (1): 1–24.

Porter argues that Kristeller's account—particularly of the shift in eighteenth-century aesthetics—is just a "Just So" story. The constellation of the "fine arts" into a core nucleus of a handful of practices, he argues, never actually took place: the fine arts have always been characterized by diverse lists of practices. Kristeller has conflated 'the modern system' with the doctrine of aesthetic autonomy, itself an artifact of his arbitrary classifications.

9. Kivy, Peter (2012). What Really Happened in the Eighteenth Century: The 'Modern System' Re-examined (Again). *British Journal of Aesthetics* 52 (1): 61–74

Kivy offers a qualified defence of Kristeller. He concedes that the eighteenth century did not see philosophers trying to establish a modern *system* of the arts according to which they were autonomous from considerations of morality or utility. Their contribution, instead, was to group some of the arts together as *fine* arts, thus sparking the search for necessary and sufficient conditions for 'art'.

10. Young, James O. (2015). The Ancient and Modern System of the Arts. *British Journal of Aesthetics* 55 (1): 1–17.

Young argues that although Batteux popularized the label of "fine art", the modern 'system' of the arts in fact dates back to Aristotle. Kristeller and others have conflated ancient talk about the arts (in general) with the *fine* arts (in particular), thereby missing the ancient category of the imitative arts. It's far from clear that this category was abandoned in the medieval era, but if it was, it was reintroduced in the *sixteenth* century, rather than the eighteenth.

15

PSYCHEDELIC SOUNDS (DEFINITION OF MUSIC)

CASE

Imagine some clever researchers develop a fantastic new recreational drug—of sorts. These researchers have discovered a particular sequence of sounds which, when played, induce a highly pleasurable psychedelic state. Suppose these sounds are easy to make for anyone who knows how to whistle. That means that anybody who knows which sounds to make, and in which order, can immediately transport anyone else into drug-induced ecstasy. I suppose that bone conduction protects the whistler from drugging themselves by boosting lower frequencies and thereby altering the whistler's own experience of the sound. Is this musical sound-drug—let's call it MSD for short—*music*?

It certainly has several properties in common with what we intuitively think music is like: it's an organized sound, it was deliberately produced, and it was designed to induce a particular kind of pleasant experience. But I doubt most of us would think of this experience as a *musical* one. So what's missing? Plausibly, the problem is that the psychedelic state we're in isn't the result of listening to the sounds as such. It's not because we're paying particular attention to them that we're transported; it's just because the tonal sequence is a key that unlocks a brute physiological reaction.

DOI: 10.4324/9781003368205-17

Conversely, let's think about *Songs of the Humpback Whale* (1970), an enormously popular album of those sounds recorded by Roger Payne. Is it music? The whales intentionally produced those sounds, to be sure, and regardless of whether they intended them as music, *Payne* certainly deliberately reproduced them for us to appreciate *as* music. But *are* they? Is there a real difference between *being* music, and just *being treated as* music?

RESPONSES

Although we have a strong intuitive understanding of what music is, few philosophers have attempted to give a definition of the concept in terms of a set of individually necessary and jointly sufficient conditions. At a first pass, we might say that music is intentionally organized sound (Godt 2005), but it should quickly become clear that this isn't quite enough. An ultrasound, for instance, uses high-energy sound waves to build a picture of the interior of the human body. The frequencies are carefully chosen to achieve their aim, but we wouldn't call them *music*. Likewise, a lion roars deliberately in order to scare off a threat or rival or to alert the pride, but that's not music either.

Still, it's at least plausible that sound and intentionality are *necessary* ingredients for music, even if they aren't *sufficient*. So, what's missing? One influential suggestion is that the sound should be made in order to produce a particular kind of experience in the listener—an *aesthetic* experience, perhaps. Put more broadly, we might say that music is intentionally organized sound produced to enhance a listener's experience of engaging with those sounds *as sounds* (Levinson 1990). So: what makes Brahms musical and the lion's roar not is just that the Brahms is intended to reward paying attention to the sounds as such, whereas the roar isn't and doesn't. Indeed, the roar is supposed to scare you off, so if you're listening to it as just a sound, divorced from the fearsome beast uttering it, you're not engaging with it correctly.

But what happens when you're learning to play an instrument and you practice your scales? You're deliberately producing sounds, but they don't really seem aimed at enriching anyone's experience of the scale (Kania 2011). Aren't you nevertheless playing music? Or consider a pianist who plays a bit of something to warm up her fingers; she certainly doesn't intend anyone to pay close attention to whatever she plays, but often it's a recognizable piece of music. Alternately, think of a score: it's a musical piece of paraphernalia, but it makes no sounds. We might worry, then, that our definition is too restrictive. Perhaps what's needed is a different twist on the experiential condition: music is an intentionally produced organized sound-event *which either has certain basic musical features or is intended to be heard as having them* (Kania 2011). The trick, then, is to avoid circularity by identifying what counts as a 'basic musical feature' without referring to music—perhaps pitch or rhythm. This yields a broader conception of music but will still exclude sounds—like a jackhammer's hammering—which don't have basic musical features, and which we aren't intended to listen to as though they did.

Given the widespread popularity of attempts to define 'art' (see *The Gallery of Red Squares* and *The Whale and the Driftwood*), it is somewhat surprising that such projects haven't taken off for the individual arts. Where music is concerned, in fact, skepticism about the entire definitional enterprise seems to be the order of the day.

Some, for example, think that 'music' is an open concept with no necessary and sufficient conditions, since the concept is subject to change in response to changes in our cultural practices (Goehr 1992). Far from being neutral, our concept of music is significantly informed by European classical music practice. So, for example, it's argued that the notion of perfect compliance with a composer's score, although it regulates contemporary musical practice, is of comparatively recent origin; and so too with the idea of standalone musical 'works' as independent objects of appreciation.

This isn't to say that anything goes, but rather, that concepts aren't independent of the practices in which they're embedded, and these practices change over time. We can't 'future-proof' the definition of music, because as our practices change over time, so too will our conception of what's necessary to it (McKeown-Green 2014). Worse, those conceptions are inextricably tied to particular socio-cultural contexts. Since there is no independent standard against which to test our definitions of music, we are left with the court of folk intuition, and we should be suspicious of its verdicts.

Levinson's account seems to rule out songs or tunes which don't call attention to themselves, such as 'Happy Birthday to You', since we don't primarily appreciate them for their aesthetic features. On the other hand, Kania's account seems to rule *in* obviously non-musical practices like Morse code, which is intentionally produced to be heard in terms of its rhythm (Davies 2012). From the struggles of attempts like these, it has been argued that we get a glimpse of the diverse elements that a definition of music must be able to incorporate, if it hopes to be adequate to the sheer breadth of uses to which the concept is put (Davies 2012). Ordinary definitions are often articulated in purely functional, operational, historical, or structural terms. Musical practices resist this kind of reduction because they extend so far into the fabric of human life; not just in terms of our patterns of consumption, but also in terms of the cultural energy devoted to music—in film, in dance, in the manufacture of musical instruments and the basics of musical education, in lulling children to sleep, etc. At every level, our music-involving practices are informed by conventions and practical considerations which aren't themselves aesthetic or musical, but which nevertheless work to shape how we conceive of music. The upshot is that we may be better off trying to articulate what could count as music at a given time and culture or tradition, rather than looking for a sufficiently broad, unitary definition.

Amidst this sea of skepticism, however, a few people have nevertheless found cause for qualified optimism. According to one proposal, for example, we can abandon the quest for necessary and sufficient conditions in favour of music's 'salient features' (Hamilton 2007).[1] So, for example, music generally has a tonal basis and exploits the listener's unprompted tendency to detach sounds from their circumstances of production ('acousmatic experience'), such that we tend to just hear *the music* as a whole rather than hear the strings, the oboe, etc.

Alternately, the success of skeptical arguments has led some towards a *pluralist* account of music, according to which there are several equally serviceable concepts of music (existing both at the same time and across time), each suited to different contexts and interests (Currie and Killin 2017). Some of these are culturally specific 'folk' concepts, others ethnomusicological, philosophical, etc. Some explanatory projects take intentions to be central, whereas others emphasize music's formal properties or its social role; depending on what we emphasize, we get different conceptions of music. If we emphasize intending the sounds to be aesthetically appreciated, for example, birdsong and lullabies may not count as music, whereas concentrating on their formal features will encourage us to include them under that particular music-concept. The appropriate question to ask of something therefore isn't 'is it music?', but rather 'does it fall under a music-concept?'

Finally, it is worth noting that most of these attempts to define music explicitly aim to rule out animal sounds as music (e.g., Levinson [1990], Kania [2011], Hamilton [2007], Davies [2012]). But we should ask ourselves whether that's an appropriate restriction. Certainly, animals don't hold piano recitals for one another; but nobody can deny that they produce complex, organized sounds. There's even evidence that some animals, at least, learn and practice their sounds, and improvise new ones (Higgins 2012, Yan 2013). It's easy to ignore how much our conception of music is shaped by cultural practices—things like listening to the music for its own sake rather than enjoying it as an accompaniment to another activity, buying albums, attending concerts, taking lessons, making instruments, composing scores, etc. We can't expect animals to share those cultural practices, but neither should we assume that they have none of their own. Nor should we place too much emphasis on the functional nature of animal sounds, since so much that we call music is also subservient to functional ends. By denying the possibility of animal music, we reinforce human exceptionalism; by accepting that animals can be more or less musical, however, we treat musicality as a naturally arising phenomenon with a biological basis (Higgins 2012). Animal music may not express important human characteristics, but that doesn't mean it doesn't express anything at all.

SUGGESTED READING

SEMINAL PRESENTATION:

1. Levinson, Jerrold (1990). *Music, Art, and Metaphysics: Essays in Philosophical Aesthetics.* Ithaca, NY: Cornell University Press.
   Levinson tackles the definition of 'music' in Ch. 11, "The Concept of Music". He defines it as sounds temporally organized by a person in order to enrich or intensify the experience of actively engaging with those sounds primarily *as sounds*.

DEFENCES:

2. Godt, Irving (2005). Music: A Practical Definition. *Musical Times* 146 (1890): 83–8.

   Godt defines music as humanly organized sound, organized with intent into a recognizable aesthetic entity aimed at being communicated to a listener (although there are some other conditions, they follow from these). He argues that music-making is a defining characteristic of humankind.

CRITIQUES:

3. Goehr, Lydia (1992). *The Imaginary Museum of Musical Works: An Essay in the Philosophy of Music.* Oxford: Oxford University Press.

   Inspired by Weitz, Goehr argues in Ch. 4 that 'music', like 'art', is an open concept: it has no necessary and sufficient conditions which are essential to it, only a cluster of properties frequently associated with its instances. The concept itself changes in response to new innovations. She argues that our musical work-concept is fairly new and is primarily correlated with the ideals embodied in the classical tradition.

4. Kania, Andrew (2011). "Definition," in *The Routledge Companion to Philosophy and Music,* Theodore Gracyk and Andrew Kania (eds.). New York: Routledge, 3–13.

   Kania offers a critical survey of the literature on definitions of music, arguing that definitions focused on identifying intrinsically musical features or on the subjective experience of music are bound to be too narrow (or, perhaps, too broad). He defines music as an event intentionally produced to be heard that either has basic musical features or is to be heard as having them.

5. Davies, Stephen (2012). On Defining Music. *The Monist* 95 (4): 535–55.

   Davies doesn't offer a definition of his own. Instead, he argues that a definition of music will have to combine several different strategies to be successful. In particular, it has to balance musical traditions with the universal elements from which they arose, as well as subsequent socio-historical, institutional, and intentional developments.

6. McKeown-Green, Jonathan (2014). What Is Music? Is There a Definitive Answer? *Journal of Aesthetics and Art Criticism* 72 (4): 393–403.

   McKeown-Green argues that appeals to intuition are only viable when the thing we are defining is determined by our conception of it—and it's not clear whether that's true of music. Certainly, we can't achieve a level of generality sufficient to future-proof a definition.

7. Currie, Adrian, and Anton Killin (2017). Not Music, but Musics: A Case for Conceptual Pluralism in Aesthetics. *Estetika* 54 (2): 151–74.

   Currie and Killin argue for a pluralist account of 'music', according to which there are several concepts of music, each suited to different contexts and interests. Music, they argue, is a disunified concept with multiple legitimate but non-equivalent meanings.

FURTHER READING:

8. Hamilton, Andy (2007). *Aesthetics and Music*. New York: Continuum.
   In Ch. 2, Hamilton argues that although there may be no necessary and sufficient conditions for music, we can nevertheless identify 'salient features' of music by thinking about its acoustic, acousmatic, and aesthetic properties. Music, he argues, lies on a continuum with non-musical sound-art.
9. Higgins, Kathleen Marie (2012). *The Music between Us: Is Music a Universal Language?* Chicago: Chicago University Press.
   In Ch. 2, Higgins argues that animals are capable of producing music. Music, she argues, seems like a defining characteristic of humanity, which is why we are quick to deny it to animals. She shows that animals are capable of deliberate and creative organized sound; our impulse to deny its musicality, she argues, stems from anthropocentrism.
10. Yan, Hektor K. T. (2013). Can Animals Sing? On Birdsong, Music and Meaning. *Social Science Information* 52 (2): 272–86.
    Yan argues that music is a fundamentally social phenomenon, and that to determine whether other animals make music we need to have a firm and explicit grasp of its social functions for humans and evaluate its social functions for animals. In denying animal musicality, we risk simply asserting that animal music doesn't express important *human* characteristics or belong to analogous animal institutions.

NOTE

1 These are similar to Kania's 'basic musical features', though not part and parcel of a definition in terms of necessary and sufficient conditions.

RETITLING ART (TITLES)

CASE

Imagine a really iconic work of art—it could be in any medium, from any period. In case you're drawing a blank, I suggest imagining something like Damien Hirst's *The Physical Impossibility of Death in the Mind of Someone Living* (1991), which is basically just a 14-foot tiger shark floating in a display case full of formaldehyde.

Now suppose it had a dramatically different title. Perhaps our shark might simply have been entitled *Tiger Shark*, *Exhibit A*, *Poseidon's Horse*, or perhaps *The Physical Impossibility of Death in the Mind of Someone Laughing*. And now for the question which completes our thought experiment: if it *had* had one of these alternate titles, would it still be the same artwork? Of course, it would have all of the same *physical* parts, but would it have the same *meaning*, the same artistic content?

Probably not, right? That's presumably because the title itself is an integral part of the work of art: it doesn't just give us something to call it, it also shapes our engagement with the work. It gives us a clue about how to approach thinking about it: not just as an exhibit in a natural history museum, but as a work of art which invites us to reflect on life, death, and our inability to conceive of the life of a lifeless form, or of our own impending doom.

DOI: 10.4324/9781003368205-18

Now consider a work like Sofonisba Anguissola's *Madonna and Child* (1598), whose title was given by a dealer or collector sometime (perhaps centuries) after its painting. Suppose some corporate entity comes into possession of it and decides to retitle it *Mary and Jesus*, to make it more accessible to a contemporary and increasingly irreligious Anglophone audience. Is it still the same painting?

Probably—all they've done is picked out a description of the scene that's equivalent to the old title (indeed, *that's just what the old title means!*). It's not like they gave it a totally bonkers title like *FSM Fodder* or *Zombie Mama*, after all. So: why does this retitling leave the work unchanged, but not the other one? It can't just be that the new title is an appropriate, non-bonkers description, since so was *Tiger Shark*, but that clearly gives us an altogether different artwork.

There are two big issues of interest here: (1) whether we can change an artwork's title without changing the artwork itself and, underlying this question, (2) whether the titles of artworks are their names. The first question is especially salient these days, because galleries and museums around the world are starting to retitle works in their permanent collections to remove offensive (primarily racist) terminology. The second is particularly philosophically thorny, because our answer to it will determine our answer to the first question. If titles *are* names, as we typically assume, then the philosophy of language tells us that retitling is no big deal; if they *aren't*, then it might be a serious problem, since that opens the possibility that changing a work's title thereby changes the work.

RESPONSES

On the classic account (Levinson 1985, Wilsmore 1987), titles are not names. This is because proper names, at least according to the majority view in the philosophy of language, are merely labels which facilitate reference to something; they're more like surface-level *properties* than deep *parts* of their bearers. As such, proper names carry no associated descriptive content; this means that it doesn't matter if I change my name from Michel to Thierry—nothing about me, myself, changes, except for the label that people use to refer to me. But some titles clearly *are* closely related to their associated artwork's identity, as we saw when we proposed retitling *The Physical Impossibility of Death in the Mind of Someone Living.* These titles have *semantic weight*, which is to say that their descriptive content has some bearing on the content of the associated object (Levinson 1985, Walton 2011). Call these *reflective* titles. But some other titles don't seem to have semantic weight—they have semantic *content*, sure, but that content doesn't really reflect upon its associated work, as in the case of *Madonna and Child* above. Let's call these *descriptive* titles. The question, then, is why some titles are reflective while others are merely descriptive: what makes (or marks) the difference?

The standard answer is that it's the person who gives the work the title who makes and marks that difference. Some titles—true titles (Levinson 1985)—are given by the artist. These titles are always integral parts of their associated artworks and thus cannot be changed without altering the work. Other titles are given by collectors, dealers and other middlemen for the purposes of selling the work. These are merely descriptive titles; they are interpretations of the work, nothing more (Adams 1987).

Others have argued that titles *are* names, but that they go well beyond a name's referring function: a title is a name whose proper function is to guide interpretation (Yoos 1966, Fisher 1984, Symes 1992). Titles thus typically have descriptive content which helps us to focus our attention on particular parts of the work to be interpreted (c.f. *Pinny the Who?*). This focus on a title's role in guiding interpretation has led some (e.g., Savedoff 1989) to take a harder line against the idea that retitling can alter an artwork, independently of the issue of whether titles are names. Visual art, so the argument goes, always supports multiple competing interpretations, and there is nothing remarkable in the fact that we can use epitextual tools to highlight one or another of these interpretations. The same is true of diagrams, after all: the same diagram can have two different descriptions or sets of labels, and we don't think it's a different diagram for all of that. There may be *some* cases where the change of title reflects a change of work, but these are cases in which the title suggests a shift to an entirely new context of evaluation (e.g., from sculpture to conceptual art).

Surprisingly, few scholars have investigated the history of our titling practices to see what insights might be gleaned from it. In large part, this is due to the fact that we have very poor extant evidence for early titling. The evidence we *do* have, however, indicates that most titles are not 'true' titles; they are descriptive titles given by middlemen. Artist-given titles are a relatively recent invention, dating back to the late eighteenth century (Yeazell 2015). Although there is some mixed evidence of (primarily descriptive) titles in ancient Greece and Rome, there is virtually none for Europe from the fifth to the fifteenth centuries, at which point we find long descriptions in what we have come to think of as the titular position (Xhignesse 2019).[1]

The evolution of our titling practices suggests another possibility: titles are indeed the proper names of their associated artworks (Xhignesse 2019). While it's true that, in the philosophy of language, proper names are purely referential, a closer look at linguistics and at our naming practices suggests that (1) just like reflective titles, many—perhaps most—names evolved from descriptions associated with their bearers (e.g., 'Ottawa' [from the Algonquin *Odàwàg*, 'to trade'], or 'Smith'), and (2) like titles, names serve distinctively social functions in addition to their referential function.

SUGGESTED READING

SEMINAL PRESENTATION:

1. Levinson, Jerrold (1985). Titles. *Journal of Aesthetics and Art Criticism* 44 (1): 29–39.

   Levinson defends four theses about the titles of artworks: (1) that they are integral parts of their associated works, (2) that they are essential to their works, (3) that title slots are replete with aesthetic potential, and (4) that the titles of artworks are *unlike* the names of persons insofar as they carry semantic weight. Levinson distinguishes between several different kinds of titles and argues that artist-given titles ('true' titles)—cannot be altered without changing their associated artwork.

DEFENCES:

2. Adams, Hazard (1987). Titles, Titling, and Entitlement To. *Journal of Aesthetics and Art Criticism* 46 (1): 7–21.

   Although Adams broadly agrees with Levinson, he goes a step further: true titles are *always* integral parts of their works. It is other titles, titles given by someone other than the artist, which are mere labels and, thus, proper names. Changes of title are merely interpretations; no true title can be altered without altering the work.

3. Wilsmore, Susan J. (1987). The Role of Titles in Identifying Literary Works. *Journal of Aesthetics and Art Criticism* 45 (4): 403–8.

   Wilsmore argues that titles are narrowly constitutive of works, such that changes of title amount to the introduction of a distinct work. Titles both are and are not parts of works; they help us to identify the work, but they ineluctably introduce the artist's intentions into the work's content. Titles, she thinks, are more than mere names and can invoke a performative aspect, too, much as a signature asserts ownership over something.

4. Walton, Kendall L. (2011). "Pictures, Titles, Depictive Content," in *Publications of the Austrian Ludwig Wittgenstein Society - N.S. 17*. Berlin: De Gruyter, 395–408.

   Walton argues that a title's semantic content helps to determine an artwork's depictive, as well as its representational, content. Consequently, titular substitutions result in different depictions—different works. Titles, he argues, clearly affect our imaginative and visual experiences of a work.

CRITIQUES:

5. Yoos, George E. (1966). Some Reflections on Titles of Works of Art. *British Journal of Aesthetics* 6 (4): 351–64.

   Yoos distinguishes different uses of titles, arguing that they give us an initial entry point into the appreciation and evaluation of any work of art. Although he accepts that titles name their artworks, he argues that their referential use is just one (relatively minor) purpose to which titles are put and, further, that the referential use of titles is not relevant to their work's appreciation.

6. Fisher, John (1984). Entitling. *Critical Inquiry* 11 (2): 286–98.

   Fisher argues that titles are names whose function is to guide interpretation, rather than merely facilitate reference. Unlike prototypical proper names, they typically have descriptive content. Titling thus facilitates discourse about art. Titles are names suited to a purpose: interpretation. *Bad* titles *mislead* us.

7. Savedoff, Barbara E. (1989). The Art Object. *British Journal of Aesthetics* 29 (2): 160–7.

   Savedoff draws our attention to the fact that visual art's pictorial surface always supports multiple competing interpretations. She argues that titles are *a* guide to interpretation, but they don't have the power to transform a work into something different simply by being altered. In the very few cases where the title does mark a change in the visual artwork, it is because it has managed to shift appreciation of the artwork into an entirely different evaluative category.

8. Xhignesse, Michel-Antoine (2019). Entitled Art: What Makes Titles Names? *Australasian Journal of Philosophy* 97 (3): 437–50.

   I chart the history of our practice of titling artworks, showing that it is of surprisingly recent origin. I argue that only some titles—reflective titles—carry semantic weight and that descriptive titles are interchangeable. I also argue that, like titles, many names *do* seem to carry semantic weight, so we should not be too quick to distinguish between titles and names. Instead, I suggest, we need to reconsider the function of names.

FURTHER READING:

9. Symes, Colin (1992). You Can't Judge a Book by Its Cover: The Aesthetics of Titles and Other Epitextual Devices. *Journal of Aesthetic Education* 26 (3): 17–26.

    Symes argues that although titles are names, they are more than mere labels: they help appreciators to frame their expectations and isolate interpretive noise. They can both identify *and* interpret; they reflect the work's content, but also work to generate interest in the work. They confer status upon works and indicate that the work is ready for appreciation. We cannot appreciate artworks separately from their titles.

10. Yeazell, Ruth Bernard (2015). *Picture Titles: How and Why Western Paintings Acquired Their Names.* Princeton: Princeton University Press.

    This is one of the *very* few historical treatments of our titling practices. Yeazell is primarily interested in developments in titulature and interpretation after the eighteenth century, since we have extensive records from that point on. She dates the earliest artist-given titles of paintings to 1796; earlier titles were provided by art dealers and other middlemen. She uses 'title' and 'name' synonymously.

NOTE

1 The situation is different in China and the Muslim world, where visual art and calligraphy were more closely related. There, we see titles cropping up somewhere between the eleventh and thirteenth centuries (Xhignesse 2019).

THE GALLERY OF RED SQUARES (DEFINING ART)

CASE

Suppose you walk into a gallery, and the first thing you see are eight identical paintings of a red square hanging around the room. At first, you think it's an installation by a single artist, and that all eight paintings together constitute the artwork; but upon closer inspection, you see that each one has a label giving it a different title from the others and that each is also by a different artist. The first is a historical painting titled *The Israelites Crossing the Red Sea* and depicts the pursuing Egyptians being drowned by the sea. The second is entitled *Kierkegaard's Mood*; the third is a landscape painting of Moscow titled *Red Square*; the fourth is a geometric Minimalist work, also called *Red Square*; the fifth is *Nirvana*, inspired by Hinduism; the sixth, a Post-Impressionist still-life, *Red Table Cloth*; the seventh, a canvas grounded with a red square by a famous artist like Giorgione, but never completed; and the eighth, an ordinary artifact that happens to have an identical-looking red square of paint on it. Suppose, further, that a young artist visits the gallery and, outraged, paints an identical-looking red square and demands it be included in the show as *Untitled* (which of course it is).

The nine objects look the same, but they're all very different. They're works in radically different traditions—Post-Impressionism,

DOI: 10.4324/9781003368205-19

Minimalism, still life, historical painting, psychological portraiture, etc.—and, thus, are each very different from one another. In fact, only seven of them are actually artworks—one is an unfinished painting, and the other an ordinary object! The question is: what makes some of these red squares artworks, and the others not?

In an early precursor to our titular thought experiment, William Kennick (1958) asked his readers to imagine being tasked with sifting through the contents of a warehouse and separating the art from the non-art objects. He observed that, while we might make a few errors at the margins, by and large, any one of us would do a reasonably good job of it. We all have a good grasp of what art is, even if we can't articulate a set of necessary and sufficient conditions which will apply universally. This, he argued, is because art is not a natural-kind term like 'gold' or 'water'—it does not have a universal essence that we can specify which will apply to all and only instances of its kind; today, we would call it a *social* kind instead. Ultimately, he argued, any attempt to find necessary and sufficient conditions for art is doomed, since the concept of 'art' is systematically vague and 'open-textured'.

Similarly, the gallery of red squares is typically taken to establish three theses: (1) for any ordinary object, we can imagine an artwork just like it; (2) for every artwork, we can imagine another just like it that is a *different* artwork; and (3) for every artwork, we can imagine something just like it which is *not* an artwork (Danto 1981). These three claims, taken together, are sometimes called the *indiscernibility thesis* (Fisher 1995), and they suggest that what makes some things artworks and others not is a matter of the structure or context in which they are embedded (which gives them meaning), rather than their perceptible properties (Danto 1981; see also *Guernicas*).

RESPONSES

One early avenue of attack targeted the relationship between an artwork and the stuff out of which it is made since, as we saw, this stuff can be a mere real thing (Margolis 1988). What does it mean, exactly, to say that the artwork and its ordinary counterpart are *indiscernible*? It seems obvious that they aren't *numerically* identical, but do we then mean that there is no difference *at all* between them, or do we mean the weaker claim that there is no *perceptual* difference between their aesthetic properties? If the former, then it seems we have no reason at all to identify one as art and the other not; if the latter, then the worry is that we're reduced to internalism about art, since there appear to be no publicly available differences between an artwork and its material counterpart.

Another early objection was that we can't generalize the lessons from the squares, which are paintings, to the other arts, especially those which are by their nature multiple (see also *The Supercopier*). The indiscernibility of some of Danto's cases (notably, Cervantes's and Pierre Menard's *Quixotes*[1]), it was thought, isn't at all troubling because *they're actually instances of one and the same work*, since the creation of the second is guided by comparison to the first (Wreen 1990). This objection is perhaps not as successful as it hopes, however, since it just shows that the Menard case is not one of indiscernibles, not that no such indiscernibles are possible. Applied to the red squares, we get the result that the ninth square, *Untitled*, is the same work as one (or all) of the others, since the artist effectively *copied* it. All of the eight coincidentally similar squares remain unaffected, however: they are indiscernible counterparts of one another.

Alternately, the thought experiment has also been criticized on structural grounds. The worry here is that it points us in the direction of a single conclusion, rather than asking us which of two or more options jibe with our intuitions (Wollheim 2012). So, while it may well be the case that the indiscernibility thesis applies to the particular case of the nine red squares, it's a whole other ball game to think it applies to all art everywhere. Although the thought experiment tells us that the squares are indiscernible, it's not clear what that means: are they indiscernible after a cursory examination, or no matter how much we learn about them? In other words, are the nine red squares still indiscernible once we know their different titles, artists, contexts, styles, genres, etc.? It seems plausible that artworks might often look like non-artworks and be initially indistinguishable to someone who only has access to their perceptual properties, but it's much harder to countenance that all artworks are ultimately indistinguishable from a material counterpart, no matter what we know about the two. If indiscernibility entails the latter claim, then it also seems to entail that we can never actually discern the trace of the artist's intentions in the work, which suggests that artworks are not, in fact, substantively dependent on the artist's intentional action (perhaps they aren't even *intention-dependent*; see *Apelles's Horses* and *The Whale and the Driftwood*).

Similarly, we might worry that the indiscernibility of the squares is predicated on the cognitive impenetrability of perceptual states (i.e., what we see is not informed by what we know; Wollheim 2012). But cognitive science shows that perception *is* cognitively penetrable (Nanay 2015)—just think of the difference that familiarity makes to your perception of a space, or that knowing something about dendrology makes to the oppressive monotony of a forest. Where the squares are concerned, knowing their titles, genres, styles, etc. plausibly makes a significant difference to our perception of each work. And if so, then it seems like any difference in a work's aesthetically relevant properties must entail a perceptual difference, too. Ultimately, then, there are no indiscernibles.

Conversely, some have drawn the more radical lesson that an artwork just is its meaning (Dilworth 2007): the material stuff of which it's made is nothing more than a vehicle for expressing that meaning. It should come as no surprise, on this model, that the same vehicle can communicate very different contents: "The peasants are revolting," after all, can mean either that peasants are gross, or that they're pretty upset. In this way, the propositional content of artworks performs the same kind of functional role as types do for multiple art-kinds (see *The Wrong Note Paradox*), without the metaphysical baggage of type theory.

Finally, two cautionary notes are in order before we conclude this discussion of the gallery of red squares. First, it should be emphasized that although the indiscernibility thesis suggests that any old 'mere real thing' can have aesthetic properties which reward critical and focused attention—even, and perhaps *especially* if the mere real thing is considered *as* art—this does not mean that mere real things *are* artworks, or can substitute for artworks which look like them. Artworks can point to mere real things and thus enrich our subsequent encounters with them, but the two are not interchangeable (Gaskell 2020), nor does this mean that artworks are reducible to the mere real things of which they are made (Fisher 1995).

Second, it is worth noting that Danto's emphasis is on the *artist's* act of creation, which locates their work in a particular (meaningful) context, not on the receiving audience's act of interpretation. Institutional theorists, by contrast, typically emphasize the context of *reception* as conferring art-status through institutional actors such as galleries, or artworld actors such as critics and scholars (see, e.g., Gaskell 2020). For Danto, this explains the *how* of artistic creation but not *what* makes it art. There is, however, a promising suggestion for doing just that, for reconciling the artist's creative, and the artworld's receptive, roles: in creating her work and locating it in a particular social context, the artist sets the terms which will govern the audience's engagement with that work, and the categories by reference to which they will evaluate it (Irvin and Dodd 2017). Art-making, then, is not just a question of *imbuing* an artifact with meaning, but also of correctly *discerning* that meaning.

SUGGESTED READING

SEMINAL PRESENTATION:

1. Danto, Arthur Coleman (1981). *The Transfiguration of the Commonplace: A Philosophy of Art*. Cambridge, MA: Harvard University Press.

    Ch. 1 opens with the gallery of red squares, which refines a series of indiscernible cases Danto began proposing in his 1964 paper *The Artworld*,[2] and which he discusses in more detail in Ch. 2. Danto uses indiscernibles to show that art-status is not conferred by an object's perceptual properties, but rather by their being embedded in networks of meaning, an "atmosphere of theory".

DEFENCES:

2. Fisher, John Andrew (1995). Is There a Problem of Indiscernible Counterparts? *Journal of Philosophy* 92 (9): 467–84.

    Fisher argues that we should be careful to distinguish the problem of indiscernibles from that of material counterparts and that indiscernibles pose a bigger challenge to formalist and institutional theories alike. The transfiguration is of an object into art by an *interpretation*; that object, however, need not be an ordinary object, nor have an ordinary object as an actual material counterpart.

CRITIQUES:

3. Margolis, Joseph (1988). Ontology Down and Out in Art and Science. *Journal of Aesthetics and Art Criticism* 46 (4): 451–60.

    Margolis worries that just what 'indiscernibility' means is unclear: is it that the artwork is artistically or numerically indiscernible from its material counterparts? Is there really no difference *at all* between an artwork and its material counterpart, or just no aesthetically relevant difference? In particular, it seems that 'mere real things' are only identified as such in contradistinction to artworks being identified as art.

4. Wreen, Michael (1990). Once Is Not Enough? *British Journal of Aesthetics* 30 (2): 149–58.

   Wreen focuses on the case of Pierre Menard, which comes from Danto via Borges's short story, *Pierre Menard, Author of the Quixote* (1939). He argues that "indiscernibles" such as this one are, in fact, merely copies or instances of the original, and thus not distinct works at all. This is because the process which generates them relies on either outright appropriation or careful editorial oversight to ensure matching.

5. Wollheim, Richard (2012). "Danto's Gallery of Indiscernibles," in *Danto And His Critics*, 2nd ed., Mark Rollins (ed.). Malden, MA: Wiley-Blackwell, 28–38.

   Wollheim takes Danto to task for the structure of his thought experiments. He argues that Danto exploits the fact that we don't have or know the conditions of application for the concept 'art' to conclude that indiscernible counterparts are always feasible. Danto may have established his *particular* cases, but it's not clear we should accept the lesson more generally: some artworks may not have indiscernible non-art counterparts, and these, then, would be art due to some intrinsic (non-relational) property they possess.

6. Nanay, Bence (2015). Cognitive Penetration and the Gallery of Indiscernibles. *Frontiers in Psychology* 5: 1–3.

   Nanay argues that the gallery of red squares is empirically inadequate: cognitive science shows us that perceptual experiences are cognitively penetrable (i.e., informed by our knowledge). This means that things like the titles of each square, the fact that they are by different artists, etc. all inform our perceptions of them; it leads us to focus on different properties of each work, and that different focus translates to a literally different perceptual experience.

FURTHER READING:

7. Kennick, William E. (1958). Does Traditional Aesthetics Rest on a Mistake? *Mind* 67 (267): 317–34.

   Kennick argues that the search for essences in aesthetics is a fool's errand, which he supports with a precursor thought experiment to Danto's: the warehouse. We all know what art is fairly easily and intuitively and can pick out artworks from ordinary objects with a fair degree of accuracy. But we don't have a similar sense that attaches to any of the properties cited by traditional definitions as universal and essential to art. Art is not a natural kind.

8. Dilworth, John (2007). In Support of Content Theories of Art. *Australasian Journal of Philosophy* 85 (1): 19–39.

   Inspired by Danto, Dilworth proposes a content theory of art: the material substrate of the artwork is just a vehicle for the meaning (content) expressed by that artwork, in the same way that the inscription 'the cat is on my lap' is a vehicle for expressing a proposition that represents the world a certain way (it's not the inscribed sentence that does so, but rather its meaning, the proposition it expresses). The artwork itself is the *content*, not the material substrate.

9. Irvin, Sherri and Julian Dodd (2017). In Advance of the Broken Theory: Philosophy and Contemporary Art. *Journal of Aesthetics and Art Criticism* 75 (4): 375–86.

   Dodd and Irvin explore the ways in which contemporary art and indiscernibles set the stage for the contextual turn in theories of art by turning the focus away from the work's intrinsic to its relational properties, particularly those pertaining to the artworld's reception of the work. They argue that this has prompted us to distinguish the artwork from its physical medium and emphasize the artist's role in setting the parameters of an audience's engagement with the work.

10. Gaskell, Ivan (2020). Works of Art and Mere Real Things—Again. *British Journal of Aesthetics* 60 (2): 131–49.

    Gaskell argues that in order to be art, an object must be received and accepted as art by some community. This means that some objects may be 'mere real things' in some communities, but artworks in others. But he cautions against generally conflating artworks with their indiscernible material counterparts: these can have aesthetic properties which reward attention, but that does not make them art. Mis-categorization actually *impedes* our ability to properly appreciate these properties

NOTES

1 Suppose a contemporary author wrote a text identical to Cervantes's *Don Quixote* (1605), but without copying or memorizing it.

2 Danto, Arthur C. (1964). The Artworld. *Journal of Philosophy* 61 (19): 571–584.

18

THE SUPERCOPIER (MULTIPLE ARTWORKS)

CASE

Let's start with your favourite painting. Since I don't know what yours is, I'll tell you mine: Jacques-Louis David's *Napoleon Crossing the St. Bernard* (1801–5).[1] It's a pretty famous painting and widely recognized as a propaganda piece equating Napoleon to Hannibal and Charlemagne.

Now, suppose you photocopied it (in colour, of course): would you now have two of the same painting? I imagine that, very sensibly, you don't think so: the original, after all, is oil on canvas, whereas our photocopy is ink on paper. But never mind that: suppose we could rig the photocopier to print in oil and on canvas; what then? I suspect you're still skeptical since, as you know, copying images involves a loss of fidelity, so that a copy of a copy of a copy of a copy may well look quite different from the original.

Similarly, no forgery is strictly qualitatively identical to its original.[2] There are always some small differences—perhaps the shade of blue over here is not quite right, or perhaps the figure's left index finger is a millimetre longer in one painting than the other; alternately, we might be able to identify the pigments used in one as being much older than

DOI: 10.4324/9781003368205-20

those in the other. On that basis, we typically ground a belief that the original is different from—typically, more valuable than—the forgery (see *Faking Nature*). But what if we could make *exact* copies?

What if we developed a really good photocopier—a *supercopier*—which didn't involve *any* loss of fidelity at all? What if the copies it printed out weren't just *perceptually* indistinguishable from the original, they were molecule-for-molecule copies (c.f. *The Gallery of Red Squares*)? Would we then be justified in thinking that we had doubled the world's stock of our favourite painting? If so, then we would have good grounds to believe that all artworks are, in fact, multiple—this conjecture is called the *Instance Multiplicity Hypothesis* (IMH; Currie 1989).

Some philosophers answer these questions in the affirmative, on the grounds that artworks are individuated by their aesthetic properties, and there can be no aesthetically relevant difference between the supercopy and the original (e.g., Strawson 2008 [1974], Zemach 1986). This motivates the further conclusion that all art-kinds[3] are, in principle, multiple (Currie 1989, D. Davies 2010)—that is to say, for any artwork in any art-kind, it is *in principle* possible for that work to have multiple instances. Multiplicity, here, is a *modal* notion: it's about what is possible in principle, not how things are in actual fact. This is a fairly counterintuitive claim, and it has further equally counterintuitive consequences: e.g., works of art are discovered, not created; when we stand in front of a painting we aren't actually appreciating—or even perceiving—*the work* itself, but rather merely one of its instances, so that when we hear Cécile Chaminade's Op. 26 *Les Amazones* (1884), we're just familiarizing ourselves with the pattern of the work, not the work itself.

RESPONSES

Others, however, have argued that the move from supercopy to universal multiplicity is insufficiently motivated. One common avenue of response takes its cue from our attitudes towards forgeries, where our preference for the original seems rooted in its causal origins rather than just its aesthetic properties (Sagoff 1978). So, for example, the reason we prefer Vermeer's works to Van Meegeren's forgeries or Tim Jenison's copies (good as they are) is that *they were painted by Vermeer's hand*.

So armed, we might take the further step of arguing that this connection to history is an integral part of aesthetic experiences of the work, so that supercopies do not, in fact, succeed in conveying all of the same aesthetic properties (Taylor 1989)—at least, not if we know that they are copies! We might then say that supercopies offer good epistemic access to a work and stand as evidence of the process of discovery that led to its creation, but that they fall short of being proper instances of the work. Indeed, it might prove useful to distinguish between a work's *epistemic* instances (instances which convey all the properties relevant to the work's aesthetic appreciation) and its *provenential* instances (instances that stand in the right kind of causal relationship to the artist's original act of creation) (see D. Davies 2010, although he takes this distinction to support the IMH).

Relatedly, we can resist the IMH by appealing to our appreciative and artistic conventions (S. Davies 2003), and to the role that an artist's intentions or sanction play in determining the categories to which their work belongs (Irvin 2008). We might then use the artist's sanction as a means of filling out what counts as a work's provenential instances and insist that these alone are proper instances of the work. On this view, we take our ontological cues from our artworld practices, which are quite diverse, and leave it to artists to determine a work's proper ontological category. This is not just a matter of simply intending that a work be singular or multiple, however: the artist must take some steps to secure that status for the work, to guide the public's reaction to it, and sometimes they may well fail (Weh 2010).

Finally, another option entirely is to deny that singularity and multiplicity exhaust all possible options. Our artistic practices are incredibly varied and complex, often contradictory, and typically built out of syncretistic amalgamations of earlier practices; any ontology which hopes to do justice to all these practices—across the world, and across human history—may need to adopt a much more nuanced division of art-kinds (Thomasson 2004).

SUGGESTED READING

SEMINAL PRESENTATION:

1. Currie, Gregory (1989). *An Ontology of Art*. London: St. Martin's.
    Currie introduces the supercopier thought experiment, arguing for two
    related theses: (1) that all kinds of artworks belong to the same ontological

category—action-types, and (2) that all art-kinds are, at least in principle, multiply instantiable. Artworks, he thinks, are individuated by the action-type which consists of the discovery of a particular structure by means of a given 'heuristic path'; and different artists, he thinks, can discover the same structure by means of the same heuristic path, in which case we will have multiple instances of one and the same artwork.

DEFENCES:

2. Strawson, Peter (2008 [1974]). "Aesthetic Appraisal and Works of Art," in *Freedom and Resentment*. New York: Routledge, 196–207.

   Strawson argues that multiple-instantiability is a modal property of artworks: any artwork, in fact, is in principle multiply instantiable, since it's a merely contingent fact that we can't make perfect copies of putatively singular artworks like paintings and (non-cast) sculptures. The distinction between singular and multiple art-kinds is misconceived: all artworks are individuals, but they are also all instances of a *type*, rather than concrete particulars.

3. Zemach, Eddy M. (1986). No Identification Without Evaluation. *British Journal of Aesthetics* 26 (3): 239–51.

   Zemach rejects the traditional distinction between multiple and singular works of art, arguing instead that artworks are *both* repeatable *and* concrete. Identification, he argues, is always relative to some sortal, and first requires us to know a thing's essential properties—for art, its aesthetic properties. And although these are rarely fully duplicated, they certainly *can* be.

4. Davies, David (2010). Multiple Instances and Multiple 'Instances'. *British Journal of Aesthetics* 50 (4): 411–26.

   Davies argues that we need to distinguish between two senses of a work's 'instances': a *provenential* sense where what matters is that the instance stands in the right causal-historical relation to the artist's original act of creation, and an epistemic sense where what matters is that the 'instance' accurately conveys all of a work's relevant perceptual properties. Davies uses this distinction to defend the instance multiplicity hypothesis.

CRITIQUES:

5. Taylor, Paul W. (1989). Paintings and Identity. *British Journal of Aesthetics* 29 (4): 353–62.

   Taylor considers and rejects the suggestion that very accurate or perfect reproductions of putatively singular artworks like paintings offer us the same aesthetic experience and, thus, that these are multiple art forms. Such reproductions, he argues, are not tokens of a type of which the original is the exemplar, the 'master' copy. Consequently, he thinks, we should resist relative identity theories in aesthetics.

6. Irvin, Sherri (2008). "The Ontological Diversity of Visual Artworks", in *New Waves in Aesthetics*, Kathleen Stock and Katherine Thomson-Jones (eds.), Houndmills: Palgrave Macmillan, 1–19.

   Irvin argues that there is no single ontological category (e.g., action-types) to which all artworks belong: artworks are ontologically diverse. This is because the identity-conditions of our artistic practices are set by our conventions, and by an artist's *sanction*, which sets our focus of appreciation.

7. Weh, Michael (2010). Production Determines Category: An Ontology of Art. *The Journal of Aesthetic Education*, 44 (1): 84–99.

   Weh argues that the existence or possibility of a notation (e.g., a score or a supercopy) does not entail that the work is multiple. Instead, he thinks that we need to look to the artist's successful intentions, as encoded in the work's production process. These fix the work's category and, thus, determine whether it is singular or multiple. Singularity and multiplicity, then, are in large part a matter of our social practices, which set the default range of our artistic intentions.

FURTHER READING:

8. Sagoff, Mark (1978). On Restoring and Reproducing Art. *Journal of Philosophy* 75 (9): 453–70.

   Sagoff wrestles with the fact that forgeries, reproductions, and restorations can be better guides to a work's original aesthetic properties. Ultimately, he argues that our preference for the original is rooted in an appreciation of the process which generated it; much like love, what matters to us is the individual itself, not just its properties.

9. Davies, Stephen (2003). "Ontology of Art," in *The Oxford Companion to Aesthetics*, Jerrold Levinson (ed.). Oxford: Oxford University Press, 155–80.

   Davies gives an overview of the debate over the distinction between singular and multiple works of art, arguing that these distinctions are fundamental to our conception of art. Although Davies agrees that multiplicity is a *modal* notion, he thinks that the conventions governing some of our artistic practices, and the context which fixes their identity-conditions, ensure that some works are nevertheless fundamentally singular.

10. Thomasson, Amie (2004). "The Ontology of Art," in *The Blackwell Guide to Aesthetics*, Peter Kivy (ed.). Malden, MA: Blackwell, 78–92.

    Thomasson offers a rich overview of the ontology of art in the analytic and continental traditions. She argues that our usual bifurcated distinctions— e.g., between abstract and concrete entities, multiple and singular works, mind-dependent, or independent entities—are insufficiently nuanced to account for our ordinary beliefs and practices regarding social objects such as artworks.

NOTES

1 Technically, the title applies to a series of five oil paintings. That's a somewhat troublesome fact, given the thought-experiment I'm about to describe, so you'll just have to bracket that information and treat it as a single painting instead. Or, better yet, use your own favourite painting instead!

2 Although most forgeries are not actually copies of works; they're new works passed off as olds.

3 'Art-kinds' is just a neutral descriptor for what we sometimes call a work's 'medium', e.g. whether it's a dance, drawing, musical work, painting, sculpture, etc. Philosophers of art try to avoid using 'medium' because it tends to be ambiguous between a work's physical and artistic media.

19

THE WRONG NOTE PARADOX

CASE

Usually, when I try to hum the theme to *Midsomer Murders* (ITV 1997-present), I get a few notes in before I start making mistakes. This might be entirely unremarkable, except for the way in which I get the tune wrong: it turns into the *Father Brown* (BBC One 2013-present) theme instead.

Their obvious similarity aside, these are clearly different pieces of music. But my inability to correctly hum the *Midsomer* theme offers a good illustration of our next paradox, the *wrong note paradox*: how much can a performance of a musical work deviate from the score (or, more generally, the prescribed sound-structure) before it stops counting as a performance of that work in the first place, and is instead a (correct) performance of a different work?

One answer is that it can't (Goodman 1968): a musical work is identified by its sound-structure, as encoded in its score or notation. Any deviation from that score would give us a different—though closely related—work, since that performance would have a different score. And yet, it seems intuitively correct that a single mistake shouldn't count against a performance being of a particular work. After all, if the third clarinet fumbles a rest in Tchaikovsky's *Swan Lake*,

DOI: 10.4324/9781003368205-21

Op. 20 (1877), it would seem hideously pedantic to insist that none of the audience had therefore heard *Swan Lake*. On the other hand, a performance with one *thousand* mistakes might not sound much like *Swan Lake* at all; there might, in fact, be no way to tell that it was a performance of *Swan Lake* apart from the performers' sincere insistence that that was what they were doing (poorly).

The wrong note paradox stems from these conflicting intuitions: on the one hand, it seems entirely fair to say that musical works are individuated by their scores and that those scores determine what counts as a correct performance of the work. On the other hand, it seems equally fair not to hold a few small deviations against a performance. But if one small deviation is acceptable, this seems to open the door to a conceptual slippery slope, since just one more deviation seems entirely innocuous, too; and a third is really not much worse than two, nor is eight really any worse than seven, which was no worse than six, etc. In this manner, we could end up with an entirely different work— e.g., *Three Blind Mice* (1609)—just one small deviation at a time. And if nothing else, *Swan Lake* is definitely *not* identical to *Three Blind Mice*! So: which of these perfectly reasonable intuitions should we jettison?

RESPONSES

The wrong note paradox is clearly something to be avoided, rather than embraced. Consequently, few philosophers have opted for the same criterion of perfect compliance to the score as Goodman. Nevertheless, there have been some efforts to rescue the Goodmanian perspective from the paradox. One strategy for defending Goodman's focus on notation rather than context or history is to subordinate performers to composers, such that the purpose of a performance of a work is to highlight the work's aesthetic value and the composer's artistic achievement (Edidin 1997). Doing so will certainly involve closely following the score, although it's possible that the strictest adherence to the score will result in a performance with slightly less aesthetic value than one which uses an unscripted flourish to highlight some element of the composition.

Alternately, it has been suggested that we should de-couple the notion of a performance from that of its underlying sound-sequence (Predelli 1999). The idea here is that what identifies a given performance as being of a particular work is not the performance's actual sound-sequence, but rather that it was intended as an instance of a particular sound-sequence type, subject to whatever is generally accepted as an acceptable degree of error. Either way, saving Goodman involves relaxing the criterion of perfect compliance somewhat in order to better capture the underlying principle that it is a work's sound-structure, rather than its history, which individuates it and its performances.

The wrong note paradox presents a particularly thorny problem for musical Platonists (see also *The Revision Puzzle* and *Unperformable Music*), who maintain that musical works are eternally-existing abstract entities individuated by their sound-structures (i.e., scores). For the Platonist, we determine which performances are instances of a work by reference to their sound-structure: same sound-structure, same work. And since abstract entities are by definition causally inert, the only way we can ever access a musical work is by hearing one of its performances. The problem here should be obvious: any Platonist who takes a hard line on score-compliance is thereby committed to the conclusion that a performance of, e.g., Beethoven's *Fifth Symphony* (1808) that's missing a note, or which has too brief a rest between notes, etc. is not a performance of the *Fifth Symphony*, but of a subtly different work. And that seems particularly unpalatable, especially in light of historical evidence indicating that the ideal of perfect compliance is quite new to classical music practices (Goehr 1992, Dyck 2014, Ravasio 2019).

Platonists have adopted several related strategies for overcoming this problem, however. A common move involves appealing to intentions: so, e.g., perhaps what perfect compliance requires is not that a performance actually *is* note-for-note identical to the elements specified by the score, but rather that performers must *intend* perfect compliance, even if they sometimes fall short in their execution (Wolterstorff 1975).

Alternately, others have tried to distinguish between instances and performances: an *instance* of the work must be perfectly compliant to the score, but a performance may deviate somewhat from this ideal (Levinson 1980). An incorrect performance would then be *of* a work (since it was intended to comply with the score) without also being one of its instances: only *correct* performances are its instances.

Similarly, some Platonists simply reject the idea that a work's context and history are irrelevant to its identity (e.g., S. Davies 2001). In particular, notational and performance conventions have been quite variable throughout history, which means that understanding their specifications requires contextual information. The result, they argue, is that performers must try to comply with *most* of the score for the performance to count as an instance of the work. Some variation is permissible, even inevitable.

A different answer which has gained some traction in recent years is that a work's identity-conditions—including the range of possible variability for its instances—is determined by our social practices (D. Davies 2012). This is not to say that anyone in particular is responsible for deciding the matter; the point, rather, is that it arises organically out of the mess of our musical practices.

SUGGESTED READING

SEMINAL PRESENTATION:

1. Goodman, Nelson (1968). *Languages of Art: An Approach to a Theory of Symbols*. Indianapolis: Bobbs-Merrill.

   Goodman presents the paradox in Ch. 5. Earlier, he distinguishes between autographic and allographic arts, arguing that autographic arts can only have a single genuine instance, whereas works are allographic if, and only if, they have or could have a notation, which gives us a decisive test for determining instances of the work. On the assumption that causal and historical facts do not help to individuate allographic works and their instances, he argues that only strict compliance with the notational system does so. To allow even a single deviation from the notation to count as an instance of, e.g., Beethoven's *Fifth Symphony* (1808) is to open the door to a conceptual slippery slope resulting in, e.g., *Three Blind Mice* (1609) counting as an instance of the *Fifth*.

DEFENCES:

2. Wolterstorff, Nicholas (1975). Toward an Ontology of Art Works, *Noûs* 9: 115–42.

   Wolterstorff defends a Platonist ontology of musical works, arguing that what matters for determining whether a given performance counts as a performance of a particular work is whether it was performed with the *intent* of perfect compliance, rather than actually *being* perfectly compliant. Properly formed instances of a work of art require an understanding of the artist's intentions concerning the production of new instances.

3. Levinson, Jerrold (1980). What a Musical Work Is. *Journal of Philosophy* 77 (1): 5–28.

   Levinson follows Goodman in arguing that perfect compliance to the score determines which of a work's performances are its instances, provided they are properly connected to that score by the performer's intentions. To count as a performance of the work, one must be "reasonably successful" at complying with the score. But not all performances of a work are its instances; some are just incorrect performances.

4. Edidin, Aron (1997). Performing Compositions. *British Journal of Aesthetics* 37 (4): 323–35.

   Edidin argues that our concept of classical music necessarily champions the importance of the composer and their achievement over the work's performers. The performer's task is just to bring out the composition's aesthetic value as much as possible, so the best performances will closely follow the score (whether they will *most* closely follow it is more complicated). If he is correct, then this allows us to build an indirect defence of perfect compliance to the score.

5. Predelli, Stefano (1999). Goodman and the Wrong Note Paradox. *British Journal of Aesthetics* 39 (4): 364–75.

   Predelli gives the wrong note paradox its name. He defends Goodman's assumption that the causal and historical facts about a musical work are irrelevant to its identification, suggesting that Goodmanians can escape paradox by denying that performances are identified with their sound-sequence. This enables him to argue that what is at issue is a performer's intention to produce an instance of a sound-sequence-type, rather than of a work, subject to a generally accepted permissibility degree specifying the number of acceptable deviations.

CRITIQUES:

6. Goehr, Lydia (1992). *The Imaginary Museum of Musical Works: An Essay in the Philosophy of Music*. Oxford: Oxford University Press.

   In Ch. 4, Goehr shows that our ideal of perfect compliance—along with a good many other intuitions we have about musical works—is of comparatively recent origin, having only come to characterize classical music since the late eighteenth century. Since then, however, we have developed what she characterizes as a "regulative work-concept"—i.e., a concept of musical works that *regulates* how we think about musical practice.

7. Davies, Stephen (2001). *Musical Works and Performances: A Philosophical Exploration*. Oxford: Oxford University Press.

   In Ch. 3, Davies argues that Goodman's focus on notation is too restrictive and that the identification and individuation of musical works requires us to also consider the work's historical context, the demands it places on performers, and the conventions which underpin it. Since notational and performance conventions change over time, some degree of reference to historical context is ineliminable. Performers must try to comply with *most* of the score, but some variation is permissible.

8. Davies, David (2012). Enigmatic Variations. *The Monist* 95 (4): 643–62.
Davies explores the problem of accounting for variations between the different instances of a multiple artwork which are fully qualified to convey its experiential properties. Ultimately, he argues that determining which variations are acceptable instances of a work is socially determined.

9. Dyck, John (2014). Perfect Compliance in Musical History and Musical Ontology. *British Journal of Aesthetics* 54 (1): 31–47.
Dyck argues that contemporary musicological research shows that our ideal of perfect compliance to a score (in classical music) is a recent phenomenon, only dating back to the very late nineteenth century. Even today, he argues, our classical music practices remain fairly pluralistic, though they tend increasingly towards perfect compliance. These facts, he argues, pose a significant problem for musical Platonism.

FURTHER READING:

10. Ravasio, Matteo (2019). Historically Uninformed Views of Historically Informed Performance. *Journal of Aesthetics and Art Criticism* 77 (2): 193–205.
Ravasio argues that a close examination of actual musical practice shows that the traditional view of historically-informed performances as being focused on compliance with the score, work-centred, and impersonal is false. The actual practice of classical music performances, he argues, is much more pluralistic than we have credited it with being.

20

UNPERFORMABLE MUSIC (MUSICAL ONTOLOGY)

CASE

Music is one of the performing arts, and so of course musical works are made to be performed and heard. Or are they?

Suppose someone composed a work consisting of a series of A# eighth notes so long that its performance would outlast the heat death of the universe.[1] It's an easy enough piece to compose, so long as we're willing to forgive its gestural quality; but it's clearly not a work which can ever be performed in full (indeed, with every passing moment, less of it can be performed). Works like this one are *nomically* unperformable—that is to say, they are unperformable given the laws of physics. Alternately, some works we compose might be *logically* unperformable—imagine, for instance, a score which demands that the oboeist play an A# and simultaneously play nothing at all or, somewhat more interestingly, a piece of doom metal which requires each instrument to play the score *slower than all the others*. Finally, other works are perhaps *medically* or *biologically* unperformable. Imagine a sonata, for instance, which is so horrifically complex that it can only be correctly played on an as-yet-uninvented stringed instrument which requires the musician to sprout two extra arms and sit inside the instrument.[2] But are these musical works?

DOI: 10.4324/9781003368205-22

Intuitively, they would be, so long as someone actually presented them as such rather than merely suggesting them as thought experiments. And yet none of them can ever be performed, let alone heard. It is perhaps tempting to think of these works as analogous to a score which a composer keeps hidden away forever, or which she ultimately destroys, since that piece, too, can never be performed or heard. But the problem of unperformable works is more acute than that of lost works since lost works are or were at least *performable* in the first place. Unperformable works, by contrast, fly in the face of all we hold dear about music.

What makes this problem so acute is one of our most basic intuitions about musical works: that they are *audible*, i.e., that they are the sort of thing which we can (or could, in principle) hear. Another basic intuition we have concerning musical works is that they are *repeatable*: we can play them on different occasions, or simultaneously but in different locations.[3] But unperformables cannot be performed; that means that they can't be repeated (you could start to play your superlong series of A#s any number of times, of course, but could never repeat the whole thing) and, worse, that they can never be heard in the first place—not even in any possible world (at least, this is definitely true where logically unperformable works are concerned). If repeatability and audibility are necessary components of music (e.g., Dodd 2007), then this is a serious problem: by virtue of what do unperformable works even count *as music*?

One possibility, of course, is that they don't. Perhaps they aren't even works at all—they're *thought experiments*, nothing more (or less). But surely they *are* (or: *can be*)—they're generated by the same kind of process of composition as regular music is, they're intended as works, and they're appreciable as works, to the extent that one can or will experience them—e.g., the slowest Doom song, above, is *really boring* (and that's saying something, considering the genre). They're appropriate objects of analysis for critics, art historians, and philosophers of art. That they can't be fully instantiated is no bar to their being partially instantiated, and it is certainly no bar to their having a score which articulates the necessary conditions for reproducing the work. What more can we ask of a work of art?

It is perhaps true that these works are better thought of as pieces of conceptual art, but then so are many works which we straightforwardly accept as musical works. This is true of John Cage's compositions, of course, perhaps the most famous of which is *4′33″*, which calls for four minutes and thirty-three second of ambient noise. But it is also true of the programmatic music of the nineteenth century, which attempted to convey an extra-musical narrative: Berlioz's *Symphonie fantastique*, Op. 14 (1830), for example, tells the wordless tale of an artist whose unrequited love drives him to opium.

RESPONSES

The dominant view of musical ontology is Platonism, which holds that musical works are abstract objects. Since it's part of the definition of an abstract object that it is causally inert—that it doesn't enter into causal relations with the material world—it's usually thought to follow that musical works cannot come into or pass out of existence, and that we cannot hear the work itself. These are counterintuitive results, and Platonists have taken pains to explain them away. Thus, some (e.g., Levinson 1980) have argued that composers indicate (but don't quite *create*) their compositions, which is a step up from merely discovering them as Leif Ericson discovered northern North America. Audibility, however, is in some ways a thornier issue, since it is arguably a more basic intuition of ours that musical works are the sorts of things we hear. But we can't hear abstract objects, since we can't enter into causal relations with them.

Platonists have tried to work around this counterintuitive result by arguing that what we hear, instead, are *performances* of the work (e.g., Levinson 1980, Dodd 2007). The suggestion here is that the work itself is a *type*, whereas each (proper) performance is just a *token* of that type. That's all well and good, of course, except that unperformable works generate types which can never have *any* tokens, meaning that they aren't audible in the first place.

A Platonist could perhaps argue that some unperformables *do* have tokens, insofar as someone could start to play a nomically unperformable work like our starting series of A# eighth notes. But these performances will be such wretchedly malformed failures as to be unrecognizable as even a badly performed token of the type. I can play *A# To Infinity and Beyond* for a few hours, for example, but that performance won't hold a candle to the actual work itself, which is supposed to outlast the universe. We wouldn't normally say that humming the first bar of a tune counts as a performance of the work.

Type-theorists are therefore better off denying that unperformables are works of music at all, since they do not satisfy the necessary condition of audibility (nor, perhaps, repeatability, depending on just how we cash it out).

One alternative to Platonism is idealism: the view that musical works (though not their performances) are mental entities (Cray and Matheson 2017). Idealism can explain unperformables as completed *ideas* which are meant to be treated the same way we normally treat musical works; whether they are ever performed, or can be heard, is entirely irrelevant to their musical status.[4]

Another option is to think of musical works as *concrete* entities. Although there are different ways of cashing this out, one fairly standard account of musical materialism (Tillman 2011) claims that the musical work just *is* every one of its performances.[5] A related strategy inspired by four-dimensionalist treatments of the metaphysics of time takes each performance, score, etc. as a single part of a larger, singular entity distributed across space and time (Moruzzi 2018). The problem, of course, is that there are no performances of unperformables, and for logically unperformables, there aren't even any *possible* performances to appeal to.

Musical materialism can get out of this pickle, but only so long as it also counts things like scores and ideas in a composer's head as constituent parts of a concrete entity, and abandons its emphasis on performances (e.g., Alward 2020). Alternately, it can bite the bullet and maintain that unperformables in particular, and unperformed works more generally, are not, strictly speaking, musical works. They are 'musical' only in a loose, analogical sense. This is not as weird a position as it first sounds, however, since even the default view in musical ontology—Platonism—has to concede that musical works are only audible loosely speaking, in an analogical sense (Davies 2009).

Unperformables might alternately prompt us to revisit our intuitions about the nature of musical works: are they *really* necessarily audible and repeatable, or have philosophers overestimated the power of these intuitions? This is a new question for experimental philosophy, but one which has garnered some recent interest. The first study of our intuitions about musical ontology focused on repeatability intuitions for popular music (Bartel 2018) and found that while laypeople seem to accept that musical works are repeatable, they have a much more restricted view of what counts as repetition than philosophers do, so that two recordings of a song which differed in their affect or connotation were judged to be entirely different works.

A subsequent collection of two larger studies of intuitions about *classical* music (Mikalonyté and Dranseika 2020) reported contrary results: folk intuitions about the repeatability of classical music appear to be quite permissive. Musically educated and lay listeners alike did not seem to attach much importance (where individuation was concerned) to the work's instrumentation or its affective and connotative properties; instead, they prioritized the sameness (or difference) of the composer and their creative actions. The differences between these studies may be attributable to the different types of music selected for study, or perhaps to the different populations studied (i.e., American vs. eastern European listeners). While we should be wary of concluding too much from such a small number of studies, these results should perhaps give ontologists of art some pause: it is not yet clear exactly which intuitions about musical ontology we should aim to preserve at the expense of which others. The mixed evidence we have found for repeatability may well be symptomatic of a similar muddle for audibility, especially when the cases presented for analysis are thought experiments rather than extant musical works.

SUGGESTED READING

SEMINAL PRESENTATION:

1. Cray, Wesley D. (2016). Unperformable Works and the Ontology of Music. *British Journal of Aesthetics* 56 (1): 67–81.
   Cray introduces the possibility of unperformable works, distinguishing between trivial, medical, nomic, and logical unperformables. She argues that these are genuine works of music, that they are composed for performance, and that their possibility poses a problem for certain accounts of musical ontology, notably type-theoretic accounts.

DEFENCES:

2. Cray, Wesley D. and Carl Matheson (2017). A Return to Musical Idealism. *Australasian Journal of Philosophy* 95 (4): 702–15.
   Cray and Matheson argue that musical works are mental entities—specifically, *ideas*. A musical work is a completed idea intended for a musical manifestation (through which indirect means we *hear* it); or, to accommodate unperformable works, a completed idea intended for the same kind of consideration as ideas which are characteristically manifestable. Unperformables

are complete ideas intended for musical manifestation and are therefore are musical works.

CRITIQUES:

3. Levinson, Jerrold (1980). What a Musical Work Is. *Journal of Philosophy* 77 (1): 5–28.

   Levinson defends a version of Platonism which aims to preserve our intuition that musical works are created by their composers. He argues that musical works are *indicated types* which take performances as their tokens: a composer (e.g., Clara Schumann) points to (indicates) a pre-existing type (e.g., *Quatre Polonaises pour le pianoforte*, Op. 1 [1831]) and thus creates a *new* type: *Quatre...*-as-indicated-by-Schumann.

4. Dodd, Julian (2007). *Works of Music: An Essay in Ontology*. Oxford: Oxford University Press.

   Dodd sets out to determine which ontological category musical works belong to, and what their identity-conditions are (see also *The Wrong Note Paradox*). He argues that we must look for an ontology that accommodates two basic facts about musical works: they are repeatable and audible. He favours a type-token theory according to which musical works are eternally-existing and uncreated abstract objects whose tokens are performances.

5. Tillman, Chris (2011). Musical Materialism. *The British Journal of Aesthetics* 51 (1): 13–29.

   Tillman defends musical *endurantism*, the view that musical works exist in toto wherever they are located; and they are 'located' at each and every one of their performances, but not at any spatiotemporal point *between* those performances. This means that each work is heard in its entirety through each performance.

6. Moruzzi, Caterina (2018). Every Performance Is a Stage: Musical Stage Theory as a Novel Account for the Ontology of Musical Works. *Journal of Aesthetics and Art Criticism* 76 (3): 341–51.

   Moruzzi defends a musical stage theory, according to which musical works are just instantaneous spatiotemporal stages, so that each performance gives us a different musical work and some of these works are connected together by a privileged causal relationship, the 'repeatability-relation'. Unperformed works—of which unperform*able* works are a subset—are not, in fact, musical works, except loosely speaking: they are would-be works.

FURTHER READING:

7. Davies, David (2009). Dodd on the 'Audibility' of Musical Works. *British Journal of Aesthetics* 49 (2): 99–108.

   Davies argues that for the type-token theory, musical works are only audible in a loose, analogical sense. Quite a wide variety of musical ontologies, he argues, can explain audibility at least as well; thus, audibility does not represent a unique or particularly compelling explanatory *desideratum* for the type-token view.

8. Bartel, Christopher (2018). The Ontology of Musical Works and the Role of Intuitions: An Experimental Study. *European Journal of Philosophy* 26 (1): 348–67.

Bartel surveys the literature on the ontology of musical works, focusing on the importance of our intuitions that musical works are created and repeatable. He presents the results of the first-ever study of lay intuitions about the repeatability of popular music, finding that laypeople seem to have a more restrictive conception of repeatability than philosophers do.

9. Mikalonytė, Elzė Sigutė and Vilius Dranseika (2020). Intuitions on the Individuation of Musical Works: An Emplyirical Study. *British Journal of Aesthetics* 60 (3): 253–82.

Mikalyonté and Dranseika conducted two studies testing lay intuitions about the repeatability of classical music. They found that musically educated and lay listeners both seem indifferent to a work's instrumentation or its affective and connotative properties for purposes of individuation, but place a high premium on the composer and their compositional process.

10. Alward, Peter (2020). Multiplicity, Audibility, and Musical Continuity. *Dialogue* 59 (1): 101–21.

Inspired by D. Davies's distinction between P- and E-instances of a work (see *The Supercopier*) Alward argues that we need a better way to account for a work's audibility by means of one of its instances. He develops a continuity relation for instances of a work which does not need to appeal to sound-pattern types.

NOTES

1 These cases of unperformable works are adapted from Cray (2016).
2 Sci-Fi fans will recognize this as Iain M. Banks's *Hydrogen Sonata*, from the eponymously titled 2012 novel in his *Culture* series. The instrument required to play it is an antagonistic undecagonstring (elevenstring).
3 See also *The Revision Puzzle*, where both intuitions are also mobilized.
4 Though it may be relevant to how they are treated that musical works are *typically* audible and performable.
5 Others may opt for mereological fusions of performances, or of performances + score + recordings + …, etc. These differences are immaterial for our purposes here.

PART III

AESTHETIC JUDGEMENTS

GENERAL BACKGROUND

Philosophers use the term 'aesthetic' in several different contexts—we talk about an object's aesthetic properties, compare our aesthetic judgements to one another, and sometimes invoke a special aesthetic attitude which we take towards works of art and scenes of natural beauty, but not towards other things. Even this book has 'aesthetics' in its title! But what, exactly, *is* the 'aesthetic'? Intuitively, it seems closely connected to the concept of beauty, but at least in some cases, it's tempting to describe certain kinds of non-beautiful experiences as aesthetically valuable: why else does *The Room* (2003) enjoy such a cult following? Upon reflection, it seems as though we find aesthetic value all around us, from paperback thrillers to picnics in the park.

The cases in this section all point to some aspect of what can broadly be described as aesthetic judgements. They tackle the nature of aesthetic properties, the possibility and desirability of aesthetic disagreements, and the nature of aesthetic appreciation, as well as the issues of what makes us count something as part of a broader style, and whether poorly executed or formulaic works can be aesthetically valuable despite or even *because of* those faults.

DOI: 10.4324/9781003368205-23

21

AESTHETIC CONCEPT ZOMBIES (AESTHETIC PROPERTIES)

CASE

In the philosophy of mind, a 'zombie' is a person who's physically indistinguishable from any other person—i.e., they have a perfectly correct physiology in fine working order—but who doesn't have an inner mental life. They walk and talk and go on dates, see movies, have cats, etc., but if you could look inside their head you wouldn't find any conscious experiences. If you think it's conceivable that such zombies could exist, but that they're missing something, then that's usually taken as a reason for you to reject physicalism (the idea that all that exists is reducible to physical processes), since it means that consciousness is distinct from brute physical processes.

What I'm calling an *aesthetic concept zombie* is roughly similar. Imagine someone who has no capacity for aesthetic judgement whatsoever—they're completely incapable of making the kinds of judgements we routinely make about movies, novels, music, etc.—and imagine further that they know this fact and want to keep it secret. (If the full-blown zombie seems too far-fetched, imagine instead someone who knows that their aesthetic judgements are consistently bad.) To hide their lack of taste, then, they spend some time paying attention to the kinds of judgements others make, and from that data, they develop an

DOI: 10.4324/9781003368205-24

elaborate system of rules for aesthetic guesswork which enables them to say more or less the right things most of the time (often enough, anyway, that nobody notices their deficiency). Although they might describe a sculpture as 'delicate', it's only ever a guess, never an observation of their own. Worse, it's a guess in which they can never have a great deal of confidence since any change at all in the object could force a need for recalculation. Thus, even though they use concepts like 'delicate' or 'pretty', they never develop an understanding of what these terms mean or when it's correct to apply them.

An aesthetic concept zombie is someone whose life is very different from ours: they have no reasons of their own to decorate their homes, dress nicely, read novels or watch movies. When they do, *we* have no reason to praise them for their taste; and when they evaluate artworks, they're engaged in a profoundly different activity from the rest of us: a robotic calculation.

If you think that this description of aesthetic concept zombies is plausible, that suggests that aesthetic properties are distinct from purely sensory properties: there's something more to them, such that we can't identify necessary and sufficient conditions for their application. Conversely, if you think the zombie should get along just as well as anybody else, that suggests that you think it *is* possible, at least in principle, to identify conditions of application for aesthetic terms.

RESPONSES

Generally speaking, there are two main schools of thought about aesthetic properties: realism, and anti-realism (see Schellekens 2012 for an overview). Pretty much everybody agrees that we make aesthetic judgements and that a work's *non*-aesthetic properties are essential to doing so—but that's as far as the agreement goes. Realists think that aesthetic properties are properties that exist independently of the viewer's mind, and the trick for them is to specify how those properties relate to non-aesthetic properties without reducing to them entirely. Anti-realists, by contrast, think that there are no special 'aesthetic' properties over and above the work's non-aesthetic properties, or our evaluative reactions to them.

On the realist side of things, Sibley (1959) argued that what distinguishes aesthetic properties (he called them 'terms' and 'concepts') from other kinds of properties is that they aren't governed by what we might now call application-conditions, and this is what explains the intuition that there can be no successful aesthetic concept zombies. In other words, there are no necessary and sufficient conditions for something to count as *garish* or *graceful*—though these terms might be *negatively* condition-governed just insofar as something that's just black and white can't be garish, or jerky movements graceful. So: there's nothing we can point to that will guarantee the presence of a particular aesthetic property, though there might be things we can point to that preclude certain properties. Aesthetic terms, for Sibley, require a judgement of taste, and it's natural for us to use them metaphorically or quasi-metaphorically.

Mothersill (1991) similarly suggests a negative test for aesthetic properties, although she characterizes them more narrowly as tied to individual objects: an object's aesthetic properties are just those which it shares with any perceptually indistinguishable object. If I claim that my rose is beautiful and that yours isn't, but then it turns out that I can't actually distinguish them, this suggests that the pleasure I take in my rose is due to something other than its aesthetic properties (all of which it has in common with your rose, since I can't tell them apart).

But these negative characterizations may well turn out to be true of some *non*-aesthetic concepts, too; how, then, do we distinguish aesthetic terms from non-aesthetic terms? And what, exactly, is the connection between a work's aesthetic and its non-aesthetic properties? Sibley's concession that there may be negative application-conditions suggests at least a conceptual connection between, say, garishness and colour. But what does this conceptual connection amount to?

Unfortunately, negative application-conditions seem to entail positive application-conditions as their contrapositives: if pastels or monochromatic pictures can't be garish, then that suggests that highly saturated colours are a necessary (though perhaps not sufficient) condition for garishness (Beardsley 1974). If we want to preserve the suggestion that aesthetic terms have no application-conditions, it seems we might be better off thinking of the connection between aesthetic and non-aesthetic properties as purely causal (i.e., colour-saturation causes garishness) and contingent (Beardsley 1974). Thus, we can say that there are no general application-conditions which guarantee the presence of a particular aesthetic property in a work. Nevertheless, it seems that aesthetic properties are causally dependent on the presence of clusters of non-aesthetic properties so that, e.g., a tune is sad because it exhibits some jointly sufficient subset of slowness of tempo, minor chords, certain kinds of interval-restricted melodies, and so on. Even if any one of these qualities, or any combination of them, isn't sufficient to explain the tune's sadness, we can nevertheless say that it *contributed* to it.

Or we might instead insist on the metaphorical and quasi-metaphorical use of aesthetic terms, using it to illustrate a very minimalistic realism about aesthetic properties (Budd 2006). On this conception, aesthetic terms have no application conditions as such. Instead, it's our perception that they fit that matters: the description of the dance as graceful changes our experience of what we see, so that now we see it as graceful where before we didn't. This doesn't mean that there is something in the dance that necessarily *makes* it graceful; rather, the dance's non-aesthetic properties simply support that attribution. We read back into our experience, using certain terms aesthetically to help us do so, and that's not something the zombie can do.

It has also been suggested that the aesthetic *supervenes* on the non-aesthetic, so that any change to a work's non-aesthetic properties entails a change to its aesthetic properties (Levinson 1984). Naturally, quite a lot hangs on just what is included among a work's non-aesthetic properties, although a first pass suggests we include among them its perceptible (but otherwise non-aesthetic) properties, its sub-structural properties (the physical properties we can't directly perceive, like molecular structure), and its contextual properties. According to this view, garishness depends on bright, saturated colours but only because we can't detect the effect without such tones, not because there's some sort of conceptual impossibility in applying the term to monochromatic pictures. Likewise, although high pitches have a particular frequency, what makes them high-pitched is just the aural experience we have of them, which is not an experience of wave frequency as such. The high pitch is not reducible to its wave frequency; doing so leaves out the aesthetic experience of the sound.

Not everyone agrees with these realists, however. In particular, the relation between aesthetic properties and their non-aesthetic bases has been pinpointed as a potential source of trouble for the idea that aesthetic properties are mind-independent (Zangwill 2000). This is because, as we saw above, aesthetic properties clearly *depend on* sensory properties like colour or sound. That is, sensory properties are *necessary*, though perhaps not *sufficient*, for aesthetic properties. But people diverge in their discrimination of sensory properties (e.g., your impressions of colours are more vivid than mine, or perhaps even entirely different, in some cases). Since it's not plausible that your experiences are 'correct' and mine 'wrong' (indeed, we're usually quite tolerant about divergent judgements of sensory qualities), we must conclude that either sensory properties are mind-dependent, or they're illusory. Either way, the same conclusion follows for the aesthetic properties dependent on them, since a property of a thing can't be more real than the thing to which it attaches.

Another significant source of disagreement concerns the distinction between aesthetic and non-aesthetic terms in the first place (Cohen 1973, Matravers 2005): on what grounds do we identify some terms as aesthetic, and others not? Sibley suggests that aesthetic terms are those which require judgements of taste for their application, but that sounds perilously close to circular. After all, isn't normal perception sufficient for us to describe something (a day, say) as 'lovely', or (e.g., a swan) as 'graceful'? If we can apply aesthetic terms in non-aesthetic contexts, then we never actually *need* a judgement of taste to apply them, and our otherwise normally functioning zombie should be just fine. So what makes a term *aesthetic* in the first place?

The answer can't be that they require an aesthetic sensibility for their application, since that's obviously circular. Perhaps, instead, there is no substantive difference here: aesthetic terms function just as non-aesthetic terms do (Kivy 1975). The difference, rather, seems to be a matter of the context in which they occur: in ordinary contexts, "square" isn't an aesthetic property, but applied to a painting, it might become one. Nor do we need some special capacity to discern the painting's squareness—the normal ability to recognize squareness will suffice. All this suggests that aesthetic properties *are* condition-governed in some way; after all, we think it's possible for something to *seem* to have an aesthetic property which it actually lacks. Aesthetic properties may not have any one thing, or any one set of things, in common which makes them aesthetic, but perhaps they are joined together by overlapping clusters of qualities. One such possible cluster is a kind of finality: to describe something in aesthetic terms is to savour it, to enjoy it under that description. And that is a capacity denied to aesthetic concept zombies. Nonaesthetic descriptions, by contrast, seem to invite further arguments, conclusions, or actions (see *The Burning Museum*).

SUGGESTED READING

SEMINAL PRESENTATION:

1. Sibley, Frank (1959). Aesthetic Concepts. *Philosophical Review* 68 (4): 421–50.
    Sibley argues that it is an essential property of aesthetic concepts that they are
    not reducible to rules or sets of necessary and sufficient conditions, although
    they do have truth values. Even though they are all tied to non-aesthetic
    properties, these non-aesthetic properties are never sufficient to guarantee
    that a particular aesthetic property is present in the work, or that a particular
    aesthetic judgement is correct.

DEFENCES:

2. Beardsley, Monroe C. (1974). The Descriptivist Account of Aesthetic Attri-
    butions. *Revue Internationale de Philosophie* 2 (8): 336–52.
    Beardsley agrees with Sibley that aesthetic terms have no general condi-
    tions of *application*, but thinks we are sometimes in a position to state suf-
    ficient *occurrence*-conditions for them in a particular case. He argues that
    there is no conceptual connection at all between aesthetic terms and their
    underlying non-aesthetic properties. The connection is purely causal, and
    contingent.
3. Levinson, Jerrold (1984). Aesthetic Supervenience. *Southern Journal of Philos-
    ophy* 22 (S1): 93–110.
    Levinson argues that aesthetic properties supervene on non-aesthetic prop-
    erties, such that two objects with different aesthetic properties must have
    different *non*-aesthetic properties, where non-aesthetic properties include
    structural (i.e., perceptible non-aesthetic properties like shape), sub-
    structural (i.e., physical but non-perceptible), and contextual properties.

CRITIQUES:

4. Cohen, Ted (1973). Aesthetic/Non-aesthetic and the Concept of Taste: A
    Critique of Sibley's Position. *Theoria* 39 (1–3): 113–52.
    Cohen argues that Sibley has not given us a compelling reason to accept his
    distinction between aesthetic and non-aesthetic terms and, thus, to accept
    that a particular judgement is aesthetic (or not). There is no principled way,
    he argues, of determining whether a descriptive term enters into a judge-
    ment because of taste or because of normal perception.
5. Kivy, Peter (1975). What Makes "Aesthetic" Terms Aesthetic? *Philosophy and
    Phenomenological Research* 36 (2): 197–211.
    Kivy argues that aesthetic terms *are* condition-governed—because the argu-
    ment for their not being so collapses. In particular, it fails to allow for the
    intuitive possibility that some object may only *seem* graceful (elegant, etc.)

without *really* being so. Aesthetic terms are those which characteristically feature in descriptions which we enjoy for their own sake.

FURTHER READING:

6. Mothersill, Mary (1991). *Beauty Restored.* New York: Adams Bannister Cox.
   In Ch. 11, Mothersill argues that our usual catalogue of aesthetic properties is mistaken: aesthetic properties cannot be captured by a simple name. Instead, an aesthetic property is the property that all perceptually indistinguishable objects share. Any two perceptually distinguishable works will have distinct aesthetic properties. What makes a property 'aesthetic' is just that we expect it to play a role in the definition of beauty.

7. Zangwill, Nick (2000). Skin Deep or in the Eye of the Beholder?: The Metaphysics of Aesthetic and Sensory Properties. *Philosophical and Phenomenological Research* 61 (3): 595–618.
   Zangwill argues that aesthetic realism requires, at minimum, that aesthetic properties be mind-independent, a requirement best fulfilled by physicalism. Aesthetic properties, whatever they are, are dependent on our sensory experiences. But the divergence of our experiences of the same stimulus indicates that they are mind-dependent and, thus, so are aesthetic properties.

8. Matravers, Derek (2005). Aesthetic Properties. Aristotelian Society Supplementary Volume 79: 191–210.
   Matravers highlights two problems for realism about aesthetic properties: (1) the ambiguity of aesthetic terms (given their supervenience on non-aesthetic properties) and (2) the autonomy of aesthetic judgements (see also *Pinny the Who?*). Although we clearly make aesthetic judgements based on distinctive perceptions caused by non-aesthetic properties, the notion of an aesthetic property is unhelpful.

9. Budd, Malcolm (2006). The Characterization of Aesthetic Qualities by Essential Metaphors and Quasi-metaphors. *British Journal of Aesthetics* 46 (2): 133–43.
   Budd picks up on Sibley's observation that some of our aesthetic ascriptions seem metaphorical or quasi-metaphorical, using it to outline a minimalist conception of aesthetic properties. Quasi-metaphorical ascriptions of aesthetic properties require only that the subject thinks the metaphor well-suited to capturing some aspect of the object's character.

10. Schellekens, Elisabeth (2012). "Aesthetic Properties," in *The Bloomsbury Companion to Aesthetics*, Anna Christina Ribeiro (ed.). New York: Bloomsbury, 84–97.
    Schellekens surveys the literature on aesthetic properties, focusing in particular on the debate between realists and anti-realists, and its division into concerns about the metaphysics of aesthetic properties on the one hand, and their epistemology on the other.

THE JEALOUS HUSBAND (THE AESTHETIC ATTITUDE)

CASE

Imagine a husband who has some reason to be jealous of his spouse (to the extent that it makes any sense to speak of justified reasons for jealousy). His spouse has been spending a fair bit of time in the company of someone rather dashing, maybe, or perhaps he caught them whispering and giggling in a quiet corner, or maybe the spouse is doing a lot of texting with *someone* (not the husband!) at all hours. Now suppose that this husband attends a performance of *Othello*.

We might expect that the close similarity between his experience and Othello's would enhance his appreciation of the play, since it would be more real for him, and he would have more direct access to the character's mindset. But we know that's not actually how that works in real life: in real life, our jealous husband is not likely to develop a finer appreciation for the play. Instead, he's much more likely to be reminded of his own jealousy, to see himself—in real life—as Othello betrayed. And that will ruin his enjoyment of the play.

The most historically popular explanation for this phenomenon (or: for the intuition that this is the case) is that the jealous husband is incapable of adopting the right mindset towards the play; his jealousy prevents him from adopting the *aesthetic attitude* (see King 2012

DOI: 10.4324/9781003368205-25

for a survey of the subject). The play hits too close to home; he can't get enough distance between the fictional events and his real life to properly appreciate what's on stage. But what, exactly, is this 'aesthetic attitude'? What makes it 'aesthetic' in the first place, and why is the jealous husband incapable of experiencing it?

RESPONSES

According to an early and extremely influential (though not widely adopted) view, the best way to understand what's going on in our thought experiment is in terms of 'psychical[1] distance' (Bullough 1912). It's probably easiest to understand psychical distance by analogy to other kinds of distance. Think of a painting: its spatial distance from us is important for its appreciation, as is made clear by the Impressionist two-step (people looking at Impressionist paintings tend to take a step closer to see the individual brushstrokes, then a step back to see the whole image come together). Likewise, the painting's subject is represented to us as being at a certain distance from the viewer's perspective, and its symbolic content may be temporally distant, in the sense that we need to know something about the period from which it comes if we're to properly understand its subject matter. 'Psychical distance,' then, is a name for how psychologically distant a work of art seems from us. If we find ourselves transported into the world of the work, there's not much distancing going on; by contrast, if we can only engage with it from a purely detached and analytical perspective, then we're quite psychologically distant from it. What makes the attitude of psychical distance 'aesthetic' is this phenomenon of putting the work "out of gear with" our practical and everyday considerations, so that we aren't just appreciating it for the ways in which it connects to our own lives. In this way, our aesthetic judgements can be said to be 'disinterested', although this does not mean they are *impersonal*. Rather, they are always personal judgements, but they are divorced from immediate appeals to practical considerations—so, for example, we don't want to eat the fruit in the still life, we just appreciate it as and for what it is.

So: the jealous husband's problem would seem to be a case of under-distancing, since he's reading too much of the play into his own experience. Narrowing psychological distance *a little* is artistically desirable, since it promotes closer engagement with the work: it's good for audiences to read their own experiences into a play or story, for example. But too much of this good thing seems to poison the well and prevent them from properly enjoying the work. Likewise, you *do* want the audience to have *some* critical distance, since you don't want them leaping onstage to save Desdemona (see *The Paradox of Fiction*), and you *do* want them to reflect on the play's themes and so on. The trick, then, is to strike the right balance between over- and under-distancing. Distancing is thus the process of coming to a "suitably contemplative" relation with the object of our attention; it's a special kind of perception (Dawson 1961). It seems, then, that there are different degrees of aesthetic appreciation tied to the degree of distance we experience (Dawson 1961). And that suggests that there isn't any single correct judgement of a work of art, but rather, that there are a range of correct judgements depending on what each individual appreciator's optimum range of distance is like.

Inspired by this analysis, others have argued that what distinguishes the aesthetic attitude from ordinary perception is not so much "distance" alone as it is our disinterested but sympathetic contemplation of an object for its own sake (Stolnitz 1961). Ordinary perception, on this view, is *interested*—it pays particular attention to the object's sensuous appeal, use, or function. This isn't to say that a disinterested appreciation is *detached*, or over-distanced. On the contrary, aesthetic experience requires us to pay attention to the deeper symbolic properties of a work, which may only be accessible to us because of our experience, or because we know something about the object's genre or use-value. We can aesthetically contemplate an ornately decorated object like a chair, but the fact that it cannot support a person's weight is an important consideration which will tend to undermine its aesthetic value, all things being equal.

These aesthetic attitude theories have been roundly criticized for introducing an elitist focus on contemporary fine art (Carroll 1997; see also *Two Societies*) and, more devastatingly, for introducing special kinds of action or attention where none exist (Dickie 1964). On what grounds, for example, do we think that 'distancing' is a special sort of action, distinctive to aesthetic experience? If I "distance" myself from *Othello*'s content, am I really doing anything more than simply paying attention to different aspects of the play? That is, am

I not just (correctly) focusing my attention on Iago's perfidy rather than on Desdemona's (perfectly innocent) actions? The jealous husband's 'under-distanced' appreciation similarly seems to just be a case of ignoring Iago's agency and focusing his attention obsessively on Desdemona instead.

The notion of 'disinterested' attention likewise seems to stipulate a special attitude where none is necessary (Dickie 1964). The jealous husband's appreciation of Othello isn't aesthetic because it's *interested*—he's reading his own experience into the play, and vice versa. It seems like we have a perfectly ordinary explanation for what is going wrong here which has no need of postulating a special kind of attitude he's not taking towards the play: he's *not paying much attention to the play at all*. His 'interest' is in obsessing over his spouse's behaviour; he's *distracted* from the play. Similarly, if you find yourself watching an animated film and thinking hard about how they managed to make the water look *like that*, you aren't paying attention to the story. Such inattention is frequent, but it's also often momentary and doesn't negatively impact our appreciation of the work as whole. It seems, then, that 'distance' and 'disinterest' are just ways of saying that one's attention is focused on the work itself. The distinction between 'distanced' or 'disinterested' and 'interested' appreciation thus seems to pick out motivational factors rather than perceptual experiences.

We might also worry that the very notion of 'disinterested' attention is incoherent: if it's the case that emotions more generally are socially constructed responses to kinds of situations, then it seems likely that our aesthetic responses are likewise socially constructed (Eaton 1995). If we accept that emotions are a way of internalizing a community's values, then to the extent that 'disinterested' appreciation is a response we learn from paradigm activities or by example, it too seems socially constructed. And that fact, if it is one, casts doubt on the legitimacy of singling it out as a special kind of perception.

More recently, some attempts have been made to revive aesthetic attitude theories and defend them from these criticisms. One alternative proposal is that the notion of 'disinterest' can be cashed out in emotional terms (Robinson 2020): what we actually experience is an *aesthetic* emotion. Such emotions are just like ordinary emotions, except that they have a different object: the work of art, and the ways in which its form shapes its content. Generally speaking, emotions tend to have specific functions (e.g., disgust prevents us from eating something harmful) and, thus, to have practical goals; at first glance, this may seem to undermine their capacity for explaining 'disinterested' appreciation. But what we mean by disinterested contemplation is just that aesthetic emotions are *consummatory* rather than instrumental: they don't motivate any particular behaviour apart from continued (pleasurable) engagement with their objects.

Another strategy is to double down on the motivational differences between the kinds of attention we pay (Kemp 1999). A film student, for example, might watch a movie with an eye to cuts, diegetic vs. non-diegetic music, etc.; this would be an 'interested' way of appreciating the film, but we wouldn't want to say that she's giving the film less than her full attention. An ordinary punter, on the other hand, is unlikely to pay much attention to the film's structural features, so although his appreciation may be 'disinterested', it also seems like a different *sort* of attention. Our ordinary attitude is 'restless' because it's driven by pragmatic concerns, and so picks out the features of an object which are most relevant to our purposes (Kemp 1999). The *aesthetic* attitude, however, engages with the whole of the work's features; it's contemplative, rather than restless. What matters is not whether our attention is interested or disinterested, but whether we attend to the object *for its own sake*, taking an interest in its intrinsic, rather than extrinsic, qualities.

Alternately, a more popular approach attempts to recast the aesthetic *attitude* in terms of aesthetic *experience* (Beardsley 1970): an aesthetic experience is just the kind of experience we have when we adopt an aesthetic point of view. An aesthetic point of view is not a special kind of attitude we take towards an object; rather, it's an attitude we take towards a special kind of object, an *aesthetic* object: to take an aesthetic point of view on *Othello* is just to take an interest in its aesthetic value. That value, in turn, can be understood as whatever value the play has as a source of aesthetic gratification. The explanatory burden is thus shifted from our psychology to the objects of our attention (in particular, to the notion of an aesthetic property—see *Aesthetic Concept Zombies*).

SUGGESTED READING

SEMINAL PRESENTATION:

1. Bullough, Edward (1912). 'Psychical Distance' as a Factor in Art and an Aesthetic Principle. *British Journal of Psychology* 5 (2): 87–118.

   Bullough argues that distancing effects can change our perception of and appreciation for art. He contends that 'psychical distance' is necessary for aesthetic appreciation. We achieve this distance by separating the object of our attention from its appeal to our selves.

DEFENCES:

2. Dawson, Sheila (1961). "Distancing" as an Aesthetic Principle. *Australasian Journal of Philosophy* 39 (2): 155–74.

   Dawson defends Bullough's account of psychical distancing, emphasizing that there are degrees of aesthetic appreciation depending on how distanced we are from an object. Although there is no universally correct distance from which to appreciate an object, each individual has a range of optimum distances for viewing a particular object on a particular occasion.

3. Stolnitz, Jerome (1961). Some Questions Concerning Aesthetic Perception. *Philosophy and Phenomenological Research* 22 (1): 69–87.

   Stolnitz distinguishes his aesthetic attitude theory from others, arguing that the core of the aesthetic attitude is disinterested and sympathetic contemplation of an object for its own sake. Aesthetic experience requires awareness that what we see is a work of art and not the thing depicted, and that we consider its symbolic relations.

4. Kemp, Gary (1999). The Aesthetic Attitude. *British Journal of Aesthetics* 39 (4): 392–9.

   Kemp defends aesthetic attitude theories from Dickie's criticisms, arguing that they are perfectly compatible with there being several different ways of attending to the object of attention. What makes some aesthetic rather than others is not disinterested attention, but whether the person is interested in their experience of the object for its own sake.

CRITIQUES:

5. Dickie, George (1964). The Myth of the Aesthetic Attitude. *American Philosophical Quarterly* 1 (1): 56–65.

   Dickie argues that the aesthetic attitude boils down to 'disinterested' attention to an object. This implies that there is such a thing as 'interested' attention, but any attempt to characterize it ultimately just describes *inattention* to the object. We can certainly focus our attention on an aesthetic object, but that isn't a special kind of attention: aesthetic attitude theories conflate a *motivational* distinction with a *perceptual* one.

FURTHER READING:

6. Beardsley, Monroe C. (1970). The Aesthetic Point of View. *Metaphilosophy* 1 (1): 39–58.
   Rather than appealing to an aesthetic *attitude*, Beardsley argues that we would be better served by talking of adopting an aesthetic *point of view*, which just means to take an interest in something's aesthetic value. An object's aesthetic value is just whatever value it possesses in virtue of its capacity to provide aesthetic gratification.

7. Eaton, Marcia Muelder (1995). The Social Construction of Aesthetic Response. *British Journal of Aesthetics* 35 (2): 95–107.
   Eaton argues that if our emotional responses are to a large extent socially constructed (and she argues that they are), then so too are our aesthetic responses, at least to the extent that they are emotional or are predicated on emotion.

8. Carroll, Noël (1997). *A Philosophy of Mass Art*. Oxford: Clarendon Press.
   Carroll defends the art-status of 'mass art', which is the kind of art that's made for mass consumption (e.g., Hollywood films). In Ch. 1, he argues that aesthetic attitude theorists have wrongly championed Kantian free beauty (experience without concepts) as the paradigm aesthetic experience, leading to a mistaken focus on disinterested appreciation and non-utilitarian objects.

9. King, Alexandra (2012). The Aesthetic Attitude. *Internet Encyclopedia of Philosophy*. https://iep.utm.edu/aesthetic-attitude/.
   King surveys the literature on the aesthetic attitude, focusing in particular on its historical underpinnings in eighteenth-century aesthetics and their twentieth-century revival in the work of Bullough and Stolnitz.

10. Robinson, Jenefer (2020). Aesthetic Emotions. *The Monist* 103 (2): 205–22.
    Robinson argues that the aesthetic attitude is fundamentally emotional: it is a case of feeling *aesthetic* emotions. Aesthetic emotions have the same structure and function as ordinary emotions but differ in their intentional objects, which are just the intrinsic qualities of a work of art and how they shape the work's content. They are consummatory rather than instrumental.

NOTE

1 'Psychical' is just a colourfully archaic term meaning 'psychological'.

THE PARADOX OF
GOOD-BAD ART

CASE

You've probably seen your share of bad movies. My stepbrothers *still* tease me about the time I made us watch Elias Merhige's *Shadow of the Vampire* (2000) (I was right and they were wrong, however). But have you ever seen one that was so bad it was actually kind of good?

The holy grail of good-bad movies is said to be Tommy Wiseau's *The Room* (2003), but there are a lot of movies like this around: Ed Wood's *Plan 9 from Outer Space* (1959), Amir Shervan's *Samurai Cop* (1991), Paul Verhoeven's *Showgirls* (1995), the Wachowskis' *Jupiter Ascending* (2015), Roland Emmerich's *Moonfall* (2022)… you get the picture. But the so-bad-it's-good phenomenon isn't limited to cinema: there's Julia A. Moore's poetry, Harry Stephen Keeler's detective stories, Rebecca Black's *Friday* (both the song and the music video), Florence Foster Jenkins's opera recitals, my little brother's heinous uncanny food replacement memes, Cecilia Giménez's restoration of the *Ecce Homo* fresco, and, of course, everything housed in the Museum of Bad Art.

Let's make no bones about it: these are all obvious cases of bad art. Nobody could possibly mistake them for anything else. And yet,

DOI: 10.4324/9781003368205-26

they enjoy a significant cult following and even acclaim. How is this possible? If they're so full of aesthetic defects, how could we possibly enjoy them, let alone think they're any good? The paradox seems especially acute because we have some evidence suggesting that repeated exposure to bad art tends to increase our dislike of it (Meskin et al. 2013).

A lot hinges on just what we mean by 'good', of course. Clearly, we don't mean that these works are well-executed masterpieces. But that's not to say that they don't have some aesthetic merit despite their obvious flaws (Kael 1969). Likewise, a lot hinges on what we mean by 'bad'. The standard model of good-bad art maintains that these works are 'bad' in the sense that they embody failures of their creators' artistic intentions: Tommy Wiseau was shooting for *Citizen Kane* (1941), but he ended up with... well, *The Room*. This failure, in turn, results in a *bizarre* work, a work for which the mismatch between ambition and ability is unimaginably vast. According to the standard model, it's this bizarre juxtaposition of intention and execution that we like. It's entirely unexpected and makes us laugh.

Perhaps, then, appreciating good-bad art is not really a matter of *artistic* appreciation at all (Kael 1969). These works are artistic failures, after all, so it wouldn't make much sense to appreciate them for their artistic features. Perhaps, instead, we are aesthetically appreciating their artistic failures (precisely because these are unintentional) (Dyck and Johnson 2017). If that's so, then good-bad art stands as a counterexample to *aestheticism*, the view that a work's artistic value is just its total aesthetic value; good-bad art seems to suggest that artistic and aesthetic value can come apart, at least in some cases.

So: these considerations suggest two related problems. The first is the apparent paradox of something's being aesthetically good because of the ways in which it is aesthetically bad. The second is a problem for appreciation: if what we appreciate in art are its *good* qualities, and if bad art doesn't have any good qualities, then how could we ever be warranted in appreciating bad art?

The standard solution is to distinguish between something's being *artistically* good or bad, and its being *aesthetically* good or bad (Dyck and Johnson 2017). Good-bad art, on this view, is *artistically* bad because it is an artistic failure—i.e., the end product does not realize the artist's vision. But despite being artistically bad, it is *aesthetically* good, because the ways in which it fails to realize the artist's vision are precisely the aspects of the work which we find it rewarding to aesthetically engage with. The mismatch between the creator's vision and their execution makes their end product *bizarre*, and that bizarreness is an aesthetically valuable property. Alternately, the artist's failure to competently execute their vision exposes new aesthetic possibilities which would have been otherwise unattainable (Tooming 2020).

RESPONSES

Some have worried, however, that the original formulation of the paradox does not do enough to distinguish the different reasons why a work of art might exhibit whatever aesthetically interesting and valuable properties it does (e.g., bizarreness). In particular, it seems that we should distinguish between those properties the work has as a result of its content from those which it has due to failures of the creative process (Algander 2018). Francis Bacon's paintings are bizarre, for example, but very deliberately so: they wear their bizarreness on their sleeve, as a result of their perverse perspective and raw-meat aesthetic; *The Room*, not so much. Nor is it entirely clear what role competence plays here: Tommy Wiseau clearly wasn't a competent director when he made *The Room*, but Gore Verbinski and the Wachowski sisters certainly were when they directed their stinkers.

Perhaps it would be useful to distinguish more carefully between the senses of 'good' and 'bad' at issue (Strohl 2022). The 'good' in good-bad art, it's thought, indicates that the work is aesthetically valuable (it is, after all, enjoyable!). Similarly, the 'bad' in good-bad art picks out a much more limited sense of 'bad'—e.g., the failure to match up one's execution with one's goals or the violation of established conventions. What makes it good-bad, then, is just that its aesthetic value partly depends on the features which make it 'bad'.

On this model, we should likewise distinguish between two reactions we have to bad art: *ridicule* and *love*. Sometimes, what we enjoy is the act of ridiculing the work; we don't find the work itself particularly aesthetically valuable. But sometimes a truly bad artwork is bad in ways which inspire us to love it, to value it aesthetically precisely because of the ways in which it's bad—perhaps, e.g., because it violates norms and expectations in new and exciting ways which capture our interest. Rebecca Black's *Friday* and Cecilia Giménez's restoration of the *Ecce Homo* fresco are objects of ridicule because of the mismatch between the artist's ambitions and their abilities, but *Showgirls* is a massive cult movie hit, thanks to its dark humour and biting satire of Hollywood's 'star is born' narratives. It's an exploitation movie dressed up as a musical, an avant-garde work of art. Our love of good-bad art thus promotes a plurality, rather than a homogenization, of aesthetic values (see also *The Uniform World*; cf. *The Paradox of Junk Fiction*).

There is some empirical support for this analysis of our enjoyment of good-bad art as parallel to our enjoyment of avant-garde art (Sarkhosh and Menninghaus 2016). One way to understand this response is in terms of genre re-categorization: if we approach *Showgirls* as we would an ordinary musical, it falls flat; but as a work of satire, it gains an enjoyable edgy irony. Similarly, when we approach avant-garde art as we would an ordinary work in the medium, it tends to garner a less than lukewarm reception; but the critics who see it as challenging genre conventions see much more of value in it. Much of our discourse about good-bad art, then, starts to look like *conceptual negotiation*, like trying to convince one another that we should see the work in a new light (Cantalamessa 2018).

This, in turn, suggests a way of rehabilitating aestheticism, the view that 'artistic value' and 'aesthetic value' are really the same thing: perhaps all we mean by these terms is the work's value considered as a member of some particular art-kind. Sometimes you just need to figure out the right comparison class to properly appreciate something (Lopes 2011; see also *Guernicas*). We want our emotional responses to be appropriate to the work in question (Livingston and Mele 1997)—e.g., we want to be moved to tears by tragedy, not guffaws. But facts about the context also seem relevant to our reactions, too, so that artistic flaws may sometimes warrant our adopting contrary responses to the work in question, e.g., by responding to pompous overreach with laughter rather than tears. Ultimately, then, *Samurai Cop* is *good* art, since it's aesthetically pleasing; but it's *unintentionally* good. Its goodness is an accidental (or perhaps incidental) property of the work.

SUGGESTED READING

SEMINAL PRESENTATIONS:

1. Kael, Pauline (1969). Trash, Art, and the Movies. *Harper's Magazine*, February 1969. https://harpers.org/archive/1969/02/trash-art-and-the-movies/.
   In this classic piece of film criticism, Kael coins the term 'good bad' and argues that most of the films we enjoy don't qualify as high Art. We become interested in films because we *enjoy* them, and we don't enjoy them primarily because of their craftsmanship or technical prowess. We just enjoy trash movies; films are about unsupervised, irresponsible enjoyment, and 'bad' films foster a sense of community based on what it is about them that we find enjoyable.
2. Dyck, John and Matt Johnson (2017). Appreciating Bad Art. *Journal of Value Inquiry* 51 (2): 279–92.
   Dyck and Johnson argue that art that's so bad it's good is an artistic *failure*: the artist did not achieve what they set out to achieve. Sometimes, an artistic failure fails in ways which make it aesthetically valuable; thus, the good-bad phenomenon. Crucially, good-bad art is good in *unintended* ways. This suggests that aestheticism is false: artistic value *is* or *can be* distinct from aesthetic value.

DEFENCES:

3. Tooming, Uku (2020). The Puzzle of Good Bad Movies. *Journal of Aesthetic Education* 54 (3): 31–46.
   Tooming argues that good-bad movies are characterized by the unwitting incompetence of their creators. The good-bad movies we genuinely love, rather than ridicule, are those which showcase aesthetic possibilities that a competent creator could not have showcased, because their competence would have gotten in the way. The visible manifestation of competence, he argues, is not essential to appreciation.

CRITIQUES:

4. Algander, Per (2018). Bad Art and Good Taste. *Journal of Value Inquiry* 53 (1): 145–54.
   Algander argues that Dyck and Johnson's solutions to the puzzles of good-bad art point to a larger puzzle that they fail to adequately resolve: to what extent should our aesthetic responses track an artwork's aesthetic value? He argues that the original appeal to bizarreness is insensitive to the different sources of bizarreness, especially bizarreness arising from a work's content versus the relation between the content and its creator's vision.
5. Strohl, Matt (2022). *Why It's OK to Love Bad Movies*. New York: Routledge.
   Of particular interest in this book-length treatment of the good-bad are Chs. 1, 3, and 6. Strohl worries that the Dyck-Johnson framing in terms of failure

risks suggesting that good-bad reactions involve disdain for their object. He argues, instead, that what makes a movie good-bad is its tendency to elicit bad movie love, such that we recognize that the film doesn't measure up to conventional standards of quality but nevertheless think that it violates these norms in amusing, exciting, or interesting ways. Good-bad art is thus avant-garde, or adjacent to it.

FURTHER READING:

6. Livingston, Paisley and Alfred Mele (1997). "Evaluating Emotional Responses to Fiction," in *Emotion and the Arts*, Mette Hjort and Sue Laver (eds.). Oxford: Oxford University Press, 157–76.

   Livingston and Mele begin with the plausible assumption that we want to respond in ways that are aesthetically relevant to the work we are considering (e.g., feeling desolated by tragedy, laughing at comedy, etc.). We want our emotional responses to be congruent with the demands of the fiction. But congruence is not sufficient to justify our emotional responses; facts about context may also be relevant. Thus, artistic flaws—including artistic *failures*—may warrant contrary (i.e., non-congruent) responses so that, e.g., we respond to what should be horrifying by barking out a laugh (as with puns).

7. Lopes, Dominic McIver (2011) The Myth of (Non-Aesthetic) Artistic Value. *Philosophical Quarterly* 61: 518–36.

   Lopes defends 'aestheticism', the view that artistic value and aesthetic value are one and the same. He does so by deflating the notion of artistic value: for him, an artistic value is just a value of a work of art as a work of some particular art-kind. In other words, he thinks that, e.g., a movie has its value as a film, a symphony as a musical work, etc. 'Artistic value' is just a term we use to designate the kind of value works have according to their associated art-kinds.

8. Meskin, Aaron, Mark Phelan, Margaret Moore and Matthew Kieran (2013). Mere Exposure to Bad Art. *British Journal of Aesthetics* 53 (2): 139–64.

   Meskin, Phelan, Moore, and Kieran empirically tested whether frequent exposure can increase our liking for *bad* artworks (psychology *has* found a mere exposure effect for *good* art). They found that exposure seemed to *decrease* liking for bad art, which makes the paradox of good-bad art especially puzzling.

9. Sarkhosh, Keyvan and Winfried Menninghaus (2016). Enjoying Trash Films: Underlying Features, Viewing Stances, and Experiential Response Dimensions. *Poetics* 57: 40–54.

   Sarkhosh and Menninghaus studied the attitudes and consumption patterns of "trash film" lovers. They found that audiences predominantly associate the term with 'cheap' films, i.e., films with low production values. They also found that trash audiences are surprisingly cine-literate and that there is a close parallel between the evaluation of trash and avant-garde cinema, with both audiences focused on their transgressive aspects.

10. Cantalamessa, Elizabeth (2018). Is This Really Art? Aesthetic Disagreement and Conceptual Negotiation. *Aesthetics For Birds*, 13 December 2018. https://aestheticsforbirds.com/2018/12/13/is-this-really-art-aesthetic-disagreement-and-conceptual-negotiation/.

Cantalamessa argues that many of the debates we have over controversial or subversive art (such as good-bad art) aren't really about the facts of whether the work is this way or that, good or bad; they're about convincing one another that we should appreciate it in some particular way, about advocating for a way of thinking about the work. This kind of conceptual negotiation reveals the values we take to be important, both in art and more generally.

THE PARADOX OF GUSTATORY TASTE

CASE

Imagine you were baking, and you combined ingredients which have no business being cooked together. Something like a mix of sweet potatoes, brown sugar, pecans, and… marshmallows.[1] This vile concoction goes by the innocuous name of 'sweet potato casserole', and presumably some people like it—but not everyone! No doubt you can tell that I think it's gross. But suppose *you* don't—which of us is correct?

There's no accounting for taste, of course, and to each their own. So, we regularly accept serious disagreements about taste as being *faultless*. Unlike an ordinary disagreement where, for example, I claim the earth is flat and you say it's more or less spherical, we don't normally think that one of us is wrong or has come to their belief by mistake. And yet, even though we accept platitudes like those above, we still do regularly disagree—and vehemently so!—about matters of taste. Consider the following exchange:

ALEXANDAR: How about I make a sweet potato casserole to go with the cranberries and stuffing? It's so good!

EMALIE: Absolutely not! It's way too sweet for a main or a side, and desserts shouldn't be gross.

DOI: 10.4324/9781003368205-27

If Alexandar and Emalie are disagreeing about the shape of the earth, that's a disagreement which can be resolved. But is it possible to resolve their disagreement about sweet potato casserole, once Emalie makes it clear that she loathes it?

Upon closer consideration, it seems that there are plenty of cases in which people try to convince one another to adopt or abandon a gustatory preference. For instance:

ISABELLE: Tofu is gross.

ERICHA: No way! It takes on the flavour of whatever you cook it in. You just have to marinate it, fry it in onions, or spice it properly first instead of just dumping it all in without doing anything to it.

ISABELLE: No, I mean it's *gross*. The texture is all slimy and when you bite into a chunk it's kind of fluffy. Fluffy slime, *eww*!

We can also imagine cases in which the participants appeal to expert judgements to convince one another (e.g., an expert's review of a wine or meal), or even in which one participant changes their mind about a taste, perhaps by having their attention drawn to aspects of the gustatory experience which they had previously neglected.

And so we seem to have arrived at something of an impasse: on the one hand, disagreements about taste often seem faultless and relatively trivial. On the other hand, at least some disagreements about taste prompt us to marshal evidence, appeal to experts, or aim to persuade an interlocutor… in other words, they give the impression that at least one participant is at fault (even if not because their claims are false or irresponsible), and that the disagreement is relatively substantial. This is *the paradox of gustatory taste*.

Matters of taste have long been a focus of aesthetics. Hume, for instance, observed that although judgements of taste vary widely, we nevertheless tend to agree about the outliers—very good or very bad works of art, for example. And, in fact, we expect others to agree with us about very good and very bad aesthetic experiences (see also *The Uniform World*). Therein lies the classical paradox of taste, which is just that we recognize our judgements to be subjective matters of personal taste but nevertheless often act as though they are objective. And Kant famously raised what he called the paradox of *aesthetic* taste, which concerns why it is that aesthetic *judgements* seem both subjective (as expressions of individual preferences) and objective (as expressions of what others *should* or *shouldn't* prefer) at the same time (see Korsmeyer 1999).

But while these classical accounts operate in the same vicinity, they should be distinguished from the paradox of *gustatory* taste (see Schellekens 2009). Although the paradoxes are structurally very similar (indeed, one is a species of the other), their objects differ in an important respect. Gustatory taste is entirely private; it is about your (or my) preferences, and only you (or I) have access to those. Aesthetic taste more broadly, however, is concerned with objects which are publicly available: a still life, for instance, looks the way it looks to everyone who is equipped with the same sensory organs (within the bounds of normal variation), whereas certain combinations of flavours and textures will appeal to me but not to you. Hume and Kant were concerned with our judgements of *beauty* (a concept with normative heft), not our palate's judgements that some dish is *tasty* (a purely personal judgement).

The classical paradox of taste thus concerns judgements which seem to have a normative aspect. The paradox of *gustatory* taste, on the other hand, zeroes in on judgements which are supposed to be paradigmatically subjective, and asks why we are nevertheless inclined to bicker over them. It concerns the conflicting attitudes we take towards taste disagreements, treating participants as sometimes being at fault, and sometimes not. What, it asks, can explain both the fault and the faultlessness of taste disagreements? If taste claims are deeply personal and disagreements are irresolvable, then why do we spend so much time trying to convince others that, although other opinions are available, some of them are just wrong?

RESPONSES

Some have treated the paradox of taste as a puzzle about what grounds judgements of beauty. One prominent suggestion in this vein is that paradoxes of taste arise because although we can and routinely do give reasons for our judgements of taste (gustatory or otherwise), these reasons aren't sufficient to compel anyone who doesn't share our opinion to come to the same judgement (Scruton

2009). The trick, then, is to identify the missing ingredient which would transform these reasons into a deductive argument which compels others to see things as we do.

Absolutists argue that there is a fact of the matter about matters of taste. The trick for an absolutist is to explain our intuitions about fault-less disagreement. One strategy for doing so is to appeal to the notion of a Humean Ideal Critic: our aesthetic disagreements are faultless when they're about things which even Ideal Critics would disagree over (Baker and Robson 2017). *Relativists*, on the other hand, argue that the truth of a proposition about taste is tied to an *assessor's* taste perspective or standard of taste, so that a proposition like 'sweet potato casserole is yummy' is *true* when you're assessing the claim, because you apply the standards from your own taste perspective (★*shudder*★), and *false* when it's me who's evaluating the claim, because I apply different standards. The content of the proposition thus stays the same, for the relativist; what varies are the standards which assessors bring to bear on that proposition. In this way, they argue, we can easily explain why taste disagreements are faultless—they simply reflect different taste perspectives, and everyone is entitled to their own taste per-spective (e.g., Macfarlane 2007, Lasersohn 2011). But if relativists are right, then it seems that no taste disagreements could ever be appro-priate—the interlocutors, after all, are expressing judgements relative to different taste perspectives. So why do we have the intuition that some disagreements *are* appropriate?

Contextualists, by contrast, have argued that taste-predicates can express *different* meanings in different contexts of utterance—so, e.g., what counts as a 'tasty' meal at home might count as 'bland' or 'boring' in a review of a restaurant with three Michelin stars. What matters are the standards of taste brought to bear by the *utterer* of the proposition *in a given situation* (e.g., Egan 2010, Sundell 2011). This means, among other things, that when you say 'sweet potato casserole is delicious', the content of that sentence can be different, depending on the situa-tion in which *you* find yourself uttering it. Unfortunately, contextual-ism can make it look as though taste disagreements are not substantive, since all that's going on is that people are talking past one another, unaware that they are evaluating some foodstuff according to different standards. Some contextualists have the resources to answer this charge, however. Sundell (2011), for instance, explains such disagreements as cases of *metalinguistic negotiation*: they're normative debates about how a particular term or concept *should* be used, rather than descriptive debates about how it *is* used.

Alternately, it has been proposed that we can resolve the paradox of gustatory taste by focusing on the purposes underlying those disagreements (Furey 2017). Recall that the paradox concerns our intuition that taste disagreements are irresolvable and faultless, on the one hand, and our disposition to appeal to experts and offer evidence for our taste claims on the other. The idea, then, is that attending to our conversational goals can help us to explain our contradictory attitudes.

By pinpointing our conversational goals, we can more easily determine whether the dispute is in principle resolvable, when someone falls short and is at fault, or whether and when it makes sense to offer evidence for one's taste claims. While judgements of gustatory taste are rooted in an individual's gustatory responses, an individual can still be wrong about what these are or will be (this tension in our beliefs is widespread and deeply rooted; see Bonard et al. 2022). Our disagreements might then aim to persuade others that there are better gustatory pleasures to be had, to determine who has more or better expertise, or even to determine whether the disagreement is in principle resolvable. The suggestion here is that taste disputes arise when we try to coordinate our taste perspectives—that is, when we try to make our taste perspective more similar to someone else's, or vice versa. The irresolvability of taste disputes, on this view, is just the result of people talking past one another or failing to pinpoint the relevant gustatory expert.

SUGGESTED READING

SEMINAL PRESENTATION:

1. Furey, Heidi (2017). The Paradox of Gustatory Taste. *Ergo: An Open Access Journal of Philosophy* 4 (17): 481–527.
   Furey distinguishes the paradox of gustatory taste from Kant's paradox of taste and argues that the real paradox concerns the fault and faultlessness of taste disagreements, and that the linguistic data often marshalled by discussions of taste and taste predicates is beside the point. Instead, she suggests that focusing on the purpose of taste disagreements suffices to explain these data and resolve the paradox.

DEFENCES:

2. Scruton, Roger (2009). *Beauty*. Oxford: Oxford University Press.

   In Ch. 1, Scruton argues that the paradox of taste arises because our judgements of beauty seem to pertain to the objects being judged and thus seem to depend on objective properties of those objects, and yet the reasons offered in support of those judgements don't seem to require anyone to come to the same judgement.

3. Sundell, Timothy (2011). Disagreements about Taste. *Philosophical Studies* 155 (2): 267–88.

   Sundell picks up on the tension between faultless aesthetic disagreements and intersubjective aesthetic evaluation. Sundell focuses on the language used to express these disagreements, rather than on the aesthetic judgements themselves, offering a contextualist account of how it is that two speakers can speak truly and yet vehemently disagree: the judgements are being expressed relative to different standards of evaluation.

CRITIQUES:

4. MacFarlane, John (2007). Relativism and Disagreement. *Philosophical Studies* 132 (1): 17–31.

   MacFarlane defends relativism about judgements of taste by appealing to the intuition that we often have faultless disagreements over such matters. He explores what it means for two or more people to disagree, arguing that, at its core, relativism is concerned to tie the *accuracy* of an assertion to a particular perspective or context of assessment.

5. Lasersohn, Peter (2011). Context, Relevant Parts and (Lack of) Disagreement Over Taste. *Philosophical Studies* 156 (3): 433–9.

   Lasersohn defends relativism about judgements of taste against the traditional position in the philosophy of language that propositions must be either true or false without qualification. In particular, he worries that contextualism cannot preserve our intuition about the existence of faultless disagreement, properly speaking; relativism, however, is chock full of faultless disagreement.

FURTHER READING:

6. Korsmeyer, Carolyn (1999). *Making Sense of Taste: Food and Philosophy*. Ithaca, NY: Cornell University Press.

   Korsmeyer tackles the subject of gustatory taste, distinguishing between the Kantian and Humean solutions to the paradox of taste and exploring the parallel often drawn between aesthetic and gustatory taste. She argues that food preparation is not a fine art and uses the science of taste to show that taste is not just inward-looking, as we typically assume; it is also outward-looking, and gustatory relativism is often oversold.

7. Schellekens, Elisabeth (2009). Taste and Objectivity: The Emergence of the Concept of the Aesthetic. *Philosophy Compass* 4 (5): 734–43.

   Schellekens summarizes the long history of the various paradoxes of taste in aesthetics and explores their relationship to gustatory taste, ultimately distinguishing between the paradox of aesthetic taste and that of gustatory taste.

8. Egan, Andy (2010). "Disputing about Taste," in *Disagreement*, Richard Feldman and Ted A. Warfield (eds.). Oxford: Oxford University Press, 247–86.

   Egan focuses on the semantics of taste attributions more generally, arguing that they reflect self-attributions (i.e., expressions of personal preference), so that disputes about taste are the result of confusion about what's being attributed to whom.

9. Baker, Carl and Jon Robson (2017). An Absolutist Theory of Faultless Disagreement in Aesthetics. *Pacific Philosophical Quarterly* 98 (3): 429–48.

   Inspired by Hume, Baker and Robson construct an absolutist semantics for aesthetics which would allow for the possibility of faultless disagreement. Aesthetic disagreements are said to be faultless when they concern matters over which Humean Ideal Critics disagree.

10. Bonard, Constant Charles, Florian Cova, and Steve Humbert-Droz (2022). "De Gustibus *Est* Disputandum: An Empirical Investigation Of The Folk Concept Of Aesthetic Taste," in *Perspectives on Taste: Aesthetics, Language, Metaphysics, and Experimental Philosophy*, Jeremy Wyatt, Julia Zakkou, and Dan Zeman (eds.). New York: Routledge, 77–108.

    Bonard, Cova, and Humbert-Droz present the results of an empirical study of the everyday concept of aesthetic taste. They found that although ordinary people are largely subjectivists about taste, they nevertheless tend to accept the objectivist idea that taste can be improved, and characterize good taste as correctly picking up on an object's aesthetic qualities.

NOTE

1 If you're a fan, then perhaps Mormon jello salad will prove less palatable: lime jelly, cottage cheese, crushed pineapple, evaporated milk, and nuts.

25

THE PARADOX OF JUNK FICTION

CASE

I really like reading historical fiction. I mean, I *really* really like it. The bloodier, the better! My favourite works are either set during the reign of the Roman Empire or during the Viking age, and they involve lots of battles and raiding and peril. The thing is, while some of these stories are of decent literary merit, most are clearly written to a template. And when a series runs to ten or more instalments, the template becomes pretty obvious. But I don't care—these are my favourite things to read!

Nor am I some weird outlier; stories like these are wildly popular (see *The Paradox of Good-Bad Art*). Bernard Cornwell, for example, has made millions writing and selling over 30 million copies of such stories, and licensing television adaptations. Others have been even more successful—just think of the authors whose works you find being sold in airports, gas stations, and Walmarts everywhere: Tom Clancy, Lee Child, Patricia Cornwell… and let's not forget all those drugstore romance novels, either! These are novels which aspire to be page-turners (and usually succeed!), but which belong to well-entrenched genres, and whose plots are perhaps best described as… formulaic. And although I'm talking about novels, we see the same

DOI: 10.4324/9781003368205-28

phenomenon in film and television, from soaps and other serials to action flicks, slashers, and zombie films. These are what we call works of *junk fiction*, and they're incredibly popular.

But if they really *are* appropriately described as 'formulaic', then this raises a difficult question, since it seems like people can't really take much of an interest in stories they already know. The situation is even worse if narrative theorists are correct that there are only a limited number of basic story types (typically 6–7).[1] I've tried to make it clear that we already know much of the junk fiction we consume. I, for one, can give you a pretty accurate description of the next novel in Simon Scarrow's *Eagles of Rome* series, even though it hasn't been written yet: Cato and Macro are sent to some godforsaken backwater of the Empire where they're given some sort of suicidal imperial mission to accomplish in the midst of a major military campaign which will see them defending a fortified position against terrifying odds (alternately, if Scarrow is feeling adventurous, they may find themselves attacking a fortified position instead). Since he writes one of these a year, we shouldn't have too long to wait!

This paradox of junk fiction should be distinguished from a clearly related paradox, the *paradox of recidivism*, which asks why it is that we enjoy reading individual *stories* over and over, even though we know everything that will happen. The paradox of junk fiction, by contrast, concerns entire *genres* of distinct individual stories which nevertheless closely resemble one another in important respects such that they are all basically the same, even if they aren't properly identical.

RESPONSES

A number of different explanations have been offered for the phenomenon (see Abbott 2008 for an interdisciplinary overview). Some of these are dismissive: e.g., people are just irrational, and there's no accounting for taste or ignorance. That irrationality, of course, needs to be explained, and many have turned to psychoanalysis for this explanation. So, for example, perhaps junk fiction is an avenue for wish-fulfillment, much like daydreaming, or perhaps it is a way for us to manifest our anxieties (Freud 1963). Since our wishes are never actually fulfilled, or since our anxieties constantly dog us, it makes sense that we would want to consume more and more junk fiction. Alternately, according to a view which was prominent in late-twentieth-century film and media studies, perhaps genre fiction's repetitiveness is a way of enforcing ideological conformity by inculcating and reinforcing certain values (Sobchack and Sobchack 1980).

More sympathetic explanations treat our engagement with junk fiction as perfectly rational. So, for example, perhaps we consume junk fiction in order to explore a genre, to probe the boundaries of the fictional background against which such stories are set, or to learn something about the world (Roberts 1990, Vidmar Jovanović 2021). So, for instance, my love of historical fiction can be explained by my love of these particular periods in history, and my desire to come to grips with what life was like for beleaguered Saxons and roving Norsemen, or what historical combat was like, and so on.

Philosophers who are drawn to make-believe accounts of fiction have a readymade explanation for our love of junk fiction: when we make-believe that the events of a story are unfolding, we are also making-believe that we do not know how it will unfold (Walton 1990, §7.4). We put ourselves in the characters' shoes, and the characters themselves don't know what's in store for them. It's this make-believe uncertainty that we enjoy, and it helps to explain why we like to play the same games over and over, again and again.

One last avenue of response draws its inspiration from a more transactional model of the value of reading and engaging with stories: we are interested in stories because of what we can do with them. They are vehicles for interpretation and inference and allow us to exercise those powers. Junk fiction invites us to guess about the story, and we enjoy guessing correctly—as well as being wrong in novel ways (Kolmes and Hoffman 2021). Notice that, on this model, junk fiction is really no different from any other kind of fiction: the value of junk fiction is exactly the same as the value of classical literature and art films (Carroll 1994, Harold 2011). Alternately, perhaps what we're after is the *emotional* (rather than the rational) satisfaction we get from correctly anticipating plot points, or having our expectations undermined in creative ways (Knight 1995).

SUGGESTED READING

SEMINAL PRESENTATION:

1. Carroll, Noël (1994). The Paradox of Junk Fiction. *Philosophy and Literature* 18 (2): 225–41.

   Inspired by Roberts (below), Carroll presents what he calls the 'paradox of junk fiction' and distinguishes it from the 'paradox of recidivism'. Carroll is primarily concerned with resisting psychoanalytic explanations of our engagement with junk fiction. He argues, instead, that the value of junk fiction is exactly the same as that of any other fiction: it offers us a site in which to exercise our powers of interpretation and inference.

DEFENCES:

2. Roberts, Thomas J. (1990). *An Aesthetics of Junk Fiction.* Athens: University of Georgia Press.

   Although Roberts coins the term 'junk fiction', the issues he addresses in this book are somewhat different from Carroll's *paradox* of junk fiction. Roberts is concerned with explaining the hypocrisy of consumers of junk fiction, who read it voraciously but disparage it at every opportunity. He argues that our enjoyment of junk fiction is best explained by our desire to explore the narrative systems of 'bookscapes' and track shifts within genres.

3. Walton, Kendall L. 1990. Mimesis as Make-Believe: On the Foundations of the Representational Arts. Cambridge, MA: Harvard University Press.

   In this landmark treatment of fiction, Walton advances the thesis that our engagement with fiction is a kind of play, participation in a game of make-believe. In §7.4 Walton tackles the issues of suspense and surprise in repeated games of make-believe, arguing that although we know, fictionally, that Charlie will be chosen as Willie Wonka's heir, it is fictional (in the game constituted by our second, third, etc. reading) that we *do not* know it.

CRITIQUES:

4. Freud, Sigmund (1963). "The Relation of the Poet to Day-Dreaming," in *Character and Culture*, Philip Rieff (ed.). New York: Collier Books.

   Freud argues that our consumption of junk fiction is fundamentally irrational and that recurrent narratives are simply symptomatic of individual human wish-fulfilment. By identifying with the protagonist, he argues, readers satisfy the urges of their psycho-social development.

5. Sobchack, Thomas and Vivian Sobchack (1980). *An Introduction to Film.* Boston, MA: Little, Brown.

   In this introduction to film studies, Sobchack and Sobchack devote Ch. 5 to genre in cinema, arguing that many genre films are deliberately designed to manipulate and reinforce an audience's existing values.

6. Knight, Deborah (1995). Making Sense of Genre. *Film and Philosophy* 2: 58–73.

   Knight argues that Carroll's resolution of the paradox of junk fiction is too narrowly focused on the question of what makes our consumption of junk fiction *rational* or intellectual. A more satisfying response, she argues, is one that recognizes that the pleasure we draw from junk fiction is primarily *emotional*: our consumption of junk fiction is motivated by the pleasure we take in emotional responses which we anticipate having gratified (and which are occasionally frustrated).

7. Harold, James (2011). Literature, Genre Fiction, and Standards of Criticism. *Nonsite.Org* 1 (4). URL = <https://nonsite.org/literature-genre-fiction-and-standards-of-criticism/>.

   Harold explores the relationship between literature and genre fiction, arguing that although there are real differences between them and the standards of evaluation appropriate to each, we are mistaken if we think that this means that Literature-with-an-L is 'better' or more aesthetically rewarding than genre fiction. The two, he thinks, give rise to different communities of readers with different goals, interests, and standards of evaluation.

FURTHER READING:

8. Abbott, Philip (2008). Genre Bending and Utopia-building. *Critical Review of International Social and Political Philosophy* 11 (3): 335–46.

   Abbott offers a useful survey of responses to the paradox of junk fiction—and of the value of genre fiction more broadly—particularly in film and media studies. He extends his investigation of the value of genres to texts in political theory, focusing in particular on the genre of utopia-building.

9. Vidmar Jovanović, Iris (2021). Fiction, Philosophy, and Television: The Case of Law and Order: Special Victims Unit. *Journal of Aesthetics and Art Criticism* 79 (1): 76–87.

   Vidmar Jovanović argues that generic, serialized fiction like L&O: SVU has substantial educational value—in particular, as a site for public philosophy. This is so, she argues, despite the (clearly false) pronouncement of fictionality which often precedes such works. It is precisely *because* a show like L&O: SVU draws from familiar real-world events that it is so popular and that it can offer philosophical insights of value to the masses.

10. Kolmes, Sara and Matthew A. Hoffman (2021). Harlequin Resistance? Romance Novels as a Model for Resisting Objectification. *Journal of Aesthetics and Art Criticism* 79 (1): 30–41.

    Kolmes and Hoffman argue that the mass appeal of Harlequin romances is due to their formulaic genre conventions, which work to offer us romantic and even erotic stories in which female subjects are not—*cannot be*—objectified, even when the content is sexually explicit.

NOTE

1 See, e.g., Christopher Booker (2006). *The Seven Basic Plots: Why We Tell Stories.* New York: Bloomsbury Academic, and Andrew J. Reagan, Lewis Mitchell, Dilan Kiley, Christopher M. Danforth, and Peter Sheridan Dodds (2016). "The Emotional Arcs of Stories Are Dominated by Six Basic Shapes." *EPJ Data Science* 5 (31): 1–12.

26

THE PARADOX OF PORN

CASE

When you stop to think about it, pornographic films have a lot in common with art films. Art films typically don't follow much of a narrative, challenge conventional morality, and feature wooden performance styles which create distance between the audience and the plot. Porn films are likewise episodic in character, go against the publicly accepted moral grain, and typically feature wooden performances. Porn even shares important features in common with art more generally: it belongs to a particular medium (film, literature, photography), it belongs to a particular genre within that medium, it aims to arouse strong emotions, etc.

Given those similarities, isn't it surprising that we don't automatically classify pornography as a kind of art? True, pornography is stereotypically bad—but that doesn't mean it isn't art! Most of the art we produce, after all, is never going to grace the walls of the Louvre or the Guggenheim, yet it still counts as art. Parents the world over proudly display their children's awkward drawings and finger-painting on the fridge door, even though these efforts are amateurish at best.

Recall, however, that pornography is actually *very* good at doing what it sets out to do: eliciting strong emotions. Normally, this is a positive

DOI: 10.4324/9781003368205-29

feature of artworks (see *The Paradox of Disgust*)—a tragedy which makes you weep uncontrollably is very good, while a comedian who doesn't make you laugh is not (see *The Paradox of Tragedy*). Since even garden-variety pornography seems to succeed in eliciting strong emotions, shouldn't it count not just as art, but as *good* art? Objectively, it seems like this *should* be the case; yet manifestly, that's not what we think at all. This is the *paradox of porn* (Brabant and Prinz 2012).

RESPONSES

There are two broad takes on the paradox of porn: compatibilism, and incompatibilism. Compatibilists argue that art and pornography are perfectly compatible and point to the proliferation of nudes and sexual content throughout art history as evidence. Incompatibilists, on the other hand, argue that art and pornography are fundamentally incompatible. Within each camp, we can distinguish between those who focus on the work's primary intended purpose and those who focus instead on the responses which the work is intended to elicit from its audience.

Among compatibilists, some have argued that there is no clear difference between art and porn at the level of its primary intended purpose (Eaton 2012): just as most pornography is produced for the purpose of sexually arousing its consumers, so too has much art been produced for that purpose, as evidenced by the panoply of sexualized female nudes throughout art history (but especially those commissioned or sold for private entertainment). Perhaps, then, we would do better to distinguish between sexual content and *objectification* (Lintott and Irvin 2016).

Other compatibilists argue that we are better served by focusing on the kind of response the work is intended to elicit from us (Maes 2011, Davies 2012; see also Nguyen and Williams 2020 on generic uses of 'porn'). If art is typified by responses which take an interrogative interest in the work's content and presentation, then it is true that most pornography is not art, since most pornography is not meant to elicit any such responses from us. But to say that most pornography *doesn't* do so is not to say that it *couldn't* do so; and that, they argue, is simply not the case. Alternately, it may be that the conventions governing certain artistic genres work to prevent audiences from adopting the kinds of objectifying responses we associate with brute pornography, motivating a different kind of engagement instead (Kolmes and Hoffman 2021).

Among incompatibilists, on the other hand, many have argued that pornography serves a primary intended purpose (sexual arousal and gratification) which is different from that served by art (e.g., disinterested aesthetic appreciation; see *The Jealous Husband*). In this respect, pornography differs from erotic art, which can titillate but whose primary purpose is artistic, and from erotica, whose primary purpose is titillation without art or gratification (Levinson 2009). Others, however, have argued that the incompatibility occurs at the level of the audience's engagement with the work: pornography and erotica do not reward taking an artistic interest in them (e.g., there is no point asking why the acting is so wooden), whereas art and erotic art do (Bartel 2010). In particular, some argue that it is the manner in which the arousal is elicited which marks the difference: pornographic interests are focused on the end result, whereas artistic interests are focused on the process or medium which *generates* the end result (Mag Uidhir 2009).

SUGGESTED READING

SEMINAL PRESENTATION:

1. Brabandt, Petra Van and Jesse Prinz (2012). "Why Do Porn Films Suck?" in *Art and Pornography: Philosophical Essays*, Hans Maes and Jerrold Levinson (eds.). Oxford: Oxford University Press, 160–90.
   Van Brabandt and Prinz characterize what they call the 'paradox of porn' and argue that the thesis of art's incompatibility with pornography has been oversold. They argue that while there is nothing incompatible about porn and art, the reason standard porn is not thought of as art is just that it does not afford an aesthetic stance, because its execution does not usually aspire to instantiate the kinds of properties typical of artworks. But it could, and perhaps should.

DEFENCES:

2. Maes, Hans (2011). Drawing the Line: Art versus Pornography. *Philosophy Compass* 6 (6): 385–97.
   Maes offers a useful overview of arguments against the compatibility of art and pornography and argues that the two can, and do, overlap. In particular, he argues that the fact that the two practices have different success

conditions is not enough to establish that some works do not belong to both categories. Satisfying the conditions for sexually arousing art seems to entail the satisfaction of the success-conditions for pornography.

3. Davies, David (2012). "Pornography, Art, and the Intended Response of the Receiver," in *Art and Pornography: Philosophical Essays*, Hans Maes and Jerrold Levinson (eds.). Oxford: Oxford University Press, 61–82.

   Davies focuses on the intended responses of consumers of art and pornography, arguing that although these are clearly different, there is no more reason to think that they cannot overlap than for religious or political art. What makes something count as art, he argues, is not its primary intended function, but rather the kind of response it elicits and the way in which that response is taken to bear on the work's content. And there is no reason why pornography cannot, in principle, elicit this kind of interrogative interest from us.

CRITIQUES:

4. Levinson, Jerrold (2005). Erotic Art and Pornographic Pictures. *Philosophy and Literature* 29 (1): 228–40.

   Levinson distinguishes between pornography, erotica, and erotic art. Erotic art aims at sexual stimulation and can reward taking an artistic interest in its content; erotica stimulates without rewarding artistic interests; and pornography simply aims at sexual arousal and satisfaction. Pornography and erotica are thus consumed, whereas erotic art is appreciated. The result is that the aims of pornography are incompatible with those of art.

5. Mag Uidhir, Christy (2009) Why Pornography Can't Be Art. *Philosophy and Literature* 33: 193–203.

   Mag Uidhir argues that while art and pornography can both share a purpose—e.g., sexual arousal—the key difference which grounds their incompatibility is that they do so in different ways. Pornography resembles advertising: what matters is the end result (e.g., sexual arousal), rather than the process. But for an artist, it is the manner in which that arousal is brought about which matters. Art is *manner-specific*, whereas pornography is *manner-inspecific*.

6. Bartel, Christopher (2010) "The Fine Art of Pornography? The Conflict between Artistic Value and Pornographic Value," in *Porn—Philosophy for Everyone: How to Think with Kink*, Dave Monroe (ed.). Oxford: Wiley-Blackwell, 153–65.

   Bartel distinguishes between different kinds of interests we can take in a work and argues that artistic and pornographic interests are incompatible. Taking an artistic interest in a work requires us to pay attention to its medium, whereas taking a pornographic interest requires us to ignore the medium and fixate on the content.

FURTHER READING:

7. Eaton, A.W. (2012). "What's Wrong With The (Female) Nude?" in Art and Pornography: Philosophical Essays, Hans Maes and Jerrold Levinson (eds.). Oxford: Oxford University Press, 277–308.

   Eaton argues that the predominant forms of artistic and pornographic depictions of the female nude are problematic in the same way: they sexualize the traditional gender hierarchy. Art's 'high' status, however, grants the female nude a particular kind of power in systems of oppression which pornography's 'low' status does not afford it.

8. Lintott, Sheila and Sherri Irvin (2016). "Sex Objects and Sexy Subjects: A Feminist Reclamation of Sexiness," in Body Aesthetics, Sherri Irvin (ed.). Oxford: Oxford University Press, 299–317.

   Lintott and Irvin offer a revisionist account of sexiness which distinguishes it from objectification. Attributing 'sexiness' to someone requires us to attend to their subjectivity, to recognize their sense of self and their sexual identity as it is expressed in their body; in other words, to see them as sexual *beings* rather than sex *objects*.

9. Nguyen, C.Thi and Bekka Williams (2020). Moral Outrage Porn. *Journal of Ethics and Social Philosophy* 18 (2): 147–72.

   Nguyen and Williams offer an account of our generic use of the term 'porn' (e.g., 'food porn') inspired by these debates on the artistic status of pornography. Generic use of the term, they argue, characterizes representations which are primarily engaged with for the sake of a gratifying reaction without the additional cost which usually attends engagement with such content.

10. Kolmes, Sara and Matthew A. Hoffman (2021). Harlequin Resistance? Romance Novels as a Model for Resisting Objectification. *Journal of Aesthetics and Art Criticism* 79 (1): 30–41.

    Kolmes and Hoffman argue, contrary to received opinion, that the artistic conventions which characterize the genre of Harlequin romances actually *preclude* the objectification of their female subjects, and do so despite the graphic nature of their erotic content.

THE PUZZLE OF
HISTORICAL CRITICISM

CASE

Snorri Kristjansson's *Swords of Good Men* (2013) is a very bad book. The story takes place in the Viking age, as Olag Tryggvasson is subjugating Norway, and sets up an apocalyptic conflict between the old gods and Christianity. There are many things which make this a dreadful read, but believe it or not, the fact that one of the Norns has a human body and leads the resistance to Tryggvasson's Christian hordes is not one of them. Nor is it that Odin, Freyja, Thor, and Loki make their own brief appearances. What bothered me the most, apart from the writing itself, was the author's brazen indifference to period detail, which led him to populate the story with any number of anachronistic and even fantastical weapons, and which led him to invent the combat and siege from whole cloth rather than basing any of it in historical fact or—heaven forbid!—mechanics.

But there's something a little puzzling about my reaction to this snore. I don't object to the gods made flesh, and I don't object to the magic, either; what I *do* object to is the gross historical inaccuracy. But if I accept that Kristjansson can write gods and magic into his story, why am I so upset that he's also written in longswords and double-bearded axes?[1] Can't a writer write whatever they want into their

DOI: 10.4324/9781003368205-30

stories? It's a work of fiction, after all, and there's no rule that says that fiction must be true to life!

And yet, the practice of criticizing works of fiction for their historical inaccuracy is quite widespread—it's not just me and this one awful book. So what explains our conflicting intuitions that fiction need not be beholden to the truth and that historical inaccuracies negatively impact a work of fiction? This puzzle is known as the *puzzle of historical criticism* (Bartel 2012),[2] and if we can't resolve it, then it seems that historical criticism of fiction is entirely unjustified. The kind of explanation we are looking for here is one which (1) can distinguish between cases where historical accuracy does and does not matter, and (2) identify a feature common to all historical criticism which explains why historical accuracy counts towards a work's aesthetic value.

RESPONSES

One possible response is to argue that historically inaccurate fiction is not *historically* inaccurate at all—a work of fiction describes a *fictional* world, and a story like *Swords of Good Men* is a perfectly *accurate* report of that particular fictional world (e.g., Gibson 2007). But that seems a little like special pleading. Consider a different case, from a different genre: Neal Stephenson's *Seveneves* (2015). Seveneves is a work of hard Sci-Fi, which is a genre characterized by a particular concern for scientific accuracy. But while Stephenson pays *a lot* of attention to the novel's physics, he's rather sloppy on the biology—to the point where he gets some basic biology (and space biology) wrong, and the novel's ending hinges on what some readers have characterized as 'biology magic'. Because it's a work of hard science fiction, however, we can't simply say that it describes a fictional world with different biological laws, *since those laws are supposed to be identical to our own.* We could try to appeal to an author's intentions to mark the difference here (Kivy 2006, Holliday 2017): Stephenson's work is flawed because his intention was to accurately report the background science, and he didn't do that where biology is concerned. On the other hand, this solution may well get Kristjansson off the hook if, for example, he's simply a dilettante who thought it would be fun to write a story with gods and Vikings in it.

Another possible explanation is that something about the story has triggered an imaginative blockage, resulting in imaginative resistance (see

The Puzzle of Imaginative Resistance): I simply refuse to make-believe that weaponry from the future was commonplace in iron-age Norway, or that a siege would be conducted and defended in such a ludicrous manner. By contrast, the truth allows us to imagine something even more vividly (Köppe and Langkau 2021). More generally, a proponent of this explanation might argue that historical inaccuracies elicit imaginative resistance when they seem to ask us to think about *real-world* history in a manner we find objectionable on moral or factual grounds. This is a promising explanation, but it's also highly subjective since it hinges on an individual's refusal to imagine. What's more, historical criticism is not limited to descriptive claims: it often seems to make *prescriptive* claims, e.g., that nobody *should* imagine longswords or double-bearded axes in iron-age Scandinavia, just as nobody should imagine AK-47s in the American Civil War.[3] Imaginative resistance struggles to adequately explain why an individual's imaginative blockage should translate into a prescriptive evaluative claim like that.

Alternately, we could point to the story's genre and the conventions which normally underpin it (e.g., Rowe 1997, Lamarque 2009, Hazlett and Mag Uidhir 2011)—in the case above, it's a work of historical fiction, so a departure from period detail is problematic. Of course, we still have to explain why I'm not bothered by the introduction of living gods and magic. And there's something of an asymmetry here because other lapses in historical accuracy are not always problematic—e.g., Bernard Cornwell's *Sharpe* series mentions British troops in India wearing shakos, when in fact they wore bicornes. Sometimes, historical inaccuracies are even quite enjoyable—e.g., Naomi Novik's *Temeraire* series is an alternate history of the Napoleonic Wars with dragons, and *Gladiator* (2000) was a great film even though Marcus Aurelius was no Republican and was not murdered by Commodus, who himself was strangled in his bath rather than killed in the arena.[4] Novik's novels can easily be assimilated to a different genre—alternate history—and we can thus explain our acceptance of Napoleonic dragons, but to do so with *Gladiator* seems like a much cheaper and less satisfying move. The more finely we start to cut up genres, the less useful they are as categorizations of broad kinds of storytelling. It is also unclear whether failing to live up to genre conventions means the work is a bad work *in that genre* (in which case the problem is its adherence to genre conventions rather than its historical inaccuracy as such), or whether it's best classified under some other genre (perhaps a new one of which it is the founding member).

Or perhaps we are wrong to expect a unified solution to this puzzle—perhaps the different sources of historical inaccuracy (e.g., sloppiness, propaganda, bias, artistic goals, etc.) can mandate different responses from us (see, e.g., Fileva 2019). Perhaps the reason I care so much about Kristjansson's inaccuracies and so little about Cornwell's is that in the work of the former, they're indicative of general sloppiness and a lackadaisical attitude towards his subject matter, whereas in the latter the shako confusion is clearly a small mistake in an otherwise carefully researched series.

Or maybe we were wrong to believe that authors have free rein to make anything whatsoever true in their stories in the first place: perhaps actual truth constrains fictional truth more than we first imagined (see *Empty and Universal Fictions*).

SUGGESTED READING

SEMINAL PRESENTATION:

1. Bartel, Christopher (2012). The Puzzle of Historical Criticism. *Journal of Aesthetics and Art Criticism* 70 (2): 213–22.
   Bartel introduces the puzzle of historical criticism and argues that the puzzle arises from our understanding of truth in fiction, according to which fictional truth is not constrained by actual truth. He argues that the genre and imaginative resistance solutions are inadequate.

DEFENCES:

2. Holliday, John (2017). The Puzzle of Factual Praise. *Journal of Aesthetics and Art Criticism* 75 (2): 169–79.
   Holliday argues that the puzzle of historical criticism applies to all fiction, since we have the intuitions that (1) fictional works are not bound by truth, but (2) accuracy can be relevant to a work's artistic value. Rather than genre, Holliday suggests that it is the author's literary intentions which determine when factual praise or criticism is appropriate.

3. Köppe, Tilmann and Julia Langkau (2021). Truth Matters, Aesthetically. *Estetika* 58 (2): 114–28.
   Köppe and Langkau argue that the truth of the statements alluded to, expressed, or implied by a work of fiction has a direct bearing on the work's aesthetic value. Truth, they contend, increases the vividness of our

imaginative engagement with the work. They argue that literary criticism should therefore pay closer attention to the truth of a text's claims.

CRITIQUES:

4. Hazlett, Allan and Christy Mag Uidhir (2011). Unrealistic Fictions. *American Philosophical Quarterly* 48 (1): 33–46.
   Hazlett and Mag Uidhir offer a principled explanation for the beliefs we import into, and export from, fiction. But, they argue, false exportations alone can't explain why we sometimes think that unrealistic fiction is aesthetically flawed. Instead, they argue, unrealistic fictions invite us to import and export inconsistent beliefs.

5. Fileva, Iskra (2019). Historical Inaccuracy in Fiction. *American Philosophical Quarterly* 56 (2): 155–70.
   Fileva offers a Gricean take on the puzzle of historical criticism, arguing that the solution is to be found in the conversational contract between the author and the audience. Just what this contract entails is determined by the work's genre.

FURTHER READING:

6. Rowe, Mark W. (1997). Lamarque and Olsen on Literature and Truth. *The Philosophical Quarterly* 47: 322–41.
   Rowe argues that Lamarque's (and Olsen's) genre-based approach to historical criticism only succeeds because it artificially restricts the range of cases to which it applies. Instead, he argues that factual truth is always relevant when we consider a work's theme. He advocates a genre-based approach that is subject to the inaccuracy's moral import.

7. Kivy, Peter (2006). *The Performance of Reading: An Essay in the Philosophy of Literature.* Malden, MA: Blackwell.
   Kivy is primarily interested in defending the idea that literary works are performances: they are *types* instantiated by their *readings*. In §24, he argues for a 'plausibility theory' of literary value, according to which the quality of an interpretation hinges on how plausible it is. Historical inaccuracies increase implausibility, decreasing a work's aesthetic value.

8. Gibson, John (2007). *Fiction and the Weave of Life.* Oxford: Oxford University Press.
   Gibson argues (especially in Ch. 4) that no fictional propositions refer to the real world; the puzzle of historical criticism, then, is an illusion, since the events related concern a world of make-believe, not the real world.

9. Eaton, Marcia Muelder (2008). Aesthetic Obligations. *Journal of Aesthetics and Art Criticism* 66 (1): 1–9.

    Although this paper is about aesthetic obligations (see *The Burning Museum*), Eaton also argues that we may sometimes have an (aesthetic) obligation to play with historical accuracy for the sake of a story's aesthetic value. Aesthetic efficacy, she argues, demands *plausibility*—'truth to,' rather than outright truth.

10. Lamarque, Peter (2009). *The Philosophy of Literature.* Malden, MA: Blackwell.

    In Ch. 6, Lamarque argues that to belong to a genre is to abide by its conventions, and one convention of historical fiction is historical accuracy (likewise for hard Sci-Fi and scientific accuracy). This only applies to genres for which historical accuracy belongs to their core conventions, however.

NOTES

1 The longsword emerged in the fourteenth century, while the Viking age ended in the middle-eleventh; double-bearded axes, on the other hand, were not used to wage war—they are a religious symbol and a fantasy weapon, nothing more.

2 'Historical criticism', here, simply denotes critiques of fiction based on their historical accuracy, not the school of literary criticism by the same name.

3 This is a central plot point in Harry Turtledove's alternate history/time travel novel *The Guns of the South* (1992).

4 It is also worth noting that many of the costumes in the film are a combination of anachronism and fantasy.

THE TRANSMOGRIFIER (STYLE)

CASE

Calvin and Hobbes (1985–95) was a comic strip by Bill Waterson featuring a six-year-old rogue and his stuffed tiger. Several of their misadventures involved a *transmogrifier*, a cardboard box that turns the user into anything at all, and whose function can be changed by altering the label. For this case, put on your *Calvin and Hobbes* hat and imagine a transmogrifier, a machine that can change specific aspects of the world. It can add or remove anything you like from the world and change it in any way you care to imagine. You can also specify which parts of the world you'd like to remain constant despite the changes you've programmed.

Now, suppose you were to select a property you think is a typical stylistic property of some composer's work—simple diatonic harmony in Mozart, say, or experimentation and counterpoint for Beethoven, etc. Let's call it *P* for short. And suppose you programmed the transmogrifier so that the world was now chock full of musical works which exhibited *P*. Would you still call *P* a stylistic property of Mozart, Beethoven, or whoever?

Conversely, suppose you took a different property of that composer's work, which you *don't* think is a stylistic characteristic of their

DOI: 10.4324/9781003368205-31

work (e.g., every piece they composed contains at least one middle D). Call it D for short. Suppose you transmogrified the world so that nobody else's music exhibits D. Would you still think D isn't a stylistic characteristic of the composer's work?

These cases are designed to put pressure on the idea that style is just a matter of a work's formal properties, of statistical regularities that obtain in an artist's *oeuvre*. In the first case, the point is that stylistic characteristics aren't brute properties of works considered in isolation: what's 'typical' of an artist's output depends not just on what they do, but on what their contemporaries do. If counterpoint is a common feature of late eighteenth-century music, then it's much less remarkable when Beethoven's work exhibits it. On the other hand, the fact that a property is uniquely attributable to someone's work, so that it identifies them as surely as a signature might, doesn't seem to amount to a style, either. The fact that Meethoven uses middle D and nobody else does makes it easy to identify a piece by Meethoven, but it doesn't really seem to count as part of his *style*.

So what *is* 'style', exactly?

RESPONSES

At first glance, it's tempting to identify an artist's style with the concrete properties of their work and the way in which some of those properties are carried over across their body of work. We might think, then, that style is a matter of resemblances (see also *The Puzzle of Depiction*) or statistical regularities which allow us to identify the work of a particular artist as being by that artist, or of a period or place as being of that period or place, etc. (Schapiro 1953, Ackerman 1962). We might then explain style as either a matter of historical forces (Schapiro 1953 canvasses, but does not endorse, several such attempts) or of an individual's imaginative approach to solving and restating the problems posed by previous generations (Ackerman 1962).

The key to this account of style is its utility for art history—both in terms of facilitating the identification and categorization of works by artist, period, nationality, etc., and for framing the history of art as a succession of increasingly refined efforts towards some goal (e.g., pictorial realism). There are questions, however, about whether this kind of historical ordering is appropriate to the many different modes of production which inform the history of our artistic practices, only some of which are later singled out and valourized as part of a grand narrative (Alpers 1990 [1979]). In particular, we need to be aware that the history of art is *ideological* as well as empirical and historical; naming a style gives it power and invites us to class similar works under its banner, even if the classification is arbitrary or historically problematic. Likewise, we should ask what marks the distinction between a *style* on the one hand, and a *genre* on the other—of all the different ways we have of classifying artworks, what makes some of them *stylistic* (Ross 2010)?

A more sophisticated treatment of style sees it as the product of an artist's action: style is a matter of how the work *appears* to have been made, of the actions of which it stands as a discernible trace (Walton 1979). Style attributions are thus based on how works *appear* to have been created (e.g., raging music appears to come from an enraged person; see *The St. Bernard's Face*). Style isn't what's *expressed*, it's the thing in the work that does the *expressing*. That thing is there to be found in the work; how we interpret its efforts, however, depends upon the context in which we find ourselves, and the background against which we interpret it. If, as in Borges's famous story, Pierre Menard writes a work that's word-for-word identical to Cervantes's *Don Quixote* (1605) from scratch, the style of the works is identical, but one will be counted as bold and exciting, the other as archaic, in view of the intervening four hundred years. The properties that make up a style are not essential to the style, although they *are* essential to the work.

A number of philosophers, however, have resisted the conclusion that we can reduce style to a checklist of properties. One problem with relying on the statistical regularity of formal features, in particular, is that many of these regularities are, in fact, entirely unremarkable when put in context (Douven 1999). It's easy enough for us to distinguish Mozart from Beethoven, and we attribute the difference to style, but each composed in a very different musical world. When we think about the ways in which Mozart differs from Beethoven, we're not usually also thinking about the ways in which his work differed from that of his contemporaries, such as Clementi, Hummel, Kozeluch, and others. Indeed, we've forgotten all about those other composers. So the statistical regularities we identify in Mozart are based on a hasty generalization from a single case, rather than on an exhaustive catalogue of the ways in which Mozart's music resembled, and differed from, the rest of the music of his day.

Another problem is that it isn't obvious that the experience of coming to grasp a style is one of ticking items off a list (e.g., elongated limbs + stylized pose + no clear perspective = Italian mannerism). Nor does it seem, intuitively, like merely possessing a given property or properties (e.g., counterpoint) suffices to place a work in a style. After all, it might turn out that a writer's work features an unusually large number of sentences whose second word starts with a consonant. This might even be a very robust statistical generalization, but that's not enough for it to count as part of the author's style; something is missing. One suggestion is that this property isn't part of how the work functions, symbolically—it's a property the work possesses, but not one it exemplifies (Goodman 1975). Style, on this construal, is entirely a matter of which features of the work's symbolic function(s) are characteristic of a particular artist, period, place, etc.

Perhaps part of the problem is that we tend to conflate the notion of a *general* style with that of an *individual* style (Wollheim 1995; see also Schapiro 1953). Statistical regularities and other such 'taxonomic' properties are fine for describing and grouping artistic traditions, but they don't describe the *artist's* style, just the properties which the work has *because* of that style. Individual style, on this conception, is a set of rules and schemata which an artist develops over time, and which she actively endorses as her way of doing things, even if she isn't always self-consciously adhering to it. Individual style is thus said to be *generative*, while general style is merely taxonomic.

The generative conception of individual style dovetails nicely with the intuition, shared by many, that style is a matter of individual expression (e.g., think of personal style). The main suggestion, here, is that an artist's way of doing things expresses their personality traits in some way (Robinson 1985). These are the kinds of attitudes, interests, and personality traits which are characteristic of the author—or, at least, of the author as *implied* by the work (see *Pinny the Who?*). Not just whatever personality traits happened to possess the artist during the moment of creation (e.g., a flash of anger), but the kinds of traits we think of as *stable standing states* for them (e.g., disciplined precision). General style, by contrast, may exhibit all of the same properties, but it has no personality behind it, no implied author whose personality it expresses.

The closer we hew to an *implied* author, the less tied we are to reading an artist's biography into their work; the work can stand for itself, even if we know nothing about its maker. By the same token, however, we start to lose the sense that a style is psychologically real for its artist, which is effectively the whole point of distinguishing the notion of individual style to begin with (Riggle 2015). If we take the analogy to personal style seriously, then it seems like having a style involves some kind of *achievement*: getting a mohawk isn't really sufficient to give you a punk style, but when you *do* have the style, you really *are* punk (in Goodman's terms, we might say that you don't just *possess* a punk aesthetic, you *exemplify* it). If style is an achievement, however, then it's more than just an expression of someone's personality. And one way to capture that 'more' is in terms of the expression of one's *ideals*: you have true punk style when you positively exude an aura of anarchism suffused with social justice, say. What matters for personal style isn't who you are, but who you strive to be; likewise, with artistic style, what matters is the way the work embodies and communicates the ideals the artist has for their art.

SUGGESTED READING

SEMINAL PRESENTATION:

1. Douven, Igor (1999). Style and Supervenience. *British Journal of Aesthetics* 39 (3): 255–62.
   Douven argues that stylistic features aren't reducible to, nor do they supervene on, local textual or perceptual qualities of a work. Mozart's 'style' isn't just a matter of the kinds of arrangements of notes and pauses he favoured, but of how it seems unpredictable and not slavishly subject to the rules which bound the work of his contemporaries.

DEFENCES:

2. Goodman, Nelson (1975). The Status of Style. *Critical Inquiry* 1 (4): 799–811.
   Goodman argues that style isn't just a matter of possessing certain intrinsic properties; it also requires that the work manifest or exemplify them. That is to say, stylistic properties are those referred to by the work itself, they're a property of the work functioning *as a symbol*. Style is not a fixed catalogue of properties.

3. Wollheim, Richard (1995). "Style in Painting," in *The Question of Style in Philosophy and the Arts*, Caroline van Eck, James McAllister, and Renée van de Vall (eds.). Cambridge: Cambridge University Press, 37–49.

   Wollheim distinguishes between general and individual style, arguing that while a taxonomic conception is appropriate to the former, the latter requires a *generative* conception. Individual style, he thinks, is psychologically real (it makes a difference to the artist), is formed rather than learned, and doesn't require active conceptualization on the artist's part.

4. Robinson, Jenefer M. (1985). Style and Personality in the Literary Work. *Philosophical Review* 94 (2): 227–47.

   Robinson argues that a style is a way of writing (painting, etc.) that expresses the personality of its implied author by appearing to express their standing (as opposed to occurrent) character, interests, and personality traits. General style may share its qualities with individual style, but it does not express a particular individual's personality traits.

CRITIQUES:

5. Ackerman, James S. (1962). A Theory of Style. *Journal of Aesthetics and Art Criticism* 20 (3): 227–37.

   Ackerman argues that style is a distinguishable group of highly changeable characteristics which nevertheless remain stable for a time, thus allowing us to identify the work of an artist, period, or place.

6. Walton, Kendall (1979). "Style and the Products and Processes of Art," in *The Concept of Style*, Leonard B. Meyer and Berel Lang (eds.). Philadelphia: University of Pennsylvania Press, 45–66.

   Walton argues that style features are parts of their works, and thus describable in terms of statistical regularities. Style is a matter of how the work appears to have been made; but how we describe that style is context-dependent. When one and the same work is described as bold and archaic, what has changed is not the work's style, but the background against which it is evaluated.

FURTHER READING:

7. Schapiro, Meyer (1953). "Style," in *Anthropology Today: An Encyclopedic Inventory*, Alfred Louis Kroeber (ed.). Chicago: University of Chicago Press, 287–311.

   Schapiro takes 'style' to refer to the constancy of form in the art of an individual or a group, the relationships between those forms, and what those forms express. Emphasizing the influence of conventions, he gives a critical overview of attempts to explain style in terms of group or individual expression, of a historical or evolutionary progression towards some goal (e.g., realism), of the expression of national or racial characters, as an imitation of great artists, and as a reflection of social life.

8. Alpers, Svetlana (1990 [1979]). "Style is What You Make It: The Visual Arts Once Again," in *The Concept of Style*, 2nd ed., Berel Lang (ed.). Ithaca, NY: Cornell University Press, 95–117.

    Alpers surveys the art historical literature on style. She is suspicious of the tendency to treat style as a kind of historical ordering or problem-solving, and of tethering an object's value to its stylistic identity. Rather than a united historical account of style, she advocates tracing the many different 'modes' operative at a time.

9. Ross, Stephanie (2010). "Style in Art," in *The Oxford Handbook of Aesthetics*, Jerrold Levinson (ed.). Oxford: Oxford University Press. 228–44.

    Ross surveys the philosophical literature on style, observing in particular that an account of *style* should distinguish it from *genre*.

10. Riggle, Nick (2015). Personal Style and Artistic Style. *Philosophical Quarterly* 65 (261): 711–31.

    Riggle argues that although personal and artistic style are closely related, neither involves the expression of one's personality. Rather, he thinks that both are matters of expressing one's *ideals*—either about oneself, or for one's art. An action is in one's style when it embodies and communicates one's ideals.

THE UNIFORM WORLD
(AESTHETIC DISAGREEMENT)

CASE

Imagine a world in which everyone likes the same things. This isn't necessarily a world where everyone only likes Beethoven, but rather one in which there's a wide range of aesthetic products on offer (including, say, Rachmaninoff, Cardi B, and Nekrogoblikon), but everyone agrees about which of those things are good, and about their relative ranking. Like ours, it's a world with Shakespeare and Agatha Christie and Louise Penny and Dan Brown, but unlike ours, it's a world in which everyone seeks out and prefers the first to the second, and so on down the list, so that only the meanest prisoners are forced to resort to *The Da Vinci Code*'s (2003) dubious powers of distraction. That's not to say there'd be no disagreement, but every disagreement about a thing's aesthetic value could be resolved.

Does that seem like a nightmare hellscape to you? If not, let's tweak the thought experiment a little bit: instead of enshrining Shakespeare and Beethoven at the top of our world's aesthetic hierarchy, let's place Dan Brown and Kenny G. (or whoever else you think is just awful). Every time you turn on the radio you hear those smooth sax tones, and every movie night it's *Angels and Demons* (2009)—*and everyone loves it.*

DOI: 10.4324/9781003368205-32

It's that last bit that matters for our thought experiment: everyone (correctly) loves the same things. Many contemporary philosophers share the intuition that such a world would be awful, dull, and awfully dull. But much of historical aesthetics conceives of our aesthetic lives as a process of ever-greater refinement, such that we aim to be the kinds of people who will make correct judgements of aesthetic value. In other words, there is a strong normative presumption that we *should* appreciate the same sorts of things, and the challenge is to explain the diversity of taste as more than mere error.

RESPONSES

Under the influence of Hume and Kant, classical aesthetics held out universal agreement with the standards of taste as the gold standard of aesthetic value (on the normative dimension here, see King 2022; see also *The Burning Museum*). We thus expect and aim for significant *convergence* in our judgements of aesthetic value. The case for convergence rests in large part on the Humean "test of time"—the fact that people of very different times and cultures tend to agree in rating certain works of art very highly (e.g., Hokusai and Shakespeare.; but see *The Problem of Genius*). Historically, this high valuation has been explained in terms of the works' *beauty*; they please universally because they are universally judged to be beautiful.

Some might think this undermines the case for universality, since judgements of beauty, like judgements of gustatory taste (see *The Paradox of Gustatory Taste*), seem deeply personal. But a proponent of convergence can maintain that although our individual ability to *discern* beauty is highly variable, the acknowledged masterpieces *are* all beautiful, and will appear so to any properly trained person who encounters them (Mothersill 1989). *You* may not find the *Iliad* beautiful, for example, but that is because your Greek is not up to the task of reading it in the original; if it were, and you did, you *would*. It's not so much that Humean ideal critics *set* the standards of taste as that they're uniquely positioned to be able to identify the features of a work that contribute to its beauty. It seems to follow that a world in which we all correctly agree on which things are aesthetically valuable is more desirable than one in which some of us are wrong to like the things we like.

But we know from our own experience that comparatively small adjustments on our part (especially to our contextual understanding of a work) can result in radically different aesthetic experiences (Kieran 2008; see also *Guernicas*). Indeed, it seems like the cultivation of some kinds of aesthetic appreciation can preclude or undermine the cultivation of others—cultivating the appreciative capacities required to appreciate pop music, for example, can impede your ability to appreciate the aesthetic properties of extreme metal. This being so, it's perfectly conceivable that works which have survived the "test of time" have done so only because we have not yet experienced the gestalt shift necessary to appreciate their real and serious aesthetic demerits. In much the same way, a joke can be funny until you realize it's quite homophobic, racist, or sexist, at which point it's no longer funny.

Similarly, it's been argued that gustatory taste may not be a good paradigm for aesthetic appreciation (Melchionne 2010). With food, we just do or don't like something, and we have immediate and infallible access to the reasons why. But cognitive science suggests that the same is not true of aesthetic judgements, which seem just as prone to error as other mental states. I might, for example, be more favourably disposed towards a bad film because I enjoyed a great pizza beforehand or saw it in good company, or I may be predisposed one way or another because of what my self-image requires. This isn't to say that our aesthetic preferences are radically unreliable, but rather that they are subject to error, and that the reasons underpinning them are not necessarily available to us in introspection. The result is that our current best guesses about what ideal critics would deem aesthetically valuable could very easily be mistaken.

Contemporary accounts of aesthetic value are largely *hedonic*: what makes something aesthetically valuable is just the particular kind of (aesthetic) pleasure it gives us (see van der Berg 2020 for an overview). This, in turn, has placed a contrary emphasis on the diversity and *divergence* of our judgements about aesthetic value. The real world seems characterized by aesthetic *dis*agreement: you like Shakespeare and Beethoven, I like Amon Amarth and Bernard Cornwell, and presumably, someone out there *really* likes Chuck Mangione and Justin Cronin, as revolting as the thought may be. But do we take the further step of thinking that *everyone* should like all and only the same things as us?

One powerful strategy for reconciling the highly individual nature of aesthetic judgement with the apparent unity of judgement over certain works is by appealing to the notion of an aesthetic community. On this model, when we make judgements of beauty we put ourselves out there, and hope for something more in return (Nehamas 2007)—judgements of beauty help us to direct our attention so that we can find what we need to better understand the reasons for our judgement, but they also invite agreement from those around us. They don't aspire to correctness by some external standard so much as acknowledgement from like-minded people.

In making the judgement we're *staking out a claim*, actively establishing our aesthetic identities. In this way aesthetic judgements are also normative: they're promises we make to ourselves to behave in certain ways, to focus some of our aesthetic attention in certain ways despite the embarrassment of aesthetic riches out there (Cross forthcoming). It's not that difference is valuable in itself; rather, it's a concern for what uniformity of aesthetic judgement would require of us. A uniform world is one in which we no longer need to discover why we think something is beautiful; it's one in which we're no longer active participants. Instead, it's one in which we strive to make our own judgements and values conform to an externally set standard—it's an echo chamber (Nguyen 2021).

While attractive, such a view does rely on characterizing aesthetic value in general, and beauty in particular, in hedonic terms: aesthetic value and beauty are *pleasures* we experience. But not all aesthetically valuable experiences are particularly pleasant—see e.g., *The Paradox of Tragedy* and *The Paradox of Disgust*. Moreover, it seems like some of the aesthetic pleasures we enjoy are the byproducts of activities we undertake for primarily non-aesthetic reasons, such as a numismatist's fascination with history. According to the *network theory* of aesthetic value, aesthetic activities each require a special kind of skill for their execution, and it is in pursuit of this expertise that we pursue them (Lopes 2017). Doing so, in turn, gives us good reason to conform to the aesthetic culture in which the action is embedded. So, for example, developing the expertise necessary to make good horror movies gives you good reasons to adhere to the tropes of the genre, rather than trying to forge your own way, since too much deviation results in something that's not recognizably a *horror* film. But developing such skills is difficult and time-consuming, so no individual can hope to master them all; we thus have good reason, at the *social* level, to distribute the labour and encourage the cultivation of different aesthetic cultures. By pursuing our own individual aesthetic interests, we ultimately contribute to a wider and better developed sphere of aesthetic possibilities for everyone else, rather than a homogenous world with comparatively few aesthetic practices.

But on the network theory, if you like romcoms or superhero movies, there's really no reason for you to start watching B-horror. Aesthetic practices yield self-sufficient worlds, such that insiders have little reason to seek out new and different aesthetic experiences. The problem, perhaps, is that the account is still too focused on *individual* aesthetic responses, rather than on the value of aesthetic practices to communities of people. According to the *communitarian* account of aesthetic value (Riggle 2022), there is no one thing that constitutes aesthetic value; aesthetic value is just whatever some community of people thinks is worthy of aesthetically valuing. For the communitarian, the very fact that there exist communities centred on valuing different practices is enough to call into question the first community's values; the fact that there exist other flourishing communities of value is reason enough for us to expand our horizons in order to enrich our aesthetic lives. At the same time, communitarianism cautions against the tendency to champion the creative output of certain impressive individuals: our aesthetic lives are much richer, and much more commonplace, than is often suggested (see also *Two Societies*).

SUGGESTED READING

SEMINAL PRESENTATION:

1. Nehamas, Alexander (2007). *Only a Promise of Happiness: The Place of Beauty in a World of Art*. Princeton: Princeton University Press.
   In Ch. 3, Nehamas argues that aesthetic value is grounded in judgements of beauty, which are characterized by their mysteriousness. Beauty constantly holds out the promise of more and deeper engagement, and making those judgements is an invitation to others to join a small community of personal taste.

DEFENCES:

2. Lopes, Dominic McIver (2017). Beauty, The Social Network. *Canadian Journal of Philosophy* 47 (4): 437–53.

   Lopes argues that hedonic accounts of aesthetic value fail to account for the wide range of aesthetic activities we undertake. These are better explained by a *network theory*: each kind of aesthetic activity requires a specialized competence, so that agents have reason to strive for excellence in their performance, and thus to conform to the relevant aesthetic culture.

3. Riggle, Nick (2022). Toward a Communitarian Theory of Aesthetic Value. *Journal of Aesthetics and Art Criticism* 80 (1): 16–30.

   Riggle argues that it's a mistake to prioritize an *individual's* aesthetic responses. According to *aesthetic communitarianism*, aesthetic value is a force that binds communities together. Aesthetic value is just whatever a community deems worthy of aesthetically valuing.

4. Kieran, Matthew (2008). Why Ideal Critics are Not Ideal: Aesthetic Character, Motivation, and Value. *British Journal of Aesthetics* 48 (3): 278–94.

   Kieran argues that the cultivation of some aesthetic virtues can preclude or undermine others required for other kinds of appreciation. Since small adjustments to our discriminatory capacities can yield outsized changes in our aesthetic evaluations of works, the "test of time" is not a good proxy for aesthetic value.

5. Melchionne, Kevin (2010). On the Old Saw 'I Know Nothing About Art But I Know What I Like'. *Journal of Aesthetics and Art Criticism* 68 (2): 131–41.

   Melchionne argues that many disputes about taste are due to our ignorance about our own tastes and their sources. Many of the reasons we give for our aesthetic satisfaction are based on guesswork or posturing; our privileged access to our own mental states doesn't guarantee their correctness or that we can reliably access them.

CRITIQUES:

6. Mothersill, Mary (1989). "Hume and the Paradox of Taste", in *Aesthetics: A Critical Anthology*, George Dickie, Richard Sclafani, and Ronald Roblin (eds.). New York: St Martin's, 269–86.

   Mothersill finds in Hume the suggestion of a new solution to the paradox of taste. To say that something is beautiful is just to say that it is individually pleasing, and judgements of taste are either true or false. Nevertheless, there are no non-trivial laws of taste; the ideal critic's job is just to explain what it is, in each masterpiece, that contributes to its beauty.

FURTHER READING:

7. van der Berg, Servaas (2020). Aesthetic Hedonism and Its Critics. *Philosophy Compass* 15 (1): 1–15.
    van der Berg surveys the literature on aesthetic hedonism, the position that something's aesthetic value is just its ability to please us in a special (aesthetic) way. Hedonism is the default position in contemporary aesthetics, but objections and alternatives have begun to surface.
8. Nguyen, C. Thi (2021). "How Twitter Gamifies Communication," in *Applied Epistemology*, Jennifer Lackey (ed.). Oxford: Oxford University Press, 410–36.
    Nguyen argues that social media platforms shape the space of our interactions, encouraging us to trade in our own values for those rewarded by engagement with the platform. This leads to a homogenization of our value landscape, rather than promoting value pluralism.
9. King, Alex (2022). Reasons, Normativity, and Value in Aesthetics. *Philosophy Compass* 17 (1): 1–17.
    King surveys the literature on aesthetic reasons and normativity. She divides theories according to their proposals about the object, source, and strength of aesthetic reasons, and asks, further, what distinguishes aesthetic from non-aesthetic reasons, what the normative force of aesthetic reasons is, and how aesthetic and non-aesthetic reasons interact.
10. Cross, Anthony (forthcoming). *Aesthetic Commitments and Aesthetic Obligations*. Ergo: An Open Access Journal of Philosophy.
    Cross argues that aesthetic value invites us to make judgements about aesthetic objects which commit us to taking certain positions and shouldering certain obligations. These are commitments we make to ourselves in view of pre-existing relationships with the aesthetic objects we care about, and which anchor our aesthetic identities.

TWO SOCIETIES
(EVERYDAY AESTHETICS)

CASE

Imagine two societies. On a political and economic level, they're identical—they're both liberal democracies with very robust social safety nets, each is as wealthy as the other, each one's citizens are as well off as the other's, etc.

Where they differ is that one society is full of meticulously designed environments and objects, each of which was crafted with the goal of facilitating pleasant interactions with users. Things just look nice, cities are easy to navigate and offer interesting views and lots of lush, well-kept greenery, there are parks everywhere, litter and dog poo are promptly picked up, computers and other devices feature intuitive design, there's little air pollution, etc. The other society, however, is the exact opposite: everyday artifacts are just slapped together with no consideration for anything but functionality, its lived environments are insensitive to people's needs or happiness, things frequently fall apart and their use is unintuitive, there are few (if any) parks, and although the cities feature lots of baseball or soccer fields, these are gravelled and stand empty year-round. The traffic is terrible, the public transportation network a pain to navigate, the buildings are ungainly blocks uncomfortable for life or work, and

DOI: 10.4324/9781003368205-33

the cities lurk inside dense brown smogs, their sidewalks caked in dog poop. You get the picture.

Now imagine you're looking down on these two societies from somewhere in the heavens and have to choose one in which to be incarnated. Suppose you don't know anything about what your life down there will be like—you don't know whether you'll be rich or poor, straight or queer, cis or trans, male or female or non-binary, what your profession will be, etc. Which society would you choose to live in?

I think it's fair to say we would pretty much all choose the first society. It just sounds a lot nicer, after all. But some aestheticians have argued that our preference for the first society isn't just a matter of it being *prettier*. Rather, they think that this simple thought experiment showcases the *moral* value we attach to the aesthetics of our daily lives. An ideal—and ideally good—society shouldn't just guarantee our basic human rights, it should also reflect those rights, and the moral values that inform them, in its built environment and in the artifacts it designs. We want our ideal society to be one that is pervaded by *care*, *respect*, and *sensitivity* to our needs. And that, in turn, encourages us to cultivate the same attitudes towards others in our environment: we're more likely to pick up after our dogs, for example, in an immaculately kept park or street than in one already saturated with effluvia.

This concern for our everyday environment lies at the heart of *everyday aesthetics*. According to its advocates, our aesthetic interactions with the world only rarely feature artworks proper; rather, most of our aesthetic encounters are with everyday objects and environments. As often as you might go to see the landscape paintings in your local gallery, you just spend more time enjoying the satisfaction of solving your daily Wordle, savouring melting ice cream on your tongue, scratching an itch, cutting tomatoes with a sharp knife, or navigating your city's streets. And that means that we need a better understanding of the aesthetics of those everyday objects and environments.

RESPONSES

Philosophical work on the aesthetic character of everyday experience traces back to John Dewey (1934), who argued that art is not necessary to have an aesthetic experience; our daily lives can suffice. Today, we can distinguish two broad trends in everyday aesthetics: one that seeks to extend the scope of things which are appropriate for aesthetic consideration, and one which has tried to articulate a new account of aesthetic appreciation peculiar to the everyday (see Saito 2021 for an overview of recent approaches).

On the first model, we should expand the concept of the aesthetic to include the everyday: everyday objects are thus appropriate targets of the kind of aesthetic consideration we normally reserve for artworks. So, for example, the very same terms we use to describe artworks also seem applicable to certain of our ordinary experiences: to say that the coffee "smells good" is to offer an aesthetic evaluation, and we say that certain experiences are "powerful" or "deeply moving" in exactly the same way we speak of theatrical or film performances (Leddy 2005).

Alternately, another way to conceive of everyday aesthetics is in terms of making the ordinary *extraordinary* (Forsey 2014 calls this 'extraordinarism'): we focus our attention on the world around us and take an aesthetic interest in it and the way it presents itself to us (Irvin 2008). In doing so, ordinary objects leave the background of our lives and come to occupy the foreground for a time (Hick 2019). Thus, it's not just that we are redirecting our aesthetic attention to a neglected subject; in doing so, we effect a change in that object, too. For extraordinarists, paying closer attention to everyday aesthetic experiences promises to enrich our lives by helping us to discover new aesthetic preferences in the world around us (Hick 2019; see also *The Uniform World*). And these, in turn, can help to fill the gap left when moral consideration tells us we should abandon certain other experiences (Irvin 2008). By learning to delight in the crunchy texture of a veggie patty, for example, one can offset the sense of loss that comes with recognising the immorality of regularly eating meat.

On the other hand, we might worry that in turning the kind of attention we normally reserve for artworks on everyday phenomena—by making the ordinary extraordinary—we are liable to lose sight of the fact that these are *ordinary* objects and experiences (Saito 2007). Perhaps, instead, we need to approach their aesthetic appreciation under a new paradigm, rather than under one which derives from our rarefied encounters with art. In other words, everyday aesthetics should be concerned with the ordinary *as it is ordinarily experienced*:

we need to notice the everyday aesthetic experiences already afforded by the ordinary, rather than construct new experiences by turning the kind of focused attention we lavish on art onto ordinary objects and experiences. And that is precisely what is most difficult about everyday aesthetics, because by nature the everyday stays hidden in the background of our lives. Usually, it is only when we find ourselves estranged from our habitual environment, or when a tool breaks down, that we take a step back and notice it and its aesthetic character (Haapala 2005). Although the appreciation of art requires a certain familiarity—with the work's genre, subject, or style, for example—everyday aesthetic appreciation seems, rather, to be grounded in a certain strangeness which prevents artifacts from "disappear[ing] into their function" (Haapala 2005: 49).

According to this view, the everyday character of our aesthetic lives highlights the moral dimension of our surroundings, whose design and maintenance directly impact our quality of life (Saito 2007). Imagine being presented with a gift that's been wrapped in plain brown paper decorated with carefully selected magazine pictures. Now compare this to the experience of being given the same item wrapped in paper from the dollar store, or to the experience of having the unwrapped item tossed in your direction. The care taken in its presentation says something, doesn't it? We don't always take the time to notice it, but the thought really does count. The way in which the gift is wrapped—or unwrapped!—expresses sensitivity, care, and consideration (or lack thereof). The same, it's argued, can be found in everyday design features (see also *The Time Machine*).

Skepticism of the everyday aesthetics movement has tended to focus on the nature of the experiences it seeks to highlight. In particular, philosophers have wondered whether they are properly *aesthetic* in the first place (Forsey 2014, Davies 2015). For example, is it that everyday experiences have a special aesthetic character of their own, which we don't typically notice, or is it that when we focus our attention on them in a particular way, we can find them aesthetically rewarding (Davies 2015)? The first strategy is consistent with the project of identifying ordinary experiences as paradigm instances of aesthetic appreciation, but without conscious attention, it isn't clear how we can discern the features that give the experience its *aesthetic* character (Davies 2015); we risk diluting the scope of aesthetic experience so much that we lose sight of how and why the aesthetic is so important to our lives (Forsey 2014). An aesthetic experience, after all, is surely not the same thing as just wallowing in sensation or dwelling unreflectively on some experience (Davies 2015). The second strategy, on the other hand, seems to commit us to treating our experiences of art as paradigm instances of aesthetic engagement, and the whole point of everyday aesthetics is to show us that this sort of focus on our comparatively rare experiences of art is misleading. The challenge for everyday aesthetics is to successfully negotiate this tension in its core commitments (Forsey 2014).

Finally, some have questioned the moral component of everyday aesthetics, as illustrated in our starting thought experiment. It's natural to focus on the utopian quality of good design, but we shouldn't forget its darker side, either. The world around us is in one in which everyday aesthetic demands are gendered, such that women keenly feel an obligation to keep up appearances—both their own personal appearances and the appearance of their domestic environment (Archer and Ware 2018; on aesthetic obligations, see also *The Burning Museum*). Now, it may be that such cases feature a conflation of what it means to go above and beyond the call of duty ("supererogation") with what is minimally or universally necessary, in which case it's plausible that paying closer attention to everyday aesthetic demands—consciously *noticing* them—will help to make us more aware of the line between the demands of duty and supererogation. But it's worth remembering that aesthetic obligations can contribute to structures of oppression if they're allowed to run unchecked.

SUGGESTED READING

SEMINAL PRESENTATION:

1. Saito, Yuriko (2007). *Everyday Aesthetics*. Oxford: Oxford University Press.
   Saito introduces everyday aesthetics, drawing inspiration from environmental aesthetics. She argues that we should pay closer attention to the aesthetics of everyday phenomena, but cautions against the tendency to extraordinarize the ordinary, enjoining us to appreciate the ordinary on its own terms (Ch. 1, 4). The trick lies in knowing when to extraordinarize, and when not, for maximum aesthetic value. She introduces our thought experiment in order to highlight the moral dimension of everyday aesthetics (Ch. 5).

DEFENCES:

2. Haapala, Arto (2005). "On the Aesthetics of the Everyday: Familiarity, Strange-ness, and the Meaning of Place," in *The Aesthetics of Everyday Life*, Andrew Light and Jonathan M. Smith (eds.). New York: Columbia University Press, 39–55.

   Inspired by Heidegger, Haapala focuses on the concept of 'place' and char-acterizes everyday aesthetics in terms of familiarity and strangeness. Because new environments are strange, we pay particular attention to their every feature, including every thing's aesthetic potential. Familiar environments, by contrast, recede into the background of our everyday awareness.

3. Leddy, Thomas (2005). "The Nature of Everyday Aesthetics," in *The Aesthet-ics of Everyday Life*, Andrew Light and Jonathan M. Smith (eds.). New York: Columbia University Press, 3–22.

   Leddy highlights the connection between everyday and environmental aesthetics and argues that everyday aesthetics is concerned with aesthetic properties as *experiences*, rather than as properties of objects. He argues that aesthetic terms do not supervene on non-aesthetic terms; whenever a puta-tively non-aesthetic term figures in an aesthetic judgement or explanation, it just is an aesthetic term—it becomes aesthetic because of its relations to other features of the work.

4. Irvin, Sherri (2008). The Pervasiveness of the Aesthetic in Ordinary Experi-ence. *British Journal of Aesthetics* 48 (1): 29–44.

   Drawing from Dewey, Irvin argues that our everyday lives are pervaded with an aesthetic character that we don't ordinarily notice. Against Dewey, how-ever, she argues that many of these experiences are quite simple, do not pres-ent as unified sensory wholes, are characterized by a fragmentary awareness, and do not afford much closure. Paying closer attention to everyday aesthetic experiences can help us to strike a better balance between our aesthetic preferences and our moral values.

CRITIQUES:

5. Forsey, Jane (2014). The Promise, the Challenge, of Everyday Aesthetics. *Aisthesis* 7 (1): 5–21.

   Forsey argues that there is a problematic tension at the heart of everyday aesthetics between expanding the range of objects subject to traditional aes-thetic attention and rethinking our understanding of aesthetic engagement in light of everyday objects and experiences. She argues that, as formulated, everyday aesthetics struggles to explain what makes ordinary pleasures spe-cifically *aesthetic*. She suggests focusing on function rather than interpretation.

6. Davies, David (2015). Sibley and the Limits of Everyday Aesthetics. *Journal of Aesthetic Education* 49 (3): 50–65.

   Davies argues that the typical characterization of everyday aesthetics risks being unable to distinguish between the aesthetic and non-aesthetic characters of the everyday things we engage with pleasurably. Drawing from Sibley, he argues that we can take an aesthetic interest in the everyday and become aware of its aesthetic character, but that this kind of attention and awareness must be consciously directed.

7. Archer, Alfred and Lauren Ware (2018). Beyond the Call of Beauty: Everyday Aesthetic Demands Under Patriarchy. *The Monist* (101): 114–27.
Archer and Ware argue for the existence of everyday aesthetic demands independent of moral obligations. That there is distinctively aesthetic disapproval suggests that we feel aesthetic obligations. But, they argue, there is a gendered imbalance in everyday aesthetic demands, and moreover we often mistake the scope of these obligations, conflating supererogatory demands with universal requirements, thus contributing to gendered oppression.

FURTHER READING:

8. Dewey, John (1934). *Art as Experience*. London: George Allen & Unwin.
In this precursor to everyday aesthetics, Dewey argues (especially in Ch. 3) that 'the aesthetic' is a property of experiences, not of objects. This capacity for aesthetic experiences is grounded in basic perceptual and emotional processes which we share with other animals and use in our everyday lives. As a result, we can have aesthetic experiences in our daily lives, absent art. Aesthetic experiences are distinguished by their complexity, unity, and sense of closure or fulfilment when they end.

9. Hick, Darren Hudson (2019). Using Things as Art. *Grazer Philosophische Studien* 96 (1): 56–80.
Hick explores the possibility of using ordinary things *as* art without believing them to be art (and without their actually *being* art). This entails taking objects from the background of our lives and placing them in the foreground, where they become subjects of focused attention and engagement. The ordinary thus becomes extraordinary.

10. Saito, Yuriko (2021). "Aesthetics of the Everyday," in *The Stanford Encyclopedia of Philosophy* (Spring 2021 Edition), Edward N. Zalta (ed.). URL = <https://plato.stanford.edu/archives/spr2021/entries/aesthetics-of-everyday/>
Saito offers a survey of the recent history of everyday aesthetics and of the many different directions in which it has branched.

PART IV

APPRECIATION AND INTERPRETATION

GENERAL BACKGROUND

Most of our ordinary talk about artworks concerns issues of appreciation and interpretation, which often go hand in hand. We like to ask what an artwork is *about* or what it *means*—for example, we might say that the novel *Jurassic Park* (1990) is about the unpredictability of complex systems like nature and evolution, whereas the film (1993) is about disturbing the proper course of nature.[1] We often disagree in our interpretations, and these disagreements colour our appreciation of the work in question: if you think Robert Eggers's *The VVitch* (2015) is about female empowerment, you're likely to view it differently than if you think it's about misogyny and oppression, and likewise you'll feel differently about it if you think it *is* misogynistic and oppressive.

Part III dealt in large measure with the core intuition that aesthetic judgements are somehow special and tied to *beauty*. Several of the cases grouped together in this section tackle the further intuition that aesthetic value is intimately tied to *pleasure*. It's common to think that we seek out aesthetic experiences because we enjoy them, but we also seem to enjoy characteristically *negative* emotions in art. After all, there's something strange about characterizing our enjoyment

DOI: 10.4324/9781003368205-34

of tragedies, gore, or cringe comedy as pleasurable, since these are straightforwardly *un*pleasant things. More generally, these ten cases point to different aspects of our appreciative and interpretative practices, from the influence of authorial intent or context of presentation to the possibility of judging without seeing and our attributions of profundity or expressiveness to non-propositional arts like music.

NOTE

1 Those were Stephen Jay Gould's interpretations, anyway—see "Dinomania," in *Dinosaur in a Haystack: Reflections In Natural History*. New York: Harmony Books (1995), 221–37.

PINNY THE WHO?
(INTERPRETATION)

CASE

Somebody is writing a children's book called *Pinny the Who?* (and it's not at all derivative!). Their target audience is about eight—the *Goosebumps* demographic, if you will. Suppose, however, that owing to their inexperience our author vastly overestimates the average eight-year-old's vocabulary. Instead of sticking to words like *bought, brought, everything, thought, through,* and *wrong,* they've peppered the text with the likes of *abhor, chasm, complement, forsake, haughty, illicit,* and—get this—*rachitic.* As a result, the work's intended audience frequently misunderstands the author's meaning: *The Tyrannosaurus's haughty attitude was complemented by acute rachitism* is taken to mean something more like *The hot Tyrannosaurus was complimented by cute ratchets.*

Surely we would say that the children have misunderstood the story, just as surely as my seven-year-old self misunderstood events in *The Hardy Boys* when, under the nefarious influence of cartoons, he mistook "framing" to mean *to smash a painting over someone's head.* It was a mistake, not unlike those made by the university students who thought that an *aerosol* was an *arrow cell,* or that Michelangelo painted *The Sixteen Chapels* (true stories!). Given their skills and experience,

DOI: 10.4324/9781003368205-35

the children above think that the author is saying one thing when in fact they're saying quite another.

If that sounds right to you, then it suggests that the meaning of a text is publicly available, rather than determined by what authors or individual audience members believe it to be. The broader issue here, then, is how we should go about fixing the interpretation of artworks: should we defer to the author's intentions, the work itself, or to some other standard?

RESPONSES

There are three main positions in this debate: anti-intentionalism, actual intentionalism, and hypothetical intentionalism (see Lin 2018 for a detailed overview).

We have already had a glimpse of *anti-intentionalism*, which maintains that an artwork's meaning must be publicly available, and that appeals to the artist's intended meaning are therefore illegitimate (Beardsley 1982). This is not to say that intention is irrelevant—art-making is by definition an intentional activity (see *Apelles's Horses* and *The Whale and the Driftwood*)—but rather that the final product just is what it is. Artists can be wrong about their achievements: I might have intended my sculpture to be a unicorn, might even genuinely believe that it represents one, but if it looks for all the world like a narwhal, then that's what it is. Actions speak louder than intentions: if my intention is successfully realized in the work, then it's plain to see in it; but if it isn't, appealing to my intention isn't enough to transform a whale into an equine. Similarly, if someone refers to you using a racist slur, while it may be of some comfort to learn that they intended it as a compliment or a neutral term, what they actually *said* is nothing of the sort.

The difficulty, however, is that once we concede that context can affect an artistic utterance's content, it seems like the same kind of consideration can be mobilized in favour of facts about the utterer, including their intentions (Stecker 1987). Such facts seem to play a role in determining the character of the utterance, such as whether it's a painting or a sculpture, representational or not, prose or poem, ironic or sincere, etc. (but see Beardsley 1982 for an anti-intentionalist solution to this problem).

Actual intentionalism, by contrast, is perhaps the most popular view in this debate, and it maintains that interpretation should pay attention to the artist's intentions. According to one version of the thesis, the meaning of a work is always ambiguous between several possibilities its content supports, so we must appeal to the author's intentions to discover which of these possibilities is correct (Hirsch 1992). Authorial intent gives us a compelling normative principle for discovering a work's meaning; the alternative is chaos, since every critic will have their own plausible interpretation. The result would be an enormous proliferation of interpretations, with no independent means of resolving disagreements. Indeed, it seems like our critical interest in contextual information is driven by a background interest in the author and their intentions in the first place (Stecker 1987).

Other intentionalists take their cue from the verbal and non-verbal world around us, where we constantly refer to someone's intentions to parse their meaning (Carroll 1992): if you tell me that you went to the bank, for example, I have to figure out whether you mean the river bank or the money bank, and it's your intention that determines which sense of 'bank' is operative. Similarly, when Marina Abramović calls a video installation of herself scrubbing a skeleton *Cleaning the Mirror* (1995), I have to figure out what she's intending to communicate to her audience. The suggestion, then, is that our engagement with art involves *communicative* as well as aesthetic (or hedonic) interests; interpretation is a kind of conversation with the work's author, and in any conversation, we want to be sure to ascertain the speaker's intended meaning. In doing so, we're aiming to foster a sense of *community* centred around the work (see also *The Uniform World*).

Finally, the position that has come to be known as *hypothetical intentionalism* finds a midway point between anti-intentionalism and actual intentionalism: a work's meaning is determined by our best hypothesis, as a suitably informed audience, about what the artist intended to convey (Tolhurst 1979, Nehamas 1981, Levinson 2002). Since we do not usually have access to artists themselves, however, or to hard evidence of their intentions (beyond the work itself), we must make do with a postulated or hypothesized author instead (but see Stecker 1987 for reasons to abandon the postulated author for the historical author). This hypothetical author must be a historically plausible character, however (Nehamas 1981). After all, we shouldn't find our-selves attributing to Shakespeare contemporary beliefs about chemis-try or quantum physics, or about dinosaurs and evolution!

Early versions of hypothetical intentionalism (e.g., Tolhurst 1979) suggested that the relevant audience is determined by the audience intended for the work by its author, so that interpreting a work requires us to put ourselves in the shoes of the intended audience and adopt the same kinds of background beliefs and attitudes. The smaller the intended audience, however, the less public a work's mean-ing; to resolve this problem, later versions of hypothetical intention-alism (e.g., Levinson 2002) appeal instead to an *idealized* audience. All versions of hypothetical intentionalism maintain that authors do not have privileged access to the meaning of their works. That meaning is publicly available in the form of the utterance before us; their inten-tions, however, *do* usually determine the *categories* to which the work belongs (Levinson 2002; see also *Guernicas*).

Notice, however, that hypothetical intentionalism appeals to our *best* hypothesis about the author's utterance meaning. This has led some to argue that hypothetical intentionalism is, at bottom, a *value maximizing* theory and, thus, closer to the anti-intentionalist end of the spectrum (Davies 2007). The value maximizing theory (also called 'conventionalism') holds that a work should be interpreted in ways that maximize its value as a work in the relevant art-kind. This is not to say that there is only ever a single best interpretation: works typi-cally support multiple interpretations, especially as they pass into the public domain and become subjects of subsequent history. And artists, of course, can be mistaken about the meaning of their utterances.

A work's identity is initially fixed by the artist's intentions and the context of its utterance, but cultural contexts change over time, and such changes can affect the work's meaning and identity (such as, e.g., when works are removed from their original contexts and dis-played in galleries and museums—see *The Problem of Museum Skepti-cism*). Indeed, the phenomenon of "aberrant influence" (Feagin 2002), which happens when a second artist is inspired by something they see in a pre-existing artwork that its creator didn't intend, is wide-spread and suggests that a work can support multiple incompatible interpretations. We should perhaps expect as much, since so much of the significance of art is retroactive, the result of subsequent cultural developments and influence, including general literacy and the development of artworld institutions and critical practices (Feagin 2002).

SUGGESTED READING

SEMINAL PRESENTATION:

1. Beardsley, Monroe C. (1982). "Intentions and Interpretations: A Fallacy Revived," in *The Aesthetic Point of View*, Michael J. Wreen and Donald M. Callan (eds.). Ithaca, NY: Cornell University Press, 188–207.

   Beardsley refines the position he and William K. Wimsatt took in *The Intentional Fallacy* (1946), arguing that the author's intentions are not relevant to determining textual meaning. We must appeal to intentions to determine what actions an author *performs*, but what those actions *represent* is entirely in the public sphere.

DEFENCES:

2. Davies, Stephen (2007). *Philosophical Perspectives On Art*. Oxford: Oxford University Press.

   Davies argues in Part II (especially Chs. 10 and 11) that the aim of interpretation is to maximize the aesthetic value of the work in question, subject to the constraints imposed by its contexts of creation and evaluation, and by the conventions of the relevant artistic practices. The result is a critical pluralism (which Davies sees as primitive): each work can support many aesthetically good interpretations. Hypothetical intentionalism, he argues, reduces to value-maximization.

CRITIQUES:

3. Tolhurst, William E. (1979). On What a Text is and How it Means. *British Journal of Aesthetics* 19 (1): 3–14.

   Tolhurst proposes an early variation of what is now called hypothetical intentionalism, according to which a work's meaning is determined by what its intended audience (understood as an ideally-situated and informed audience) takes to be the best hypothesis about the artist's intended meaning.

4. Carroll, Noël (1992). "Art, Intention, and Conversation," in *Intention & Interpretation*, Gary Iseminger (ed.). Philadelphia: Temple University Press, 97–131.

   Carroll argues for a conversational account of interpretation, according to which engaging with art is a conversational encounter with its creator. Just as a genuine conversation requires us to do what we can to understand our interlocutor's meaning, so we have a conversational interest in pursuing the aesthetically-best interpretation possible that is consistent with our best hypotheses about the author's intentions.

5. Hirsch, Eric Donald (1992). "In Defense of the Author," in *Intention & Interpretation*, Gary Iseminger (ed.). Philadelphia: Temple University Press, 11–23.
Hirsch defends actual intentionalism, the view that we *must* appeal to the author's intentions to figure out what their work means. Any work will have multiple possible meanings; it will be necessarily ambiguous. We can only narrow the field of possible meanings down by appealing to the author's intentions. To fail to do so is to vest individual critics with the power to determine meaning and, thus, to proliferate a work's meanings.

6. Levinson, Jerrold (2002). "Hypothetical Intentionalism: Statement, Objections, and Replies," in *On the Single Right Interpretation*, Michael Krausz (ed.). University Park: Pennsylvania State University Press, 309–18.
Levinson explains and defends hypothetical intentionalism, the view that literary works are public utterances made by culturally- and historically-situated authors. Their meaning is therefore a kind of utterance meaning, rather than textual or intended meaning, understood as what an appropriately situated audience would most reasonably take the speaker to be saying.

FURTHER READING:

7. Nehamas, Alexander (1981). The Postulated Author: Critical Monism as a Regulative Ideal. *Critical Inquiry* 8 (1): 133–49.
Nehamas argues for what would now be recognized as hypothetical intentionalism (he calls it 'critical monism'). Interpretation requires us to place the text in a context that accounts for as many of its visible features as possible, and to see it as the product of an author's intentional action. It requires us to see it as the product of a historically plausible postulated author.

8. Stecker, Robert (1987). Apparent, Implied, and Postulated Authors. *Philosophy and Literature* 11 (2): 258–71.
Stecker tackles the notion of a hypothetical author whose intentions we try to discern in interpretation, arguing that any attempt to license contextual factors in interpretation also licenses appeals to the author and their intentions. Although sympathetic to intentionalism, Stecker thinks that interpretation can have many different goals and need not yield one, and only one, correct interpretation of a work.

9. Feagin, Susan (2002). "Tossed Salad: Ontology and Identity," in *Is There A Single Right Interpretation?* Michael Krausz (ed.). University Park: Pennsylvania State University Press, 360–80.
Feagin argues that visual artworks can gain or lose meanings over time, as their place in a culture changes or as they enter into new cultural contexts. Irrespective of the artist's intentions, culture and history can change not just the interpretation, but even the ontology of an artwork if the work has a

cultural significance the artist doesn't know or understand, or insofar as it's embedded in a system of practices identified at the cultural, rather than the individual, level.

10. Lin, Szu-Yen (2018). Art and Interpretation. *The Internet Encyclopedia of Philosophy*. https://iep.utm.edu/art-and-interpretation/#:~:text=A%20 compromise%20between%20actual%20intentionalism, made%20by%20 a%20selected%20audience.

Lin surveys the literature on the interpretation of art, with a particular focus on interpreting literature. He argues that contemporary approaches are dominated by a commitment to contextualism, and shows that, under the influence of the philosophy of language (especially Grice's work on meaning and implicature) intentionalism remains the most popular solution.

THE PARADOX OF DISGUST

CASE

It's widely agreed that disgust is an emotion that's universally rec-ognized in human cultures: it's a 'basic emotion'. Unlike other basic emotions such as anger, sadness, or fear, however, it's often thought that disgust is 'transparent' (c.f. *Dinosaurs in the Jungle*)—that is, that things which are disgusting in real life are also disgusting when repre-sented in art.[1] A painting of rotting meat, then, is disgusting because real-life rotting meat is disgusting; or, on a stronger formulation, the painting of rotting meat is every bit as disgusting as real rotting meat.

The *paradox of disgust* hinges on this transparency: it concerns the fact that people seem to have *positive* emotional experiences of works with disgusting content. But if the transparency thesis is true, then disgusting content should produce an immediate and *un*pleasant phys-iological reaction. It's obviously true, however, that we sometimes do have some sort of positive reaction to disgusting art, since works like Damien Hirst's *A Thousand Years* (1990) or Gaspar Noé's *Irréversible* (2002) have enjoyed great critical acclaim. The question, then, is how it's possible for us to enjoy such a bad feeling.

Structurally, the paradox of disgust is very similar to the *Paradox of Tragedy*, which asks how and why we like sad narratives, given that

DOI: 10.4324/9781003368205-36

sadness is an unpleasant emotion. Both might be said to be species of a more general paradox of aversion, which captures the phenomenon of having positive reactions to unpleasant artistic content. All of our negatively valenced emotions are aversions of some sort and thus invite a similar paradox.

It is worthwhile considering the paradoxes of tragedy and disgust separately, however, because they draw our attention to distinct features of the cases. The paradox of tragedy draws our attention to fictionality and the *distance* it creates between us and the object of our emotions; the paradox of disgust, on the other hand, draws our attention to disgust's transparency and the *closeness* it creates between us and the object of our aversion.

Disgust is sometimes thought to be unique among our emotional reactions in the degree of its transparency: disgusting representations are said to be every bit as disgusting as the real thing (Korsmeyer 2010). If that's true, then it suggests that disgust-elicitors put us into closer contact with an artwork's representations than the elicitors of other strong emotions, such as fear, pity, or sadness. It is also sometimes thought that disgust is unique in its conceptual focus on contamination (rather than, e.g., danger), which suggests a strong imaginative association.

RESPONSES

Not everyone has accepted the paradox's framing conditions. Some, for instance, have argued that the paradox is predicated on a fallacy: in asking how and why we enjoy unpleasant or 'painful' art, we are begging the question by assuming that we *do*, in fact enjoy it (Smuts 2009). Whether we do so seems like an empirical question, after all (for a survey of recent empirical results, see Strohminger 2014). In particular, we should not assume that people are motivated exclusively by pleasure, since we often act against pleasure but out of a sense of duty, for example, or anger, compassion, honour, love, retribution, spite, etc. (just think of heroic sacrifices or vengeance pursued to the utmost). If we recognize that people are motivationally complex, then the paradox disappears entirely, although questions remain about what our motivations are and why we prefer painful art to its real-life counterparts.

Also at issue is whether disgust is transparent in the first place. It is unclear, first, that disgust is particularly unique among strong emotions in its apparent transparency—fear or pity, for example, seem equally transparent (consider *The Paradox of Fiction*). But also, much of the empirical evidence suggests that disgust is not just sensory, but also—perhaps even primarily—*ideational*: it concerns how we *imagine* the object of disgust in relation to ourselves (Contesi 2016). Although a picture of a cookie touched by a maggot is disgusting, it's not obvious that it's every bit as disgusting as an actual cookie placed before you with a maggot writhing on it.

For those who have accepted its framing conditions, solutions to the paradox have tended to mirror those offered to *The Paradox of Tragedy* and can be usefully divided into those which posit competing emotions, one of which (pleasure) overcomes the other (disgust), and those which posit that the unpleasantness of disgust is somehow integral to the pleasurable experience of the work. Solutions of the first kind are called 'co-existentialist', and those of the second 'integrationist' (Iseminger 1983). On both the co-existentialist and the integrationist models, philosophers have attributed a great deal of value to a sense of distance from, or of control over, the encounter with the object of disgust.

On the co-existentialist side, we find broadly Humean approaches to the paradox. These are sometimes called 'conversion' theories because Hume's thought was that the artwork converts our disgust into pleasure—although whether he meant outright pleasure or overall pleasure is a matter of some debate. At least some commentators, however, have argued that we should understand Hume as suggesting that there are degrees of conversion, so that sometimes the entire feeling of disgust is converted to pleasure, whereas sometimes only some of it is (Dadlez 2016). Something like this full conversion might be at work, for example, in our experience of cringe comedies like *The Office* (BBC Two 2001–3), *Peep Show* (Channel 4 2003–15), or *Curb Your Enthusiasm* (HBO 2000-present): the social awkwardness is deeply painful, but we laugh through our fingers (or, in my case, with my head in my shirt). Such experiences might also fall under the category of 'benign masochism', safely enjoyable pain (Strohminger 2014).

But if our reactions of disgust are visceral, automatic, and sensory, as some have argued (Korsmeyer 2010, Robinson 2014), then it is difficult to see how they could ever be pleasant in and of themselves. One way of explaining it is to appeal to a special aesthetic category which is rooted in a particular kind of feeling of disgust. 'Aesthetic disgust', it has been suggested, is the kind of disgust which we feel in experiences of the 'sublate' (Korsmeyer 2010). The sublate is like an anti-sublime: whereas the sublime converts feelings of abject *terror* into aesthetic *delight*, the sublate converts aesthetic disgust into insight. What is converted, then, is not so much the emotion itself—the disgust is still present—but rather its capacity: skilled artistry enables disgust to signify in particular ways, to highlight certain features of our aesthetic experience, so that it does more than merely disgust us.

On the integrationist side of things, philosophers tend to explain disgust's contributions to aesthetic appreciation as indirect. It isn't the disgust as such that we enjoy, but rather the disgusting objects viewed as humorous, or terrifying, or interesting, etc. (Robinson 2014). The disgusting is thus an integral part of our aesthetic appreciation because it is the object of our appreciative interest, and triggers our more pleasing reflections. Something like this may be at work, for example, for the women who report entirely positive experiences of Jenny Saville's paintings of large, fleshy, and veined women. Although their visceral reactions may be displeasing (and to be clear, it's not obvious that this is universally the case), the paintings afford (especially female) audiences an opportunity to reflect critically on that reaction, and on the culturally-determined standards of beauty which underpin it, as well as the pervasive social association of disgust with the feminine. The disgust, then, acts as a source of social and political insight which audiences can use to valorize non-idealized feminine beauty (Meagher 2003; see also Dadlez 2016). The disgusting thus contributes to a positive experience of the work as a whole.

The role of negative affect in general, and of disgust in particular, has also been considered in environmental aesthetics, where it has been observed that a great deal of nature is not, in fact, particularly pleasant (Rolston 1988). Not all landscapes are equally scenic, of course, and what counts as 'scenic' in the first place reflects culture to a great extent. But also, any picture of a landscape will include myriad individual dead and dying things, even if they aren't all readily apparent. Indeed, it's not uncommon for outdoor enthusiasts to come across rotting corpses or scattered bones. These individual objects are clearly not pleasant; they may even be revolting. A popular response, however, is that our proper aesthetic and appreciative focus should be the ecosystem as a whole: although the rotting elk carcass is individually disgusting, considered holistically it is part of a beautiful ecosystem, since its decomposition offers the raw materials for new life and flourishing. The trick, then, is to move past our individual or species-level gut reactions to consider the unpleasant from a broader perspective in which that ugliness is integrated into a complex and beautiful whole (Rolston 1988).

The virtue of this approach is that it sees us overcoming our selfish and anthropocentric tendency to view nature as a (visual) resource for entertainment, and to recognize it and appreciate it on its own terms (Saito 1998). The difficulty, however, is that in doing so we lose sight of just what our aesthetic object is supposed to be: is it the carcass, the forest, or perhaps the planet's entire ecosphere? The broader the perspective we take on the carcass, the more our actual perceptual experience drops out of the picture. Likewise, we should be wary of the division fallacy: the thesis that the beauty of the whole entails the beauty of its individual parts. Rather than seeing all nature as unambiguously aesthetically positive, perhaps instead we should acknowledge that nature's ugliness can sometimes be overwhelming, but that its aesthetic appreciation is helped by distancing effects (see *The Jealous Husband*) and by consideration of the scientific story that individually ugly elements are telling us (Saito 1998; see also *Faking Nature*).

SUGGESTED READING

SEMINAL PRESENTATION:

1. Korsmeyer, Carolyn (2010). *Savoring Disgust: The Foul and the Fair in Aesthetics*. New York: Oxford University Press.
   In Chs. 1–4, Korsmeyer argues that disgust is just as sensitive to imagined as to real content. The mere perception of sensory features which characteristically elicit disgust, she argues, suffices to elicit disgust, regardless of whether the elicitor is actually present or merely represented. She argues for the existence of a special feeling of disgust called 'aesthetic disgust', which informs the new aesthetic category of the 'sublate'.

DEFENCES:

2. Dadlez, Eva M. (2016). A Humean Approach to the Problem of Disgust and Aesthetic Appreciation. *Essays in Philosophy* 17 (1): 55–67.

   Dadlez thinks that a Humean conversion theory can account for the aesthetic value of disgust, particularly as an intensifier of aesthetic experiences. She argues that we should understand Hume's conversion theory as allowing degrees of conversion or transformation: sometimes the entire feeling of disgust is converted to pleasure, but sometimes only part of it is. Arousing disgust can help to drive social and political insights, including disgust's long association with the feminine.

CRITIQUES:

3. Robinson, Jenefer (2014). Aesthetic Disgust? *Royal Institute of Philosophy Supplement* 75: 51–84.

   Robinson surveys scientific and social scientific work on the physiology and origins of disgust. Although she embraces disgust's transparency, she argues that experiences of disgust cannot, in themselves, be sources of pleasure or be converted into them. Like other negative emotions, disgust's contributions to aesthetic appreciation are indirect. Feelings of disgust are the same in both life and art.

4. Contesi, Filippo (2016). Disgust's Transparency. *British Journal of Aesthetics* 56 (4): 347–54.

   Contesi argues that both strong (representations are *as* disgusting as the real thing) and weak (representations are disgusting *if* the real thing is) readings of the transparency thesis are implausible. He argues that empirical evidence suggests that disgust is primarily ideational rather than sensory and, thus, is directed at the subject of representation and elicited by our imaginative capacities—just like other strong emotions, such as fear or pity.

FURTHER READING:

5. Iseminger, Gary (1983). How Strange a Sadness. *Journal of Aesthetics and Art Criticism* 42 (1). 81–2.

   In this brief reply to Eaton's control theory (see *The Paradox of Tragedy*), Iseminger usefully distinguishes between solutions to the paradox. Co-existentialist solutions posit the co-existence of competing emotions (viz. disgust and pleasure), one of which overpowers the other. Integrationist solutions, by contrast, maintain that the unpleasantness we feel can somehow contribute to the pleasure we take in the work.

6. Rolston, Holmes III (1988). *Environmental Ethics: Duties to and Values in the Natural World*. Philadelphia, PA: Temple University Press.

   In Ch. 6, Rolston considers the aesthetics of nature. Ruminating on the imaginary elk carcass, he argues that any natural scene is filled with unpleasant discrete elements. Taken as such, the experience is unpleasant; but our proper aesthetic focus should be holistic, centred on its role in the ecosystem, which reveals the beautiful whole.

7. Saito, Yuriko (1998). The Aesthetics of Unscenic Nature. *Journal of Aesthetics and Art Criticism* 56 (2): 101–11.

   Saito argues that not everything in nature is aesthetically positive: some ugliness can overwhelm our senses. But distancing effects can help us to overcome our negative initial reactions and to recognize (thanks to natural history and science) that nature's story-telling power is always aesthetically positive. Aesthetically appreciating nature means backtracking the scientific story to the sensuous.

8. Meagher, Michelle (2003). Jenny Saville and a Feminist Aesthetics of Disgust. *Hypatia* 18 (4): 23–41.

   Meagher argues that although disgusted responses are predicated on an innate bodily reaction, the objects of disgust are often culturally or socially determined, especially in the domain of aesthetics (where it concerns the appearance and depiction of women, in particular). The physical shock of disgust offers us an opportunity to interrogate the origins of our bodily response, and to consider the social constraints and obligations that may be involved.

9. Smuts, Aaron (2009). Art and Negative Affect. *Philosophy Compass* 4 (1): 39–55.

   Smuts surveys the literature on what he calls the 'paradox of painful art', arguing that it has tended to focus on a motivational reading that begs the question: the issue is not *why* we enjoy painful art, but *whether* we enjoy it in the first place. Since humans are not exclusively motivated by pleasure (motivational hedonism), there is no real paradox here.

10. Strohminger, Nina (2014). Disgust Talked About. *Philosophy Compass* 9 (7): 478–93.

    Strohminger surveys scientific and social scientific work on disgust, focusing on contemporary developments. In particular, she observes that disgust seems to fix our attention on certain objects and even amplify our enjoyment in some contexts, rather than repelling us entirely. One suggested explanation is that we can experience disgust as a 'benign masochism': we can enjoy unpleasant things as novelties so long as they are safe (benign).

NOTE

1 Whether disgust really is unique in this way is another matter.

33

THE PARADOX OF FICTION

CASE

When he was 17 or 18, one of my stepbrothers saw *The Ring* (Gore Verbinski's 2002 remake of Hideo Nakata's 1998 Japanese original, *Ringu*). I'm not entirely sure why he saw it—horror isn't really his thing. I wasn't there, but what I *am* sure of is that he didn't think any part of it was real. Nevertheless, for the next couple of years he covered the television in his bedroom with a blanket, just in case. He was *terrified* that Samara's vengeful spirit might crawl out of the TV and murder him.

On the one hand, my stepbrother's reaction is clearly silly—if I'm being honest, we teased him mercilessly over it.[1] After all, *The Ring* is only a movie; it's not real. There's no such thing as ghosts, let alone Samara: she's a fictional character, made up out of whole cloth. But it's also a perfectly common reaction—who among us *doesn't* check the back seat for knife-wielding psychos before driving? Who *hasn't* worried about a creak outside their room at night,[2] a thump in the closet,[3] or a monster under the bed?[4] But, again, let's be clear: these are unfounded worries, because they're centred on things that don't exist (viz., psychos hiding in the car; boggarts in the closet; monsters under the bed). In this respect, the situation seems analogous to one

DOI: 10.4324/9781003368205-37

in which you tell me that something terrible happened to you when you were a child, only to later tell me that nothing of the sort ever happened. It would be weird and irrational for me to still be upset on your behalf once I know that I have no cause to be upset (see also *The Paradox of Tragedy* and cf. *The Paradox of Disgust*).

But now consider the kinds of feelings we have about other non-existent things, such as fictional characters. It doesn't seem particularly silly of me to say that I felt sorry for Asmodean in *The Wheel of Time* (1990–2013), that I was terrified for Damaya in *The Fifth Season* (2015), that I was upset about Anna's treatment in *Downton Abbey* (2010–5), or that I can't stand the character of Tim Fleming in *Heartland* (2007-present). In fact, this kind of emotional engagement with fiction seems both perfectly commonplace and entirely *desirable*. But fictional characters don't exist, so why is it silly for someone to be afraid *of* them in the real world, but not to feel sorry *for* them (see also *The Parable of the Pawn*)?

The tensions at work here are commonly called the *paradox of fiction*. The core idea behind this paradox is that we seem committed to three propositions, not all of which can be true at the same time:

1) We have emotional responses to fiction (whether characters, situations, events, etc.).
2) We don't believe that fictional things exist.
3) To have an emotion towards something requires us to first believe that it exists.

Each proposition seems independently plausible, but when we look at them in the cold light of day, it's clear that they aren't all mutually compatible.

Calling it *one* paradox may be a bit of misnomer, however. There may well be a significant difference between being scared by a horror film—a terror that affects us and our behaviour *outside* the fiction, in real life—and worrying about a character, feeling sad about their demise or misfortunes, etc. Although the two puzzles are often treated together, it may be worth keeping the distinction in mind.

Similarly, there may be a significant difference between the irrationality puzzle and the full-on paradox of how it's possible to have these reactions, given our beliefs. It's clearly *irrational* to be worried about the fate of someone who doesn't exist—just as it's irrational to have a phobia of quicksand or peanut butter sticking to the roof of your mouth—but we know that it's perfectly *possible* to do so, since we do it all the time (and, indeed, people genuinely have phobias, no matter how irrational they seem; c.f. also *The Gamer's Dilemma*). There is a normative puzzle here, which is that we seem to routinely engage in behaviour that, upon reflection, seems irrational (but which is entirely normal and desirable from the reader's perspective). The challenge, then, is to explain why it is that our emotional engagement with fiction isn't just irrational, given that we would so describe parallel situations concerning real life. The full paradox comes in when we endorse both the belief that we have genuine emotional responses to fiction and the belief that it is only possible to have genuine emotional responses to extant entities. In that case, the challenge is to explain whether and how genuine emotional responses to fiction are even possible in the first place.

RESPONSES

One obvious response is simply to accept that our engagement with fiction is irrational (e.g., Radford 1975). Most philosophers tackling the problem, however, have tried to show that we *aren't* irrational; that our emotional engagement with fiction is perfectly rational. One way of doing so is to deny the first proposition. This is the kind of strategy famously employed by Walton (1978), who argues that what we feel towards fiction is not genuine emotion, but rather quasi-emotion: we are *making-believe* that we feel real fear for Damaya or genuine sympathy for Asmodean.

Alternately, we could deny the second proposition, perhaps either by accepting that fictional entities are real (in some suitably adjusted sense of 'real') or by arguing that when we consume fiction we *temporarily* believe in their existence. Both these claims seem somewhat dubious, however: fictions aren't real (that's the point), and we clearly don't forget that fact since we don't try to save Anna Karenina or warn Othello about Iago's machinations. But perhaps something in their vicinity is true: perhaps it makes a difference that we recognize that certain events, the fates of fictional characters, etc. *are true in the world of the story* (Langland-Hassan 2020). In that case, so the argument goes, we have good reason to respond the way we do so long as the things we're responding to are true in the story. Similarly, my stepbrother would have had good reason to be afraid of Samara coming to get him *if The Ring were a true story*; but it isn't, so he didn't. It's precisely because we recognize that fiction *isn't* real that our responses are appropriate (i.e., we don't take appropriate real-life steps to deal with the situation), rather than an obstacle to understanding them. In other words, the point is that we don't all of a sudden discover that the objects of our emotional responses don't exist; we knew it all along, and took those objects to be fictional characters and events (see also *The Jealous Husband*).

Finally, the most popular approach to dissolving the paradox has been to deny the third proposition and argue that emotional responses do not, in fact, require us to believe the relevant entities exist. These approaches can be roughly divided into two further camps: those who take themselves to be tackling a metaphysical reading of the third proposition, and those who take themselves to be answering a normative reading.

On the metaphysical reading of the proposition, genuine emotional responses can only be had towards extant objects and events, so it's ontologically problematic that when we react to fiction we're reacting to something that doesn't exist. In order to dispel the problem, philosophers have taken to showing that we *can* have emotional responses to nonexistents, including towards a thought we imagine, or towards *possible* people or states of affairs (e.g., Lamarque 1981, Gendler and Kovakovich 2005, Robinson 2005, Dadlez and Haramia 2015). In other words, our reactions to fiction depend on the same mental wiring as our emotional responses to real things, and this wiring permits us to anticipate or adapt to possible future situations. We can't help our responses to fiction, and that's an evolutionarily good thing.

On the normative reading, our reactions to fiction are irrational in the same way that arachibutyrophobia is irrational: it's not that we *can't* be afraid of peanut butter sticking to the roof of our mouths—obviously, some people are!—but rather that we *shouldn't* be. It's a pointless fear, in much the same way that taking candy from a baby is pointless,[5] or that the cat's looking for a door into summer is pointless. In that case, we need to pay closer attention to the norms that govern our aesthetic engagement with fiction, since it is these which will determine whether our affective responses are rational and appropriate (Yanal 1994, Willard 2019, Friend 2020). And when we do that, we can't help but recognize that it would be profoundly weird for us not to love and admire some characters, to fret about or loathe others, to feel profound melancholy in response to tragedy, or to mourn the death of a beloved character. After all, a horror movie that isn't scary despite its best efforts isn't much of a horror movie.

SUGGESTED READING

SEMINAL PRESENTATIONS:

1. Radford, Colin (1975). "How Can We Be Moved by the Fate of Anna Karenina?" *Aristotelian Society Supplementary Volume* 49 (1): 67–80.
   Radford first formulates the paradox and countenances a number of possible solutions to it. Ultimately, however, he concludes that our emotional responses to fiction are irrational, since their objects don't exist and we are clearly aware of that fact. He does not, contrary to some reports, deny that we have genuine emotional responses to fiction.

2. Walton, Kendall L. (1978). Fearing Fictions. *Journal of Philosophy* 75 (1): 5–27.
   Walton argues that we *make-believe* our emotional responses to fiction; what we feel are *quasi*-emotions. We make-believe the same sort of response we would have in real life, if we believed that the same events befell real people, except that we know that none of it is true. Quasi-emotions can manifest in exactly the same way as "real" emotions, but without the same connection to the belief that these things are *really* happening.

DEFENCES:

3. Yanal, Robert J. (1994). The Paradox of Emotion and Fiction. *Pacific Philosophical Quarterly* 75 (1): 54–75.
   Yanal connects Radford's and Walton's puzzles together into a single paradox. He argues that to resolve the paradox we must reject the proposition that emotional responses require a genuine object. In particular, he thinks we must take care to note that, as consumers of fiction, we are not participants; we are on the outside looking in.

CRITIQUES:

4. Lamarque, Peter (1981). How Can We Fear and Pity Fictions? *British Journal of Aesthetics* 21 (4): 291–304.

   Lamarque shifts the focus away from what we believe and to the stories themselves, concentrating his attention on the question of what it is that we are actually responding to. He argues that we are responding to something real and in the world: a thought, or mental representation, which we imagine. This is sometimes called the "thought theory".

5. Robinson, Jenefer (2005). *Deeper than Reason.* Oxford: Oxford University Press.

   Robinson argues that emotions are not essentially cognitive—they don't necessarily involve beliefs or judgements, just automatic "affective appraisals". In Ch 5 she argues that our affective appraisals of fiction precede any judgements about whether a character is real, and are thus perfectly emotionally rational, since they promote similar responses in the real world.

6. Langland-Hassan, Peter (2020). *Explaining Imagination.* Oxford: Oxford University Press.

   In Ch. 11, Langland-Hassan argues that our emotional responses to fiction are generated by a combination of what we take to be true in the story plus what we *want* to be true; in other words, by norms which govern our appreciation of fiction. What matters, from the perspective of rationalizing our emotional reactions, is that something happens *in the world of the story*; that is enough to warrant our reactions.

7. Friend, Stacie (2020). Fiction and Emotion: The Puzzle of Divergent Norms. *British Journal of Aesthetics* 60 (4): 403–18.

   Friend argues that Radford has been systematically misread, and that the paradox of fiction is misconceived: the problem isn't the so-called irrationality of our emotional responses to fiction, but rather that we apply different standards of rationality depending on the context in which they are made. In fiction, our emotions aren't just sensitive to what's generally true; they're sensitive to what's true *in the story*, too.

FURTHER READING:

8. Gendler, Tamar Szabó and Karson Kovakovich (2005). "Genuine Rational Fictional Emotions," in *Contemporary Debates in Aesthetics and the Philosophy of Art*, Matthew Kieran (ed.). New York: Blackwell. 241–53.

   Gendler and Kovakovich canvas empirical work which shows that there are distinct cognitive benefits to being able to respond affectively to imagined situations. They argue that we cannot help but to respond in this way to fiction, and that's a good thing: it helps us to develop and train the relevant emotions and decision-making skills.

9. Dadlez, Eva M. and Chelsea M. Haramia (2015). Fictional Objects, Future Objectives: Why Existence Matters Less Than You Think. *Philosophy and Literature* 39 (1A): 1–15.

Dadlez and Haramia explain emotional responses in terms of our existing (general) commitments and beliefs, such that our responses to fiction are neither irrational nor imaginary. These responses, they argue, seem grounded in evaluative beliefs concerning *possible* (rather than particular) experiences— just like many of the beliefs and responses we think we hold in daily life. We have genuine emotional responses to fiction when the particulars of the story cause us to access more general evaluative beliefs. And evaluative beliefs can elicit genuine emotions and even obligations.

10. Willard, Mary Beth (2019). Reclaiming the Paradox of Fiction. *Debates in Aesthetics* 14. http://debatesinaesthetics.org/reclaiming-the-paradox-of-fiction/. Willard argues that the existence of the object of our emotions is not a necessary precondition for those emotions. Instead, she argues that the rationality or irrationality of our response depends on our compliance with the norms that govern aesthetic engagement with the work of art.

NOTES

1 In the interest of evening the scales somewhat, I was absolutely petrified by Sam Raimi's *The Evil Dead* (1981), which I saw as a fully-grown adult. I still break out in sweat when watching films that reference it (though not the sequels, which are comedies).
2 It's a cat.
3 Also a cat.
4 A cat again. Nor am I convinced that Pseudo *isn't* both a monster *and* a murderous psycho.
5 Unless, of course, the cruelty is the point, or unless someone is preventing the baby from eating the candy (since babies shouldn't eat candy).

34

THE PARADOX OF PORTRAITURE

CASE

A picture is worth a thousand words, but are one thousand words enough to convey the essence of a person? That's the gamble a portrait makes.

The paradox of portraiture concerns the mismatch between portraiture's goals and its means of attaining those goals: it aims to capture the essence of a living subject, but must use base physical materials like paint, photo-sensitive paper and chemical emulsions, or bits and bytes to do so. In doing so, we turn a *subject*—a living person—into an *object*: a painting or photograph, to be sure, but also an object of aesthetic attention and appreciation (see also *The Paradox of Porn*). The paradox is thus more a puzzle than a paradox proper. One way to think about it is as a tension between subjectivity and objectivity, or mind and body, which reflects the debates over dualism in the philosophy of mind (Freeland 2007). Similarly, we might speak of a tension between the aims of faithful but revelatory representation of the sitter and the artist's creative expression.

Historically, however, this tension was expressed as the tension between the different representational capacities of painting and poetry (i.e., the literary arts): the medium of painting is constrained to

DOI: 10.4324/9781003368205-38

present its subjects in a single instant, whereas poetry can show us its subjects as they change over time (Guyer 2020). In other words, a portrait can only show us one small part of a person (usually the front of their face) at a single moment of the sitter's life, whereas poetry enjoys more freedom to sample from a person's countenance and life. The puzzling thing, then, is just how it is that a portrait, given so little to work with, so often succeeds in giving some insight into the character of the sitter. What do we mean when we speak of portraits as being "revelatory", as capturing the "air" of the sitter?

The puzzle becomes rather more pronounced—and approaches a paradox proper—when we consider the art of caricature. A caricature is by definition inaccurate, since it involves grossly exaggerating some of the subject's features and under-emphasizing others. Nevertheless, we can immediately identify caricatures of people whose faces we know, and their pointed use in political cartoons suggests that we think of them as a relatively powerful representational vehicle. How is it, then, that caricatures can work so well?

Portraiture did not really emerge as a distinct genre of painting until the seventeenth century, at which point it became restricted to human subjects and turned its attention from external details to trying to express the sitter's psychology. Early portraits primarily documented the patron's power and status, but in the early twentieth century, they came to feature ordinary people, too, and were destined for sale to the artworld at large, rather than reserved for the patron and his family (Freeland 2007). But what *is* a portrait, exactly?

RESPONSES

At a first pass, it seems like portraits are pictures of people. But not all pictures of people are portraits; in fact, it's common for artists to use models to stand in for someone else (e.g., Napoleon), or as a generic and non-specific human being. A common way of cashing out this difference is in terms of how much of the sitter's subjectivity is on display (Freeland 2007, Spinicci 2009, Maes 2015). The model is destined to be anonymously transparent, a tool through which the artist depicts someone else, or highlights some other feature of the work. A portrait's sitter, however, is expected to stare back out of the painting at us; we expect to see something of the person glinting behind those eyes. A portrait seems to require not just that its artist treat their sitter as a subject, but that viewers be invited to do so, as well.

That said, it seems like much the same is true of pictures of the natural world, too (or, indeed, of built environments): they aren't posed, obviously (only *com*posed!), but they very often *do* aim to communicate the essence or "air" of a place (Matthes 2020). A parallel paradox seems to attend landscape portraiture, since a landscape is such a vast area, both in terms of geographical and temporal spread, and since so many of its aesthetically-relevant properties are non-sensory. How can a single picture, focusing on a tiny portion of a landscape for just an instant of its life, possibly hope to convey the character of a place? And yet, clearly, they do: sometimes a landscape portrait succeeds in immersing us in the place, in conveying its dynamic and complex character without relying on background scientific knowledge (cf. *Guernicas*).

But how does a portrait manage to reveal something about its subject? One natural suggestion is that portraits aren't all that different from other genres of artworks in this respect and that the "paradox" of portraiture is not unique to our experience of portraits (Maynard 2007). Just as we immediately recognize that some objects are natural objects, and others are artifacts (see *The Whale and the Driftwood*), so do we immediately recognize what a portrait is: a work of art that *displays* its sitter. Armed with this important contextual cue, we naturally look for hidden meaning in the picture, so that there is no real mystery in how artists balance the demands of representation and creativity, or subjectivity and objectivity. It's immediately clear to viewers that portraits are the result of an *interaction* between artist, sitter, and audience, whereas the model largely drops out of the equation outside portraiture (Guyer 2020). The heavy lifting is all done by context; the artist just produces an object that directs us to imagine that by seeing it, we are in fact seeing its subject.

We might also wonder, however, whether there is a tension between the demand of faithfulness of representation, and the fact that so many portraits are *posed* (Guyer 2020). Posing, after all, means deliberately selecting the face we present to the world, and that face may not be representative of our character considered as a whole. If we understand the paradox as concerning how the artist can condense the whole of a life into a single still image, then posing seems to raise it anew, since the pose captures or suggests particular character traits which may be present, but not dominant, in the person as a whole. The tendency to pose thus seems to undermine a portrait's capacity to act as a vehicle for knowledge about the sitter.

On the other hand, it also seems plausible that artists can use posing as a technique to draw out deep character traits (Debaene 2021). A heavily *edited* picture might undermine the truthfulness of the portrait by introducing too great a mismatch between the surface features of the depiction vs. the reality; but posing, because it involves deliberately presenting oneself a certain way, can identify and communicate otherwise hidden character traits, often by exaggerating them.

Philosophers have not (yet) had much to say about caricature, but the genre features many close parallels to portraiture which might prove instructive. So far, we've mostly been considering realistic portraits, but a good caricature is a lot like a good portrait in that it requires us to recognize its subject and should work to say something about that person's character. But caricature is also more clearly paradoxical than portraiture since it must perform these tasks despite being a deliberately *inaccurate* representation of the subject. Caricatures are false by definition: they exaggerate or under-emphasize various aspects of the subject's physiognomy. And yet we often think they say something true about the subject.

One possibility is that caricatures are a kind of portraiture; and just as we have more and less realistic landscapes (e.g., think of Rosa Bonheur's pastoral scenes vs. Cézanne's ubiquitous mountain), caricatures are just unrealistic portraits (Ross 1974; see also Spinicci 2009). And just as we don't have to work out by careful inference who the subject of a realistic portrait is (provided they're known to us), neither do we need to work backwards to identify the subject of a caricature: we just recognize them, and the choice of misrepresentations tells us something about them (Ross 1974).

Alternately, maybe caricatures are more like visual metaphors, or visual hyperbole, in which case they should be explained in the same terms as these linguistic phenomena (Caldarola and Plebani 2016). One popular such explanation is that they do require a little work to understand: we immediately see *that* a caricature is a misrepresentation and must work to understand *why* the artist misrepresented their subject. Doing so engages us in a game of make-believe in which we take the picture as a prop so as to figure out why it is the way it is. And doing that triggers a higher-order game of make-believe in which people who are like the subject in certain respects (e.g., they are greedy) also have the same strange attributes (e.g., huge mouths filled with something valuable) (Caldarola and Plebani 2016).

The trouble is that these reflections on caricature actually *sharpen* our paradox: because caricatures are by definition misrepresentations, then to the extent that we rely on them for knowledge about someone, our beliefs are *unwarranted* (Mag Uidhir 2013). Worse, it seems like caricatures exploit audiences' pre-existing beliefs about someone, which suggests that their revelatory potential is trivial. If these observations are correct, and if caricature is a kind of portraiture, then this spells trouble for the idea that portraits are revelatory of their subjects.

SUGGESTED READING

SEMINAL PRESENTATION:

1. Freeland, Cynthia (2007). Portraits in Painting and Photography. *Philosophical Studies* 135 (1): 95–109.[1]
   Freeland observes that portrait painting turns a person—a subject—into an object—a painting. She then asks how it is that a mere object can successfully capture the essence or "air" of a living subject. She argues that portraits can "show" people by being accurate likenesses, testifying to their presence, evoking their personality, or presenting their uniqueness.

DEFENCES:

2. Maynard, Patrick (2007). Portraits As Displays. *Philosophical Studies* 135 (1): 111–21.
   Maynard posits that recognizing objects as artifacts rather than natural objects is a basic human skill, and with it comes the natural inclination to perceive the object as the result of intentional activity and ask about how it satisfies human goals and purposes. We immediately understand that portraits are *displays*, and this means that every facet of the portrait is laden with hidden meaning. There is thus nothing strange in their subjective objectification.

3. Guyer, Paul (2020). "Portraits, Persons, and Poses," in *Portraits and Philosophy*, Hans Maes (ed.). New York: Routledge, 47–61.
   Guyer argues that the paradox is best formulated in terms of the distinction between parts and wholes, rather than minds and bodies. The challenge of portraiture is to condense an entire life into a single captured moment.

Doing so situates the paradox in the historical debate over the differing representational capacities of painting versus poetry.

CRITIQUES:

4. Maes, Hans (2015). What Is a Portrait? *British Journal of Aesthetics* 55 (3): 303–22.

   Maes argues that accounts of portraiture such as Freeland's and Spinicci's struggle to handle non-paradigmatic cases. In particular, both ascribe too much significance to posing, which Maes argues is not necessary for portraiture. Instead, he argues that 'portrait' is not a kind-term that tracks a single, consistent concept, but rather one which has changed over time.

FURTHER READING:

5. Ross, Stephanie (1974). Caricature. *The Monist* 58 (2): 285–93.

   Ross argues that we identify caricatures directly, just as we do everyday objects or the subjects of portraits; we don't need to engage in any process of imagination or work backwards by reversing exaggerations and understatements, etc. Caricatures are simply less realistic portraits which ask us to see reality in the terms they set out.

6. Spinicci, Paolo (2009). Portraits: Some Phenomenological Remarks. *Proceedings of the European Society for Aesthetics* 1: 37–59. http://proceedings.eurosa. org/1/spinicci2009.pdf.

   Spinicci argues that what makes a picture a portrait is a matter of the social conventions which govern our use of it. Paradigmatically, he argues, portraits aim to shed light on their sitter's subjectivity, and the easiest way to achieve this end is by staging a pose, so that the sitter "narrates" themselves in the first person, in a moment of "temporary inaction" during which they achieve a compromise between how they *do* and how they'd *like* to appear.

7. Mag Uidhir, Christy (2013). Epistemic Misuse and Abuse of Pictorial Caricature. *American Philosophical Quarterly* 50 (2): 137–51.

   Mag Uidhir argues that caricatures are epistemically defective because they're distortions which are typically used to exploit cognitive biases. Caricatures exploit an audience's cognitive biases to make a moral or political point which their audiences already associate with the subject. This means that any belief informed by a caricature is, to that extent, unwarranted.

8. Caldarola, Elisa and Matteo Plebani (2016). Caricatures and Prop Oriented Make-Believe. *Ergo: An Open Access Journal of Philosophy* 3 (15): 403–19.

   Caldarola and Plebani argue that caricatures are best explained by a make-believe account of figurative language. Caricatures are depicted metaphors and hyperbole. Metaphors and hyperbole and literally false, and trying to understand what they could mean instead engages us in a game of make-believe.

9. Matthes, Erich Hatala (2020). "Portraits of the Landscape," in *Portraits and Philosophy*, Hans Maes (ed.). New York: Routledge, 128–39.

Matthes argues that landscapes can be the subjects of portraits so long as they evoke the natural or built environment's character, understood not as an inner quality but as its aesthetic character. There is a parallel puzzle in landscape portraiture, since landscapes are vast and include sensory features beyond the merely visual, but in portraits are purely visual.

10. Debaene, Aurélie J. (2021). The Truthful Portrait: Can Posing be a Tool for Authenticity in Portraiture? *Journal of Aesthetics and Art Criticism* 79 (4): 440–51.

Debaene argues that posing can exert significant influence over our understanding of a portrait. Posing involves the deliberate and performative presentation of a bodily configuration, and is truthful when it identifies and communicates important aspects of the sitter's character. Unlike heavily-edited social media photographs, a posed portrait can be *more* truthful to the sitter.

NOTE

1 Although Freeland introduces the paradox in this article, she first names it in her subsequent book, *Portraits and Persons: A Philosophical Inquiry* (OUP 2010).

35

THE PARADOX OF TRAGEDY

CASE

Tragedies are really popular. Not real-life tragedies, you understand—those are just sad. But fiction is chock full of tragedies, and people love to consume them. There's the story of King Arthur, for example, which leaves me in floods pretty much no matter how bad the adaptation. But maybe it was Peter Heller's *The Dog Stars* (2012) that did it for you, or Emily St. John Mandel's *The Glass Hotel* (2020). If Cli-Fi is your thing, then maybe it was J.G. Ballard's *The Drowned World* (1962), John Brunner's *The Sheep Look Up* (1972), or Karen Thompson Walker's *The Age of Miracles* (2012).

If you're a theatre buff—or if you survived high school English—then you know that Shakespeare's tragedies (*Othello, Macbeth, Romeo and Juliet*, etc.) translate better for modern audiences than his comedies (*As You Like It, A Midsummer Night's Dream*, etc.), and are considered his very best works. Where films are concerned, if you're of a certain age, you'll remember the frenzy that accompanied James Cameron's *Titanic* (1997), the accolades for Ang Lee's *Brokeback Mountain* (2005), or, more recently, the success of Greta Gerwig's adaptation of *Little Women* (2019).

DOI: 10.4324/9781003368205-39

These are all sad stories, but they're also massively popular. So what gives? Why do we like unpleasant content so much—to the point that we seek it out and consume it over and over and over? This is known as the *paradox of tragedy*. It's no exaggeration to say that this is one of the oldest problems in philosophy, with a pedigree reaching back at least as far as Aristotle, who explained our love of tragedy as a way for us to release pent-up emotions (1981 [c. 335 BCE]). The emotions themselves are unpleasant, he thought, but their release comes as a relief. The paradox received renewed attention in the eighteenth-century thanks to Hume, who argued that the experience of tragedy is composed of many discrete parts, some of which are indeed unpleasant, but whose narrative purpose is to highlight the beauty of the skilled representation before us, so that our feelings of unease about particular moments in the tragedy are transformed into an overall pleasant experience (1987 [1757]).[1]

Since then, the paradox of tragedy has remained a popular topic of discussion. It has exerted considerable influence on the discussion of related topics, such as the *Paradox of Fiction* and the closely related *Paradox of Disgust*. The paradox of tragedy, however, asks how it is we can take so much pleasure from the sad events we find in fiction. Not the kind of masochistic pleasure we can sometimes take in pain, mind you, or the thrill of schadenfreude we feel an at enemy's misfortune, but honest-to-goodness bog-standard pleasure.

RESPONSES

Contemporary attempts to resolve the paradox have tended in two broad directions: the different-objects solution, and the distance solution. Let us take these in turn.

The different-objects solution simply posits that our unpleasant emotional reactions to tragedy take different objects from our pleasant reactions. The suggestion has its roots in Hume's observation that we take pleasure in the skill on display, rather than in the unpleasantness itself: we don't enjoy *what* is represented but *do* enjoy *how* it's represented (1987 [1757]). So: one possibility is that the delight and satisfaction we feel when we consume tragedies is a higher-order feeling: the tragedy makes me sad (if it's any good!), but what I enjoy is the fact that it has made me sad, that I am the kind of person who does and would respond to the situation represented with the appropriate emotions (Feagin 1983). The pleasure we feel is thus a kind of self-satisfaction at the confirmation that we are, after all, pretty decent people. We like tragedy, then, because it's so closely tied to morality, which we think is of paramount importance. Good art should be consistent with our moral views; an unfavourable meta-reaction, however, would suggest that the work is immoral (c.f. *The Paradox of Good-Bad Art*).

A similar suggestion is that sad art, in particular, acknowledges sadness in a way that we find comforting (Evers and Deng 2016): it involves recognizing the existence of life's tragedies and honouring them. The creation and consumption of sad art is a commemorative act, if you will, which sees us representing sad events both as being sad, and as being significant. Anyone who has experienced similar events, or who can imagine experiencing them, can then take some comfort from this commemorative act, and that is the pleasure we take in tragedy.

If either of these solutions is correct, however, then presumably they ought to generalize across our entertainments, rather than being limited to tragedy and sad art: I ought to feel joy at being happy for a character's good fortune, and so on. But while there's clearly something to this thought, it's not obvious that it translates well across types of narratives. In particular, it seems to yield the wrong results for comedy, which usually sees us laughing at someone's expense and which should therefore provoke an *unfavourable* meta-reaction.

An alternative different-objects solution shades closer towards the Aristotelian, and limits itself to unpleasant narratives, such as tragedy and horror. In particular, the suggestion is that the delight we take in horror stories lies in the role that the unpleasantness plays in the narrative, particularly as a device for producing and releasing tension (Carroll 1990). We don't enjoy the unpleasantness as such but recognize it as being an important structural element, and so accept it. For horror stories, in particular, disgust (usually aimed at the monster) is the price we inevitably pay for the disclosure of the unknown, for the satisfaction of our curiosity and the revelation of the impossible. Our fascination with horror is intimately tied to its disturbing nature.

A second set of solutions take their inspiration from Hume's observation that tragedy's fictionality seems to make a difference to our reactions, since we (presumably) wouldn't applaud quite so enthusiastically if the events of *Romeo and Juliet* were actually unfold-ing around us. Fictionality creates a kind of distance between us and what's depicted (see also *The Jealous Husband*); but while that reduces the unpleasantness, it doesn't yet explain how it turns into outright pleasure. Hume's suggestion is that distance diminishes unpleasantness, and a little unpleasantness serves to highlight the work's outstanding aesthetic achievements, provided there's not so much of it that it overpowers the distancing effect of fictionality. The overall experience is thus pleasant, even if some of its component parts were unpleasant.

Alternately, it has been suggested that distancing effects can help to explain all kinds of aesthetic appreciation, not just that of tragedy in particular. On the control theory (Eaton 1982), for example, it is our sense of being in control of the encounter that allows us to focus our attention on its aesthetic properties. This sense of control is granted by our distance from the work: fictionality is one way of creating distance, of course, but physical and temporal distance can achieve the same effect. As long as it isn't *my* house that's on fire, for instance, or safe in the knowledge that the footage is from years ago, it's relatively easy for me to admire the play of the flames.

This is an important insight, because just as closer inspection reveals that we can take this kind of paradoxical pleasure from lots of different kinds of art—not just narrative tragedies—it also seems likely that we can have such experiences to *real* events, too (Friend 2007). A biogra-phy or documentary, for example, could easily be structured to afford us the same sense of tragedy as a fictional story, or to elicit similar feelings of fear and disgust as horror. There are, after all, more things in heaven and earth than dreamt of in anyone's philosophy.

Recently, cognitive scientists have proposed the inelegantly-named 'distancing-embracing model' of our enjoyment of painful art (Menninghaus et al. 2017). According to this model, two sets of factors combine to allow us to enjoy painful art: distancing and embracing factors. Distancing factors work to create distance between us and the work. They include things like the work's fictionality, but also its cultural, physical, and temporal distance from us, as well as the awareness that it is an artwork. Embracing factors include all of those mentioned earlier, and more: catharsis, the cohesion of the work's structural elements, its novelty, the skillfulness of its representation, the meta-satisfaction we feel in response to our negative emotion, etc. The awareness of distance allows us to focus on the work's embracing factors. Crucially, this model is not limited to explaining our reactions to painful art: it is a model which tries to explain aesthetic engagement more generally and, in particular, how it is that negative emotions can be turned to a work's advantage.

What these distancing accounts seem to get right is that the 'paradox of tragedy' is inaptly named: it seems to cover a much broader set of experiences than that of consuming fictional tragedies. What they still leave out, however, is an explanation of why we seek out such experiences in the first place. It is this question that the 'rich experience theory' tries to answer with an 'all of the above' strategy: our motives are a complex hodge-podge which, ultimately, boil down to a desire to seek out strong emotional reactions, and for many of us painful emotional responses are particularly affectively, intellectually, and perceptually engaging, for exactly the reasons cited by Menninghaus et al. (Smuts 2007).

SUGGESTED READING

SEMINAL PRESENTATIONS:

1. Aristotle (1981 [c. 335 BCE]). "Poetics", in *Aristotle: Rhetoric and On Poetics*, Ingram Bywater (trans.). Exton, PA: The Franklin Library, 201–44.
   Aristotle argues that the paradox of tragedy is resolved by reflecting on the function of tragedy, which is to arouse emotions like pity and fear in order to cathartically purge them. The negative feelings themselves are not pleasant as we experience them; what we enjoy is the relief of catharsis. The best tragedies achieve this through their plots and the resolution of narrative arcs rather than sheer spectacle; the beauty of tragedy lies in its being complete and self-contained.

2. Hume, David (1987 [1757]). "Of Tragedy", in *Essays: Moral, Political, and Literary*, Eugene F. Miller (ed.). Indianapolis: Liberty, 216–25.
   Hume breathes new life into the paradox of tragedy, treating it as a distinct problem worthy of consideration. He observes that knowing the unpleasant events are fictional can allow us to take pleasure in them, though the effect is not guaranteed. Likewise, we take pleasure in the skill on display, in the novelty of representations; a little sorrow or difficulty helps to highlight these, so long as it isn't allowed to overpower them.

DEFENCES:

3. Eaton, Marcia Muelder (1982). A Strange Kind of Sadness. *Journal of Aesthetics and Art Criticism* 41 (1): 51–63.

   Eaton posits a 'control theory' according to which what allows us to enjoy negative emotions in art is the feeling that we are in control of the encounter. The control afforded by distance allows us to more carefully attend to something's aesthetic properties. Fictionality can help to create the needed distance, but the phenomenon is much more widespread, and not limited to experiences of art or the consumption of fiction.

4. Feagin, Susan L. (1983). The Pleasures of Tragedy. *American Philosophical Quarterly* 20 (1): 95–104.

   Feagin distinguishes between the different kinds of pleasure we can take in things, arguing that the profound satisfaction we feel after consuming a good tragedy is a *meta*-response to our *direct* response (of sadness) to the work's unpleasantness. The pleasure we take in tragedy is thus a kind of self-satisfaction that we're having the right kind of response to the work.

5. Carroll, Noël (1990). *The Philosophy of Horror, or, Paradoxes of the Heart.* New York: Routledge.

   In Ch. 4, Carroll takes up the paradox of horror, which closely parallels that of tragedy. He argues that we genuinely find the horrific aspects of the story unpleasant; our delight is in the role these elements play in the overall narrative. What we like about horror, he thinks, is its narrative arc of discovery, proof, and confirmation of the monster, a structure which excels at producing and releasing tension.

CRITIQUES:

6. Friend, Stacie (2007). The Pleasures of Documentary Tragedy. *British Journal of Aesthetics* 47 (2): 184–98.

   Friend argues that the paradoxical pleasure we take in tragedy can be aroused by non-fictional works, too. The crucial ingredients, she argues, are the story's subject and structure; in particular, sad narratives which offer a sense of closure (such as documentary tragedies) can enable us to experience tragic pleasure.

7. Smuts, Aaron (2007). The Paradox of Painful Art. *Journal of Aesthetic Education* 41 (3): 59–77.

   Smuts tackles what he calls the 'paradox of painful art' in general, arguing that its traditional framing begs the question: what's really at issue is why we seek out painful art in the first place, and 'pleasure' is just one of many possible answers. He argues, instead, that the best solution is a rich experience theory: painful art simply represents an easy way for us to access incredibly rich experiences of strong emotional reactions.

8. Menninghaus, Winfried, Valentin Wagner, Julian Hanich, Eugen Wassiliwizky, Thomas Jacobsen, and Stefan Koelsch (2017). The Distancing-Embracing Model of the Enjoyment of Negative Emotions in Art Reception. *Behavioral and Brain Sciences* 40: 1–15.

   Menninghaus et al. make the empirically-grounded case that the experience of the paradox of tragedy is grounded in the combination of two broad factors which generally help to make our enjoyment of art more acute: a distancing and an embracing component. The distancing component creates space between us and the work, allowing us to set aside any immediate concerns we might otherwise have, and thus allowing us to pay particular attention to the embracing components on display.

FURTHER READING:

9. Dadlez, Eva M. (2013). "The Pleasures of Tragedy," in *The Oxford Handbook of British Philosophy in the Eighteenth Century*, James A. Harris (ed.). Oxford: Oxford University Press. 450–67.

   The eighteenth century saw a flurry of scholarly activity on the paradox of tragedy. Dadlez canvasses the most typical issues raised, with particular attention to Hume and interpretations of, and responses to, his work.

10. Evers, Daan and Natalja Deng (2016). Acknowledgement and the Paradox of Tragedy. *Philosophical Studies* 173 (2): 337–50.

    Evers and Deng answer the paradox by arguing that sad art *acknowledges* the sad aspects of life. Like monuments to real tragedies, sad art acknowledges sad events by representing them as such, and as being important. In doing so, the work adopts a perspective on its content which it invites us to share, which is comforting for those of us who have had similar experiences.

NOTE

1 For an excellent overview of the paradox's eighteenth-century antecedents, see Dadlez (2013).

THE PROBLEM OF MUSEUM SKEPTICISM

CASE

Some art is *site-specific* art; this just means that the work was designed to exist in a particular place and no other. To move a site-specific artwork, then, is to significantly alter it, perhaps even to destroy it. In its infancy, the term predominantly referred to publicly commissioned sculptural works designed for particular urban locations (e.g., Richard Serra's *Tilted Arc* [1981]), although it came to be associated with performance art (e.g., Dennis Oppenheim's *Two Jumps for Dead Dog Creek* [1970]) and landscape or environmental art as well (e.g., Marco Casagrande's *Sandworm* [2012]).

But what if *all* or *most* art is actually site-specific? After all, the Sistine Chapel's ceiling is supposed to be in the Sistine Chapel, not the Louvre or some billionaire's basement. Miniature portraits don't hold the same significance outside their lockets; altar pieces and religious scenes don't transform their associated spaces in the same way when hung on museum walls rather than adorning a church; presented outside its architectural or cultural context, a Kwakiutl house post or Tlingit shame pole inaptly become "totem poles". Many of the most iconic paintings of the Italian quattrocento were likewise painted to adorn particular spaces, especially in particular chapels. Thus, Piero's

DOI: 10.4324/9781003368205-40

Resurrection (1463–65) fresco would lose much of its effect if displayed on a wall of the Guggenheim rather than on the interior wall facing the entrance to the Palazzo della Residenza in Sansepolcro. Just think of the Elgin marbles, those sculptures which used to adorn the roof of the Parthenon in Greece but whose broken forms now live in the British Museum: they're impressive, sure, but they just aren't the same housed inside a room full of tourists as they were atop an architectural marvel—in fact, some might argue that in this particular case, they become independent artworks in their own right, and are more amenable to visual examination (Rodrigues 2016).

Nevertheless, the point is that these are all works which transform their associated spaces into spaces where certain kinds of activities—prayer, meditation, reverence, reflection, etc.—are sanctioned. In museums, however, they become objects of aesthetic contemplation from which we merely take visual pleasure.[1] This raises an interesting philosophical puzzle: once these works are moved to the museum or gallery, have they changed in some fundamental way? Have they lost some of their original *meaning* (and, if so, isn't that a *bad* thing)? In particular, does the move to the museum impede our ability to gain knowledge of the work and its history? This is *the puzzle of museum skepticism*.

Among art-historians (where it is often called the problem of 'decontextualization' or of 'museumization'), museum skepticism dates back to the late seventeenth century, with the advent of mass exhibitions in museum settings (Quatremère de Quincy 2021 [1815], Carrier 2006, Rodrigues 2016). Paintings (in particular) would be crammed cheek-by-jowl on every wall, pillar, and pilaster, with no accompanying object labels or identifying information (they were given numbers corresponding to catalogue entries in the mid-eighteenth century). Works were thus stripped of their context and put to work establishing the new narrative of art history (Duncan and Wallach 1980). As an art-historical concern, museum skepticism has been quite widespread, having been articulated in passages from Goethe and Valéry to Bourdieu, Dewey, and even Heidegger (Carrier 2006).

The first museum skeptics were particularly concerned with the state appropriation, resale, and display of clerical and aristocratic collections (Quatremère de Quincy 2021 [1815]). More recently, however, the issue has resurfaced in philosophical aesthetics in debates over public and street art (Baldini 2016) and cultural appropriation (Eaton and Gaskell 2009). It is particularly pressing in this latter context, where the question becomes whether the cultural artifacts of colonized cultures belong in Western art museums, especially if their placement there compromises their meaning through decontextualization (see also *The Puzzle of Cultural Appropriation*).

RESPONSES

Before we can talk about museum skepticism, we need to pause for a moment and consider *aesthetic cognitivism* (see *Faking Nature*), a constellation of different views which can be roughly characterized as holding that art has and conveys significant cognitive content, such that we can learn something about the world and its history simply by contemplating it. For a time, cognitivists argued that art can give us the same kind of propositional knowledge of the world as science; since non-literary artworks seldom make actual statements, however, cognitivists typically argue that these statements are implicit. But this view runs into some trouble from the fact that (1) implicit statements seem awfully close to testimony, which is often not sufficient on its own for knowledge, and (2) even in literary works, the statements being made are understood to be literally false, and thus have no real cognitive value. These problems have led some cognitivists to opt for an exemplification theory, according to which artworks exemplify certain properties—but, of course, some thing cannot exemplify properties it does not literally have (e.g., I work out a lot, so I don't particularly exemplify smallness or weakness).

A promising alternative argues that art *can* give us knowledge, but only of a specialized kind that doesn't figure in law-like generalizations, as scientific knowledge does (Young 2001). This is because art—especially visual art—makes no arguments; the best it can do is to offer us an *illustrative demonstration* of some point or perspective. In doing so, art makes a particular perspective on something available to its audience, guiding them to a position from which they can judge for themselves whether something is true or false, right or wrong.

Having outlined the bare bones of cognitivism, we can turn our attention back to museum skepticism. On the art-historical side of things, museum skepticism has been motivated primarily by intuitions and bare assertions. In philosophical aesthetics, however, it first came to prominence as a skeptical response to cognitivism (Feagin 1995). It has found a particular justification in *contextualism*, which emphasises the role that contextual and historical factors have in determining a work's aesthetic properties (see: *Guernicas, Pot People, Basket Folk*): if non-perceptible contextual properties underpin a work's aesthetic properties, then changes to some of those contextual properties (such as moving the work to a new location) may fundamentally alter the work's aesthetic properties, and prevent us from gaining knowledge of the work and its history (Feagin 1995). In particular, moving a work from, say, a chapel to a museum makes it into an object of pure perception, rather than an object which transforms its associated space into one where certain kinds of actions, responses, and rituals are called for. In much the same way, a tiger in captivity is a different beast entirely from one in the wild; the roar which is pitiful in the former context is glorious and terrible in the latter. Our experience of art also seems to involve an important first-personal dimension: we want and need to be put in direct contact with great art, rather than replicas (Korsmeyer 2016). Our assessments of aesthetic value are intimately bound up with judgements about an object's origins: genuine originals are of greater aesthetic value because they put us into contact with the past in a way that replicas don't and can't.

Contextualism, then, seems to invite us to emphasize art's site-specificity, thereby discounting the ideal of disinterested appreciation of works as self-contained autonomous entities (Gaiger 2009). In response, however, a number of aestheticians have argued that contextualism need not push us quite so far. So, for example, while it's true that removing a work to a museum changes something about its context of appreciation, we should remember that artworks are always changing over time (Carrier 2006): Rembrandt's *Militia Company of District II under the Command of Captain Frans Banninck Cocq* (1642), for example, is known as the '*Night Watch*' because it was thought to depict a night scene until the 1940s, when it was discovered that it was a day scene covered in a varnish that had darkened considerably over the centuries. In this respect, then, artworks are no different from ordinary objects, and even people, which also change over time: so long as there is some sort of physical continuity between earlier and subsequent stages, we are comfortable identifying, say, *Michel* as one and the same person as that baby way back when. In fact, placing the work in a museum—especially when care is taken to craft sensitive accompanying materials and to group it with other works from the same culture—may allow us to see more of it (and more often) than was accessible to its original culture, giving us a *better* perspective on the work's aesthetic and historical properties and facilitating visual comparisons (Carrier 2006, Eaton and Gaskell 2009, Rodrigues 2016).

SUGGESTED READING

SEMINAL PRESENTATION:

1. Quatremère de Quincy, Antoine Chrysostôme (2021 [1815]). *Quatremère de Quincy's Moral Considerations on the Place and Purpose of Works of Art: Introduction and Translation.* Louis A. Ruprecht, Jr. (trans.). New York: Lexington Books.
   This treatise represents the first major articulation of museum skepticism in art history. Writing at a time when the property of the clergy and the aristocracy was being confiscated by the state and sold off to collectors—and when the Louvre was being converted into a museum—Quatremère de Quincy argues that artworks are essentially tied to their contexts of origin, so that removing them from those contexts entails a loss of meaning.

DEFENCES:

2. Duncan, Carol and Alan Wallach (1980). The Universal Survey Museum. *Art History* 3 (4): 448–74.
   Duncan and Wallach canvas the history of 'universal survey' museums, arguing that they structure the space of our engagement so that it facilitates a ritualized encounter with artworks one by one, stripped of their context and power to speak. Artworks thus become ceremonial monuments to state ideology, and visitors play the part of ideal citizens.

3. Feagin, Susan L. (1995). Paintings and their Places. *Australasian Journal of Philosophy* 73 (2): 260–8.
   Feagin's primary concern is the question of whether art can give us knowledge, which she argues is confused. She highlights the presuppositions we make when we ask that question; in particular, she observes that most artworks have a strong degree of site-specificity but are displayed and experienced outside their original sites. This alters our experience of the work. The point of paintings is to transform the spaces in which we act, not to give us knowledge.

CRITIQUES:

4. Carrier, David (2006). *Museum Skepticism: A History of the Display of Art in Public Galleries*. Durham, NC: Duke University Press.

   Carrier coins the term 'museum skepticism'. Ch. 3 gives a wide-ranging overview of the history of museum skepticism, going back to Quatremère de Quincy. In Ch. 4, he argues that museum skepticism is misguided since a work's meaning is determined by its creator's intentions and actions. The work's significance may change over time, but so long as there is a degree of continuity with its physical matter it remains one and the same thing.

5. Eaton, A. W. and Ivan Gaskell (2009). "Do Subaltern Artifacts Belong in art Museums?" in *The Ethics of Cultural Appropriation*, James O. Young and Conrad Brunk (eds.). Malden, MA: Wiley-Blackwell, 235–67.

   While they concede that displaying subaltern artifacts in art museums recontextualizes them, Eaton and Gaskell argue that doing so is not necessarily harmful—provided they are treated sensitively. Artifacts outlast the intentions of their original makers and can take on new functions and significances without compromising their identities: they can be *exapted* for new purposes.

6. Rodrigues, Alda (2016). People and Things: Questions Museums Make Us Ask and Answer. *Royal Institute of Philosophy Supplement* 79: 199–216.

   Rodrigues tackles an apparent contradiction between two of Quatremère de Quincy's texts, arguing that although museums *do* decontextualize works, doing so can call our attention to particularly interesting features of the works which would be missed *in situ*. Museums, she thinks, can prompt us to think of art as having a broader cultural bearing than that suggested by the world whence it came, or the intentions which shaped it.

FURTHER READING:

7. Young, James O. (2001). *Art and Knowledge*. New York: Routledge.

   In Ch. 3, Young argues that the propositional theory of art and the exemplification hypothesis cannot adequately explain art's cognitive value. He argues, instead, that art can only provide knowledge by acting as an illustrative demonstration, by guiding audiences to take a particular perspective on something.

8. Gaiger, Jason (2009). Dismantling the Frame: Site-specific Art and Aesthetic Autonomy. *British Journal of Aesthetics* 49 (1): 43–58.

   Gaiger surveys the origins of the ideal of the aesthetic autonomy of artworks and of site-specificity in art, arguing that site-specificity is a response to aesthetic autonomy. In other words, it is part and parcel of the move away from formalist theories of art and allows us to reclaim the social function of art from exile.

9. Baldini, Andrea (2016). Street Art: A Reply to Riggle. *Journal of Aesthetics and Art Criticism* 74 (2): 187–91.

   Baldini responds to the characterization of street art as being essentially characterized by being outside the art world, such that 'the street' is internal to its meaning. Inspired by Feagin, he argues that we should understand this street art as a direct challenge to the idea that art does or should function as a prop facilitating disinterested appreciation; instead, it inspires us to reinscribe a space with new meaning and to engage with it differently.

10. Korsmeyer, Carolyn (2016). Real Old Things. *British Journal of Aesthetics* 56 (3): 219–31.

    Even though we can't directly perceive authenticity, Korsmeyer argues that it has significant aesthetic value. We value authentic objects more than perfect replicas; authenticity is a kind of contextual property that we assume objects possess, and being disabused of that assumption comes with negative judgements. The ability to touch an authentic object gives us a kind of contact or relationship with history.

NOTE

1 Or testaments to the might of empire, though this is perfectly consistent with their also being objects of aesthetic appreciation.

THE PUZZLE OF ACQUAINTANCE

CASE

> In the case of Angels and Demons, there's a radical re-invention of the old formula. And the radical re-invention this time is that they run *and* explain things at the same time. [...] They point as they're running because they run and point and explain things at the same time. Because clearly, there was a board meeting in which somebody said, "You know this standing around pointing and explaining things? Everybody in their reviews said that that wasn't very good, but they liked the running a little bit more, so let's run but we have to explain things."[1]

So begins Mark Kermode's review of Ron Howard's *Angels and Demons* (2009)—a rant of such epic proportions that it literally woke one listener from his coma.[2] With that review in mind, why bother watching the film? I, for one, already know everything I need to know about it: it's a stinker!

Now, imagine instead that someone is telling you about a painting they saw recently—let's say it's William Baziotes's *Cyclops* (1947), an abstract-expressionist work. Suppose that person tells you that this hideous work looks like it was painted by a child who couldn't yet colour inside the lines, and whose ambition stretched to painting a flesh-coloured number eight on a darkish green background, gave it a

DOI: 10.4324/9781003368205-41

weird blue eye, and threw in a few yellow triangles for good measure. Do you need to actually see the painting for yourself before concluding that it's not very good? Would a reproduction suffice? Or, conversely, would it be appropriate for you to conclude that it is *beautiful* without first seeing it for yourself?

Has something gone wrong in these examples? Perhaps a critic's review seems like a good basis for deciding whether to *watch* a movie, but not such a great basis for deciding whether it's any good. A friend's hot take about a painting likewise seems like useful information but not sufficient to make up my own mind about the work. Nor does it seem like popular opinion should substitute for my own. What if I googled a picture of the painting? Could I then come to a judgement about its aesthetic value, even though I've never seen it in person and so might be missing out on some of its aesthetic properties (e.g., maybe it has interesting topographical or impasto features)?

The typical diagnosis of what is going on in these cases is that our judgements seem to violate an intuitive rule of aesthetic engagement called *the acquaintance principle* (Wollheim 1980). According to this principle, we have to arrive at judgements of aesthetic value for ourselves, based on first-hand experience rather than on the basis of someone else's testimony, however accurate it may be. There are, however, different ways of articulating the acquaintance principle, depending on just what it is that one is worried about transmitting—aesthetic judgements, in the classic case, but also knowledge, justification, etc., depending on the nature of the debate in which the acquaintance principle is being invoked. The principle rises to the level of a puzzle because we aren't usually skeptical about the value of testimony *in general*. If I tell you that I saw a stag last night, odds are you'll believe me—especially if I have no obvious reason to lie about it, and if you know that I live somewhere rural with a large deer population. Indeed, you'd be equally justified in believing that last assertion!

Those who accept the acquaintance principle are usually called *pessimists* about aesthetic testimony; *optimists*, by contrast, believe that we can gain aesthetic knowledge through testimony. While blanket pessimism is rare, pessimists typically worry that aesthetic experience and engagement are governed by special norms which are not relevant to other kinds of testimonial knowledge, and which cannot be satisfied second-hand. It would be silly, they think, to claim that *Angels and Demons* is a stinker or *Cyclops* is hideous while admitting, in the same breath, that one had never seen them.

One natural way of tackling the problem is in terms of the statement's content: perhaps when I say that '*Cyclops* is hideous', I am implying that I have seen the painting for myself (or at least a sufficiently detailed reproduction). Pessimism thus offers us an attractive diagnosis of the problem: we are jumping the gun and violating certain conventions governing what we can say (norms of assertion). But that seems somewhat beside the point: our interest, here, is not so much in norms of assertion as it is in the norms which determine which beliefs we subscribe to: the issue is not whether I am warranted in *asserting* that *Angels and Demons* is a bad film on the basis of testimony alone, but whether I am warranted in *believing* it. More specifically, we might also wonder whether a high-quality photograph of *Cyclops* (such as you might find in an art history text) can substitute for a visit to the Art Institute of Chicago (see also *Faking Nature* and *The Supercopier*).

There is also an interesting asymmetry at work here, since not all aesthetically-relevant judgements are impacted in the same way. While it seems inappropriate to conclude that *Cyclops* is beautiful without seeing it, it seems perfectly appropriate to conclude on the basis of someone else's testimony that it's an abstract expressionist painting, that its "eye" is blue, or that it's composed of oil on canvas. In fact, I imagine that *you* may be doing so yourself right now, unless you're already familiar with the work or took the time to look up a picture. So: what is going on?

RESPONSES

Despite its initial intuitive plausibility and widespread acceptance (see e.g., Mothersill 1991, Hopkins 2011, Konigsberg 2012), contemporary philosophers are generally (but not universally!) skeptical that the acquaintance principle really does apply to our experience of art and our aesthetic judgements.

Some have argued that the acquaintance principle only applies to aesthetic *properties*, such as complexity, elegance, gaudiness, or gracefulness, rather than to judgements of aesthetic *value* (Levinson 2005).

So while I can tell you that I think *Cyclops* is drab and ungainly, that is not enough, on its own, to justify a similar claim on your part, even if my judgement that it is a bad artwork suffices for you to express the same judgement. Others have argued that the acquaintance principle's plausibility is domain-specific—in other words, it varies depending on what we're talking about (Konigsberg 2012). According to this view, some art forms, like conceptual art, don't require direct acquaintance at all, and so the acquaintance principle is unlikely to apply to them. The performing arts, by contrast, *do* seem to require some measure of direct experience for their proper appreciation. And concrete works of visual art often seem to, as well, although we might make allowances for photographs which successfully convey the work's visual content.

Other philosophers reject the acquaintance principle entirely, arguing that the debate has conflated different senses of 'judgement', the norms governing different kinds of assertion, or ordinary testimony with reasons and justifications (e.g., Budd 2003, Gorodeisky 2010, Robson 2015). For some of these, aesthetic judgements are perfectly transmissible, provided their purveyors are in possession of adequate evidence and explain the reasons underpinning their judgements—just as a film critic does. The suggestion, then, is that perhaps the reason we were initially inclined to disdain testimonial belief in aesthetics was just that we were thinking of it as being hasty or uninformed belief instead.

Finally, some philosophers have sought to reconcile the optimistic and pessimistic takes on aesthetic testimony. One way of doing so is to draw further distinctions at the level of our *goals*—i.e., are we aiming for aesthetic *knowledge*, or for aesthetic *judgement* (Ransom 2019)? Testimony seems sufficient for knowledge, after all, but not for an aesthetic judgement. Another approach is to further clarify our starting principle: are we talking about aesthetic *acquaintance*, which demands that our judgement derive from our experience of the work, or aesthetic *autonomy*, which demands that our judgements be the product of our own efforts (Nguyen 2020)? In other words, are we concerned to ensure that we experience a thing for ourselves, or that we draw our own conclusions? Each may involve a different process that makes different demands on us.

SUGGESTED READING

SEMINAL PRESENTATION:

1. Wollheim, Richard (1980). *Art and Its Objects*. Cambridge: Cambridge University Press.

   Wollheim names and defends the acquaintance principle in Ch. 6. This is the *locus classicus* for contemporary discussions of the issue, although versions of it date back as far as Kant.

DEFENCES:

2. Mothersill, Mary (1991). *Beauty Restored*. New York: Adams Bannister Cox Pubs.

   Mothersill argues (especially in Ch. 3) that aesthetic judgements are avowals and thus imply that the speaker has had a direct, pleasurable acquaintance with the work. Testimonial judgements would therefore be highly misleading.

3. Hopkins, Robert (2011). How to be a Pessimist about Aesthetic Testimony. *Journal of Philosophy* 108 (3): 138–57.

   Hopkins argues that aesthetic judgements—unlike more mundane judgements—are governed by a norm which ensures they are intransmissible, though he concedes some limited exceptions such as lost works and past performances.

4. Konigsberg, Amir (2012). The Acquaintance Principle, Aesthetic Autonomy, and Aesthetic Appreciation. *British Journal of Aesthetics* 52 (2): 153–68.

   Konigsberg severely restricts the application of the acquaintance principle, arguing that it is properly applied only to works for which a perceptual dimension is aesthetically essential to the experience of the work.

CRITIQUES:

5. Budd, Malcolm (2003). The Acquaintance Principle. *British Journal of Aesthetics* 43 (6): 386–92.

   In this touchstone rejection of the acquaintance principle, Budd argues that aesthetic judgements—especially judgements about a thing's aesthetic properties—are perfectly transmissible.

6. Robson, Jon (2015). Norms of Belief and Norms of Assertion in Aesthetics. *Philosophers' Imprint* 15 (6): 1–19.

   Robson argues that we needn't be pessimists about aesthetic testimony to explain the impermissibility of certain kinds of aesthetic assertions; all we need is a different, more plausible norm of assertion to the effect that we should not misrepresent someone else's aesthetic labour as our own.

FURTHER READING:

7. Levinson, Jerrold (2005). Aesthetic Properties. *Aristotelian Society Supplementary Volume* 79: 211–27.

   Levinson defends realism about aesthetic properties, which he argues are manifest higher-order ways of appearing. Levinson argues, further, that the supposition of aesthetic properties undermines the plausibility of the acquaintance principle.

8. Gorodeisky, Keren (2010). A New Look at Kant's View of Aesthetic Testimony. *British Journal of Aesthetics* 50 (1): 53–70.

   Gorodeisky argues that the problem of aesthetic testimony is not best conceived along epistemic or expressivist lines; her emphasis, instead, is on the judgement's aesthetic character, which is governed by different norms.

9. Ransom, Madeleine (2019). Frauds, Posers And Sheep: A Virtue Theoretic Solution to the Acquaintance Debate. *Philosophy and Phenomenological Research* 98 (2): 417–34.

   Ransom argues that we can reconcile optimism and pessimism about aesthetic testimony by recognizing that although we can gain aesthetic *knowledge* by testimony, aesthetic *judgement* requires direct acquaintance. She introduces a performance model of virtue aesthetics according to which aesthetic judgement is the exercise of aesthetic competence, whereas testimonial aesthetic knowledge comes from exercising general testimonial competence.

10. Nguyen, C. Thi (2020). Autonomy and Aesthetic Engagement. *Mind* 129 (516): 1127–56.

    Nguyen distinguishes between aesthetic acquaintance and *autonomy* (the idea that we should arrive at our aesthetic judgements ourselves, not by deferring to experts) and argues that the primary value of aesthetic appreciation comes from engaging in the *process* of appreciating for oneself, rather than in coming to the "correct" judgements.

NOTES

1 You can listen to the entire rant at: https://www.youtube.com/watch?v=VdKWoi0PMWg.

2 Those looking for confirmation will find it approximately five minutes into the November 26, 2010 episode of the podcast: https://www.bbc.co.uk/programmes/b00w17yq.

THE PUZZLE OF DEPICTION

CASE

Think of a painting you know well—a realistic representational painting, not an abstract or entirely non-representational painting. If one isn't leaping to mind, then Goya's *Portrait of the Duke of Wellington* (1812–4) will do—it's a half-length portrait with Wellington in three-quarter profile, wearing his red military coat and several decorations from his exploits in the Napoleonic Wars up to that point. The *puzzle of depiction* asks: what and how does the portrait *depict*?

Obviously, it's a portrait of Arthur Wellesley, 1st Duke of Wellington. But what does it mean, exactly, to say that the painting *depicts* him? How can mere splotches of oil paint amount to showing us a human being? Factor in the consideration that without a title, very few of us would know that it was the Duke of Wellington depicted (as opposed to a generic nineteenth-ish-century man), and the case for its depicting him starts to get downright shaky (that is to say, the title seems to do more depictive work than the painting itself).

At a first pass, we might say that it looks like him: if we had been sufficiently acquainted with the Duke at the time of the portrait, we would say that the painted man bears a striking resemblance to the real man. But what does that mean, exactly? After all, the shapes and

DOI: 10.4324/9781003368205-42

colours used to represent the Duke of Wellington two-dimensionally in the painting aren't *really* all that much like those which composed his three-dimensional body. We should ask for further specification: resembles him *in what respect*? In terms of shapes and colours? In terms of texture, character, or wit?

Worse, resemblance is a reflexive and symmetrical relation (Goodman 1968): any object will resemble itself more than anything else, and anything it resembles will resemble *it* just as much. But depiction is neither reflexive nor symmetric: the portrait resembles itself more than anything else, but it doesn't *depict* itself, and Wellington (the man) doesn't depict the portrait. Even worse: strictly speaking the portrait resembles any other portrait more closely than it does the actual human being we say it depicts. So why does it represent *him*, and not some other portrait (say, one of David's equestrian portraits of Napoleon)?

There are two main difficulties any theory of depiction must overcome, but which present a particular challenge for resemblance theories (Lopes 1996). First, the theory must be able to account for the wide variety of depictions—that is to say, it shouldn't just commit itself to saying that only photo-realistic pictures depict, since our use of pictorial representation is much more widespread and employs many more and varied styles of depiction. Second, whatever explains depiction, it should allow for the fact that we can recognize depictions and resemblances without having any prior knowledge of depictive content.

RESPONSES

One of the first responses to resemblance theories was the conventionalist account of depiction, which construed pictorial representation in the same way as denotation in language: in other words, pictures refer in the same way that words refer (Goodman 1968). On this model, both pictures and language are systems of symbols, and the meaning of any individual item (symbol) in each system is ultimately arbitrary, a matter of convention. But a pictorial system, unlike a linguistic one, is richer in the sense that it assigns (or can assign) meaning to *every* mark on the pictorial surface, so that even the thickness of a line can make a difference to meaning; in language, by contrast, an O is just an o. So although different instances of a letter or word can look very different from one another but still mean the same thing, any difference at all between pictures entails a difference in what they represent.

More recently, Kulvicki (2006) follows Goodman in arguing that pictures have a non-semantic *syntax*, a set of rules governing their abilities to represent, grounded in the picture's structural properties (its 'bare-bones content'). This allows us to identify a set of individually necessary and jointly sufficient conditions for depiction: *repleteness* (how many of a symbol's properties are relevant to its syntactic identity), *sensitivity* (how much change a symbol can undergo while preserving its syntactic identity), *richness* (how many denotations a system has relative to its syntactic types), and *transparency* (representations are syntactically identical to their objects; see also *Dinosaurs in the Jungle*). Adding transparency allows us to restrict our definition of representation to pictorial systems alone, and helps to explain depiction's connection to realism, since by perceiving a picture we gain access to its bare-bones content. Realism is a matter of how many of a picture's surface-features are relevant to its interpretation.

Psychological accounts of depiction, by contrast, explain depiction in terms of the kinds of experiences pictures cause in their viewers. One influential approach maintains that what distinguishes experiences of depiction from real experiences of the depicted subject is a kind of doubled awareness ('twofoldness') of our experience: we are simultaneously aware of seeing *a picture* and seeing its subject (Wollheim 1998). Pictures are marked surfaces which enable *seeing-in*, a basic visual ability which allows us to see content in a representation. A marked surface only depicts what can be seen in it, which is determined by the artist's intentions and execution. Seeing-in is also permeable to thought, however, which means that we likewise have the capacity to see one thing *as* another if it's suggested to us.

Another popular psychological theory maintains that we use pictures as props in games of visual make-believe, so that they guide us in imagining a fictional world whose content is determined by whatever we correctly imagine ourselves seeing in them (Walton 1973). In other words, Goya's portrait of Wellington depicts him because it encourages us to imagine seeing him as he is shown by the painting. This means, however, that depiction is never independent of a background which sets implicit rules for our games of pictorial make-believe—in other words, depiction relies on pre-existing conventions which we have all sufficiently internalized to play the relevant games (e.g., it requires us to see cross-hatching as indicating shading rather than a veil of mesh).

A different kind of psychological account rests on the structure of the mind, especially its recognitional capacities (Lopes 1996, Newall 2006). On this construal, the key to depiction is furnishing the viewer with visual information that is sufficiently similar to that furnished by the thing depicted to trigger recognition. Successful depiction is a matter of a picture activating the viewer's capacity for visual recognition: artists suggest similarities such that, when seen, they trigger recognition of the thing depicted. Because the human brain has evolved to recognize objects under a wide variety of very different conditions, verisimilitude is not required (Newell 2006): the hues need to be close enough to the real thing to trigger recognition, but need be no closer. Likewise, an outline needs to be close enough, but need not be perfect (as with caricatures—see *The Paradox of Portraiture*). What distinguishes *pictorial* representation from other depictive systems (such as description) is that pictures are necessarily selective, since in choosing to represent some visual information artists are precluded from conveying other kinds of visual information (Lopes 1996).

This said, resemblance theories are far from dead in the water. In fact, several recent accounts of depiction start from the premise that resemblance—a similarity relation between the picture and what it depicts—is the key to understanding depiction.

One way of reintroducing resemblance is by arguing that depiction rests on viewers experiencing resemblance (Peacocke 1987, Hopkins 1995). But what is it that we experience as resembling something else? One candidate is *shape in the two-dimensional visual field* (Peacocke 1987): so long as we experience the depicted object as occupying a similar region of our visual field to one in which the real object could be presented to us, then we have a successful depiction. This experience need not be consciously noticed: it's purely perceptual and immediate. A similar candidate is the object's *outline shape* (see also Hyman and Bantinaki 2018, which gives a detailed account of Hyman's related *occlusion shape*), an objective geometrical property of objects that we always see but which we seldom explicitly acknowledge. Coupled with an artistic intention to the effect that the pictorial surface induce the same kind of experience of outline shape as the thing depicted, we have the makings of a theory of depiction. So: when I see Goya's portrait, I experience it as showing an object whose outline shape is similar to Wellington's, and it has that similar outline shape because Goya intended it to (i.e., I'm not just seeing faces in the clouds).

Alternately, it has been argued that resemblance theories can meet the challenge of specifying which aspects of resemblance are relevant head-on (Abell 2009). All we need to do is recognize that the scope is narrowed by the artist's intentions, and by the stylistic conventions governing the production of the work. An impressionist's painting of Wellington would not look very realistic, since it would use small brushstrokes and colour contrasts to convey the play of light; but it *would* depict him because (1) that's what the artist was trying to do (c.f. *Apelles's Horses*), subject to (2) their ideas about communicating colour and light. Our painting resembles Wellington in terms of the colour and light as he sat for the artist, if not in terms of strict appearance.

SUGGESTED READING

SEMINAL PRESENTATION:

1. Goodman, Nelson (1968). *Languages of Art: An Approach to a Theory of Symbols*. Indianapolis: Bobbs-Merrill.
    In Ch. 9, Goodman attacks the resemblance theory of depiction, arguing instead that pictorial representation is akin to denotation in language: for a picture to represent something, it must be a symbol for/stand for/refer to that thing. Resemblance is never necessary or sufficient for denotation; instead, depiction is like a description of an object, and like any object, descriptions are artificial and subject to conventions.

DEFENCES:

2. Kulvicki, John (2006). *On Images: Their Structure and Content*. Oxford: Oxford University Press.
    Kulvicki argues that perceptual accounts of representation are unsuccessful, defending instead a structural analysis of pictures inspired by Goodman's conventionalist treatment. What makes a picture representational are its syntactic and semantic relations to other pictures in the same system of representation. He identifies four necessary and jointly sufficient conditions for pictorial representation: relative repleteness, syntactic sensitivity, semantic richness, and transparency (see Chs. 1–3 and 6).

CRITIQUES:

3. Walton, Kendall (1973). Pictures and Make-Believe. *Philosophical Review* 82 (3): 283–319.

   Walton argues for an experiential treatment of depiction grounded in games of make-believe: when a picture depicts something, it invites us to use it as a prop in a pictorial game of make-believe which prescribes that we imagine a particular content. To see something in a picture is thus to *imagine* actually seeing it, or something of the same kind.

4. Peacocke, Christopher (1987). Depiction. *Philosophical Review* 96: 383–410.

   Peacocke argues that depiction is a matter of subjective, rather than objective, similarity. The account is purely perceptual: viewers need not be familiar with any background conditions or information. The more realistic the depiction, the richer the experience of the visual field's similarities.

5. Hopkins, Robert (1995). Explaining Depiction. *Philosophical Review* 104: 425–55.

   Hopkins argues that depiction rests on the similarity between the *outline shape* of the depiction and the depicted object. As long as we experience the outline shape of the depiction as similar to that of the thing depicted, and as long as someone intended the depiction to resemble its object in this way, then we have a successful depiction.

6. Wollheim, Richard (1998). On Pictorial Representation. *Journal of Aesthetics and Art Criticism* 56 (3): 217–26.[1]

   Wollheim argues that depiction is primarily a visual phenomenon and that grasping what a depiction represents is a matter of perception, not interpretation. He explains the centrality of the perceptual skill of 'seeing-in' to his account of depiction: seeing-in is logically and historically prior to representation, and leaves us aware of both the marked surface *and* the content it represents, but remains permeable to thought (to seeing-*as*).

FURTHER READING:

7. Lopes, Dominic (1996). *Understanding Pictures*. Oxford: Oxford University Press.

   In Ch. 1, Lopes argues, first, that a theory of depiction must account for the full range of styles and genres employed in making pictures (the diversity constraint); and, second, that viewers must be able to notice depictions and resemblances without prior knowledge of depictive content (the independence constraint). He argues that pictures present *aspects* of their subjects, that our ability to recognize what they depict is related to our ability to recognize those objects in real life, and that our ability to interpret pictures depends on our familiarity with the styles and systems in question.

8. Newall, Michael (2006). Pictures, Colour, and Resemblance. *Philosophical Quarterly* 225: 587–95.

   Focusing on similarities of colour, Newall argues that depiction is rooted in the viewer's psychological makeup: a depictive picture activates the viewer's pre-existing recognitional skills, which evolved to recognize objects under a wide variety of conditions. Depiction only requires that pictures be similar enough to their subject to trigger our recognitional system.

9. Abell, Catharine (2009). Canny Resemblance. *Philosophical Review* 118 (2): 183–223.

   Abell advocates for a resemblance account of depiction. She argues that instances of depiction can be governed by resemblance in any of many respects and that the field of possible resemblances is significantly narrowed by (1) the artist's communicative intentions, and (2) the stylistic conventions used.

10. Hyman, John and Katerina Bantinaki (2021). "Depiction," in *The Stanford Encyclopedia of Philosophy* (Fall 2021 Edition), Edward N. Zalta (ed.). https://plato.stanford.edu/archives/fall2021/entries/depiction/.

    Hyman and Bantinaki survey the extensive literature on depiction, starting from the early resemblance accounts in Plato, Pierce, Langer, and Hospers. Their focus is primarily on the debates that followed Gombrich and Goodman's skepticism about resemblance, especially from the 1990s until today.

NOTE

1 The ideas here are refinements of those introduced in Wollheim's earlier work, notably *Painting as an Art* (1987: Princeton University Press), repackaged here in an easily accessible format.

THE PUZZLE OF MUSICAL PROFUNDITY

CASE

Suppose someone claims that James Joyce's *Ulysses* (1922) is profound, but that Emily St. John Mandel's *Station Eleven* (2014) is not.[1] They're different works, of course: *Ulysses* is an unforgiving brick of a modernist novel about... well, *something*. *Station Eleven*, on the other hand, is a breezy dystopian read about a post-pandemic world. So, what makes one of them profound, and the other not?

One intuitive explanation is that *Ulysses* deals with profound subject matter, whereas *Station Eleven* doesn't, and that marks the difference between them. Profundity depends on your subject matter, and what you *say* about it. But, of course, plenty of *bad* art has profound subject matter (see *Good-Bad Art*), so we need a way to restrict profundity to the good stuff. Here again, literature can help us: *Ulysses* is incredibly difficult to read because it's so chock-full of allusions and parodies, does weird things with the English language, has a very particular structure, etc. *Station Eleven*, by contrast, is a straightforward narrative unfolding at two different times.

Extrapolating from literature, then, we might say that for an artwork to be profound, it must (1) be about something, (2) that something must be profound, and (3) it has to deal with its profound subject in a

DOI: 10.4324/9781003368205-43

particularly exemplary manner, or a manner that 'fits' the importance of its subject matter (Kivy 1990).

This is a promising gloss on profundity, but it runs into trouble outside of literature—especially with music. That's because it's quite common for the 'musically learned' to say that certain works are profound—usually works in the 'classical' tradition of instrumental music, although there is no reason why other musical genres cannot also be profound. The trouble is that *instrumental* music isn't *propositional*; it doesn't *say* anything, and so can't really be *about* anything in the first place. It's just nice sounds. So, despite the pronouncements of the musically learned, it seems like instrumental music, at least, can't be profound. Profundity seems to require words. But if *any* music is profound, surely Beethoven's is a better candidate than Britney Spears's?

One way to salvage the profundity of instrumental music is in terms of its structural properties: if there are ways for music to refer to itself, then it can satisfy the aboutness criterion. And one suggestion for doing so is through *counterpoint* (Kivy 1990). In counterpoint, several melodic voices are made to complement one another despite acting independently. The result is a textured polyphony, with several simultaneous but independent lines of melody. A classical example is Bach's *Well-Tempered Clavier* (1722), but we can also find counterpoint in the *Star Wars* theme (the brasses are doing one thing, and the strings, basses, and percussion another). What makes counterpoint musically challenging is the task of juggling a number of different melodies, each of which remains intrinsically interesting on its own. A skilled composer can combine one melody with itself, with a version of itself that's augmented or diminished, with an inverted version of itself, or even with itself back to front. In doing so, we get a work that is plausibly 'about' itself and shows us the possibilities hidden in a theme.

Pulling this off requires supreme craftsmanship, of course. Generalizing to the rest of music, it seems plausible that supreme craftsmanship is what all the music we call 'profound' has in common, from classical instrumental music to jazz standards, and that what supreme craftsmanship does is to show us the possibilities hidden in the music (Kivy 1990). This is surely interesting, and certainly important; but is it *profound*? Recall the second condition above: the work's subject should itself be profound. And usually, when we say something is profound, we mean that it cuts to the heart of the human condition. The 'profound' problems are things like the meaning of life, the existence of free will, and the problem of evil; in that company, an interest in musical possibilities seems somewhat misplaced. So, although instrumental music seems capable of satisfying conditions (1) and (3), it struggles to justify itself against condition (2). The result, then, is that it cannot be profound (Kivy 1990).

RESPONSES

Perhaps unsurprisingly, much of the subsequent discussion of musical profundity has focused on Kivy's second condition. The problem, these philosophers argue, lies in thinking that 'aboutness' requires propositional content: if we grant that something can be about something without expressing any propositions about it, then we can sufficiently weaken condition (2) to allow some musical works to count as profound.

One popular suggestion is that music's expressive qualities allow it to be 'about' something profound: human emotional life (Levinson 1992; see also *The St. Bernard's Face*). Music's expressive qualities, it's argued, can draw attention to fundamentally important extra-musical concerns, such as death or the ravages of time, by prompting listeners to focus and reflect upon its emotional qualities (Levinson 1992).

A different way of cashing this out is to say that profundity in general isn't really propositional; rather, it's *dispositional*, it's about the kinds of responses it elicits in an audience (Dodd 2014). The literature we describe as 'profound', like Joyce's *Ulysses*, abides by the English teacher's dictum: *show, don't tell*. When literature tells us something that's supposed to be profound, it comes out trite; but when it *shows* us, either by exemplifying its thesis or putting it on display, the effect is deeply moving. Profound artworks thus demand that we interpret their *artistic* meaning, not their propositional content. And what makes that artistic meaning profound isn't the message itself, but rather the way in which the work's details compel us to reflect seriously upon that meaning so that we come to appreciate it more deeply.

In fact, perhaps profundity doesn't require 'aboutness' at all—perhaps profundity requires a *connection* to something of human importance, but needn't take that thing as its subject (Davies 2002). Consider chess: chess is an incredibly rich game with the capacity to engage the human mind more fully than many other activities. It seems perfectly plausible to describe some games of chess, or some moves, as 'profound'; but chess isn't about anything at all. It's just a game (c.f. *Utopia*). So: perhaps profundity is something that is shown in someone's actions or in the quality of their judgements and valued for what it shows us about the agent behind that action or judgement. Profound music, then, is music we value for what it shows us about its composer and the superlative capacities of the human mind.

Another way to cash out the insight that profundity doesn't require aboutness is in structural terms (Ridley 1995). Profoundly-held beliefs are beliefs that stand at the centre of a network; they are so deeply embedded in a person's identity and world-view that they shape everything they touch. To say that a belief is profoundly held is to say that it stands at the heart of a web, structuring the many other beliefs which depend upon it. By analogy, we can say that profound art, or profound music, exhibits similar structural relations, with some element standing in a central structural relation to a wider context. In music, expressive properties seem particularly well-disposed to this kind of structuring: they anchor the piece, determine its various movements, and offer listeners hints about new ways to look at the world around them.

But if we take the analogy to literature seriously, another possibility emerges. Profound literary works like *Ulysses* are relatively *inaccessible*: aesthetically engaging with them takes *a lot* of work (Nanay 2021). They reward that effort—indeed, they *invite* it, which is why we do it in the first place—but they also actively resist it. Water is deep when you can't see its bottom, and so, too, with art: works are profound when they actively frustrate straightforward interpretation but nudge us on to keep interpreting them. This account has the advantage of explaining why profundity is unevenly distributed across genres: comedies, pop music, and thrillers make their artistic aims obvious, whereas modern novels, tragedies, and instrumental music tend not to do so (see also *The Paradox of Tragedy*).

Or perhaps profundity isn't any single property and thus isn't amenable to any single, unified account (White 1992, Reimer 1995,

Sharpe 2000, Bicknell 2009). In fact, empirical work on profound musical experiences suggests that we describe many very different experiences as 'profound', including having a new and altered perception of the world, significant sensory-motor responses (e.g., shivers), a narrowing of perception, and feeling a deep emotional connection to the music (Reimer 1995). We clearly use 'profundity' as an intensifier, meaning that a given work is *deeply* depressing or *thoroughly* enjoyable (White 1992; see also Reimer 1995). Experiences of profundity thus seem to be intense experiences which we'd like to repeat. And repetition serves to make the structure of the experience apparent, since it allows us to deploy our *memory* of parts of the composition, say, in order to *anticipate* its future directions.

Nor should we get too hung up on the problem of instrumental music, since our judgements of it are never purely formal (Sharpe 2000): they require knowledge of the work's history, development, and cultural context, as well as comparisons to its predecessors and its contemporaries. Profound works *demand* interpretation, and we satisfy that demand by noticing all of these extra-musical associations. This is why we apply the term 'profound' in so many different ways, to works which break new ground and show us new possibilities, or which demonstrate remarkable skill (e.g., jazz), etc. 'Profound' seems to mean different things in different contexts; but perhaps we should be careful to distinguish intense emotional (i.e., sublime) experiences, which need not be 'about' anything at all, from profound ones, which seem to imply a cognitive component (Bicknell 2009).

SUGGESTED READING

SEMINAL PRESENTATION:

1. Kivy, Peter (1990). *Music Alone: Philosophical Reflections on the Purely Musical Experience*. Ithaca, NY: Cornell University Press.
   Kivy introduces the puzzle of musical profundity in Ch. 10, arguing that for something to be profound it must be about something, that something must be profound, and it must treat its subject in an exemplary manner, or in a manner adequate to the subject. Since music isn't propositional, it cannot be profound.

DEFENCES:

2. Bicknell, Jeanette (2009). *Why Music Moves Us*. London: Palgrave-Macmillan.
   Bicknell argues that the empirical evidence shows that music does in fact
   arouse strong emotions, and that an important part of the explanation for
   this phenomenon is social. In Ch. 7 she distinguishes between experiences
   of sublimity (intense emotional reactions) and profundity (which is tied to
   knowledge).

CRITIQUES:

3. Levinson, Jerrold (1992). Musical Profundity Misplaced. *Journal of Aesthetics
   and Art Criticism* 50 (1): 58–60.
   Levinson takes aim at Kivy's 'aboutness' criterion, arguing that the expressive
   qualities of music can draw attention to themselves, and thus music can be
   'about' the expression of emotion. Profoundness is not just a matter of structural properties: it's a matter of providing a particular kind of experience or
   vision of fundamentally important human possibilities.

4. Davies, Stephen (2002). Profundity in Instrumental Music. *British Journal of
   Aesthetics* 42 (4): 343–56.
   Davies takes issue with Kivy's second condition, arguing that restricting
   'aboutness' to propositional content is too strict. Chess isn't 'about' anything,
   but certain moves or games can be profound. Profundity is something shown
   in an action or a judgement; music is profound because of what it shows us
   about its composer, and what it reveals about the capacities of the human
   mind.

5. Nanay, Bence (2021). Looking for Profundity (in All the Wrong Places).
   Journal of Aesthetics and Art Criticism 79: 344–53.
   Taking seriously the analogy to literature, Nanay argues that a work's profundity is primarily a function of its inaccessibility to audiences. Profound
   works resist our efforts to interpret them, but also *invite* interpretation.

6. Ridley, Aaron (1995). "Profundity in Music," in *Arguing About Art*, Alex Neill
   and Aaron Ridley (eds.). New York: McGraw-Hill, 260–72.
   Ridley argues that the 'aboutness' criterion is entirely mistaken: profundity
   isn't tied to something's subject matter, but rather to the fact that it stands in
   a central structural relation to a wider context. Music is profound in virtue
   of its expressive properties, which hint at different ways to structure our
   views of the world.

7. Dodd, Julian (2014). The Possibility of Profound Music. *British Journal of
   Aesthetics* 54 (3): 299–322.
   Dodd argues that profundity isn't to be found in the propositions a work
   expresses, but rather in the kinds of responses it elicits (and justifiably so)

from an understanding audience. Profundity isn't a matter of *expressing* truths about the world but rather of *portraying* them in a manner that compels us to appreciate them more deeply.

FURTHER READING:

8. White, David A. (1992). Toward a Theory of Profundity in Music. *Journal of Aesthetics and Art Criticism* 50 (1): 23–34.

White argues that there is no independent property of works picked out by the term 'profundity'; instead, we use it as an intensifier, to mean, e.g., that the work is *deeply* melancholy or *very* joyful. Profound aesthetic experiences are those of enjoyment modulated by a desire to encounter the work again, so that we can experience it as a whole and anticipate its movements.

9. Reimer, Bennett (1995). The Experience of Profundity in Music. *Journal of Aesthetic Education* 29 (4): 1–21.

Reimer surveys empirical research on experiences of musical profundity, which suggests that such experiences come in different forms. He argues that in addition to the music's formal structure, the individual's constitution and dispositions and the context of hearing all shape experiences of profundity, which he defines as 'being moved deeply' by the music.

10. Sharpe, Robert Augustus (2000). Sounding the Depths. *British Journal of Aesthetics* 40 (1): 64–72.

Sharpe argues that there can be no single, unified account of profundity in music. We use the term to pick out works which break new musical ground and show us new possibilities, to denote enormous technical skill (though this doesn't seem sufficient), and as an intensifier, to denote works which we find greatly moving. Profundity, he thinks, implies interpretation.

NOTE

1 I don't endorse this claim!

THE ST. BERNARD'S FACE (MUSIC AND EMOTION)

CASE

Imagine a picture of a St. Bernard: it's looking up at you, staring with those big brown eyes, its ears flopped down and its jowls drooping well below its chin. Doesn't it look sad?

It's not, of course, *expressing* sadness, since that's just the way a St. Bernard *looks*, regardless of how it's feeling. It doesn't look sad because it *is* sad, either, or because it makes *us* sad to see it. Presumably, it looks sad because its face has certain structural properties—primarily droopiness, but maybe also big, moist eyes—which we associate with sad *human* behaviours. Now try to imagine someone who thought it looked overjoyed—it's hard to do, right? We might disagree about whether the dog looks melancholy, lonely, or petulant, but we're not very likely to think it looks happy, grateful, or serene.

Now imagine a sad piece of music. Anything you know well will do. I used to think that Israel Kamakawiwoʻole's *Somewhere Over the Rainbow/What A Wonderful World* was unbearably haunting. My partner disagrees: she thinks it's joyful. I've mostly come around (although I still think it has a mournful or melancholy tone), so maybe Josh Ritter's *The Curse* is a better example. Is there anything strange or puzzling in claiming it's sad? The lyrics are about loneliness and love

DOI: 10.4324/9781003368205-44

outlived, which certainly aren't happy themes; Kamakawiwoʻole's mashup, by contrast, has predominantly hopeful lyrics (hence my partner's take). But what, if anything, does the music itself contribute to the expressive quality of the song?

The commonsense explanation of musical expressiveness is just that music *resembles* the emotions in various ways (c.f. *The Paradox of Portraiture* and *The Puzzle of Depiction*). This is known as the *resemblance theory* of musical expressiveness. In particular, musical expression is said to resemble human emotion in the same way that St. Bernard's face looks sad; that is to say, by being broadly similar to human expressive behaviour (Kivy 1980[1]). For example, sad voices fall in pitch, so that falling melodies are appropriate for expressing sadness, whereas joy or trepidation quicken the pulse, so that a quick beat is appropriate for expressing those emotions. To say that the music is sad is thus to say that we recognize the ways in which it resembles how we typically express sadness, or some convention which originated in a behavioural expression of sadness. Music therefore expresses what it does independently of the emotions it leads us to feel, or those felt by the composer.

But music alone (i.e., without text) doesn't seem able to make fine-grained distinctions between the emotions it expresses—e.g., between hope and excitement, or fear and anxiety. For that reason, this theory is sometimes called the *contour theory*, since music resembles the emotions in its broad contours. That's not to say that we're necessarily aware of performing these comparisons, however: according to the contour theory, we have a brute, evolved tendency to 'animate' music, in much the same way that we tend to see faces in the clouds or patterns in events.

RESPONSES

As it stands, the contour theory stakes out two significant empirical claims: (1) that we consistently recognize similarities between musical passages and expressive human behaviour, and (2) that this process is largely automatic. In fact, there is a fair bit of empirical evidence suggesting that perceptions of musical expressiveness are widely shared, with listeners generally agreeing in their descriptions of the music's expressive and extra-musical content (Young 2014). This evidence suggests that even instrumental pure music can arouse a wide range of emotions beyond the simplest and most basic. Whether the arousal of emotion in the listener is a byproduct of the music's expressive character, or whether its expressive character is a byproduct of arousal, however, remains an open question. On the other hand, the animation claim requires a kind of synaesthesia, whereas the perceptual phenomena in question may be more closely tied to each individual sensory modality (Ravasio 2018). Moreover, it seems like perceptions of musical expressiveness require an *attenuated* resemblance—if Ritter starts to sob uncontrollably in the middle of singing *The Curse*, then it's no longer clear that we're dealing with a *musical* expression of sadness.

'Appearance emotionalism' attempts to ditch some of this baggage while sticking to the contours of a resemblance theory. According to this model, the musical work's expressive qualities are *response-dependent* properties of the work (Davies 2011): they have the expressive quality they have in virtue of their ability to produce a relevantly related characteristic response in typical auditors under suitable conditions. What makes some music sad, then, is just that it tends to produce, say, a watering about the eyes of its listeners, or at least a melancholy feeling. And it does so by resembling, in its dynamic and temporally-extended way, the kinds of expressive behaviours we evince when we're sad—e.g., moving slowly, as at a funeral procession.

The resemblance isn't based on an absolute measure of similarity, but rather on our experience of similarity, especially as conditioned by the contexts in which certain behaviours count as appropriate emotional responses and displays. Where instrumental pure music is concerned, we can't expect fine-grained distinctions between complex emotions—e.g., despair vs. depression—but we nevertheless find widespread congruence between people's musical experiences of more basic emotions. This is explained by the fact that there are only a limited range of emotions which we can individuate based on bodily movement alone, without accompanying context or verbal indications.

So-called 'arousal' theories[2] instead maintain that we feel emotions in response to perceptual properties in the music, and this causes us to perceive the music as expressive. These emotions are aroused in us directly, rather than about or for some intentional object (Radford 1991; Matravers 2011). Because they lack intentional objects, these emotions are just non-cognitive mental states: they're *feelings*. As a result, they're perhaps better characterized as 'moods', to distinguish them from more complex (cognitive) emotions.

On the other hand, even though there may not be much of an affective or physiological difference between certain complex emotions (e.g., depression vs. melancholy), there may still be significant *cognitive* differences between them which music can indicate, provided we consider musical works as *wholes* rather than focusing on a few bars here and there (Robinson 1994). Individual passages thus directly arouse 'primitive' emotions like sadness or startlement, but when joined to a succession of such emotions over the length of an entire composition, they function to tell us something about expressiveness in the work as a whole. They offer a clue to the work's more complex cognitive content, inviting us to speculate.

It has also been suggested that the imagination plays a crucial role in establishing music's expressiveness. According to the *persona theory*, for example, we hear music as the expression of someone's mental states—that is, when listening to music we imagine a persona who tells us how they feel by means of the music (Levinson 2006). Much as the contour theory had us 'animating' the music, the persona theory contends that we hear an agent in the music, even if they are relegated to the background. But we might wonder: why stop at one persona (Davies 2011)? Why can't a piece feature several duelling personas? Alternately, perhaps what's needed is a more general *imaginationist* account (Trivedi 2017). On this view, we might say that personas are a sufficient, but not a necessary, explanation for musical expressiveness. In addition to personas, perhaps the imagination can generate musical emotion by personifying the music itself and attributing the relevant mental state to it, or by making it seem like it's *our own* mental states which are being expressed (not unlike how we seek out music to fit our moods).

Finally, it is worth mentioning the *formalist* alternative, which primarily finds its justification in the failings of other theories (Beardsley 1958): if other theories don't quite work, then all we're left with is the music itself. According to the formalist, our appeal to emotions is just a way of *describing* the music we hear, a kind of metaphor. These descriptions can help us to imagine the music more concretely if we haven't yet heard it, but it's better still to be able to point to the music itself. Terms like 'express' are thus redundant: it's enough to say that the music is joyous, and to say that it *expresses* joy just confuses the matter by needlessly multiplying entities.

SUGGESTED READING

SEMINAL PRESENTATION:

1. Kivy, Peter (1980). *The Corded Shell Reflections on Musical Expression.* Princeton: Princeton University Press.
   According to Kivy's *contour theory* of musical expressiveness, music expresses by imitating expressive behaviours—so, e.g., sad music and sad gestures both tend to be slow, and happy music and gestures fast. We hear it as appropriate for expressing a particular emotion, e.g., sadness. And what makes it appropriate for the expression of sadness is just its structural similarities to our own expressions of sadness (its 'contour'; see especially Chs. 6–7).

DEFENCES:

2. Young, James O. (2014). *Critique of Pure Music.* Oxford: Oxford University Press.
   Young argues that music's aesthetic value is typically due to its representation of extra-musical (i.e., non-formal) content. In particular, he defends the contour theory of musical expressiveness, arguing that empirical evidence confirms its basic tenets (see especially Chs. 1 and 2).
3. Davies, Stephen (2011). "Artistic Expression and the Hard Case of Pure Music," in *Musical Understandings: And Other Essays on the Philosophy of Music.* New York: Oxford University Press, 7–20.
   Davies argues for a resemblance theory he calls 'appearance emotionalism', according to which a musical work's expressive qualities are objective but response-dependent properties of the piece. Music is expressive insofar as its dynamic structure tends to prompt us to recall expressive human behaviour, especially the body's air, attitude, carriage, and gait under certain circumstances.

CRITIQUES:

4. Radford, Colin (1991). Muddy Waters. *Journal of Aesthetics and Art Criticism* 49 (3): 247–52.
   Radford argues for what has been called 'arousalism', the view that music can arouse the emotions it expresses—in other words, sad music tends to make us sad, happy music happy, etc. We aren't sad or happy *about* the music, or *for* it, but rather are made sad or happy directly *by* it.

5. Ravasio, Matteo (2018). On Evolutionary Explanations of Musical Expressiveness. *Evental Aesthetics* 7 (1): 6–29.

   Ravasio outlines several problems facing Kivy's suggestion (also adopted, to some extent, by Davies, Levinson, and Young) that we are evolutionarily hard-wired to automatically animate inanimate things. In particular, he argues that the 'wiring' in question seems to be closely tied to individual sensory systems so that no single phenomenon can explain automatic uptake across all sense systems, or cross-modal resemblances.

FURTHER READING:

6. Beardsley, Monroe C. (1958). *Aesthetics, Problems in the Philosophy of Criticism.* New York: Harcourt, Brace & World.

   Beardsley does not offer a positive thesis about emotion in music; instead, in Ch. 7, §18 he argues against the image-evocation, expression, and the signification theories. By process of elimination, he thinks we are left with a formalist theory of music: emotional talk is descriptive and backed up by the music itself, to which we should pay attention.

7. Levinson, Jerrold (2006). "Musical Expressiveness as Hearability-as-Expression," in *Contemplating Art: Essays in Aesthetics,* Jerrold Levinson (ed.). Oxford: Oxford University Press, 91–108.

   According to Levinson's *persona theory,* to hear music as expressive is to hear it as someone's personal expression of their mental state. Music invites us to posit a person (not the music itself, nor the composer; a hypothetical person) expressing themselves by its means.

8. Matravers, Derek (2011). "Arousal Theories," in *The Routledge Companion to Philosophy and Music,* Theodore Gracyk and Andrew Kania (eds.). New York: Routledge, 212–22.

   Matravers surveys the contemporary literature on arousal theories of musical expression. He tackles the problem of negative emotion, arousal in non-arousalist theories, and distinguishes 'simple' from 'sophisticated' arousal theories depending on the scope of their central claim.

9. Robinson, Jenefer (1994). The Expression and Arousal of Emotion in Music. *Journal of Aesthetics and Art Criticism* 52 (1): 13–22.

   Robinson develops an inference-based arousal theory, according to which music directly arouses simple emotions in us (e.g., joy, sadness, startlement, etc.). The interplay of such snatches of music and simple feelings can contribute to more complex emotions by giving us clues about the formal and expressive structure of the piece as a whole.

10. Trivedi, Saam (2017). *Imagination, Music, and the Emotions: A Philosophical Study.* Albany, NY: SUNY Press.

    Trivedi argues, especially in Ch. 6, that musical expressiveness is a matter of imagination: either (1) personifying the music and imagining it to be sad,

(2) imagining that it's *as if* someone were expressing the relevant emotion, or

(3) imagining that the music is expressing our mental states.

NOTES

1 Note, however, that Kivy later abandoned this theory.

2 Or 'neo-arousalism', to distinguish it from its eighteenth-century antecedents.

PART V

ETHICS AND VALUE

GENERAL BACKGROUND

The cases surveyed in the previous parts have shown the importance of artists and their intentions to the nature of their final product, as well as how a context of display or reception can influence our judgements of artworks. They've also shown that our appreciation and interpretation of art are often tied up in judgements about the influence of those facts. We use art to express ideas and register disagreement, to explore possibilities, and to indulge our fantasies. Because art is made by and for human beings, it responds to human interests and social practices; it's not surprising, then, that it's so often tangled up in moral and political considerations.

This final section groups together cases which focus on ethical issues in art, as well as broader questions about aesthetic value. They invite us to consider the ways in which we engage with art, and whether our responses are morally appropriate, but they also ask us to consider why we think it's important to have access to certain kinds of aesthetic experiences. Is it wrong for us to root for evil protagonists or to do things in the context of a game which we'd otherwise think are morally reprehensible? Is it morally wrong to appropriate the styles or motifs of other cultures? Why should we care what an animal or landscape looks like, and why do we care so much about virtual objects?

DOI: 10.4324/9781003368205-45

THE PARADOX OF *BAD*-BAD ART (MORALISM/IMMORALISM)

CASE

Imagine a horror movie. Not the kind of cattle prod cinema characterized by jump-scares, but a piece of psychological terror that leaves audiences devastated in its wake. Suppose further that this film's guiding objective was to make *kittens and rainbows* the central feature of that utter devastation.[1]

It's a hard sell, isn't it? You can sort of imagine it being done in the abstract, but it's hard to imagine it being done particularly successfully. That's because the response that the film prescribes—abject terror and utter desolation—is not one that's usually warranted by depictions of rainbows and kittens. It takes a lot more work for a film about kittens and rainbows to earn its keep as a horror film; one might get most of the way there with a film told from the perspective of small rodents, but the rainbows remain a sticking point. At any rate, the point here is not that such a film is impossible to conceive, but rather that there's an incongruity between the attitude the film recommends for its audience and the circumstances it uses to justify that attitude. This incongruity gets in the way and makes the entire project seem ridiculous; it's an aesthetic flaw.

DOI: 10.4324/9781003368205-46

The same kind of problem, it's thought, can arise from an artwork's moral flaws: the moral flaws can or will (depending on how strong the formulation is) amount to aesthetic flaws, because they will inhibit audience uptake. But whereas our initial case involved some far-fetched imagining, we don't have to work too hard to find real cases of artworks whose moral flaws are plausibly also aesthetic flaws: just think of Leni Riefenstahl's *The of Triumph of the Will* (1938), William Luther Pierce's *The Turner Diaries* (1978), or Paul Bernardo's *A MAD World Order* (2015). There's absolutely no question that these are *morally* flawed works, but are they *aesthetically* flawed? The last two are, frankly, not very good, but they're aesthetically bad independently of whether their moral flaws make them even worse. *The Triumph of the Will* is a much more interesting case, because the film is beautiful and masterfully executed. If it *is* aesthetically flawed, the only plausible source of those flaws is ethical. We now have our puzzle: do *The of Triumph of the Will*'s moral flaws amount to aesthetic flaws? It's obviously a *morally* bad film, but does that make it *aesthetically* bad? In contrast to *The Paradox of Good-Bad Art*, then, we might call this *The Paradox of Bad-Bad Art*.

RESPONSES

An influential strand of art criticism maintains that artworks are independent, self-contained entities, and that we should confine our criticism to the work itself. This view is sometimes called '*autonomism*', and readers will recognize formalism as its main branch (see *Guernicas*). Autonomism would have us bracket our responses to *Triumph*'s message and the perspective it urges us to adopt and recognize it as beautiful independently of its moral viciousness.

Moralism, by contrast, is the view that moral flaws can sometimes count as aesthetic flaws (Carroll 1996). According to moralists, this happens when a work sets out to elicit a particular kind of response from its audience, but the work's moral flaws prevent the audience from successfully adopting the prescribed response. This is a failure of design and, thus, an aesthetic failure (or, following Dickie 2005, an *artistic* failure). If one of the artistic goals of *The Triumph of the Will* is to get me to see the glory of Hitler's vision for Germany, then it fails in that respect since I simply *cannot* shrug off my beliefs about how bad Nazism is (see also *The Puzzle of Imaginative Resistance*).

Ethicism takes a somewhat stronger tack: any moral virtue or vice that is relevant to the work's appreciation is an aesthetic virtue or vice (Gaut 1998). Artworks, on this view, often prescribe that their audiences adopt certain moral perspectives; this is especially true of the narrative arts. A work's attitudes will be reflected in the responses it prescribes to its audience; so, for example, *The Triumph of the Will* wants to convince us to become Nazis, so it's bad, whereas Henry Bean's *The Believer* (2001) makes it clear that we should not approve of its Nazi protagonist. Only the first constitutes a moral flaw in the work. Similarly, although Swift's *A Modest Proposal* (1729) makes a heinous suggestion, it does not prescribe that we endorse that suggestion—on the contrary, properly understanding the work means recognizing it as satire and, thus, *condemning* the callous attitude people have towards the poor. When a work prescribes a response which it hasn't merited, then that is an artistic flaw: thrillers that don't thrill us are aesthetically flawed. And sometimes, a work's prescribed response is subject to ethical criteria; if it hasn't earned that sort of response, then that's an artistic failure.

Alternately, several philosophers have observed that moral flaws can sometimes *enhance* a work's value: this view is usually called *immoralism*. Sometimes, for example, a joke's offensiveness is an integral part of what makes it good; it's transgressive, and that's what makes it funny (Jacobson 1997). Similarly, many narrative works feature 'rough' heroes, protagonists who are irredeemably bad, like Tony Soprano or Walter White,[2] and whose exploits *audiences are meant to cheer on*. These works ask us to endorse an aberrant moral perspective, and that is surely a moral failing—but when it works, it also constitutes a singular aesthetic achievement (Eaton 2011). It is no easy task to make audiences like the morally despicable and want more of it, while they nevertheless recognize it *as* despicable. The work's immorality seems like an important part of the explanation for why it captivates us so.

Then again, perhaps we should be more careful: the *characters* are morally flawed, and the narrative is structured so as to make us root for them, but that doesn't mean that the work itself is morally flawed. The characters' moral turpitude is on obvious display, and while the works prescribe that we view them in a sympathetic light, unlike *The Triumph of the Will* it doesn't usually aim to convince us to be like them (Dadlez 2017). Indeed, the fact that rough heroes are fictional, whereas *Triumph* is a documentary, seems to mark an important difference in the moral perspectives being prescribed. *Triumph*'s moral flaws are intrinsic to the work itself. Nor is it clear that it *could* be sanitized, its moral and aesthetic content separated (Jacobson 1997, Devereaux 1998): every single detail contributes to the film's vision and effect. Understanding the work requires us to open ourselves to it and its message (Devereaux 1998); it's a *beautiful* film, but its beauty is *terrible*.

It has also been suggested that autonomism can be saved in various ways, however. One suggestion is that the autonomist should adopt a 'narrow' understanding of what counts as 'aesthetic', such that only a work's perceptual properties count as aesthetic, and none of its contextual properties do (Dickie 2005). Moral flaws might then lead to *artistic* flaws, but not aesthetic ones. The difficulty here, however, lies in specifying an account of aesthetic properties (Smuts 2011). If they're response-dependent, then they are akin to powers to cause us to have certain reactions. But if emotional responses contribute to aesthetic value, then conflicting responses can detract from it, and surely moral flaws can lead us to have conflicting responses. So moral flaws seem like a plausible 'defeater' of aesthetic properties, which is all moralism requires. Alternately, perhaps aesthetic properties (e.g., gracefulness) supervene on primary qualities (e.g., shape or colour). But if contextualism about art is right, then some contextual properties (e.g., art-kind, originality) must also be included in the supervenience base; and if that's so, then we have no principled reason to exclude moral properties as potential aesthetic defeaters. All moralism needs to show, then, is that there's some sort of causal or explanatory chain linking a work's moral flaw(s) to its aesthetic flaw(s).

Finally, some philosophers have argued, instead, for a more moderate account. According to this *moderate autonomism*, moral considerations are perfectly legitimate grounds for the criticism of art, but those grounds are distinct from aesthetic considerations (Anderson and Dean 1998; see also *The Puzzle of Moral Persuasion*). That is to say, moral considerations can *inform* aesthetic considerations, but they aren't themselves also somehow aesthetic. In particular, a moderate autonomist can observe that the moralist's use of 'prescribed' responses is ambiguous: does it mean that the response is endorsed, elicited, or both (Stear 2020)? If it's endorsement, then the work is ethically, but not yet aesthetically, flawed; if it's elicitation, then it's aesthetically (i.e., artistically), but not yet ethically, flawed. And if it's both, then the moralist's argument rests on an equivocation and is thus unsound. Endorsing seems like the best candidate, but then all the moralist can show is that the work's moral and aesthetic flaws have a common cause, not that the moral flaw *is* an aesthetic flaw.

SUGGESTED READING

SEMINAL PRESENTATION:

1. Carroll, Noël (1996). Moderate Moralism. *British Journal of Aesthetics* 36 (3): 233–8.
   Carroll distinguishes between radical autonomism, which maintains that moral considerations are never appropriately applied to art, and moderate autonomism, which maintains that moral and aesthetic considerations are separate kettles of fish. He argues for a moderate moralism, according to which some art-kinds, including the narrative arts, typically or even necessarily involve a moral dimension. For those art-kinds, moral flaws can turn out to be aesthetic flaws: they are failures at the level of design.

DEFENCES:

2. Gaut, Berys (1998). "The Ethical Criticism of Art," in *Aesthetics and Ethics: Essays at the Intersection,* Jerrold Levinson (ed.). Cambridge: Cambridge University Press, 182–203.
   Gaut argues that an artwork's ethical merits and demerits constitute artistic virtues and vices, provided they are relevant to its appreciation. In particular, he argues that some artworks prescribe the kinds of responses their audiences are supposed to have, including certain kinds of moral evaluation. It is an artistic merit when an artwork succeeds in provoking the intended response and when that response is merited, and a demerit when it doesn't or isn't.

3. Dickie, George (2005). The Triumph in Triumph of the Will. *British Journal of Aesthetics* 45 (2): 151–6.
   Dickie agrees with Carroll and Gaut that an artwork's moral perspective and content are important subjects of critical consideration. But he argues that moral flaws, to the extent that they are failures of design, are not *aesthetic* flaws: they are *artistic* flaws. Leni Riefenstahl's *The Triumph of the Will* (1935)

is deeply morally flawed, but it's also perfectly coherent. None of its *aesthetic* qualities is a moral defect; as an *artistic* project, however, it is odious.

4. Smuts, Aaron (2011). Grounding Moralism: Moral Flaws and Aesthetic Properties. *Journal of Aesthetic Education* 45 (4): 34–53.

   Smuts argues that moral properties are relevant to art's aesthetic evaluation regardless of how we choose to characterize aesthetic properties (viz., as response-dependent or supervenient). Quite simply, moral flaws become aesthetic flaws when they defeat the operation or uptake of aesthetic properties.

CRITIQUES:

5. Jacobson, Daniel (1997). In Praise of Immoral Art. *Philosophical Topics* 25 (1): 155–99.

   Jacobson surveys a wide swathe of the debate between formalism (or 'autonomism') and moralism, including its spillover into philosophical thinking about humour. He argues that just as a joke's offensiveness is sometimes inseparable from its funniness, so too is it the case that sometimes moral flaws actually *increase* an artwork's aesthetic value (immoralism).

6. Anderson, James C. and Dean, Jeffrey T. (1998). Moderate Autonomism. *British Journal of Aesthetics* 38 (2): 150–66.

   Anderson and Dean argue that moralism does not succeed in showing that a work's moral defects *are* aesthetic defects. Instead, they argue that it simply shows that moral defects can be the *basis of* aesthetic defects. The result is that they advocate a moderate autonomism: while ethical criticism of art is appropriate, it is distinct from aesthetic criticism.

7. Stear, Nils-Hennes (2020). Fatal Prescription. *British Journal of Aesthetics* 60 (2): 151–63.

   Stear argues that the usual arguments in favour of moralism cannot establish the conclusion that ethical flaws are aesthetic flaws. What they show, instead, is that ethical flaws can be obstacles to aesthetic appreciation. This is because moralism relies on different senses of a 'prescription' at different points in its arguments. Moralism's reliance on 'merited responses' gives away the game: it is not with respect to manifesting or prescribing an unethical attitude that these works are flawed.

FURTHER READING:

8. Devereaux, Mary (1998). "Beauty and Evil: The Case of Leni Riefenstahl's 'Triumph of the Will,'" in *Aesthetics and Ethics: Essays at the Intersection*, Jerrold Levinson (ed.). Cambridge: Cambridge University Press. 227–56.

   Devereaux argues that in appreciating *The Triumph of the Will* we cannot bracket its moral perspective and real-world implications. To do so would require us to ignore the essence of the film; appreciating its beauty requires us to see it as it was intended to be seen, to attend to its artistic vision and respond to it as art. Although the film's utter moral failure is a significant artistic defect, it also underpins its value.

9. Eaton, A. W. (2011). Rough Heroes of the New Hollywood. *Revue Internationale de Philosophie* 258 (4): 511–24.

Eaton argues that some works of fiction are aesthetically valuable precisely because of their moral flaws. In particular, she thinks that rough heroes—irredeemably *bad* protagonists—present us with cases where we both recognize how awful they are, but also cheer them on. And that, she thinks, represents a significant artistic achievement. The conflicted state we are left to inhabit, she argues, is properly described as an *aesthetic* one.

10. Dadlez, Eva M. (2017). Hume, Halos, and Rough Heroes: Moral and Aesthetic Defects in Works of Fiction. *Philosophy and Literature* 41 (1): 91–102.

Dadlez contends that works featuring rough heroes, although often of greater aesthetic interest for that fact, are not themselves *immoral*: there is no moral flaw (at least, not typically). The characters are morally flawed, but the works are so only occasionally, when they tend to reinforce such behaviour in their audiences. Rough narratives seem to better reflect real people's mixed characteristics and our real reactions to them.

NOTES

1 This example is suggested in Dadlez (2017).

2 I take it that this is the point of *Breaking Bad* (AMC 2008–13), at any rate; Jesse is redeemable, but White, though he begins the series an antihero, so thoroughly compromises his (and our) values throughout the series that he becomes a monster proper. In contrast, Alex from *A Clockwork Orange* (1962) is often cited as a rough hero, but the whole point of the story is that he is redeemable, as suggested in the epilogue.

HOW THE ZEBRA LOST HER STRIPES (ENVIRONMENTAL AESTHETICS)

CASE

Depending on whom you ask, there are three or four species of zebras: Grévy's zebra, the plains zebra, the mountain zebra, and Hartmann's zebra (sometimes classified as a subspecies of the mountain zebra). Each species has a distinct conservation status, and the plains zebra is not considered endangered or vulnerable. But imagine it was. Imagine, in fact, that *all* zebras are endangered because they are extensively hunted for their striped coats.

Imagine further that we decide to save the zebra by selectively breeding individuals to lose their stripes. These stripeless zebras would look a bit like weird mules, but they'd still be Grévy's, Hartmann's, mountain, and plains zebras. We'd have saved zebras, but the question is: have we actually preserved everything we *ought* to have preserved? Put another way: it seems obvious that a world with stripeless zebras is a better world than one with no zebras at all, but has something of value been lost in the process of creating the stripeless–zebra–world?

I suspect most of us would think so: in losing its stripes, the zebra has lost something that we care about—not, perhaps, the stripes themselves, but rather their overall effect on our idea of the creature and

DOI: 10.4324/9781003368205-47

its ingenious evolutionary history. The lesson we can draw, then, is that we don't just care about species for the sake of raw, numerical diversity: we care about them for aesthetic reasons as well (Russow 1981). The value we attach to species and biodiversity is not just intrinsic.

This is not to say that species are valuable insofar as they are beautiful. A goblin shark, for example, is absolutely hideous, and so is a Bobbit worm (*shudder*). Aesthetic value is wide-ranging and can cover things which are of interest to us because they look weird, because they inspire awe or terror, because of their historical significance, because of how they fill their ecological niche, etc. (see also *Faking Nature*). Nor is this to suggest that aesthetic value is absolute—it's just that we usually think twice before destroying something of aesthetic value, to ensure that the benefits outweigh the costs (see also *The Burning Museum*).

Applied to issues of conservation, this appeal to species' aesthetic value might justify the differential treatment of certain species. Mosquitoes, for example, are of low aesthetic value, whereas blue whales are of high aesthetic value; so we should exert more effort to preserve the latter than the former, since their loss would be more keenly felt (on an aesthetic level). What we seem to lose, however, is a sense of why a species' being *endangered* matters, if its members are not of any special aesthetic value. Why should its brute *numbers* compel us if its appearance doesn't?

RESPONSES

One answer is just that certain species hold special cultural significance for certain groups of people (e.g., bald eagles for Americans, beavers for Canadians, Bengal tigers for Indians, and the… unicorn?… for Scots), and so those people are compelled to preserve these animals for that reason (see, e.g., Sagoff 1974; cf. Parsons 2007). Alternately, perhaps what we value is our aesthetic relation to the expressive qualities we attribute to animals—the lion's courage, the dolphin's joyful grin, the purity and masculine power of the unicorn, etc. (Brady 2014; see also Greaves 2019).

Or perhaps we are misidentifying the target of our aesthetic appreciation: perhaps it isn't the *species*, but rather *individual members* of a species (e.g., Russow 1981, Sober 1986). In other words, perhaps what we really care about is that there exist certain individual creatures with particular properties (which we later identify as typical of the species). We care about the zebra's stripes because they look nice and because zebras' razzle-dazzle camouflage represents a really cool defensive adaptation, among other reasons (Parsons 2007). And one reason why we should care that there are fewer of them in the world is because that means our chances of encountering them—and thus of appreciating their aesthetic value—are lower. Since animals die, if we want to keep encountering their aesthetically valuable features in the world, then we should ensure that they have the means to reproduce both themselves *and* their features of interest.

The problem, however, is that the rarer an animal or environment is, the less likely anyone is to encounter it—and, thus, the less likely anyone is to appreciate its aesthetic value (Parsons 2015). According to this kind of instrumentalist defence of a species' aesthetic value, it looks as though the last unicorn should have *less* aesthetic value than the lowest worm. One way to avoid this problem is to pivot to a species' *intrinsic* value instead. An instrumentalist alternative, however, is to claim that preserving species allows the few who do encounter them to become better judges of aesthetic value, which ultimately benefits us all (provided judges deign to share their newfound expertise) (Parsons 2015).

There is a potential ethical tension here, however. It is all well and good to say that some species matter more because they have more aesthetic value to us, but isn't that *speciesism*? In other words, isn't this just discrimination on the basis of species-membership (see Hettinger 2010)? And if it is, isn't that arbitrary and bad? Many will have the intuition that it is, by analogy to racism and sexism. Perhaps, then, we'd be better off arguing that aesthetic appreciation comes bundled with certain responsibilities—e.g., with duties of care—or flows from a particular virtuous character trait (Vice 2017).

Finally, yet another possibility is that in identifying aesthetic value as the value of a species, we have relied on the wrong analogues: perhaps the proper analogue to a species is not an individual art*work*, but rather an entire art-*kind*. On this model, the value of a species is like the value of an artistic genre or tradition, so that the extinction of a species—even one as aesthetically unappealing as the Bobbit worm, or as reviled as the mosquito—is like the loss of an entire artistic genre or medium (Carter 2010).

SUGGESTED READING

SEMINAL PRESENTATION:

1. Russow, Lilly-Marlene (1981). Why do Species Matter? *Environmental Ethics* 3 (2): 101–12.
   Russow introduces the possibility of stripeless zebras to show, first, that our concept of species is ambiguous, and second, that our concern for endangered species is not driven solely by concerns about biodiversity. She argues that the value of a species is driven by aesthetic considerations.

DEFENCES:

2. Sagoff, Mark (1974). On Preserving the Natural Environment. *The Yale Law Journal* 84 (2): 205–67.
   Sagoff argues that the aesthetic qualities of natural objects come from their cultural value. Insofar as a culture values what some creature has come to stand for (e.g., the bald eagle and freedom), then that culture has strong aesthetic reasons to preserve that species.
3. Hettinger, Ned (2010). Animal Beauty, Ethics, and Environmental Preservation. *Environmental Ethics* 32 (2): 115–34.
   Hettinger argues that aesthetic merit is an important, legitimate, and morally acceptable basis for species preservation. He defends this view against the charges that (1) it is discriminatory, and (2) the natural world is full of aesthetic *demerits* like animal death and suffering (see also *The Paradox of Disgust*).

CRITIQUES:

4. Parsons, Glenn (2007). The Aesthetic Value of Animals. *Environmental Ethics* 29: 151–69.
   Parsons considers several sources for the aesthetic value of animals, such as their strangeness or symbolic value, but argues that these are superficial modes of appreciation which do not reflect the animal's own nature and our relation to that nature. Instead, he argues that animal beauty is primarily functional: it is grounded in 'fitness for function'.
5. Carter, Alan (2010). Biodiversity and All That Jazz. *Philosophy and Phenomenological Research* 80 (1): 58–75.
   Carter surveys several aesthetically-grounded arguments for species-preservation, arguing that they either secure too little or depend upon a

flawed conception of 'species' as genotypes or phenotypes. The results are defences of species grounded in inappropriate artworld comparisons. Instead, Carter argues that a cladistic understanding of species yields the result that species-extinction is akin to the extinction of entire artistic genres.

FURTHER READING:

6. Sober, Elliott (1986). "Philosophical Problems for Environmentalism," in *The Preservation of Species: The Value of Biological Diversity*, Bryan G. Norton (ed.). Princeton: Princeton University Press, 173–94.
   Sober argues that environmental and aesthetic value are more than merely instrumental, and draw instead upon the connections we form to places and things. He also considers the importance of context and environmental 'fit' / site-specificity, the value of rarity, and the influence of human culture on the appreciation and valuation of art and nature.

7. Brady, Emily (2014). "Aesthetic Value and Wild Animals," in *Environmental Aesthetics: Crossing Divides and Breaking Ground*, Martin Drenthen and Jozef Keulartz (eds.). New York: Fordham University Press, 188–200.
   Brady is concerned that accounts of animal beauty leave out our aesthetic relation to the expressive qualities we attribute to animals (e.g., the mournfulness of a loon's cry or a dolphin's happy mien). In particular, she thinks that wild animals evoke the sublime and its associated aesthetic responses.

8. Parsons, Glenn (2015). Why Should We Save Nature's Hidden Gems? *Journal of Applied Philosophy* 32 (1): 98–110.
   Parsons observes that if a place is too remote, or a species too rare, its inaccessibility means it can have little (instrumental) aesthetic value. He argues that instrumentalists can overcome the problem by recognizing that the Humean 'true judges' of aesthetic value whose aesthetic judgements set the standards for our own need to have access to the full range of kinds of beauty.

9. Vice, Samantha (2017). The Ethics of Animal Beauty. *Environmental Ethics* 39 (1): 75–96.
   Vice develops an account of animal beauty that rests on their *animation* (i.e., that they are animate, rather than inanimate, matter). The aesthetic pleasure we take in animals and their animateness, she argues, comes replete with certain ethical obligations, including an obligation not to harm animals or cause their death or extinction. The value of a species, then, is aesthetic, and rooted in individual organisms' animation.

10. Greaves, Tom (2019). Movement, Wildness and Animal Aesthetics. *Environmental Values* 28 (4): 449–70.
    Inspired by Merleau-Ponty, Greaves argues that judgements of animal 'wildness' and aesthetic value are grounded in our perception of the way they manifest their animal qualities by moving through their environments.

43

THE BURNING MUSEUM
(AESTHETIC NORMATIVITY)

CASE

Oh no, the Guggenheim is on fire!

You're inside and have the time to save just one painting. But which one should it be—Kazimir Malevich's *Morning in the Village after Snowstorm* (1912), Hilma af Klint's *No. 15* from *The Atom Series* (1917), Francis Bacon's *Three Studies for a Crucifixion* (1962), or perhaps Helen Frankenthaler's *Canal* (1963)? Probably the Malevich? Yes, definitely—but wait! The museum guard's ageing dog has got its leash caught on *Morning in the Village after Snowstorm*—should you save the dog instead?

Then again, perhaps the time pressure in these thought experiments is warping the outcome. So imagine, instead, that you're a restorer who is faced with a painting where something has been painted over top of something else, and both paintings are of significant art historical interest and value (for a real-life analogue, think of the decision to leave the fig leaves covering Christ's genitals on the Sistine Chapel's ceiling, even though it was a later addition).

The object of these thought experiments is to discern whether we think we have *aesthetic* obligations—to artworks, ourselves, society, or anything else. But perhaps the dog case is a little misleading, since it

DOI: 10.4324/9781003368205-48

seems to invoke a *moral* obligation where the dog is concerned, so let us return to the pure artwork cases instead. Suppose that the moral value of the paintings in question is identical—identically *nil*, perhaps. Do we have any kind of aesthetic obligation to save one or the other—or either one?

Our intuitions about burning-museum-type cases certainly seem to *suggest* that we have aesthetic obligations (Eaton 2008; see also *Two Societies*), but where do they come from, exactly? And are they distinct from moral obligations? One long-standing explanation (of sorts) has its roots in Kant: its proponents simply stand firm and argue that we have an obligation to appreciate what is beautiful, where 'appreciation' can be cashed out in different ways, some of which may sometimes mandate specific action and others of which may not (Press 1969). The trick is to be sure that the duties in question are aesthetic and don't reduce to moral duties such as Kant's duties of self-respect or self-perfection. Thus, a more modern version of this view takes aesthetic reasons to be self-contained: they are simply reasons to appreciate something, to feel a certain way, not reasons to act or judgements about what others ought to believe (e.g., Gorodeisky and Marcus 2018; c.f. *The Uniform World*).

Another, increasingly popular, explanation is relational: aesthetic obligations are obligations we have towards someone or something in virtue of the kinds of people we are or take ourselves to be. In other words, the aesthetic obligations we have derive from the role that aesthetic considerations play in our self-conceptions. If, for example, I think of myself as a fan of the melodic death metal band Nekrogoblikon, then I *ought to* listen to their new album. But this obligation, such as it is, is one which I incur by virtue of how *I* relate to the band, or perhaps to the musical genre; it is not incurred automatically by the existence of the new album itself. So, although I experience an obligation, that obligation is not Kantian in form since it is conditional (it depends on how I relate to the object of my appreciation) and non-universal (it applies only to those who share the same relation to the object of appreciation). To fail to live up to this kind of obligation may threaten my self-conception as a fan, but that is as far as the wrongdoing goes (if we can call it that).

As simple as it seems, there are different ways of cashing out this relational strategy. According to one model (Kubala 2018), aesthetic obligations are *promises* we make to ourselves, such that they *concern* aesthetic objects, but are not obligations *to* those objects themselves. As above, my obligation is to *myself* (as a fan of the band), not to Nekrogoblikon or their album. Alternately, it has been suggested that perhaps aesthetic obligations are incurred in virtue of standing in a particular relationship to some object—namely, a *loving* relationship (Cross 2017). So: it is because I *love* Nekrogoblikon that I should listen to their new album, or because I *loved* the Harry Potter books that I should see the films.[1] Aesthetic obligations are thus parasitic on having a pre-existing relationship with certain artists, genres, or works. A similar suggestion is that what generates the obligation is my commitment to integrity (McGonigal 2018): it's because I think of myself as a Potterhead that I ought to see the films or, conversely, because I don't that I needn't. We owe it to ourselves to honour whatever our aesthetic preferences are, and one way of doing so is to seek out more of the same experiences, or experiences which will express, reflect, or sharpen our practical identities.

RESPONSES

One classic response is simply to deny that there are any aesthetic obligations akin to moral obligations (e.g., Hampshire 1954). To the extent that we can articulate aesthetic obligations, these seem trite by comparison to moral obligations. After all, 'don't play polka at a funeral' doesn't have quite the same ring to it as 'thou shalt not kill'.

One way to explain this apparent disparity—without also dismissing the intuitive pull of the polka rule—is to concede that not *all* reasons are deontic, that is, that not all reasons make demands we would be wrong to ignore (Dyck 2021). Some reasons might, for example, make the activity they recommend seem attractive or fun; but these enticing reasons do not compel any particular behaviour from us, the way reasons typically do in the moral sphere. Because these enticing reasons are not universally applicable—unlike moral rules!—they cannot have deontic force. On this strategy, we need not deny that there are aesthetic obligations, just that they are purely aesthetic. To the extent that they seem to compel us to do something, it is because, e.g., the moral or social domains have bled through. In a similar vein, it has been argued that to the extent that our aesthetic judgements motivate us to act in certain ways, this motivation does not follow solely from the content of our judgements (aesthetic internalism); it follows from the content of those judgements in conjunction with other desires and beliefs (aesthetic externalism; see King 2018). So, for example, my motivation to read all of Ursula K. LeGuin's work is not solely driven by the aesthetic content of the first of her works I read, *The Left Hand of Darkness* (1969), but also by my disposition towards completionism, my interest in the Sci-Fi and fantasy genres and the histories of their development, by an elitist inclination to read all and only good stuff, or to be the kind of person who's read LeGuin's corpus, etc. The content and aesthetic value of the stories features prominently in my motivations, but it is inextricably mixed with other commitments of mine.

On the other hand, if we think that distinctively aesthetic obligations really do exist, then so too must it be possible for us to go above and beyond the call of our aesthetic duties (this is called *supererogation*) (Archer and Ware 2017). Indeed, it does seem like we can go above and beyond the call of aesthetic duty, and in ways which are not also morally praiseworthy: think, for example, of an artist like van Gogh, who gives himself wholly over to his art and sacrifices his own well-being and personal relationships on that altar. While these sacrifices seem *morally* wrong, they may nevertheless be counted as *aesthetically* good. Conversely, vandalism (such as the repeated attacks on Edvard Eriksen's statue, *The Little Mermaid* [1913]) is not just morally or legally wrong; it also uglifies (or even destroys) something aesthetically valuable.

SUGGESTED READING

SEMINAL PRESENTATION:

1. Eaton, Marcia Muelder (2008). Aesthetic Obligations. *Journal of Aesthetics and Art Criticism* 66 (1): 1–9.

   Eaton argues that the existence of aesthetic dilemmas (such as burning museum cases) implies the existence of aesthetic obligations. As a second datum, she argues that we readily recognize when we are obligated to tell good stories about people (e.g., in eulogies or obituaries). An obligation is said to be 'aesthetic' when it is a thing's aesthetic properties which demand our consideration.

DEFENCES:

2. Press, Howard (1969). Aesthetic Obligation. *Journal of Philosophy* 66: 522–30.
   Press distinguishes between three kinds of aesthetic obligation: obligations to action, feeling, and character. He argues that we have at least one purely aesthetic obligation: to appreciate what is beautiful. 'Appreciation' here can be articulated in a variety of ways, from cultivating an aptitude to detect beauty or developing our sensibilities to actively seeking out experiences of the beautiful. But moral and aesthetic sensibilities are united in aesthetic experience.

3. Cross, Anthony (2017). Obligations to Artworks as Duties of Love. *Estetika* 54 (1): 85–101.
   Cross argues that aesthetic obligations are duties incurred by virtue of standing in a loving-relationship with particular works of art. Certain artworks are important to our practical identities, and we develop the same kinds of relationships to and with them as we ordinarily do with people, making commitments to them based on their value to us.

4. Kubala, Robbie (2018). Grounding Aesthetic Obligations. *British Journal of Aesthetics* 58 (3): 271–85.
   Kubala argues that aesthetic obligations are like promises—but promises we make to ourselves, in virtue of our practical identities as fans and experts. So, e.g., if I love Iron Maiden's music then I owe it to myself to see the band live, especially since they are primarily a touring, rather than a recording, band. This means, however, that it is the *promise*, and not my experience of a demand, that obliges me in certain ways.

5. McGonigal, Andrew (2018). "Aesthetic Reasons," in *The Oxford Handbook of Reasons and Normativity*, Daniel Star (ed.) New York: Oxford University Press, 908–36.
   McGonigal accepts that there are aesthetic obligations, and presents 'drowning artwork' cases in support of that intuition: when the cost to oneself is small, we should opt to preserve beautiful artworks. These obligations derive from a duty we have towards ourselves to honour and authentically express our aesthetic preferences.

CRITIQUES:

6. Hampshire, Stuart (1954). "Logic and Appreciation," in *Aesthetics and Language*, William Elton (ed.). Oxford: Basil Blackwell, 161–9.
   Hampshire argues that there is a significant disanalogy between the notions of moral and aesthetic obligations: moral problems involve serious practical decisions with real consequences, while aesthetic decisions are 'gratuitous' and leave artists under no pressure to justify their actions. There are moral laws, but not aesthetic laws; thus, there are no aesthetic obligations.

7. Dyck, John (2021). There are No Purely Aesthetic Obligations. *Pacific Philosophical Quarterly* 102 (4): 592–612.

Dyck argues that aesthetic reasons do not, in fact, have deontic force—they can entice us to do something, but not compel us to do so. Aesthetic reasons, he argues, are simply evaluative. To the extent that aesthetic reasons may sometimes seem to entail obligations, these are not *purely* aesthetic reasons— nor is this surprising, since our obligations to one another can extend into the aesthetic realm.

FURTHER READING:

8. Archer, Alfred and Lauren Ware (2017). Aesthetic Supererogation. *Estetika* 54: 102–16.

Archer and Ware argue that there is such a thing as aesthetic supererogation— actions which go above and beyond the call of aesthetic obligations. They argue that there is a distinctively aesthetic kind of blameworthiness or outrage which is occasioned by failing to meet our aesthetic obligations, and which is distinct from whatever *moral* blameworthiness might also be occasioned.

9. Gorodeisky, Keren and Eric Marcus (2018). Aesthetic Rationality. *Journal of Philosophy* 115 (3): 113–40.

Gorodeisky and Marcus argue that aesthetic reasons only involve reasons to appreciate, not duties to act. An aesthetic judgement is simply appreciative; it is not a judgement about what to believe (e.g., "everyone should agree that *MacBeth* [c. 1606] is Shakespeare's best play") or what to do (e.g., "I should preserve Elías García Martínez's *Ecce Homo* [c. 1930]"). Aesthetic reasons are simply reasons to feel a certain way.

10. King, Alex (2018). The Amoralist and the Anaesthetic. *Pacific Philosophical Quarterly* 99 (4): 632–63.

Aesthetic *internalism* is the view that motivations to act follow directly from the content of our aesthetic judgements. King, however, argues that we should be motivational *externalists* about aesthetics—i.e., that our motivations to act, such as they are, derive from our aesthetic judgements *in conjunction with* other desires and beliefs. Aesthetic motivational externalism suggests that we should reject the close link between normativity and motivation more generally.

NOTE

1 I did, and I haven't.

44

THE GAMER'S DILEMMA (GAMING ETHICS)

Content Warning: *the thought experiment described here sets up a contrast between murder and child abuse, a contrast discussed in detail in many of the recommended readings. I will briefly touch upon the example here, since it is key to the dilemma's original formulation, although I will aim to give a broader characterization of the dilemma.*

CASE

Imagine you're playing *Skyrim*, and you decide to kill an NPC.[1] Now, you haven't murdered anyone, exactly, since fictional characters don't exist in the real world. You have, however, committed a game-world murder, since it would count as murder if the game-world *were* real. But have you done anything wrong? You aren't really supposed to murder NPCs in Skyrim, but you can; *should* you?

I, personally, have a very strong sense that I *shouldn't*, even though I have, at times, tried (unsuccessfully!) to role-play a villainous cur. I know it doesn't actually matter, but I guess I feel like I shouldn't mistreat fictional people (just in case!). This conviction is so deeply held, in fact, that I generally avoid player dialogue which would

DOI: 10.4324/9781003368205-49

constitute a lie, or which might hurt an NPC's feelings. I always accept the side-quest to help someone find their lost kitten.

But not everyone feels this way! Here, for example, is how one gamer described their approach to *Fable 2* on *Reddit*:

> I used to flirt with NPCs, lure them to my home, have sexy times, then behead them. Marry several people, have their houses right next to each other, wait for the inevitable confrontation, lure them all to your house, have an orgy, murder them all, then watch as your children freak out. Some good times there.
> <https://www.reddit.com/r/gaming/comments/2be48c/any_open_world_games_that_allows_you_to_freely/ > (accessed 22/06/2021)

Nor is this user alone in feeling this way, as the replies and any number of YouTube videos and Twitch streams testify. I suspect, in fact, that I'm something of an outlier here. If that's right, then it seems like there's not really anything wrong with virtual murder; nor, presumably, is there anything wrong with trying to enslave the world as the Confederate States of America in *Victoria II*, or playing one of the axis powers in *Hearts of Iron IV*.

There are some deep moral questions to be asked about why we think that bad things are permissible in fictional contexts, including interactive fictional environments such as games (c.f. *The Paradox of Bad-Bad Art* and *The Puzzle of Moral Persuasion*). And there is likewise a great deal to be said about doing bad things to player-characters, such as PKing[2] them in ostensibly cooperative games.

But the *gamer's dilemma* only arises when or if we concede that some things might be so bad as to be impermissible in interactive fictional environments, too. Let us suppose we are agreed that virtual murder is okay (it's not murder, after all); would virtual child abuse also be okay (Luck 2009)?

Philosophers writing on this topic generally think that the answer is 'no': virtual murder may be permissible, but virtual child abuse is not, even if no actual children are harmed. But while this may seem like a perfectly sensible intuition, it is surprisingly difficult to articulate a principled justification for it.

RESPONSES

We can distinguish at least three general sets of putative solutions to the gamer's dilemma. The first group of solutions are those which aim to find a morally relevant feature which can help to distinguish between morally acceptable and unacceptable game-actions (e.g., Bartel 2012, Patridge 2013). These include, for instance, arguing that some actions one undertakes in a video game may also constitute morally objectionable *depictions*; so even if the virtual action is permissible because no real people are harmed, the depiction which results from it may cause real-world harm, and is thus impermissible.

Another group of solutions take issue with the structure of the gamer's dilemma, arguing that its framing invites confusion and conflation of several different and structurally important features. Ali (2015), for instance, argues that we should not buy the intuition that virtual murder is permissible and virtual child abuse not, since the permissibility of virtual actions is sensitive to the context in which they occur. The gamer's dilemma, he argues, invites us to conflate storyworld actions with simulations. Davnall (2020), by contrast, argues that we are conflating our intuitions about images with our intuitions about real actions when what is needed is a focus on just what it is that the gamer actually does when she chooses to do something potentially morally objectionable. In other words, realism makes a difference to our willingness to do certain things in a game, as does the structure of the game itself; e.g., a player-vs-player first-person shooter can't be played without consenting to virtual murder (Ramirez 2020).

Finally, a third approach is to worry about the kinds of aesthetic and moral engagement required of players. We might worry, for instance, that simulated wrongdoing is *always* wrong, since it involves adopting attitudes which are disrespectful towards members of the categories involved (Tillson 2018). Alternately, we might worry that the choices we make in a game require us to adopt a certain first-person perspective (Dadlez 2015) or reflect decisions we make about how to represent our agency and how those choices connect up to our desires (Bourne and Caddick Bourne 2019; see also *Utopia*). The worry, then, might be that vicious virtual choices reflect a certain viciousness of character on our part.

SUGGESTED READING

SEMINAL PRESENTATION:

1. Luck, Morgan (2009). The Gamer's Dilemma: An Analysis of the Arguments for the Moral Distinction between Virtual Murder and Virtual Paedophilia. *Ethics and Information Technology* 11 (1): 31–6.
   Luck introduces the gamer's dilemma, framing it as a mismatch between our intuitions about the permissibility of virtual murder and virtual child abuse. Luck surveys five kinds of arguments we might give to explain our intuition that the former is acceptable and the latter not, arguing that unless we can find a moral distinction between kinds of virtual action, then we must treat them all the same way.

DEFENCES:

2. Bartel, Christopher (2012). Resolving the Gamer's Dilemma. *Ethics and Information Technology* 14 (1): 11–6.
   Bartel argues that we can draw a principled distinction between virtual murder and child abuse insofar as the latter constitutes child 'pornography,'[3] which is of course itself a morally bad thing, whereas the former does nothing of the sort. Virtual child abusive material is morally objectionable because it harms *women* (rather than children) by eroticizing inequality.
3. Patridge, Stephanie L. (2013). Pornography, Ethics, and Video Games. *Ethics and Information Technology* 15 (1): 25–34.
   Patridge argues that virtual child abuse is not child-abusive material and that characterizing the harms of virtual child-abusive material as harm to women does not do enough to distinguish it from pornography. She argues that the problem stems from the fact that the game seems to reflect our lived moral reality but asks us to behave in a contrary manner (see *The Puzzle of Imaginative Resistance*).

CRITIQUES:

4. Ali, Rami (2015). A New Solution to the Gamer's Dilemma. *Ethics and Information Technology* 17 (4): 267–74.
   Ali argues that we should not accept the starting intuition. Instead, he argues that we must distinguish between storytelling and simulation; the context in which the virtual action occurs matters, so that some virtual murders may be permissible and others not. As long as the game's representations and viewpoint are not objectionable, neither are actions which fall under the game's storytelling constraints.

5. Tillson, John (2018). Is it Distinctively Wrong to Simulate Doing Wrong? *Ethics and Information Technology* 20 (3): 205–17.

   Tillson argues that consuming representations of wrongdoing is not morally objectionable in itself. *Simulating* wrongdoing for oneself, however, *is*, irrespective of the player's goals or intentions. Tillson adopts a deontological approach to the dilemma, arguing that even *justified* simulated wrongdoing—e.g., killing zombies—is morally objectionable.

6. Bourne, Craig and Emily Caddick Bourne (2019). Players, Characters, and the Gamer's Dilemma. *Journal of Aesthetics and Art Criticism* 77 (2): 133–43.

   Bourne and Caddick Bourne argue that a more profitable approach is to consider the kinds of aesthetic engagement mandated by the games in question. They argue for a sharper distinction between player-action (i.e., pushing buttons) and character-actions (e.g., virtual murder). What is at issue, for them, is how a game's interactive environment allows a player to deploy their fiction-making resources, and how these choices reflect on the player and their actual desires.

7. Davnall, Rebecca (2020). What Does the Gamer do? *Ethics and Information Technology* 23 (3): 225–37.

   Davnall argues that the problem stems from a metaphysical confusion. Inflationary views treat game worlds as ontologically similar to the real world, so that virtual murder is a kind of murder. Deflationary views, by contrast, just worry that game *images* are real images. She argues that neither set of views is adequate; instead, we need to think of the gamer as a *performer* empowered to decide which sorts of performances it is morally permissible to enact.

FURTHER READING:

8. Dadlez, Eva M. (2015). "Make-Believe Wickedness vs. Wicked Making-Believe: RPGs, Imagination and Moral Complicity," in *How to Make-Believe: The Fictional Truths of the Representational Arts*, J. Alexander Bareis (ed.). Berlin: De Gruyter, 309–23.

   Dadlez draws out parallel concerns about moral wickedness in live and tabletop RPGs, which require players to participate in the construction of a fictional world. The problem with moral wickedness, she argues, arises because of the first-person vantage point players adopt, and how invested players are in their character creation. She distinguishes between games in which we imagine that a *character* is nefarious and those in which we imagine *being* nefarious.

9. Kania, Andrew (2018). Why Gamers are not Performers. *Journal of Aesthetics and Art Criticism* 76 (2): 187–99.

   Kania argues that despite games' interactive nature, and despite the fact that many video games are played for an audience (e.g., via Twitch or YouTube), gamers are not performers in any sense like that in which actors, dancers, and musicians are. Games, unlike works of music and other performance art, do not prescribe a *role* for their 'performer' to play.

10. Ramirez, Erick Jose (2020). How to (Dis)solve the Gamer's Dilemma. *Ethical Theory and Moral Practice* (23): 141–61.

Ramirez argues that the gamer's dilemma fails to take into account the distinction between realistic and unrealistic representations of violence. Realistic depictions of murder or abuse, he thinks, are both likely to elicit resistance from players. Likewise, players typically consent to virtual murder, but children can't consent to abuse.

NOTES

1 A 'non-player' or 'non-playable' character. These are computer-controlled characters who are not immediately hostile to the player character (i.e. they aren't 'enemies'). They typically offer up information, goods, or services to the player, request their help for side-quests, or just help to fill in the fictional world's background.

2 'Player killing'. PKing can describe consensual player-versus-player play or killing a player-character who has not consented to a duel. Sometimes, as in the *Diablo* franchise, a subsidiary goal may be to steal the dead character's gold or items, which are dropped upon death. Many players seem to PK primarily for the joy of making it impossible for others to play the game (also known as 'griefing').

3 'Pornography' is an inapt name for what is, in fact, more properly called 'child abusive material'.

45

THE PARABLE OF THE PAWN (VIRTUAL VALUE)

CASE

Imagine you're playing a game of chess (though hnefatafl will do, if you prefer). Is the pawn real? Obviously, the figure you're moving is real; but is *the pawn itself*? The figurine, after all, is not identical to 'the' pawn. If it were lost, any old object would do to replace it—you could even play chess with coins, if you wanted to. Pawns might then be pennies, knights nickels, bishops dimes, rooks quarters, the queen a loonie, and the king a toonie (or whatever your local equivalents are).

Whatever token you use to indicate a chess piece, that's all it is: it isn't *the* piece in Platonic chess heaven, it's just a prop you're using to keep track of relative board positions. If you had the free processing power to devote to it, you could even play chess entirely in your head, with no physical objects whatsoever (the record, incidentally, is 48 *simultaneous* games of blindfold chess). But even in that game, the pawns would move to different positions on the game grid. This suggests that the game-object does not exist: it's imaginary. What exists is a token, a prop we use to keep track of the game-object throughout the game.

Whatever else it is, this '*parable of the pawn*' is at least a plausible analysis of the ontology of chess. And it seems clear that these insights can be generalized to many (perhaps even most or all) other games. But it

DOI: 10.4324/9781003368205-50

raises a puzzle: presumably, only existent things are valuable, and imaginary objects by definition don't exist. But imaginary objects can be valuable—your king is your most valuable chess piece, after all (in one sense, since it's also the least useful), and your queen is the most useful (and thus in another sense the most valuable). Similarly, we attach a great deal of value to the relative emptiness of soccer nets. The puzzle becomes even more acute, however, when we consider the value we attach to things like the contents of a Pokédex, the legendary amulet Haunt of Vaxo, or to cryptocurrencies. These are virtual objects, but the fact that we attach so much value to them seems to entail that they all exist. (See also *The Paradox of Fiction*, which has a similar structure, and *The Gamer's Dilemma*, which trades on similar concerns.)

This is *the puzzle of virtual value*. How can we explain our tendency to act as though some things—especially imaginary objects—are really, *really* important, even as we rush to say, when pressed, that they don't really matter? It's a tendency that's particularly acute in the context of video games, but we can also raise the same question about games more generally (see *Utopia*), the value of virtual reality (VR) and virtual experiences, our cheering for certain sports teams, or the brave new world of non-fungible tokens (NFTs).

RESPONSES

One striking feature of the value we attach to kings in chess, to legendary amulets in-game, and to our preferred sports team winning is that we're generally prepared to admit, upon reflection, that it doesn't actually matter very much at all. A natural way of explaining why we seem to care about such trivial things is that we *don't*—not really. We *pretend* to care for the sake of the activity we're undertaking—for the sake of enjoying the game, say—but it's really all just make-believe (Walton 2015, Wildman and McDonnell 2020). The chess piece and the legendary amulet, in particular, are mostly worthless objects, interchangeable with any other which performs a similar function, that function being to act as a prop for a particular game of make-believe. The pretence gives us a good, genuine reason to care about game-outcomes, which in turn helps to increase our enjoyment of the activity.

On the other hand, there are plenty of ordinary situations in which we find ourselves caring quite a lot about something that doesn't matter at all—the outcome of a practical joke, for example, or losing a parking spot to someone else on a crowded day. The same phenomenon of disproportionate care is at work in these situations, but it seems a stretch to explain them in terms of pretence, which suggests that the make-believe solution overgeneralizes (Stear 2017). In fact, the games we play offer a clear showcase for the fact that we quite easily take on and shrug off new goals and motivational attitudes, even when they aren't our own (because, e.g., they're the ones baked into the game by its designers) (Nguyen 2019). Perhaps a better general explanation, then, is just that our motivational attitudes are volatile, and tend to outpace the actual importance we attach to things (Stear 2017).

Now, normally, we can offer extended chains of reasons in support of the importance of some activity (Stear 2017): I care about being on time for class because I care about having enough time to cover the day's material, and I care about that because I care about my students doing well, and I care about that because I care about them developing their critical reasoning skills and because that's what I'm paid to do, and I care about that last because I need the money for food and shelter, etc. Conversely, when we're talking about the importance of a legendary amulet or a sports outcome, my chain of reasons is somewhat more truncated: my caring is not parasitic on so many of my other commitments. And this seems to explain the strange disparity between our behaviour and what we avow is important: when we game (or cheer on a team), we temporarily adopt someone else's goals as our own and behave accordingly (Nguyen 2019).

Others have taken a different tack, arguing that virtual value just is, or is comparable to, real value (Cogburn and Silcox 2014, Chalmers 2017). In particular, life in virtual worlds is replete with the same kinds of interpersonal interactions that we find in the real world, even when those interactions are mediated through a game or augmented by technology; but they are no less real for all that. One way to explain how virtual and real value can coincide is simply to note that virtual events can correspond to real events, such as when we spend hours grinding for better fictional equipment; in that case, the legendary amulet reflects hours of real effort (Strikwerda 2012). Likewise, I might spend real money to acquire the same amulet. Or, indeed, I might find that my VR gear's haptic feedback is generating real sensations (Mooradian 2006). Similarly, a budding friendship with another player but conducted through a virtual environment is actually a budding *real-world* friendship (Chalmers 2017). In all these cases, virtual value is grounded in real events involving me and my real-world actions.

Similarly, it has been argued that the ontology of virtual environments is socially constructed, which suggests that virtual value—that is, the value of objects and experiences in virtual worlds, as well as the value of game-objects and experiences—is socially constructed (Brey 2003, Simpson 2021). What gives objects and experiences their value, it's argued, is social reality, and social reality need not draw hard lines between the real and the imaginary. Money, after all, is valuable because we behave around it in ways that make it so, by using and accepting it as a medium of exchange, by hoarding it, by measuring things against it, by building institutions around it, and so on. Its value is partially constituted by the things we collectively believe about it, but it's also independent of any one person's thoughts and behaviour.

Social realities exist relative to some community of believers who recognize the entity in question for what it is, and accept it as such. For social ontologists, then, the reasons we value kings in chess, legendary amulets in *Diablo 3*, the outcomes of sporting events, and the reason people are willing to pay millions of real dollars for NFTs—a glorified deed for some unique digital object, usually encoded in some instance of meme-art—is just that that's the kind of thing people do in chess, in *Diablo 3*, in a crowded bar, or with their investments in cryptocurrencies. Our caring doesn't make much sense *out* of context, but *in*-context it's perfectly real and rational. If we're not playing a game of chess, then I don't have much reason to care about the white or black king's position. If I'm playing *Diablo 3*, then having +128–63 dexterity, strength, or intelligence along with a 3–4% increase in my critical hit chance, to say nothing of summoning shadow clones and three other random magic properties, is really quite useful. If I'm in a crowded bar and everyone is watching the game, then cheering for one side or the other allows me to participate in an exciting event. And in an investment context, maybe it makes sense for me to buy an artificially scarce digital token that points back to a blockchain (well, okay, it doesn't).

SUGGESTED READING

SEMINAL PRESENTATION:

1. Wildman, Nathan and Neil McDonnell (2020). The Puzzle of Virtual Theft. *Analysis* 80 (3): 493–9.

    Wildman and McDonnell argue that the puzzles of virtual theft and virtual value conflate game-objects with the props we use to identify them. Game-objects are imaginary, but the props which stand in for them—including bits and bytes—are not. What is lost when the prop is stolen—what is valuable to us—is the make-believe experience for which that prop is necessary.

DEFENCES:

2. Walton, Kendall (2015). "'It's Only a Game!': Sports as Fiction," in *In Other Shoes: Music, Metaphor, Empathy, Existence*. New York: Oxford university Press, 75–83.

    Walton notes the disparity between the value that we seem to attribute to sports outcomes versus that which we are ready to avow for them. He argues that the best explanation for this disparity is that we are engaging in make-believe: we pretend to care a lot in order to better enjoy the spectacle, to have a reason to genuinely prefer one outcome over another.

CRITIQUES:

3. Mooradian, Norman (2006). Virtual Reality, Ontology, and Value. *Metaphilosophy* 37 (5): 673–90.

    Mooradian is concerned with VR in particular rather than digital objects in general. He argues that most of the value we attach to VR experiences is grounded in things that happen to *us*, to *our* bodies. Thus, VR value seems hedonistic: the valuable VR activities are those in which we care about *sensations* rather than skilled performance (e.g., virtual sex vs. virtual karate).

4. Chalmers, David J. (2017). The Virtual and the Real. *Disputatio* 9 (46): 309–52.

    Chalmers argues that VR is a kind of genuine reality, that virtual objects are real, and that virtual experiences are entirely real. Virtual value is thus comparable to real value; no make-believe is necessary although it's certainly possible, just like in real life.

5. Cogburn, Jon and Mark Silcox (2014). Against Brain-in-a-Vatism: On the Value of Virtual Reality. *Philosophy and Technology* 27 (4): 561–79.

    Cogburn and Silcox argue that life in VR—"brain-in-a-vat-ism"—is just as valuable as real life. The arguments against VR value, they argue, rest on impoverished conceptions of the nature and function of VR environments.

FURTHER READING:

6. Brey, Philip (2003). The Social Ontology of Virtual Environments. *The American Journal of Economics and Sociology* 62 (1): 269–82.
   Brey argues that the ontology of virtual environments is a social one modelled on Searle's, according to which social facts come into existence when we collectively impose a function on something, thus creating artifacts and institutions. Brey argues that the richness and interactive nature of virtual objects precludes their being merely fictional.

7. Strikwerda, Litska (2012). Theft of Virtual Items in Online Multiplayer Computer Games: An Ontological and Moral Analysis. *Ethics and Information Technology* 14 (2): 89–97.
   Strikwerda examines the legal status of virtual theft, arguing that virtual objects can count as someone's property in both the virtual *and* the real world. A virtual object's real value depends on how it was acquired, e.g., through real and virtual effort (real hedonic value), or by purchase (real pecuniary value).

8. Stear, Nils-Hennes (2017). Sport, Make-Believe, and Volatile Attitudes. *Journal of Aesthetics and Art Criticism* 75 (3): 275–88.
   Stear identifies the related 'puzzle of sport' and argues that make-believe accounts of sport's mixed value to us overgeneralize to other cases where there is clearly no make-believe at work. Instead, he argues that our motivational attitudes are volatile, which explains why they tend to outstrip the actual importance we attach to their objects. The puzzle arises when we adopt a synoptic perspective from which we try to make sense of our behaviour and our variable self-conceptions.

9. Nguyen, C. Thi (2019). Games and the Art of Agency. *Philosophical Review* 128 (4): 423–62.
   Nguyen argues that when we play games, we temporarily adopt the ends specified by the game for the sake of the experience of pursuing those ends. In fact, many games see us adopting a variety of fictional *and* real-world goals, which demonstrates just how easily we can adopt and shuck different motivational attitudes and goals. Games have both fictional and real value.

10. Simpson, Jack (2021). The NFT: A Wealth And Poverty Of Imagination. *Aesthetics for Birds*, March 18, 2021. https://aestheticsforbirds.com/2021/03/18/nfts-a-wealth-and-poverty-of-imagination/.
   Simpson considers the case of NFTs, which have been selling for millions. Part of their value lies in their economic activity: as tokens which point to a blockchain, they enable the tracking of royalties and can act as digital deeds; because they're non-fungible, they are artificially scarce. Ultimately, he argues, their perceived value is grounded in social reality.

46

THE PUZZLE OF CULTURAL APPROPRIATION

CASE

Are you familiar with poke? It's a Native Hawaiian dish of raw fish—kind of a fish salad seasoned with traditional condiments like candlenut and limu. In 2016, a Chicago restaurant chain calling itself 'Aloha Poke' trademarked the words 'aloha' and 'poke' and began sending cease-and-desist letters to restaurants across the United States—including in Hawai'i—using those words in their name. (Note that both 'aloha' and 'poke' are Hawaiian words.) I think it's fair to say that there's something transparently wrong about this situation. One way of articulating that wrongness is in terms of cultural appropriation: Aloha Poke appropriated a native Hawaiian dish and two Hawaiian words, and sought to restrict their use in Hawai'i and elsewhere, all for commercial gain.

Consider now the case of the writer Joseph Boyden, who writes books about Indigenous people and culture, usually inspired by true stories. Boyden has claimed Mi'kmaq, Métis, Nipmuc, and Ojibway ancestry, but has struggled to prove that ancestry. Boyden has often spoken publicly on behalf of Indigenous peoples, and has accepted awards and prizes and collected speaking fees intended for Indigenous people. To clarify matters a little, let's imagine someone like him

DOI: 10.4324/9781003368205-51

and stipulate that he has no actual Indigenous ancestry or social and cultural ties: in that case, we have a situation in which someone takes Indigenous stories and tells them for his own gain, and speaks on behalf of Indigenous peoples and takes resources intended for them. All that seems transparently wrong, too, and might also be described as 'cultural appropriation'.

Finally, consider the case of the famous Haida artist Michael Nicoll Yahgulanaas, who is the author of *RED: A Haida Manga* (2009), a graphic novel that blends a Haida narrative and Indigenous iconography with the Japanese manga style. The novel sold out immediately in Japan. This looks like a case of cultural appropriation, since a distinctively Japanese form of storytelling is being used, but it's not clear that it's morally objectionable in the same way that the other two cases are. But why not? Now compare this case to that of Adidas' 2013 line of tracksuits, which featured 'totem pole print'—cartoonized versions of design motifs from the First Nations of the Pacific Northwest.[1] I suspect that this case will strike most of us as rather less acceptable— but why? How can we explain our conflicting intuitions about these cases? What is it, in short, that makes cultural appropriation wrong (if indeed it is)?

We should begin by broadly distinguishing several different kinds of cultural appropriation: (1) *object* appropriation involves taking another culture's artifacts, (2) *subject* appropriation involves taking other cultures and their stories, real or fictional, as one's artistic subject matter (often leading to worries about 'voice' appropriation), and (3) *content* appropriation, which involves someone reusing an idea from another culture (e.g., a style or motif) in their own work, motifs, etc. (Young 2008). The wrongs we associate with object and subject appropriation are relatively clear: theft, for object appropriation, and misrepresentation and stereotyping for subject appropriation (Keeshig-Tobias 1990; see also *The Problem of Museum Skepticism*). In seeking to deny Hawaiians the commercial use of words in their language, and of a characteristically Hawaiian dish, the Aloha Poke case seems to shade into *object* appropriation (see also *The Puzzle of Cultural Property*). Boyden's case, on the other hand, is clearly one of *subject* appropriation, and the criticism he has faced has been formulated in large part as a concern with voice appropriation. Our attention in this section will focus, instead, on the case of *content* appropriation, since the wrong associated with it is much less clear. Yahgulanaas, for example, has engaged in a measure of content appropriation, but has he done anything wrong? Styles, motifs, and media are an inexhaustibly reusable resource, after all; but then, why *shouldn't* Adidas use them to sell tracksuits?

RESPONSES

One possibility is that content appropriation is often *offensive*, but not usually morally *wrong* (Young 2008). We can be unjustifiably offended by something, for example, such as licking a spoon or loving someone of the same sex. That something is offensive gives us a good reason to avoid doing it, but that reason is defeasible—easily so, in the case of unjustified offence. Where art is concerned, possible defeaters might include greatness or social value (e.g., Shakespeare's work can be offensive, but it's also of undeniably high quality). But since so much art is also an artist's self-expression, we might also think that offence is a price worth paying for freedom of expression (see Young 2008, Táíwò 2018). Things are different, too, when someone rubs your face in something offensive, rather than keeping it mostly to themselves.

The upshot, then, would be that a great deal of content appropriation is not, in fact, wrong. To find a wrong, we would do better to identify a harm. Yahgulanaas seems to have harmed no one by using the medium of manga; indeed, Japanese audiences seem to have been rather interested in his work. Adidas, on the other hand, *may* have caused some harm by using garish and low-quality renderings and thus devaluing the meaning and quality of the source material, and also by ensuring that none of the profits are distributed to source communities.

The dominant explanation of the harms of misappropriation is in terms of group power dynamics. According to this view, there is nothing wrong about cultural appropriation in and of itself; what is wrong is the way in which it plays into, reflects, and maintains structures of oppression (Matthes 2019). Many Indigenous peoples, for example, have suffered not just the theft of their land and their concomitant economic subordination, but have also survived a long (and only recently ended) system of cultural genocide. Stacked against this history, cultural appropriation looks a great deal like the theft of identity and of a scarce economic resource (Todd 1990). The commodification of minority culture promises recognition and reconciliation, but too often mass culture strips it of social and political meaning, to say nothing of directing profits away from the community in question (hooks 2015 [1992]). The moral issue at stake, then, can be characterized as exacerbating underlying inequalities (Jackson 2019, Matthes 2019), or perhaps as the threat of assimilation and cultural hegemony by a dominant group (Rowell 1995). It is the Haida's relative lack of power, then, and Adidas' surfeit of power, that explains why the first case is morally acceptable, and the second not. A Haida manga does not contribute to or manifest oppression, whereas the corporate use of Indigenous motifs without consultation or profit-sharing does.

Another way of thinking about when appropriation is wrong here is in terms of *toleration*: if a group is generally happy to share their cultural products with outsiders, as Japanese people are with manga, then there's no harm and no foul. If, on the other hand, several members of a cultural group vociferously contest the appropriation of its culture, and do so in a sustained and public manner, and citing culturally specific explanations, then the act of appropriation is morally wrong because the appropriators are at best culpably ignorant of the harm they cause (Lenard and Balint 2020). The degree to which it is morally wrong, however, is another matter. Most appropriation is relatively harmless, but contextual factors (including inter-group power dynamics and financial benefits) can amplify this wrongness. Although obtaining consent is an important step towards toleration, we can't quite use it as a proxy for contestation, since so much cultural engagement and transfer takes place beyond our notice (see also Táíwò 2018, Jackson 2019; cf. Matthes 2019).

One last approach argues that we should focus on the appropriators themselves: when they are acting out of disrespect for or indifference to a culture, or are culpably negligent, then they have *mis*appropriated a culture's content (Tuvel 2021). The toleration- and power-based approaches both locate appropriation's wrongness in factors external to the agent, and this, in turn, makes it more difficult for us to determine whether a given act of appropriation was wrong. But determining community tolerance, establishing community members' identities, and registering contestation are difficult and time-consuming tasks. By contrast, the agent-centred approach requires us only to examine the appropriator's attitudes and their reasons for appropriating. This isn't to say that the toleration- and power-based accounts don't identify real harms; rather, the thought is that these harms are secondary to that of *disregard* for other cultures. Our feelings of profound offence are thus responsive to someone's disregard for our culture: Yahgulanaas acted out of an interest in Japanese material culture, whereas Adidas exhibited an offensive disregard for Indigenous peoples and motifs.

SUGGESTED READING

SEMINAL PRESENTATION:

1. Young, James O. (2008). *Cultural Appropriation and the Arts.* Malden, NY: Wiley-Blackwell.
   Young distinguishes between several different kinds of cultural appropriation, arguing that most aspects of a culture can, in fact, be appropriated without doing anything immoral. In Ch. 5, he focuses on claims that appropriation is profoundly offensive, arguing that although an action's profound offensiveness is a *prima facie* reason to think it's morally wrong, a work's social value or its status as the artist's self-expression can counterbalance the offensiveness it may cause.

DEFENCES:

2. Táíwò, Olúfẹ́mi O. (2018). Artworld Roundtable: Is Cultural Appropriation Ever Okay? *Aesthetics for Birds.* https://aestheticsforbirds.com/2018/08/22/artworld-roundtable-is-cultural-appropriation-ever-okay/#taiwo
   Táíwò worries that the debate over cultural appropriation is overly hostile to artists and art and that the terms of debate are set by people whose standing relative to the creative processes in question is quite peripheral, and who hope to benefit from their vigilance. All this, he argues, serves to obscure the fact that most music, in particular, is the result of a diverse collaborative process in which all but a few frontmen remain invisible (see also *The Puzzle of Multiple Authorship*).

CRITIQUES:

3. Jackson, Lauren Michele (2019). *White Negroes: When Cornrows Were in Vogue… and Other Thoughts on Cultural Appropriation.* Boston, MA: Beacon Press.
   In this wide-ranging discussion of cultural appropriation, Jackson surveys the many different realms in which culture is appropriated, including music, fashion, and art, but also language and internet (especially meme) culture. She argues that most acts of appropriation are done unconsciously and

beneath our notice, and that cultural transportation is not in itself ethically problematic. The problem comes with the discourse of power in which many acts of appropriation are embedded.

4. Matthes, Erich Hatala (2019). Cultural Appropriation and Oppression. *Philosophical Studies* 176: 1003–13.

    Matthes argues that cultural appropriation is wrong when it manifests or exacerbates inequality, marginalization, and oppression. Cultural appropriation, he argues, has no distinct wrong particular to itself; rather, when it's wrong, it's because it exacerbates underlying inequalities, such as those which are the legacies of colonization or slavery. The fact that the group making an appropriation claim is oppressed establishes a normative foundation for that claim.

5. Lenard, Patti T. and Peter Balint (2020). What is (the Wrong of) Cultural Appropriation? *Ethnicities* 20 (2): 331–52.

    Lenard and Balint advocate a 'contestation account' of cultural appropriation, according to which something counts as cultural appropriation when the appropriator knows what they are doing and the act of appropriation itself is the subject of significant contestation from a cultural community. They argue that appropriation itself is often only trivially wrong, but that contextual factors can amplify that wrongness.

6. Tuvel, Rebecca (2021). Putting the Appropriator Back in Cultural Appropriation. *British Journal of Aesthetics* 61 (3): 353–72.

    Tuvel argues that we should focus our attention on appropriators and their reasons for appropriating. What makes misappropriation wrong, she thinks, is the attitude evinced by the appropriator—specifically, attitudes of disrespect, indifference, or culpable neglect.

FURTHER READING:

7. hooks, bell (2015 [1992]). "Eating the Other: Desire and Resistance." in *Black Looks: Race and Representation*. Boston, MA: South End Press, 21–39.

    hooks diagnoses the appropriative impulse as issuing primarily from desire rather than hatred; in particular, a desire to be *changed* by contact with the social Other. In this way, acts of appropriation manifest an imperialist nostalgia and re-enact the colonizing journey. hooks is particularly concerned about the link between appropriation and commodification.

8. Keeshig-Tobias, Lenore (1990). "The Magic of Others," in *Language in Her Eye: Views on Writing and Gender by Canadian Women Writing in English*, Libby Scheier, Sarah Sheard, and Eleanor Wachtel (eds.). Toronto: Coach House Press, 172–7.

    Keeshig-Tobias offers some context for thinking about the harms of literary appropriation, which she characterizes as a kind of voice appropriation. She worries that this voice appropriation falls hard on the heels of land appropriation and cultural genocide, and seems to treat Indigenous stories as just another resource to be sold off ("to the Americans"—175).

9. Todd, Loretta (1990). Notes on Appropriation, *Parallelogramme* 16 (1): 24–33.

Todd ties cultural appropriation to the colonial appropriation of Indigenous lands, arguing that the Indigenous imagination is what colonialism takes when it runs out of material resources. She suggests that we look to Aboriginal Title to guide our thinking about cultural appropriation.

10. Rowell, John (1995). The Politics of Cultural Appropriation. *Journal of Value Inquiry* 29 (1): 137–42.

Rowell considers proposed revisions to the Canada Council's funding guidelines for the arts, which asked artists to be aware of cultural appropriation (the revisions failed). He argues that the primary moral issue at stake is the threat of cultural hegemony by a dominant group, which government funding should not facilitate.

NOTE

1 Note that (1) 'totem' poles are neither totems nor totemic, and (2) that 'Pacific Northwest' is an American term not used in Canada (though I have reproduced it here as a more or less descriptive shorthand).

THE PUZZLE OF CULTURAL PROPERTY

CASE

Imagine a culture—let's call them the Util—with very few remaining members, say just 200. Imagine, further, that one of the most significant artworks ever produced by this culture was in the possession of a major museum, like New York's Metropolitan Museum of Art. Should the work be returned to the Util?

A straightforward utilitarian calculation would suggest not. Even if the work is worth 10,000 hedons[1] to each member of the culture, that only gives us a total hedonic value of two million. But if the work is worth just one hedon to every New Yorker, that still means the work is more than four times more valuable to New York, to say nothing of the rest of the world. And yet, this conclusion does not sit well with most of us.

Consider, now, a different case: a Spanish museum is in possession of an ornate Viking-age goblet of probable Norse origin. Should the goblet be returned to Norway? Our intuitions, I suspect, pull in the other direction here—or, if they don't, then certainly their pull is not quite as strong as in the first case.

What these thought experiments illustrate is *the puzzle of cultural property*: who owns it, exactly? Can cultures as a whole have a claim

DOI: 10.4324/9781003368205-52

to own their cultural products? The issue is a difficult one which is closely tied to *The Puzzle of Cultural Appropriation*. It is significantly complicated, however, by the fact that for many artifacts, the cultures which produced them are extinct or discontinuous with their modern-day descendants: who, then, should have them? What constitutes a cultural group, anyway, and do they have any grounds for restricting the use and disposition of their cultural output?

RESPONSES

Several philosophers have expressed skepticism about repatriating cultural property. One species of skepticism concerns the epistemic difficulty of determining what needs repatriating, and to whom (see Young 2007). Even if we agree that stolen art and artifacts should be returned to their rightful owners, it can be exceedingly difficult to determine whether a particular artifact was stolen, extracted under coercive conditions, bought and sold in the usual, approved way, or simply abandoned and discovered. Appeals to the legal notion of inheritance are unlikely to be of much help since, absent testamentary records, we are not warranted in simply stipulating that some people and not others would have been intended beneficiaries.

This problem is especially acute when we also consider the metaphysics of cultural groups. Modern cultural groups and nation-states, after all, are not especially coextensive with their ancient forebears (Appiah 2006). Today's Norwegians, for example, have virtually nothing in common with ninth-century Vikings, apart from the geographic regions they inhabit and the language they inherited. After a thousand years of immigration and emigration, many modern-day Norwegians may not even be particularly close descendants of the iron-age pirates.

Worse, some long-dead peoples might have strenuously objected to their cultural artifacts falling into the hands of their most hated enemies (typically their neighbours): how happy would the Athenians be, for example, at the prospect of all Greeks—including the Spartans and Thebans—coming into possession of the Parthenon friezes (Young 2007)? They may well have preferred their outright destruction! Likewise, it's worth noting that artifacts stolen from one people may become quite important to another: Stonehenge is currently in the hands of the descendants of (several successive waves of) the people who conquered its builders, and the Koh-i-Noor has spent more time embedded in the British crown than it ever did in the hands of its original miners, the Delhi Sultanate. As Anthony Appiah puts it, "patrimony, here, equals imperialism plus time" (2006).

This skepticism typically feeds the conclusion that the value of cultural property is to people, not peoples—that these artifacts belong to all of humanity, rather than to some particular unspecifiable subset of people (Appiah 2006, Young 2007; c.f. *The Problem of Museum Skepticism*). This conclusion is commonly expressed in museums' mission statements, which claim an obligation to make these works accessible to all of humanity. But if this view is correct then it seems as though museums are failing in their missions, since so many artifacts moulder in their basements, unseen by anyone (Matthes 2017). Nor is it obvious why so much cultural wealth should be concentrated in the hands of so few institutions: perhaps these artifacts should be repatriated to ensure a fairer and broader distribution, and to secure wider access to humanity's cultural patrimony. In doing so, we can also help to redress historical wrongs. It's not just that the acquisition of artifacts has been conducted primarily through violent and coercive means, that their distribution skews to museums, and that those museums are mostly located in Western nations; it's also that these museums have a long and ongoing history of cultural marginalization (Matthes 2017). Non-western art, for example, is typically relegated to anthropological, rather than art, museums, and is often labelled 'primitive' (see *The Paradox of Authenticity*).

There may be a role here for the digitization of museum collections to ensure wider access—but we should be careful not to conflate this kind of diffuse loss of control with repatriation, especially when museums remain in possession of the artifacts themselves or hold intellectual property rights over them (Crouch 2010). Radically redistributing these artifacts doesn't just facilitate broader access to them, it can also facilitate the recognition of historically marginalized groups and return artifacts to people who hold them in greater esteem. Not only might an artifact hold greater cultural significance for some people than others, but its significance may even be enhanced by the facts surrounding its appropriation, so that it comes to stand, e.g., as a symbol of one people's domination by another (Young 2007). Under such circumstances, it is hard to see why the artifact *shouldn't* be repatriated, given the tangible goods served by repatriation.

Although the universalist impulse is intuitively attractive, we must be sensitive to the fact that it has historically been used to carry water for the imperialist acquisition of cultural property and to control access privileges (Wylie 2005). Accepting the universalist impulse should not, by itself, override the moral and political concerns which attend the acquisition or display of any given piece of cultural property (Glass 2004). Indeed, it has been suggested that a commitment to the universal value of art is a way of emphasizing a heritage that transcends particular interests and desires, and which helps us to ensure our descendants are afforded the same sorts of opportunities to form meaningful connections with their human heritage (Thompson 2004). Those who subscribe to such a universalist view should likewise recognize that even cultural groups who *don't* share the universalist impulse have an interest in being able to forge the same sorts of connections with *their* heritage. Allowing them to do so may sometimes mean seeing particular artifacts become inaccessible to the rest of us.

Another tack which has gained popularity recently involves explaining the value of artifacts and practices for certain cultural groups in terms of the identity or intimacy of these groups, and the relationships they forge with and through those artifacts and practices (Coleman 2010, Nguyen and Strohl 2019, Thomas 2021). We might then explain that certain cultural groups have a sense of ownership over certain artifacts because they have invested them with a great deal of 'symbolic density' (Coleman 2010), so that these artifacts are part and parcel of what it means to be a member of the relevant group and demands for their repatriation help to reinforce the boundaries of a group's identity (Nguyen and Strohl 2019). This is just how heirlooms function for families, for example: the meaning invested in an object or practice gives its investors a stake in its disposition, even if it does not necessarily give them *property rights* over it (Coleman 2010). But it also suggests that cultural property can take on significance for new groups of people, and that old groups may sometimes divest their symbols of their meaning, just as a wedding band may lose some sentimental value after the dissolution of the marriage it symbolized.

SUGGESTED READING

SEMINAL PRESENTATION:

1. Young, James O. (2007). Cultures and Cultural Property. *Journal of Applied Philosophy* 24 (2): 111-23.

   Young argues that most arguments for the cultural ownership of artifacts are unsuccessful. In particular, he targets arguments from inheritance, cultural practices, and collective production. Nevertheless, he argues that some artifacts may be of sufficiently great value to extant cultures to ground claims of ownership; this 'cultural significance principle', however, only applies to tangible artifacts, not to motifs, styles, musical compositions, stories, etc.

DEFENCES:

2. Appiah, Kwame Anthony (2006). Whose Culture is it? *New York Review of Books*, 9 February 2006: 53 (2).

   Appiah offers a skeptical take on the concept of cultural property, arguing that the modern-day inhabitants of nation-states are culturally nothing like the people who produced the cultural artifacts under discussion, even if they are sometimes descended from them. Except in cases where the acquisition was unjust and recent, he argues that we are better off treating cultural artifacts as belonging to all of humanity.

CRITIQUES:

3. Thompson, Janna (2004). Art, Property Rights, and the Interests of Humanity. *The Journal of Value Inquiry* 38 (4): 545-600.

   Thompson asks what reason could justify the intuition that humanity's interests trump an individual person's right to destroy a great artwork, but not an individual culture's right to dispose of their works as they see fit. She argues that a culture's commitment to universalism (or lack of such a commitment) prescribes certain restrictions on what people are entitled to claim and do with cultural property.

4. Coleman, Elizabeth Burns (2010). "Repatriation and the Concept of Inalienable Possession," in *The Long Way Home*, Paul Turnbull and Michael Pickering (eds.). New York: Berghahn Books, 82–95.

   Coleman argues that the moral case for repatriation is grounded in the special kinds of 'identity' relationships that groups of people form with artifacts, investing them with 'symbolic density'. This sense of ownership is necessary for people to claim rights in relation to an object but is not a sufficient reason to do so. Coleman argues that recognizing Indigenous autonomy means recognizing that cultural patrimony is *alienable*.

5. Matthes, Erich Hatala (2017). Repatriation and the Radical Redistribution of Art. *Ergo: An Open Access Journal of Philosophy* 4: 931–53.
Matthes argues that concerns about cultural discontinuity have been divorced from their political contexts and the background of historical and ongoing injustice which informs them. He agrees that cultural artifacts are the patrimony of all of humankind but argues that this premise should motivate radical repatriation informed by principles of distributive justice.

6. Nguyen, C. Thi and Matthew Strohl (2019). Cultural Appropriation and the Intimacy of Groups. *Philosophical Studies* 176 (4): 981–1002.
Nguyen and Strohl focus on style appropriation, arguing that claims of cultural property are grounded in the intimacy of social groups. Group intimacy results in certain prerogatives, just as interpersonal intimacy does, some of which may be to restrict, or to spread, the relevant item of cultural property. Appropriation claims, they argue, are often expressive, and help to assert the boundaries of group intimacy.

FURTHER READING:

7. Glass, Aaron (2004). Return to Sender: On the Politics of Cultural Property and the Proper Address of Art. *Journal of Material Culture* 9 (2): 115–39.
Glass argues that, for cultural groups subjected to violent oppression and genocide, the repatriation of their patrimony can symbolize an assertion of their agency, identity, and power of self-determination, as well as facilitate community healing, remembrance, and personal closure.

8. Wylie, Alison (2005). "The Promise and Perils of an Ethic of Stewardship," in *Embedding Ethics*, Lynn Meskell and Peter Pels (eds.). Providence: Berg Publishers, 47–68.
Wylie surveys the history of the development of the concept of an 'ethic of stewardship' in archaeology. She observes that its early development reaffirmed archaeologists' privilege of access to and control over sites and materials and lent itself to justifying museums' acquisition of cultural goods. She is skeptical of appeals to a universal public interest which function to shield scientific work from moral and political concerns.

9. Crouch, Michelle (2010). Digitization as Repatriation. *Journal of Information Ethics* 19 (1): 45–56.
Crouch explores the National Museum of the American Indian's (NMAI) decision to digitize its artifacts and photographs in a searchable online collection. Although she is optimistic that the consultative process and increased access to archival records will prove a net boon to originating communities, she worries that digital repatriation preserves the museum's intellectual property rights.

10. Thomas, Joshua Lewis (2021). When does Something 'Belong' to a Culture? *British Journal of Aesthetics* 61 (3): 275–90.

Thomas asks what makes an artifact or practice 'of' or 'from' a culture, in the sense of affiliation. He argues that Belonging is rooted in the meaning an object or practice has for a culture: the stronger and more numerous these connections are, the more the object or practice Belongs to that culture. Belonging alone, however, does not tell us who should *own* an object or practice.

NOTE

1 A hedon is a single unit of pleasure.

48

THE PUZZLE OF IMAGINATIVE RESISTANCE

CASE

It's pretty easy for us to imagine stories about astronauts stranded on Mars, ships hurtling through hyperspace at speeds faster than light, wizards who cast spells by waving a wand and chanting nonsense Latin, and pretty much anything else, really (although see *The Puzzle of Historical Criticism*). But now try to imagine the following (very short) story instead:

Loving-Kindness

Yesterday, I woke up sleeping. My little sister had just had breakfast so I threw her to the crocodiles, whose frenzied chomps beat the water to bloody froth. It wasn't pretty, but I had to do it because that's what kindness is. It's doing something for someone else because you can.

Did you imagine a world in which the narrator was kind because of what they did? Did you imagine them awake and sleeping at the same time? If you were unwilling or unable to imagine these things, then you have just experienced what is known as *the puzzle of imaginative resistance.*[1]

DOI: 10.4324/9781003368205-53

A number of slightly different puzzles are associated with the broader label (Weatherson 2004). The first of these (the *imaginative puzzle*) concerns why it is that we resist imagining what we are asked to imagine; the second (the *fictionality puzzle*) concerns why we have such a hard time believing that it's true in the story-world that feeding one's sister to the crocodiles is a kind thing to do; the third (the *phenomenological puzzle*) asks why we find the story's last two lines so jarring; and the fourth (the *aesthetic puzzle*) asks whether the fact that we resist some of the story's claims makes it a worse or less interesting story.

So what, exactly, is going on here? Some have argued that imaginative resistance is just a case of *unwillingness* to imagine (Gendler 2000); others, that it instead features an *inability* to imagine (Weatherson 2004). Some have postulated that the phenomenon might just be an automatic reaction prompted by the way our brains process imaginative content, while others are convinced that it's primarily a conflict between an emotion engendered in us by a story (e.g., revulsion) which demands that we feel a different emotion instead (e.g., approbation). We might also ask whether imaginative resistance is sometimes justified and sometimes not, and whether we can or should overcome cases where it isn't (Tuna 2020). As Kendall Walton (2006: 146) has observed, just about the only part of the puzzle of imaginative resistance that anyone agrees about is the word 'of'!

RESPONSES:

Focusing on the cases prompted by a mismatch between the moral principles we endorse and those which the story seems to endorse, we might be tempted to think that imaginative resistance arises primarily due to our reflexive background endorsement of moral realism, such that the mere suggestion that our moral principles might be wrong is unimaginably shocking (Todd 2009; see also *The Paradox of Bad-Bad Art* and *The Puzzle of Moral Persuasion*). The more interesting question would then be why the author has asked us to imagine such a flagrantly false proposition: what are they trying to achieve, conversationally speaking? And there is good empirical reason to believe that we *do* import certain key beliefs—such as the belief in moral realism—into our stories, as a kind of background against which we read the story and construct the story-world (Weisberg and Goodstein 2009).

The evidence is especially strong for scientific and mathematical facts, however, which suggests that these, too, should trigger imaginative resistance. And, indeed, subsequent efforts have shown that it can arise in response to a wider set of claims, including especially those which we believe to be wholly impossible. It has also been observed that we don't just experience imaginative resistance when we have a deep-seated commitment to the falsity of some candidate proposition: we can also experience it when we *don't know* whether the proposition in question really is true (Mahtani 2012; see also *Empty and Universal Fictions*).

This has prompted a more general approach to the puzzle rooted in the cognitive architecture of our brains. According to these responses, the puzzle isn't, properly speaking, an *imaginative* puzzle at all: our unwillingness or inability to imagine the proposition in question is due to different elements of our cognitive architecture entering into conflict with one another (Meskin and Weinberg 2011). The phenomenon arises when the text asks us to add a belief to our arsenal, but the cognitive mechanism that checks for consistency among our beliefs identifies a potential conflict. When the conflict can't be resolved—because, e.g., the text keeps insisting that the resistant proposition is true—we end up with an imaginative blockage, and unless the author offers us a way to bypass the blockage, our only option is to refuse the invitation to imagine the resistant proposition.

Conversely, it seems like there are many cases where we *should* experience imaginative resistance but *don't* (Skow 2021); e.g., children don't usually refuse to believe that Eric Carle's very hungry caterpillar **<spoiler alert>** becomes a beautiful butterfly at the end of the story, even though it builds and emerges from a *cocoon* rather than a *chrysalis* (suggesting it is in fact a moth), and even though its wings are obviously upside down (and thus, presumably, non-functional). The natural explanation here seems to be that children—and most adults—don't know enough about insect behaviour and development to notice the inconsistency, so the claim goes unnoticed by the brain's belief-monitoring system. And while many adults do notice that the butterfly's wings are upside down, we tend to shrug it off because, well, maybe some butterflies look like that. Who knows?

A related suggestion has it that perhaps we find ourselves pulled in different directions, able and willing to imagine certain kinds of complex propositions (e.g., $1 + 1 = 3$), but not at the level of detail required to grasp the more basic facts upon which they would ordinarily depend for their truth (e.g., the basic mathematical theorems required) (Weatherson 2004, Stock 2005). When authors don't supply us with a ready workaround, we implement our own by stipulating that the resistant proposition is somehow (indirectly) satisfied. So, for example, I might imagine a newspaper headline announcing that $1 + 1 = 3$ and accept *that* as satisfying the prescription that I imagine the proposition, without engaging in any of the sophisticated mathematical work that would be required to directly imagine it.

SUGGESTED READING

SEMINAL PRESENTATION:

1. Gendler, Tamar Szabó (2000). The Puzzle of Imaginative Resistance. *Journal of Philosophy* 97 (2): 55–81.
   Gendler names the puzzle and explores some of its historical antecedents. She argues that, at least in moral cases, imaginative resistance is the result of our unwillingness to take up an author's invitation to imagine some morally deviant scenario. Imagining, she argues, requires us to participate in the imagined scenario in a way that mere supposition does not. The result is that we are unwilling to imagine morally deviant scenarios because we are unwilling to adopt points of view we repudiate.

DEFENCES:

2. Weatherson, Brian (2004). Morality, Fiction, and Possibility. *Philosophers' Imprint* 4: 1–27.
   Weatherson distinguishes between four different puzzles which may be involved in imaginative resistance, arguing that the phenomenon is not limited to morally deviant propositions and our responses to them. Instead, he argues that the problem arises when we are presented with higher-level concepts, but without the means to imagine the more fundamental, lower-level facts on which they would depend for their truth.

CRITIQUES:

3. Stock, Kathleen (2005). Resisting Imaginative Resistance. *Philosophical Quarterly* 55: 607–24.
   Stock diagnoses imaginative resistance as a failure to understand some proposition. The problem is not that the proposition is a conceptual impossibility,

but rather that readers cannot conceive the surrounding context which would make it true.

4. Walton, Kendall (2006). "On the (So-Called) Puzzle of Imaginative Resistance," in *The Architecture of the Imagination*, Shaun Nichols (ed.). Oxford: Oxford University Press, 137–48.

Walton revisits Weatherson's four puzzles, arguing that the imaginative and fictionality (Weatherson's 'alethic') puzzles are closely intertwined. Walton argues that the kind of resistance we display in the fictionality puzzle is not properly *imaginative* at all—our resistance, rather, is to *accepting* the relevant claim(s).

5. Todd, Cain (2009). Imaginability, Morality, and Fictional Truth: Dissolving the Puzzle of 'Imaginative Resistance'. *Philosophical Studies* 143: 187–211.

Todd argues that the primary factor driving imaginative resistance is the reader's moral realism. Imaginative resistance, he thinks, is prompted by story-context. Thus, the question we should ask ourselves when faced with a resistant proposition is not why it isn't true in the story, but rather why the author is trying to tell us that it *is*.

6. Meskin, Aaron and Jonathan M. Weinberg (2011). "Imagination Unblocked," in *The Aesthetic Mind: Philosophy & Psychology*, Elisabeth Schellekens and Peter Goldie (eds.). New York: Oxford University Press, 239–53.

Meskin and Weinberg argue that the architectural model of the imagination offers the best analysis of imaginative resistance. The key phenomenon, they argue, is that of imaginative *blockages*, which occur when different pieces of the cognitive architecture (notably the belief inputting and updating mechanisms) operate at cross-purposes.

FURTHER READING:

7. Weisberg, Deena Skolnick and Joshua Goodstein (2009). What Belongs in a Fictional World? *Journal of Cognition and Culture* 9 (1–2): 69–78.

Weisberg and Goodstein empirically investigate how readers construct fictional worlds from the texts they read, focusing on the kinds of facts they import from the real world. They find that even in stories which diverge significantly from the real world, readers mostly treat scientific and mathematical facts as invariant; they suggest that the same may well be true of what readers believe to be moral facts.

8. Mahtani, Anna (2012). Imaginative Resistance Without Conflict. *Philosophical Studies* 158: 415–29.

Mahtani argues that we can experience imaginative resistance without experiencing a conflict between our beliefs and the resistant proposition, since we sometimes experience imaginative resistance when we don't know whether the proposition is true. The solution is to rethink the background we import into stories and to notice that we only import the general moral principles we believe to be true.

9. Tuna, Emine Hande (2020). "Imaginative Resistance." *The Stanford Encyclopedia of Philosophy* (Summer 2020 Edition), Edward N. Zalta (ed.). https://plato.stanford.edu/archives/sum2020/entries/imaginative-resistance/.

   Tuna offers a useful survey of the debate over imaginative resistance, the different positions which have been staked out, and promising alternatives and topics for future investigation.

10. Skow, Bradford (2021). Questioning Imaginative Resistance and Resistant Reading. *British Journal of Aesthetics* 61 (4): 575–87.

    Skow offers a diagnosis of many failures of resistance: the claim to be resisted is simply not salient to the reader. This might be because the resistant claim is not foregrounded in the text (e.g., perhaps it's too sophisticated a claim for the story's intended audience, whose focus is elsewhere), or perhaps because it's not clear that the resistant claim is false in the first place.

NOTE

1 Whether imaginative resistance is a question of inability or unwillingness to imagine is a matter of some debate, on which we need take no position here. For a detailed summary of this debate, see Tuna (2020).

49

THE PUZZLE OF MORAL PERSUASION

CASE

Jonathan Swift's *A Modest Proposal For Preventing the Children of Poor People From Being a Burthen to Their Parents or Country, and For making them Beneficial to the Publick* (1729) is a staple of English literature classes everywhere. It's crucial to properly understanding the essay that the reader get that it's a work of (Juvenalian) satire; anyone who thinks Swift is actually advocating that the poor should cannibalize their children has *gravely* misunderstood him. But it doesn't stretch the imagination *too* much to imagine that someone *could* misread the text that way—a child unaccustomed to satire, irony, and sarcasm, say, or maybe an adult who came across it in a strange context, alongside other, more forthright works. Now: what if this not-so-modest Swift *actually convinced them* of his solution to poverty?

We probably wouldn't go so far as to say that *A Modest Proposal* is a morally corruptive work, since our hapless reader did, after all, grossly misunderstand it (see also *Pinny the Who?*). But what if the essay wasn't at all satirical? Or what if our reader had instead read a work of fiction with the same perverse aims?

If it seems difficult to imagine, just think of all the children who report having waited with bated breath for their letter of admission

DOI: 10.4324/9781003368205-54

to Hogwarts, of worries about copycat crimes after certain films are released, or about violent media (especially video games) leading to increased aggression. Conversely, think of how we credit Harriet Beecher Stowe's *Uncle Tom's Cabin; or, Life Among the Lowly* (1852) with widely changing American attitudes towards slavery. If fiction can convince us to be better moral agents, then it can convince us to be worse, too. But how? This is *the puzzle of moral persuasion.*[1]

RESPONSES

One possibility, of course, is that art—and literature in particular—affords no general knowledge whatsoever, whether moral or otherwise (Beardsley 1958). This is because art, while it can *suggest* a hypothesis, cannot marshal evidence in its defence. Even in literature, where we might find evidence in propositional form, must remember (1) that the narrative is typically *designed* to support any general theses it might advance, thus begging the question, and (2) that fiction is characteristically *made up*, or false (Lamarque and Olsen 1994). Thus, the quality of the evidence is both suspect and indirect, so that if knowledge is anything like a justified true belief, art will struggle to properly justify its claims. Nor is literary practice focused on uncovering and communicating truths; its aims are rather different, and vary from one social group to another (Lamarque and Olsen 1994). The best art can manage, then, is to suggest hypotheses about the kinds of cases it represents, or to catalogue the historiography of value.

Many philosophers of art have been more optimistic about art's capacity for moral education, however. Among optimists today, the more or less standard suggestion is that art educates by engaging our imaginative capacities in some way. As far as fiction is concerned, the suggestion is that it persuades us by getting us to imagine a similar moral or immoral perspective to the one depicted (Currie 1995). When I'm reading about Uhtred of Bebbanburg in Bernard Cornwell's *Saxon Stories* (adapted for TV as *The Last Kingdom*), for example, I'm *simulating* what it would be like to be a maligned pagan warlord in ninth-century Britain, murdering priests, pillaging unwary towns, and feeding Danish armies to the ravens. I'm effectively donning Uhtred's helmet for a few hours to see what it was like, without *actually* having to harm any priests or Danes.

So long as we believe that imagining can help to change our moral outlook, then it seems clear that fiction can do so by guiding our imaginings. A closely related suggestion has it that imagination is crucial to moral understanding in general; our theoretical understanding of morality, with all its general moral principles, derives from our ability to imagine what it's like to be someone in different (worse) circumstances (Kieran 1996). Because art and fiction are tools for guiding our imaginings, it follows that art and fiction can play an important role in shaping our moral outlook. Indeed, the particular value of art is that it gives us a chance to imaginatively engage with unfamiliar subjects which we might not otherwise consider for ourselves. Art directs our moral gaze, and therein lies the trouble since it seems like we might be persuaded to love or do bad things (such as crushing Danish armies). Gregory Currie (1995) calls this dark side of moral persuasion the "pathology of fiction".

A different reason to be optimistic about fiction's capacity for moral education is that philosophy often relies on thought experiments and other narrative examples and counterexamples (Carroll 2002). And if *philosophy* can yield knowledge—admittedly conceptual rather than empirical—then it seems there should be no barrier to art doing the same. Even if we concede that a narrative's morally educational aspects are organizational structures, the point is that understanding these structures and the role they play in the narrative involves the kind of conceptual reflection required for moral persuasion.

Other explanations for moral persuasion are available, of course, particularly for the more pathological sort of persuasion. One such is imitative: we might worry that although immoral fiction may not explicitly convince us to embrace the bad, it might encourage us to do so by way of imitation. I might, for example, try to be more like Uhtred, and I might do so in ways of which I am not immediately cognitively aware. The empirical literature on imitation suggests that our imitative mechanisms operate largely automatically and unconsciously, which makes it hard for us to accept that we are behaving imitatively (Hurley 2004). And since the enormous literature on the subject indicates that exposure to violent media tends to increase aggression (see Hurley 2004 and Hopkins and Weisberg 2017, although these latter note several important caveats), perhaps we should worry about a "chameleon effect" leading us down the garden path to immorality. The solution, according to the empirical literature, seems to be for people to explicitly override these tendencies—which requires us to first accept that we are subject to them. Whether art has a productive role to play in doing so is a matter of some debate.

So far, the responses surveyed have focused on realistic fiction. But does non-realistic fiction have the same capacity for pathological persuasion? One important suggestion is that a work's genre (including whether it is fiction or non-fiction) exerts significant influence over the kind of information readers extract from stories (Liao 2013). Knowing that we're reading hard science fiction, for example, tells us to import most of what we know about science (except where the story violates what we know of physical laws for the sake of the narrative)—but it also tells us that we can *export* the same kinds of facts back to our understanding of the real world. There is a certain symmetry between what we can import into and export out of fiction. A Sci-Fi world similar to ours with respect to morality but not physics is one according to which we can import real-world moral norms, but not necessarily physical laws and, likewise, one which allows us to draw real lessons about morality, but not physics. Genre helps to determine the work's relation to the real world. Likewise, knowing whether something is a work of fiction or non-fiction helps us to determine which of the attitudes it prescribes are available for export back to the real world, and which are to be quarantined as "just a story"—provided the work's context of creation allows such an interpretation (Clavel-Vázquez 2020).

A genre's conventions will constrain which inferential patterns are appropriate to the work and inform our expectations about what it is appropriate for us to imagine (Liao 2013). This is why it's so important for readers to recognize that *A Modest Proposal* is satire. Satire, in particular, exploits imaginative resistance (see *The Puzzle of Imaginative Resistance*) to halt our imaginative identification with a character in its tracks, to jar us into adopting the author's perspective instead (Harold 2007). Indeed, this can be an advantage of unrealistic over realistic fictions, since realistic fiction usually sees us adopting a character's inner perspective as the vehicle of our emotional engagement.

The empirical evidence (primarily from studies of children) seems to confirm genre's influence (Hopkins and Weisberg 2017). Children predictably struggle with "the reader's dilemma" of identifying which information to export from the fiction and which to quarantine, but adults are not immune to such struggles either. Decisions about which information to export and which to quarantine seem to be influenced by a work's genre and other contextual factors, as well as the reader's firsthand experience. The evidence likewise suggests that children do apply the lessons they learn from fiction to their real-world interactions, although they seem to do so mostly implicitly rather than explicitly; this may be consonant with lessons from the science of imitation (see Hurley 2004), or simply an artifact of studying small children who struggle to explicitly articulate and extrapolate general themes from narratives. Children seem susceptible to learning both prosocial and antisocial behaviours from realistic and non-realistic fiction, but the effects are often short-lived, and the way in which they are assessed also seems to make a difference to the outcomes measured, since assessments tend to co-vary with the lessons taught (Hopkins and Weisberg 2017).

SUGGESTED READING

SEMINAL PRESENTATION:

1. Currie, Gregory (1995). The Moral Psychology of Fiction. *Australasian Journal of Philosophy* 73 (2): 250–9.
   Currie argues that imagination plays a central role in art's capacity for moral instruction. In particular, he argues that we are morally persuaded by *simulating* a character's beliefs and desires, by imaginatively projecting ourselves into the fictional situations and being encouraged to imagine they are about *ourselves*.

DEFENCES:

2. Kieran, Matthew (1996). Art, Imagination, and the Cultivation of Morals. *Journal of Aesthetics and Art Criticism* 54 (4): 337–51.
   Kieran argues that the imagination is crucial to moral understanding in general, where it substitutes for a reliance on general theoretical principles. Imaginative engagement with exemplars conveys more and richer information than simply applying moral principles.
3. Hurley, Susan (2004). Imitation, Media Violence, and Freedom of Speech, *Philosophical Studies* 117 (1): 165–218.
   Hurley argues that we need to pay closer attention to the cognitive psychology of imitation to explain fiction's moral persuasiveness. She surveys the empirical literature on imitation as well as on the effects of violent media,

arguing that the increased aggressiveness observed from the consumption of violent media is best explained as imitative.

CRITIQUES:

4. Beardsley, Monroe C. (1958). *Aesthetics*. New York: Harcourt, Brace, & World. Beardsley offers a notoriously pessimistic appraisal of art's cognitive value and its prospects for moral education in Ch. 21. While he grants that art can exemplify certain general themes, he argues that the best that non-propositional arts like music and painting can do is to suggest hypotheses which need external confirmation.

5. Lamarque, Peter and Stein Haugom Olsen (1994). *Truth, Fiction, and Literature: A Philosophical Perspective*. Oxford: Oxford University Press.
In Chs. 11–15, Lamarque and Olsen argue that the general beliefs expressed in literature are there to organize the text, not to educate us. Literary practice, they argue, is not preoccupied with the truth of literary claims or their educational potential.

6. Carroll, Noël (2002). The Wheel of Virtue: Art, Literature, and Moral Knowledge. *The Journal of Aesthetics and Art Criticism* 60 (1): 3–26.
Carroll defends art's cognitive value from a trio of objections, arguing that art can function as a thought experiment, example, or counterexample. Philosophers frequently use such tools—often narratively structured—as well as examples taken from fiction to advance their arguments, so fiction (and art) clearly *can* advance persuasive arguments.

7. Liao, Shen-yi (2013). Moral Persuasion and the Diversity of Fictions. *Pacific Philosophical Quarterly* 94 (3): 269–89.
Liao argues that prior empirical and philosophical work gives us an incomplete picture of moral persuasion through fiction because of its narrow focus on realistic fiction. Liao argues that fiction's persuasive abilities and mechanisms will vary according to genre.

8. Harold, James (2007). The Ethics of Non-Realist Fiction: Morality's Catch-22. *Philosophia* 35 (2): 145–59.
Harold argues that realistic and non-realistic fiction employ different techniques for moral persuasion. Satire exploits imaginative resistance to pull us out of our ordinary passive reading habits and our imaginative identification with characters, so that the morally persuasive perspective is the author's rather than the characters'.

FURTHER READING:

9. Hopkins, Emily J. and Deena Skolnick Weisberg (2017). The Youngest Readers' Dilemma: A Review Of Children's Learning From Fictional Sources. *Developmental Review* 43: 48–70.

Hopkins and Weisberg give a comprehensive overview of the empirical literature on children's learning from fiction, as well as some work on adult learning. Although children struggle to explicitly draw moral lessons from fiction, this seems tied to their difficulties spontaneously drawing *general* lessons; implicitly, they do seem to alter their behaviour in light of stories.

10. Clavel-Vázquez, Adriana (2020). The Diversity of Intrinsic Ethical Flaws in Fiction. *Journal of Aesthetics and Art Criticism* 78 (2): 143–56.

   Clavel-Vázquez distinguishes between a work's intrinsic and its extrinsic ethical flaws, arguing that the focus on intrinsic flaws has left us unable to distinguish between works which exhibit the same flaws but are of different aesthetic merit. Our focus, she argues, is better directed at whether a work's defects are fictional or actual.

NOTE

1 On whether morally bad art can be aesthetically good see *The Paradox of Bad-Bad Art*; on responding positively to unpleasantness, see *The Paradox of Disgust* and *The Paradox of Tragedy*.

UTOPIA (GAMES)

CASE

Imagine a post-scarcity utopia.[1] Every single inhabitant of this utopia can have more or less whatever they want, whenever they want it. All the work, including household chores, is automated and done by machines. Powerful and benevolent artificial intelligences (AIs) take care of the administrative tasks of detecting needs and deputizing machines to take care of them. Technological advances in nanotechnology and fabrication ensure that any material object can be produced to precise specifications, and is available to anyone and everyone. As a result, there is no need for anyone to perform work in our ordinary sense; the machines and fabricators take care of all that.

Suppose, further, that this techno-utopia has managed to solve all of our interpersonal problems: there is no more depression or addiction, no more violence and trauma, no more envy or jealousy, etc. As a result, nobody needs to compete for admiration, affection, approval, attention, or love any more. Everyone can be and live exactly as they wish to be and live.

So far, I trust that this all sounds pretty good. But consider this: in a world where nothing bad can happen to anyone, there's no need for

DOI: 10.4324/9781003368205-55

morality. And if we think that the production of art requires us to be able to reflect on our passions, our dreams and hopes, our tragedies and fears, our moral and interpersonal shortcomings, and so on—well, a world without any of those things seems like a world that won't have much, if any, art in it. The non-representational art that's left once we've subtracted all of these human travails could just as easily be churned out by AIs, and thus wouldn't require any human emotions for its production at all (on whether such works would be art, see *Apelles's Horses* and *The Whale and the Driftwood*). Similarly, we can stipulate that all that's knowable is already known in Utopia (if not by individuals, then by the AIs running things).

Now that we've purged it of all of these instrumentally valuable goals (goals we value for some external reason, like pleasure or wealth), our Utopia is starting to look more than a little boring (or perhaps even like a total hellscape—see *The Uniform World*). What is there for Utopians to *do*?

Well, they can still play games. Games present us with obstacles we have to overcome for the sake of playing the game—in other words, a game's instrumental and its intrinsic value are inseparable. It seems to follow, then, that the ideal existence is one consumed entirely by the playing of games.

But what about people who don't want to durdle around conquering the world in *Risk*, winning the Cold War in *Twilight Struggle*, solving a murder in *Orient Express*, directing armies in *Medieval: Total War*, or competitively stacking weird shapes in *Bandu*? What about the people who enjoy building things for themselves, or cleaning, or whatever else it is that people enjoy doing? All this is still possible in Utopia, it's just that the motivational structure underlying these activities is subtly different. Before, even if we enjoyed them, we did them because we *had to* in some sense. In Utopia, however, nobody 'has to' do anything—instead, everyone is free to choose to do whatever they wish. Utopians always have the ability to push a button (or whatever) and have their wish fulfilled, but some of them set themselves arbitrary restrictions. They voluntarily undertake to overcome wholly unnecessary obstacles: in Utopia, all the world's a game, and all the men and women merely players.

RESPONSES

Responding to Wittgenstein's infamous skepticism about the definability of 'games', Bernard Suits (1978) argued that all games share certain structural features in common. Players aim to achieve a specific state of affairs (the *prelusory goal*;[2] often, the game's win-conditions). Moreover, they seek to do so using only the means allowed by the rules of the game (the *lusory means*). These rules prohibit players from achieving their lusory goals in the most efficient manner possible, demanding that they use less efficient means instead (e.g., you make money in Monopoly by charging rents and passing 'Go', not by taking what you want directly from the bank; these are the game's *constitutive rules*). This restriction is important, because it's what marks the difference between a game and a 'technical activity', an activity such as work which we want to complete as efficiently as we can. Finally, games are also characterized by the fact that players voluntarily accept these restrictions in order to make play possible (they adopt a *lusory attitude*).

This characterization of games and of utopia has come under fire from a number of quarters. Two dominant threads of criticism argue that Suits's utopia is either incoherent or circular (or both). It is incoherent because it makes no room for the possibility of failure, disappointment, and negative emotions (Thompson 2004). Our experience of the real world clearly shows us that many of the pursuits we value most are painful and filled with negative emotions (see *The Paradox of Tragedy*). Similarly, many of the games we like most are incredibly challenging, and we enjoy them *because of* that challenge (van de Mosselaer 2019). The same is true in sports, where the skills required for high-level competition come at considerable personal expense, and require that some people *lose*, thus experiencing intense disappointment (Thompson 2004). Since Utopian society allows everyone the freedom to choose their experiences, it seems like there is no possibility of anyone failing to meet the challenges they set themselves, thus undermining the very concept of a challenge.

This objection seems misapplied, however. It's crucial here to remember that Utopia is a place where we willingly undertake the activities we do for their own sakes; and, because they are games, we voluntarily accept inefficient means for achieving our goals. Thus, nobody in Utopia *arbitrarily* experiences failure, loss, or pain; but they may *voluntarily* accept those risks so as to play particular games (Vossen 2016). Playing competitive games requires us to accept a certain amount of disappointment for the sake of playing the game. Indeed, we often seem to suspend our everyday agencies in order to adopt the temporary agencies required by the game (Nguyen 2020; but see Kukla 2021 and *The Gamer's Dilemma* for some limits). Monopoly, for example, tends to bring out the worst in everyone who plays it (and that's the point). This is true of many non-competitive games as well, such as puzzles; they can be incredibly frustrating, but as long as players perceive them as stemming from the game's proper functioning, they are insulated from that negativity (van de Mosselaer 2019). So there is plenty of room for real challenges and failures in Utopia, it's just that Utopians must choose to risk them rather than being subjected to them unwillingly.

The circularity objection, on the other hand, stems from the worry that Utopia's setup saw us stipulating that gameplay is the only activity we undertake for its own sake, thereby pre-theoretically ruling out other plausible candidates such as reading or writing (Holowchak 2007). In other words, the thought experiment doesn't *show* that gameplay is the ideal of human existence, it just concludes that it is. Similarly, we might also wonder whether we have grounds to believe that a society entirely without instrumental activities is utopian. Once again, other intuitions may be available.

To this objection, it can be replied that in Utopia, at least, these other candidate activities *are* games: if a Utopian reads a novel rather than immediately downloading its content into her mind, it's because she wants to savour the act of *reading*. She is choosing to set herself unnecessary obstacles for the sake of the activity of reading—in other words, reading, for her, is a game. When we read or watch mysteries, for example, we like to speculate about the culprit rather than skipping to the end, and this is a game we play with ourselves (Hurka 2019). So too with writing, thinking, scientific inquiry, sex, and so on. Now, this invites the worry that the definition of a game has become overbroad, especially since it turns out that in Utopia *every* non-game human activity has a counterpart that *is* a game (c.f. *The Gallery of Red Squares*). But it's not clear that this should worry us overmuch, since it's in virtue of sharing a common structure that these activities count as games, and that structure isn't realized outside of Utopia itself (Hurka 2019).

Another objection stems from Suits's puzzling argument that art would be absent from Utopia since the motivational spurs underlying its creation would be absent. It's not obvious, however, that Utopians couldn't make art as part of a game, just as some play at working (Wildman and Archer 2019). A more troubling version of the argument maintains that the structure of a game is incompatible with that of being an artwork, so Utopia *must* be entirely devoid of art (Rough 2018). There are at least three reasons to think this might be the case. First, games and artworks have different constitutive goals (viz., some prelusory goal vs. understanding and aesthetic appreciation). The goals of a game must be specified independently of the game itself, but the goal of art is entirely bound up in the artwork. Second, art-making cannot be arbitrarily inefficient, since all of an artwork's properties are potentially aesthetically relevant. Finally, it seems like games and artworks prescribe that we adopt incompatible attitudes towards their objects: adopting the lusory attitude is sufficient to make something a game but would not suffice for engaging with an artwork-game (an artistic or aesthetic attitude would also be necessary; see *The Jealous Husband*). If successful, this suggests a more general threat: perhaps there are other everyday activities whose structure is incompatible with gameplay—e.g., love, friendship, science, philosophy, and so on. If that's right, then Utopia may be quite boring after all.

By way of response, however, it seems like we can imagine at least a few gamified ways to smuggle art back into Utopia (Wildman and Archer 2019). We can imagine, for example, *art-inclusive* games, which are just games which contain works of art (e.g., the art on the faces of *Magic: The Gathering* cards), or we can imagine *art-production* games, whose playing entails creating and appreciating artworks (e.g., drawing 30-second animals).

Finally, it is worth noting that even a game-playing Utopia is not immune from becoming a terrifying hellscape. Because they temporarily adopt game-defined agencies and values, gamers are, in many respects, at the mercy of game designers, who structure their games so as to facilitate the adoption of some agencies and values, and to impede others (Nguyen 2020, especially Ch. 9). There is thus a danger of value- or agency-capture, of substituting the simpler values or agencies coded into the structure of the games for our own (Nguyen 2020, Kukla 2021; see also *The Puzzle of Moral Persuasion*). In the real world, gamifying our everyday tasks can help to alleviate their monotony, but rather than take us a step towards Utopia, doing so tends to see us sacrificing our well-being on the altar of corporate profit.

SUGGESTED READING

SEMINAL PRESENTATION:

1. Suits, Bernard (1978). *The Grasshopper: Games, Life and Utopia*. Peterborough: Broadview Press.
   Suits offers a definition of games, arguing they are characterized by the voluntary attempt to overcome unnecessary obstacles (Ch. 5). To play a game is to achieve a particular end-goal using only a restricted set of means which are less than maximally efficient, because to do so makes it possible for us to adopt the 'lusory attitude'. Suits presents Utopia as proof that game-playing is the only human activity we undertake wholly for its own sake (Ch. 15).

DEFENCES:

2. Vossen, Deborah P. (2016). Utopia is Intelligible and Game-Playing is What Makes Utopia Intelligible. *Journal of the Philosophy of Sport* 43 (2): 251–65.
   Vossen stresses that the difference between the work undertaken in the real world versus that undertaken in Utopia is attitudinal: non-Utopians work because we have to, whereas Utopians work *only* because they *want* to. Utopia's need-free ideal doesn't *impose* a work-free existence upon Utopians or doom them to trivial undertakings; it allows them to choose what they do and why they do it, and frees them to find intrinsic value in it all.
3. Hurka, Thomas (2019). "Suits on Games: Slightly Revised, Slightly Restricted," in *Games, Sports, and Play: Philosophical Essays*, Thomas Hurka (ed.). Oxford: Oxford University Press, 13–32.
   Hurka defends Suits's analysis of game-playing against the charges that it is over- or under-inclusive, arguing that it has the virtue of finding a common structure for everything that *does* fall under its purview and brings to the fore the intrinsic good of achievement. Lusory attitudes may sometimes be determined at the level of community, rather than individual, engagement.
4. Nguyen, C. Thi (2020). *Games: Agency as Art*. New York: Oxford University Press.
   Nguyen expands on Suits's characterization of games, arguing that games are an art-kind whose medium is the player's agency. In playing games, we adopt disposable ends, sometimes for aesthetic reasons. We pursue temporary goals in order to engage in the *means* of their pursuit (rather than those goals

themselves), and this can yield aesthetic experiences. Of particular interest are Chs. 8 and 9, in which Nguyen outlines the social structure of gaming and explores the dangers of value capture through the gamification of real work and spaces.

CRITIQUES:

5. Thompson, Keith (2004). Sport and Utopia. *Journal of the Philosophy of Sport* 31 (1): 60–3.

   Thompson argues that the concept of a utopia is incoherent because it makes no room for failure and negative emotions—both of which are necessary elements of high-level sports and gameplay. Moreover, he argues that value pluralism necessarily rules out utopia.

6. Holowchak, M. Andrew (2007). Games as Pastimes in Suits's Utopia: Meaningful Living and the "Metaphysics of Leisure". *Journal of the Philosophy of Sport* 34 (1): 88–96.

   Holowchak argues that Suits's account of Utopia is circular and incoherent. In particular, he accuses Suits of begging the question by stipulatively ruling out other activities which are candidates for meaningful autotelic activity, such as reading and writing. Experience shows that game-playing is just one of several ends which people pursue for itself.

7. Rough, Brock (2018). The Incompatibility of Games and Artworks. *Journal of the Philosophy of Games* 1 (1): 1–21.

   Rough argues that something's being a game is incompatible with its being an artwork, for three reasons: (1) games and artworks must have different constitutive goals, (2) artworks cannot be arbitrarily inefficient, and (3) games and artworks prescribe that we adopt incompatible attitudes towards their objects.

8. Wildman, Nathan and Alfred Archer (2019). Playing with Art in Suits' Utopia. *Sport, Ethics and Philosophy* 13 (3–4): 456–70.

   Wildman and Archer present three kinds of games which, they think, can introduce art into Suits's Utopia: dual-natured, art-inclusive, and art-productive games. By spending their time playing games, Utopians can therefore create art, or indeed perform any other instrumental activity.

FURTHER READING:

9. van de Mosselaer, Nele (2019). Only a Game? Player Misery Across Game Boundaries. *Journal of the Philosophy of Sport* 46 (2): 191–207.

   van de Mosselaer responds to the paradoxes of fiction and tragedy by arguing that players' lusory attitude typically sees them bracketing their in-game emotions from their real-world selves. Emotions induced by game elements are part of the player's make-believe; when they don't perceive the source of negative emotion as being part of the game, however, it is no longer bracketed.

10. Kukla, Quill Rebecca (2021). Sculpted Agency and the Messiness of the Landscape. *Analysis* 81 (2): 296–306.

Against Nguyen, Kukla argues that gameplay is inextricably linked with its cultural, material, and social contexts, so that gameplay is not typically insulated from interpersonal moral considerations or instrumental reasons. They argue that everyday life is structured in many of the same ways often taken to be distinctive of games.

NOTES

1 If you're struggling, just think about Sci-Fi. Iain M. Banks's *Culture* universe, as described in *The Player of Games* (Macmillan 1988), fits the bill particularly well.

2 'Lusory' is an archaic word derived from the latin '*lusus*', meaning '*to play*'.

INDEX